CW00953588

THE GLOBALIZATION OF HATE

THE GLOBALIZATION
OF HATE

INTERNATIONALIZING
HATE CRIME?

EDITED BY
JENNIFER SCHWEPPE
AND
MARK AUSTIN WALTERS

OXFORD
UNIVERSITY PRESS

OXFORD
UNIVERSITY PRESS

Great Clarendon Street, Oxford, OX2 6DP,
United Kingdom

Oxford University Press is a department of the University of Oxford.
It furthers the University's objective of excellence in research, scholarship,
and education by publishing worldwide. Oxford is a registered trade mark of
Oxford University Press in the UK and in certain other countries

Published in the United States of America by Oxford University Press
198 Madison Avenue, New York, NY 10016, United States of America

British Library Cataloguing in Publication Data
Data available

Library of Congress Control Number: 2016933495

ISBN 978-0-19-878566-8

Printed and bound by
CPI Group (UK) Ltd, Croydon, CR0 4YY

ACKNOWLEDGEMENTS

The editors would like to thank the participants at the Inaugural conference of the International Network for Hate Studies held at the University of Sussex in May 2014 for their input and engagement. They would also like to thank the authors for their excellent contributions to this text, and for attending and participating in the Globalization of Hate workshop at the University of Sussex in May 2015. Thanks also to our editor, Lucy Alexander from Oxford University Press for her help and support through the process, and to Mahalakshmi Kathirreshan, who oversaw the production of the text.

Jennifer would like to thank her husband, James, and son, Findlay, for their love and for ensuring life is full of laughter. Mark would like to thank his husband, Daniel, for his love and patience during the many weekends he spent editing this collection.

TABLE OF CONTENTS

List of Contributors   ix

Introduction: The Globalization of Hate   1
Jennifer Schweppe and Mark Austin Walters

PART I THE GLOBAL DIMENSIONS OF HATE CRIME

1 Defining Hate Crime Internationally: Issues and Conundrums   15
  Jon Garland and Corinne Funnell

2 Conceptualizing Hatred Globally: Is Hate Crime
  a Human Rights Violation?   31
  Thomas Brudholm

3 Hate Crime Concepts and Their Moral Foundations:
  A Universal Framework?   49
  David Brax

4 White Pride Worldwide: Constructing Global Identities Online   65
  Barbara Perry and Ryan Scrivens

5 Global Terrorism Events and Ensuing Hate Incidents   79
  Kathryn Benier

6 How 'Hate' Hurts Globally   96
  Paul Iganski and Abe Sweiry

PART II GLOBAL ISSUES, NATIONAL EXPERIENCES

7 Covered in Stigma? Exploring the Impacts of Islamophobic Hate Crime
  on Veiled Muslim Women Globally   111
  Irene Zempi

8 Hate Crime in Transitional Societies: The Case of South Africa   126
  Duncan Breen, Ingrid Lynch, Juan Nel, and Iole Matthews

9 The Problematization of Hate Crime Legislation in Turkey:
  The Re-emergence of Legitimate Victims   142
  Bengi Bezirgan

10 Internationalizing Hate Crime and the Problem of the Intractable State:
  The Case of Ireland   157
  Amanda Haynes and Jennifer Schweppe

11 Do Some Identities Deserve More Protection than Others?
    The Case of Anti-LGB Hate Crime Laws in Poland   174
    Piotr Godzisz and Dorota Pudzianowska

12 Policing Hate Crime: Transferable Strategies for Improving Service
    Provision to Victims and Communities Internationally   190
    Paul Giannasi and Nathan Hall

PART III INTERNATIONAL RESPONSES
TO HATE CRIME

13 National Monitoring of Hate Crime in Europe: The Case for
    a European Level Policy   213
    Michael Whine

14 The European Court of Human Rights and Discriminatory
    Violence Complaints   233
    Jasmina Mačkić

15 How Should We Legislate against Hate Speech? Finding
    an International Model in a Globalized World   247
    Viera Pejchal and Kimberley Brayson

16 Regulating Hate Crime in the Digital Age   263
    Chara Bakalis

17 State-sponsored Hatred and Persecution on the Grounds
    of Sexual Orientation: The Role of International Criminal Law   277
    Ruby Axelson

18 Challenging Orthodoxy: Towards a Restorative Approach
    to Combating the Globalization of Hate   294
    Mark Austin Walters

Conclusion: Towards an International Response to Hate Crime   314
Jennifer Schweppe and Mark Austin Walters

Index   319

LIST OF CONTRIBUTORS

EDITORS

Jennifer Schweppe is a lecturer in law at the University of Limerick. She is co-founder and co-director of the International Network for Hate Studies. She is also co-founder and co-director of the University of Limerick-based Hate and Hostility Research Group, the only academic research group in Ireland dedicated to exploring and understanding hate crime in an Irish context. She has published widely in the area of hate crime, and her work explores the experience, understanding, and potential future reform of hate crime in an Irish context. Her work in the area of hate crime has been funded by the Irish Research Council (*Monitoring Hate Crime: Analysis and Development of Online Third Party Reporting*), the Irish Council for Civil Liberties (*Out of the Shadows: 360° Evaluation of Hate Crime in Ireland*), and the European Union (*The Life Cycle of a Hate Crime: Best Practice in the Prevention and Prosecution of Hate Crime*).

Mark Austin Walters, PhD is a Reader in Criminal Law and Criminal Justice at Sussex University. He is also co-founder and co-director of the International Network for Hate Studies. Mark has published widely in the field of hate crime, focusing in particular on the criminalization of hate-motivated offences, criminological theories of causation, and the use of restorative justice for hate crime. His monograph *Hate Crime and Restorative Justice: Exploring Causes, Repairing Harms* was published by Oxford University Press in 2014. Mark is currently involved in a number of empirical studies on hate crime, including: *The Indirect Experience of Hate Crime: the Victim Group Response*; *The Life Cycle of a Hate Crime: Best Practice in the Prevention and Prosecution of Hate Crime*; and *Policing Hate Crime: Modernising the Craft, an Evidence-Based Approach*.

CONTRIBUTORS

Ruby Axelson graduated with a LLB in Law with International Relations and an LLM in International Law from the University of Sussex. She has since worked as an intern at the International Criminal Tribunal for the former Yugoslavia. She is currently working as a legal assistant for Global Rights Compliance LLP.

Chara Bakalis is a Senior Lecturer in Law at Oxford Brookes University. Her current research interests lie broadly in the field of hate crime and hate speech with an emphasis on legal regulation. In particular, she is interested in the interaction between technology, criminal law and hate crime/speech. She has written on legal reform of English law as well as on the underlying principled rationale for hate crime legislation. She has recently published a report on cyberhate for the Council of Europe's Commission against Racism and Intolerance (ECRI).

Kathryn Benier is a Research Fellow on the Australian Community Capacity Study at the University of Queensland, Australia. Her PhD dissertation focused on the neighbourhood factors influencing the incidence of hate crime in Australia, and the effect of victimization on the individual's interactions and perceptions of their neighbourhood. Her research interests include hate crime, the neighbourhood ecology of crime, immigration and ethnicity, terrorism, fear of crime, and the effects of victimization.

Bengi Bezirgan completed her PhD in Sociology at London School of Economics and Political Science in 2015. Her PhD research examines the Armenian question in Turkey by focusing on news discourse in three national newspapers and the narratives of Armenian interviewees concerning their past and present experiences. Previously Bengi received her MS degree in Sociology from Middle East Technical University in 2010. She obtained her BS degree in Sociology from Middle East Technical University and also completed a European Studies minor program in the Department of International Relations in 2007. Her research interests include nationalism and national identity, race and ethnicity, qualitative research, sociology of media, hate speech and hate crime, and sociology of memory.

David Brax holds a PhD in practical philosophy from Lund University, Sweden, and has specialized in the philosophical aspects of Hate Crime and Hate Crime Legislation since 2011. He is currently doing a post-doctoral project on Hate Crime Legislation in Europe at the Centre for European Research, the University of Gothenburg (CERGU). He is a member of the advisory board for the International Network for Hate Studies. He teaches at the Department of Philosophy, Linguistics, and Theory of Science, the University of Gothenburg, Sweden.

Kimberley Brayson is a lecturer at the University of Sussex, where she is a member of the Centre for Human Rights Research and co-ordinator of the Gender, Theory and Politics stream of the Centre for Gender Studies. She completed her PhD at Queen Mary, University of London and holds a Masters in Legal Theory from the European Academy of Legal Theory, Brussels. She completed her undergraduate degree in English Law and German Law at the University of Kent. Kimberley has worked as a legal researcher at the College of Europe in Bruges and was also research fellow on an EU Framework 6 project entitled Juristras.

Duncan Breen is a human rights and refugee protection practitioner currently based in the Middle East. In South Africa, where he served as an advocacy officer with the Consortium for Refugees and Migrants in South Africa (CoRMSA), his work included measures to address regular outbreaks of xenophobic violence. This led him to found the Hate Crimes Working Group, a lobbying group seeking to address multiple forms of hate crime in South Africa. Duncan's recent work has included efforts to strengthen protection for lesbian, gay, bisexual, transgender, and intersex (LGBTI) refugees as well as other refugees facing high risks of violence, increase accountability for perpetrators of xenophobic violence, and address human rights abuses of refugees and migrants by states at international borders. Duncan is currently involved in the response to the refugee and migration crisis in Europe.

Thomas Brudholm is Associate Professor at the University of Copenhagen, Institute for Cross-Cultural and Regional Studies. Although a philosopher by training, he regularly leaves the armchair and expertise in transitional justice and the ethics of reconciliation has led to engagements in South Africa, Northern Ireland, Rwanda, Bosnia, China, and Greenland. Thomas is author of *Resentment's Virtue: Jean Améry and the Refusal to Forgive* (Temple University Press, 2008) and co-editor of several books, including *The Religious in Responses to Mass Atrocity* (Cambridge University Press, 2009). Currently, Thomas is focusing on questions of hatred, combining philosophical sources with legal and political discourses on hate crime and hate speech, genocide, and reconciliation. In relation to this, he is co-editing *Hate, Politics, Law* (Oxford University Press, expected in 2016). He has published in, e.g., *Journal of Applied Philosophy, Law & Contemporary Problems, Journal of Human Rights*, the *Hedgehog Review*, and *Criminal Law and Philosophy*.

Corinne Funnell is a senior lecturer in criminology at the University of the West of England. Corinne has researched hate crime and also illegal drug markets and has worked as a government policy and practice advisor in these and related fields. Her ESRC-funded PhD, undertaken at Cardiff University, explored victims' perceptions of racist hate crime and the impact of these experiences on their lives. Corinne is particularly interested in ethnographic research methods and, in relation, the challenges this method raises for researchers, including the potential social, emotional, and physical harms. Corinne's current research activities include a mixed methods inquiry into gender and policing and an ethnographic investigation of police hate crime detectives. She is also interested in the applicability of bringing the real world into the teaching of criminology and criminal justice.

Jon Garland is a Professor in Criminology in the Department of Sociology at the University of Surrey. His main areas of research are in the fields of hate crime, rural racism, community and identity, policing, and victimization. He has published six books: *Racism and Anti-racism in Football* (with Mike Rowe); *The Future of Football* (with Mike Rowe and Dominic Malcolm); *Youth Culture, Popular Music and the End of 'Consensus'* (with the Subcultures Network); and (all with Neil Chakraborti) *Rural Racism; Responding to Hate Crime: The Case for Connecting Policy and Research*; and *Hate Crime: Impact, Causes, and Consequences* (now onto its second edition). He has also had numerous journal articles and reports published on issues of racism, the far-right, hate crime, policing, cultural criminology, and identity. He is on the Editorial Board of *Ethnic and Racial Studies* and *Law, Crime, Justice and Society*.

Paul Giannasi works in the Ministry of Justice in the United Kingdom. He leads the cross-government Hate Crime Programme, which brings all sectors of government together to co-ordinate efforts to improve the response to hate

crime across the criminal justice system. Paul is the UK National Point of
Contact to the Office for Democratic Institutions and Human Rights on hate
crime and has worked to share good practice within the OSCE region and within
Africa. Paul has 30 years' experience as a police officer and is a member of the
Association of Chief Police Officers (ACPO) Hate Crime Group. He manages
True Vision (www.report-it.org.uk) on behalf of the police and is the author
of the 2014 *Police Hate Crime Manual,* which offers guidance to all UK police
officers and partners. He is the co-editor of the 2014 *Routledge International
Handbook on Hate Crime.* Paul was awarded an OBE in the 2014 New Years
Honours list for services to policing, equality, and human rights.

Piotr Godzisz is a hate crime consultant with experience in research, policy, and
capacity building projects. He co-operates with civil society and international
organizations working in the field of tolerance and non-discrimination across
Europe. He holds a master's degree in political science from the University
of Warsaw. He has published in the area of hate crime. For his PhD project at
University College London, he examines the development of national hate crime
policies in Poland. Specifically, he is looking to answer the question why hate
crime laws in this country cover hate speech and hate crimes based on racism
and xenophobia, but leave out homophobic, transphobic, or disablist violence.
For this reason, he has analysed the arguments used by opponents of the
expansion of hate crime laws, evaluated advocacy strategies of civil society groups,
as well as examined the influence of international bodies on the development of
national hate crime measures.

Nathan Hall, PhD is Associate Head of Department at the Institute of Criminal
Justice Studies at the University of Portsmouth. He has published widely
in the field of Hate Crime, and is a member of the Cross-Government Hate
Crime Independent Advisory Group, the National Police Chief's Council Hate
Crime Working Group, and the Crown Prosecution Service's Wessex Hate
Crime Scrutiny Panel. He has also acted as an independent member of the UK
Government's delegation to the Organization for Security and Co-operation in
Europe (OSCE).

Amanda Haynes, PhD is a senior lecturer in sociology at the University of
Limerick, Ireland. Her research interests centre on the analysis of discursive,
classificatory, and physical violences, and their relationship to prejudice. Her
current research and writing projects centre on hate crime, policing, stigma, and
public political discourse on minority issues. Her works include *Legislating for
Hate Crimes in Ireland* (with Jennifer Schweppe and James Carr, 2014). She has
been published in the *Journal of Housing and the Built Environment, Journalism:
Theory, Practice & Criticism,* and *New Media and Society.* She is a co-director
of both the Hate and Hostility Research Group and the Power, Discourse and
Society Research Group at the University of Limerick. She co-edits a book
series entitled Discourse, Power and Society, published by Rowman Littlefield
International. Her research has been funded by the European Union and the
Irish Research Council.

Paul Iganski, PhD is Professor of Criminology and Criminal Justice in the Lancaster University Law School, UK. For a decade-and-a-half he has specialized in research, writing, teaching, and public engagement about hate crime and hate speech. His books include *Hate Crime. A Global Perspective* (2015 with Jack Levin), *Hate Crime and the City* (2008), *Hate Crimes against London's Jews* (2005 with Vicky Kielinger and Susan Paterson), and the edited volumes *Hate Crime: The Consequences of Hate Crime* (2011) and *The Hate Debate* (2002). He particularly applies a victim-centred harms-based approach focusing on the impact and consequences of hate crime and hate speech. He mostly conducts his research in collaboration with, or commissioned by, NGOs and the equalities sector.

Ingrid Lynch, PhD is a research psychologist and works as a research specialist at the Human Sciences Research Council, South Africa. She is also an affiliate researcher in the Rhodes University Critical Studies in Sexualities and Reproduction research programme. Her research interests include same-sex sexualities, feminist approaches to researching sexual- and gender-based violence, and sexual and reproductive health and rights. Prior to her appointment at the HSRC, she worked in the non-profit sector as a research and policy manager and has presented at local and international conferences. Her research on sexualities has been published in international and South African journals and she has also written extensively for civil society research and advocacy publications.

Jasmina Mačkić graduated in criminal law and criminal procedure and European law from the University of Leiden. She also studied at Queen Mary and Westfield College in London. After her graduation she worked for the Council of State of the Netherlands. In 2010 she was awarded a Mozaïek subsidy (a personal grant with the maximum amount of EUR 200,000) from the Netherlands Organization for Scientific Research to carry out PhD research. Her research focuses on the evidentiary system of the European Court of Human Rights in the context of allegations of discriminatory violence. Mačkić has also taught various courses related to Dutch criminal law and criminal procedure, international and European law, and human rights law.

Iole Matthews is Director of the Independent Projects Trust, an NGO working in the Refugee, Human Rights, and Criminal Justice Sectors. An experienced facilitator and project manager, Iole chaired the South African National Hate Crimes Working Group during 2012/2013 and was Secretary in 2014. Over the last nineteen years she has managed a Unity through Youth Programme, the Mediation Training Programme for Schools, a five-year Criminal Justice Strengthening Project and numerous projects around improved service delivery within local and provincial government. Since 1998 she has variously served on the KwaZulu Natal Provincial Victim Empowerment Forum and the National South African Police Service Committee responsible for providing oversight on the development of in-service victim support training for police members and the national Integrated Child Justice Forum. Previous work includes managing, monitoring, and evaluating a range of projects including the National

Prosecuting Authority's Restorative Justice and Community Prosecution Projects.

Juan Nel is a registered clinical and research psychologist and employed as Professor of Psychology at the University of South Africa (UNISA). His expertise in sexuality and gender—in particular, lesbian, gay, bisexual, transgender, and intersex (LGBTI) mental health and well-being, as well as in hate crimes and victim empowerment and support, more generally—is recognized. His related research, tuition, advocacy, and community participation have contributed to improved theory, professional practice, policy changes, and community mobilization. Juan is passionate about equality and human rights, and the strengthening of healthcare service provision. He is a founding member of eight related government-led and civil society structures and organizations, including the SA Victim Empowerment Programme (VEP), Hate Crimes Working Group, OUT LGBT Well-Being, and the Department of Justice-led National Task Team aimed at addressing gender- and sexual orientation-based violence targeted at LGBTI persons. Juan's academic citizenship, community engagement, and related advocacy efforts are increasingly focused on the discipline of Psychology. In 2013, Juan was elected as President Elect of the Psychological Society of South Africa (PsySSA); he served as PsySSA President in 2014–2015, and as of September 2015 is the PsySSA Past President.

Viera Pejchal is a lawyer and a political scientist (both titles from the University of Granada, Spain). She has been awarded several research excellence awards which allowed her to study in the USA, Russia, and Switzerland. During her academic studies, she worked at different positions in international governmental and non-governmental organizations, including the UN Office of the High Commissioner for Human Rights and the Red Cross. Her main areas of research include Constitutional and Human Rights Law. She has published articles related to Freedom of Expression, Discrimination, and Hate Speech. Her PhD thesis is entitled: 'The Regulation of Hate Speech in Transitional Democracies'. Currently she works at the University of Geneva at the Department of Public Law as a teaching and research assistant.

Barbara Perry is Professor in the Faculty of Social Science and Humanities at the University of Ontario Institute of Technology. She has written extensively on hate crime, including several books on the topic, among them *In the Name of Hate: Understanding Hate Crime,* and *Hate and Bias Crime: A Reader.* She has also published in the area of Native American victimization and social control, including one book entitled *The Silent Victims: Native American Victims of Hate Crime,* based on interviews with Native Americans (University of Arizona Press). She has also written a related book on policing Native American communities: *Policing Race and Place: Under- and Over-enforcement in Indian Country* (Lexington Press). She was the General Editor of a five-volume set on hate crime (Praeger), and editor of *Volume 3: Victims of Hate Crime* of that set. Her work has been published in journals representing diverse disciplines: *Theoretical Criminology, Journal of Social and Behavioral Sciences, Journal of*

History and Politics, and *American Indian Quarterly*. Dr Perry continues to work in the area of hate crime, and has begun to make contributions to the limited scholarship on hate crime in Canada. Most recently, she has contributed to a scholarly understanding of anti-Muslim violence, hate crime against lesbian, gay, bisexual, trans, and queer (LGBTQ) communities, the community impacts of hate crime, and right-wing extremism in Canada.

Dorota Pudzianowska studied law and sociology at the University of Warsaw and Ecole Normale Supérieure in Paris. Currently she is an assistant professor at the Faculty of Law, Warsaw University. She specializes in human rights law with a special focus on anti-discrimination law and immigration law. Since 2006, she has been affiliated with the Helsinki Foundation for Human Rights (Warsaw); she currently heads the Anti-Discrimination Programme. She has been involved in domestic and ECHR litigation. The cases she has worked on had a significant impact on human rights protection in Poland and concerned, inter alia, discrimination on the basis of sexual orientation, ethnicity and race, disability, as well as overcrowding of prisons, freedom of assembly, religious freedom, and statelessness. In 2008–2012, she was an alternate member of the Management Board of the EU Fundamental Rights Agency. She has worked as the legal expert within FRANET network, Council of Europe, European Commission, and private law firms. She has authored books and numerous articles and chapters on human rights. She co-authored the first Equal Treatment Bench Book for judges and prosecutors in Poland.

Ryan Scrivens is a PhD student in the School of Criminology, Simon Fraser University (SFU), and a researcher with the International CyberCrime Research Centre (ICCRC). His current research interests include: right-wing extremism, terrorists' and extremists' use of the Internet, research methods and methodology, data-mining, and classification. He has gained valuable experience in the field, not only by documenting the online and offline activities of the far-right, but also by interviewing former white supremacists and police officers.

Abe Sweiry, PhD is Senior Research Associate in Law in the ESRC Centre for Corpus Approaches to Social Science (CASS) at Lancaster University, UK. He is a former Research Fellow in the European Institute for the Study of Contemporary Antisemitism (EISCA), London, and recipient of a Felix Posen Research Fellowship from the Vidal Sassoon International Center for the Study of Antisemitism (SICSA), The Hebrew University of Jerusalem. He conducts sociological research on contemporary antisemitism, hate crime, and racism, and is a specialist in using the methodology of corpus linguistics to analyse hate speech online.

Michael Whine is the Government and International Affairs Director at the Community Security Trust, and a member of the Hate Crime Independent Advisors Group at the UK Ministry of Justice. He is also a member of the advisory Platform of the European Union Agency for Fundamental Rights (FRA). Between 2010 and 2012 he acted as Lay Advisor to the Counter Terrorism

Division of the Crown Prosecution Service, and in 2013 was appointed to the Hate Crime Scrutiny and Involvement Panel of the London Crown Prosecution Service, which assesses and evaluates hate crime prosecutions. He has represented the UK at OSCE conferences and National Point of Contact on Hate Crime meetings at the OSCE since 2008. In September 2013, he was appointed the UK member of the Council of Europe Commission against Racism and Intolerance.

Irene Zempi is a Lecturer in Criminology in the Sociology Division at Nottingham Trent University. She has a PhD in Criminology and an MSc in Criminology from the University of Leicester, and a BSc in Sociology from Panteion University of Social and Political Sciences in Athens, Greece. Irene has published widely on issues of Islamophobia and anti-Muslim hate crime. She is the co-author of the book *Islamophobia, Victimisation and the Veil* (Palgrave Macmillan, 2014 with Dr Neil Chakraborti). Her most recent research project involves the first ever study to examine both online and offline experiences of anti-Muslim hate crime of 'visible' Muslim men and women in the UK, with Dr Imran Awan. This study was commissioned and funded by the Measuring Anti-Muslim Attacks (Tell MAMA) Project. As a practitioner, Irene has extensive experience working with victims of anti-social behaviour, hate crime, domestic violence, and volume crime at Victim Support in Leicester.

INTRODUCTION: THE GLOBALIZATION OF HATE

Jennifer Schweppe and Mark Austin Walters

Over the past twenty to thirty years we have learned much about what is now commonly referred to as 'hate crime'. Yet most of the knowledge accretion about hate crime is based on country-specific analyses that have used jurisdiction-specific definitions of the phenomenon. Scholarship in the United States and the United Kingdom has to a large extent monopolized the theorization of the concept, and it is in these jurisdictions that governments have arguably led the way in establishing specific policies to address hate-motivated offences (see, e.g., Chakraborti and Garland 2015; Lawrence 1999). Other Western jurisdictions throughout Europe, and countries including Canada, Australia, and New Zealand, have also been fertile ground for research on hate crime (see relevant chapters in Hall et al. 2014). In particular, there is a growing body of research that examines the impacts of hate crime victimization in these jurisdictions (see, e.g., Iganski and Lagou 2015; McDevitt et al. 2001), while a burgeoning literature has also developed on the practical and theoretical arguments for and against the enactment of hate crime legislation (see Schweppe and Walters 2015 for an overview). Smaller pools of scholarship have developed on: the causes of hate crime (Perry 2009); new forms of hate such as cyber-hate (Citron 2014); and the use of alternative justice measures to address the causes and consequences of hate-based conflicts (Walters 2014). There is, of course, much more to learn. In particular, there is currently very little information on the effects that globalization has had on both the proliferation of hate crime and how we as a global society should go about combating it. This book attempts to fill this lacuna through a comprehensive exploration of both the globalized dynamics of hate, and the internationalization of the concept of hate crime.

Globalization generally refers to the increasing interconnectedness of societies throughout the world. More specifically, it can be characterized as an expanding international economic, legal, political, and cultural connectedness that is increasingly fuelled by transnational mobility, technological advancements in communication, and the dismantling of jurisdictional trade barriers (Findlay 2008). Our ever growing globalized society means that what happens on one side of the world can have impacts on the other—in some cases almost instantaneously. A great deal has been written about the effects that globalization is having on all of our lives (Held et al. 1999; Martell 2010). There are immense benefits to our growing cultural, political, and economic connectivity—not least new opportunities to create wealth, the dissemination of knowledge and ideas, and the ability to travel to pastures new. However, with benefits there are disadvantages to opening up international borders of both a physical and virtual nature. More specifically, the rapid expansion in international (virtual) mobility has facilitated new opportunities for some of the most damaging of criminal activities. Common amongst these have been the proliferation of cybercrime, organized criminal activity, green crimes, human trafficking, and terrorism. This has resulted in an expansion of criminological discourse on international crime control measures for these types of crimes (see, e.g., Findlay 2013). Yet broadly absent from most of the critical analysis on the globalization of crime is any detailed examination of the proliferation of hate speech, hate crime, and more broadly hate-based conflicts.

In many respects one need not scrutinize the effects of globalization too deeply to comprehend its impacts on the spread of hate crime. The hate-motivated attacks in Paris at the beginning and end of 2015, which together left nearly 150 people dead are cases in point. These mass murders provided fuel to a polarizing public debate that has pitted Western concepts of freedom of speech against the so-called Islamization of Western civilization.[1] Similar incidents in Denmark (BBC 2015) and in Australia (Ralston 2014) illustrate how quickly hatred, with its devastating consequences, can spread throughout the world. These events, and many others like them, have been directly correlated with geo-political conflicts, or what are often referred to as 'trigger events'[2] (Copsey et al. 2013). The impacts of such events, such as the Charlie Hebdo massacre, quickly ripple out as social media and traditional media outlets spark interest, outrage and in turn violent retaliation in locations across the globe (see, e.g., Copsey et al. 2013; CST 2014). Others have pointed to the ongoing conflict, including alleged war crimes, between Israel and Palestine during recent times as being directly causal to the sharp increases in the number of antisemitic and Islamophobic hate incidents that have been reported in a number of jurisdictions (CST 2014; FRA 2014).

Other recent geo-political events have similarly resulted in the proliferation of hate-based conflicts. The rise of the militant group Islamic State (also commonly referred to as IS, Isis or Isil) has galvanized support amongst those who feel a sense of indignation resulting from regional geo-political and religious-based conflicts, as well as the aggressive international policies of the US and Europe. The Islamic State group is spreading across Syria and Iraq, where they have brutally murdered 'non-believers', gay and lesbian people (Duffy 2015), and those who resist the group's 'restoration of the Caliphate' (Al-Marashi 2015). Islamic State is the epitome of globalized hate. It is an international movement that has created a global army of jihadists who have travelled from all corners of the world to fight in a so-called holy war. Those who oppose or who fall outside of their strict rules are ruthlessly vanquished, pushed off buildings (Duffy 2015), beheaded, shot, or hung in public places (Shaheen and Black 2015).

---

[1] For a list of commentary see, e.g., http://www.theguardian.com/world/charlie-hebdo-attack

[2] i.e. Violent incidents that catch the attention of the media and which, in turn, result in the proliferation of retaliatory identity-based violence.

Intertwined with these ideological wars is the global economic and humanitarian crisis that began in earnest during the late 2000s which has led to mass global migration. The surge in the number of those travelling to Europe from Africa, for example, has led to a humanitarian crisis in Europe not seen since the Second World War. This situation has caused immense public and political unrest in European countries concerned about the impacts that mass immigration has on national cultures and local prosperity. Such concerns, magnified by the media, have given rise to increased support for far right parties across the continent which vociferously resist immigration (Vasilopoulou and Halikiopoulou 2015). In some countries extremist hate groups (such as the Golden Dawn in Greece) have penetrated mainstream politics, typifying the growing hostilities felt amongst certain sections of society towards the 'foreigners' who arrive at their shores daily (Vasilopoulou and Halikiopoulou 2015).

Though globalization has clearly produced new avenues through which identity-based prejudices and hostilities are spread, it has simultaneously enabled groups of people to create global movements that are aimed at forging new alliances between marginalized groups, thereby giving once silenced communities a more powerful political voice. For example, the proliferation of LGBTQI[3] rights groups across Western countries has enabled a persecuted minority to vocalize their experiences of oppression and abuse. It is this voice that has gradually penetrated broader public consciousness about LGBTQI people, finally giving rise to public support for the enactment of new laws protecting people from anti-LGBTQI discrimination and supporting equality through access to social institutions such as marriage (Duggan 2015). While this is most definitely a welcome step in the fight for equality for LGBTQI people, we need also be mindful of the consequences that these developments have globally. In France, for example, the introduction of marriage equality has resulted in increases in homophobic violent attacks (SOS Homophobie 2014). The situation is even worse in countries such as Russia and Uganda (to name but two jurisdictions), where global pressure to protect LGBTQI people has been met with vociferous opposition and further vilification against those deemed to have caught the 'Western disease' (see, e.g., de Vos 2015).

INTERNATIONALIZING HATE CRIME

So what is to be done to quell the global proliferation of hate-motivated violence? The increased international knowledge base on hate speech and hate crime has led to the beginnings of international efforts to address it (Perry 2015a). As we will see throughout this collection, there are now international laws (e.g., European Union Framework Decision on combating certain forms and expressions of racism and xenophobia by means of criminal law (2008)), transnational crime control policies (e.g., OSCE 2009), and the beginnings of comparative analyses of experiences of

---

[3] Lesbian, Gay, Bisexual, Transgender, Queer, and Intersex.

hate crime victimization as well as the laws that are aimed at tackling them (see FRA 2012, 2013, 2014; OSCE 2013).[4] This means that we are now witnessing the beginnings of what this book terms the 'internationalization of hate crime'. That is to say, hate crime—both as a concept and as a specific criminal offence—has been recognized as a social problem that is being addressed collectively at the international level.

This approach by the international community has led to new attempts to engage criminal justice agencies, policy bodies, and NGOs across borders who together are formulating new ways to better deal with hate crime (see Perry 2015a, 2015b). However, researchers must also play their part in the dissemination of ideas and research findings in order that society as a whole has a better understanding of the problem, including how we as a global society can better address hate-based conflicts (Perry et al. 2015). One such attempt to bring international partners together to do just this is the creation of the International Network for Hate Studies (INHS). The Network is led by academics, policy experts, and practitioners, and aims to provide a platform through which researchers, policy makers, and practitioners (and the public) can share knowledge about hate and hate crime globally.[5] The INHS website states, '[h]ate has no borders and, with the proliferation of online sources and resources, its study needs a multi-disciplinary and international focus as well as one which examines local and jurisdiction-specific causes and responses.'[6] The Network continues to support its aims via a biennial international conference,[7] an edited online blog, an extensive online library of resources, and workshops to facilitate international research collaboration.

While there have been international efforts to combat hate speech and hate crimes for several years now, these laws, policies, and practices have been subjected to very little detailed critical analyses. As mentioned at the start of this introduction, the current body of literature, though expanding, has tended to focus on Western conceptions of hate crime. Several authors and editors have attempted to break this mould by publishing works that take a more international perspective on hate crime. For example, in 1994 Mark Hamm edited a collection entitled *Hate Crime: International Perspectives on Causes and Control*, which gave focus to the disparate nature of hate crime victimization within Europe and the US. Hamm believed that the conceptualization of hate crime globally should be done via the lens of 'an international youth movement toward racism'. He added that 'this is because it is racism (not homophobia, and certainly not misogyny) that fuels neo-Nazi skinhead violence from Rostock to London, from Amsterdam to Paris, and from Stockholm to Dallas' (Hamm 1994: 175). This narrow approach to conceptualizing hate crime is reflected in two other international collections on hate crime, both published in 1998: Jeffrey

  [4] For a list of international research studies on hate crime see: http://www.internationalhatestudies.com/current-research-studies

  [5] The INHS has four key aims: sharing information; public policy engagement; collaboration in research; and improved understanding of hate crime globally (see http://www.internationalhatestudies.com/about-us/aims-and-objectives-of-the-network).

  [6] www.internationalhatestudies.com

  [7] This book is the result of the INHS' first international conference, Understanding Hate Crime: Research, Policy and Practice, held at the University of Sussex on 7–8 May 2014.

Kaplan and Tore Bjørgo's *Nation and Race: The Developing Euro-American Racist Subculture* and Robert Kelly and Jess Maghan's *Hate Crime: The Global Politics of Polarization*. While both collections advanced further the scope of hate crime scholarship by including essays on the plights of 'Homeless Palestinians' in Israel and the Arab world, social cleansing in Colombia, hate crimes in India, as well as the more typical European and American analyses, they too suffered from the narrower lens of Hamm's 1994 book.

It was not until the early 2000s that the hate crime umbrella was forced open to embrace a more diverse range of prejudices and identity characteristics beyond racism. This is now reflected in the newer contributions to the field. For instance, Nathan Hall and others published their *International Handbook on Hate Crime* (2014), which provides chapters on a range of hate crimes including anti-LGBT, disablist, anti-Roma, and crimes targeted against individuals belonging to alternative sub-cultures. The book also includes a section on 'the international geography of hate' (Part Two). This part of the book includes chapters on Europe, the UK, the US, Canada, Australia, and New Zealand (as well as a chapter on global antisemitism). More recently, Paul Iganski and Jack Levin published their book entitled *Hate Crime: A Global Perspective* (2015). This too is a more inclusive text which identifies a number of 'common' types of hate crime that occur across the world, while also providing a 'snapshot' of some of the countries where hate violence is particularly problematic. Perhaps most innovatively, it begins to highlight the effects of globalization by focusing on religious hatred and the impacts of extremist violence globally.

Together these newer contributions offer a more comprehensive evaluation of the international geography of hate crime. Nonetheless, there remains a paucity of research on hate crime in Africa, Asia, and South America. As Perry and others noted recently, '[t]he time has come to widen our geographical lens' (2015: 3). This book aids such an endeavour by examining how hate crime manifests (and how it is challenged) within a number of jurisdictions across the world—including in Eastern Europe, Africa, and Asia. However, readers should note that it is *not* the purpose of this book to provide a comprehensive discussion of hate crime around the world. Rather, the focus of this book is to consider more specifically the dynamics of *globalization*; including whether universal principles and global explanations help us to conceptualize hate crime. Contributors additionally explore how global forces impact upon the ways in which hate crime is caused and is responded to (or not) in different locales. Finally, we ask not just how hate is being globalized but whether the concept can be truly internationalized—and perhaps more pertinently whether a global response can help to combat its spread.

STRUCTURE OF THE BOOK

The book is divided into three separate parts, each explained below, that collectively aim to challenge our understanding of hate crime. Of course, this is really just the start of a (global) conversation about hate crime. The editors acknowledge that much more needs to be done to ensure that the debate is opened further to be more inclusive of different perspectives from different parts of the world.

PART I

Part I of this book examines the global dynamics of hate. It is here that our contributors begin to analyse whether hate crime can be defined globally, whether universal principles can be applied to the phenomenon, how hatred is spread, and how it impacts upon our global society.

In Chapter 1, Jon Garland and Corinne Funnell consider the issues and conundrums raised by the different conceptualizations of hate crime that have been developed throughout the world. They argue that the causes and consequences of hate crime are both an international as well as a domestic phenomenon. Through a brief analysis of the international instruments and policies aimed at combating hate and hate crime, the authors assert that a 'top down' human rights-based approach to combating hate crime internationally has failed to gain the traction some have hoped for, resulting in uneven protection for victims across borders. Instead, the authors argue that local communities should concentrate on grass roots initiatives based on a 'politics of justice' approach that will allow for a more inclusive and jurisdiction-specific response to hate crime to develop.

In Chapter 2 Thomas Brudholm turns our attention squarely onto a human rights perspective of hate crime by asking the question as to whether it should be conceptualized globally as a human rights violation. Distinguishing between two schools of thought in human rights discourse (the 'power-regulative conception' versus what he labels the 'dignitarian conception'), Brudholm argues that while 'ordinary' hate crimes (i.e. those committed between/against private citizens) may be conceived as a human rights 'issue' they do not amount to human rights violations. This, he concludes, does not mean that hate crime should not be addressed at the international level, but rather the legal framework for human rights violations is a misnomer for hate crime; one which also potentially undermines the purpose and utility of human rights instruments.

In Chapter 3 David Brax moves away from human rights discourse and asks whether it is possible to develop a universal framework for understanding hate crime. Brax uses the current literature and philosophical theorization of hate crime to outline five separate, but interlinking, concepts of the phenomenon. He summarizes the concepts for the reader before offering additional moral foundations for sustaining a concept of hate crime. Brax concludes that in order to develop an international framework of hate crime legislation, policy, and even scholarship, we must create greater clarity as to hate crime's conceptual and normative basis.

In Chapter 4 the book moves on from asking how we define hate crime to asking how hatred and hate crime are spread globally. Barbara Perry and Ryan Scrivens offer new insight into the world of cyber-hate, detailing the ways in which hate groups disseminate their ideologies online, constructing collective identities as they do so, and in this case, (re)establishing 'White Pride Worldwide'. Perry and Scrivens discuss how online platforms help to construct common identities by building solidarity and, somewhat paradoxically, challenging globalization by forming a globalized 'White Nation' that is based on the white Aryan cultures of Western Europe.

Chapter 5 adds to our understanding of globalized hate by offering insight into the 'ripple effects' of terrorist events. Kathryn Benier presents a comprehensive review of the evidence that links global terror events with increases in hate crime incidents. Benier illustrates how these studies have shown a temporal relationship between terrorism and more localized incidents of hate. However, using original empirical research conducted by the author in Australia, the chapter offers a slightly different perspective, with the results from the study showing little correlation between terrorist acts overseas with domestic incidents of retaliatory hate crime; suggesting that the effects of terrorism (at least in the Australian context) may be less global than we have previously assumed.

In Chapter 6, Paul Iganski and Abe Sweiry complete Part I of the book by offering a comprehensive overview of research on the harms caused by hate violence globally. Highlighting in particular the various spatial and psychosocial impacts of different types of hate violence across the globe, the deleterious effects that such incidents have on our global communities' health and wellbeing are emphasized by the authors. In fact, such are the devastating impacts of hate violence that Iganski and Sweiry argue that it should be conceived as a global health problem that requires the formation of new public health interventions.

PART II

Part II of the book moves beyond the broader questions of globalization to jurisdictional examples of how globalization impacts upon both our understanding of, and also our responses to, hate crime. It is here that we are able to explore in greater detail what is happening around the world and how the international concepts of hate crime are being operationalized locally. As mentioned above, this part of the book is not intended to be a comprehensive review of hate crime across the world. Rather, it is aimed at drawing out themes of globalization and internationalization as evidenced by a number of jurisdictions from Europe (West and East), the US, Asia, and Africa.

Chapter 7 begins this endeavour with an exploration of the impacts of Islamophobic hate crimes against women in the UK. Irene Zempi presents empirical data from her qualitative study conducted in Leicester, England, and analyses her findings through the 'notions of worldwide, transnational Muslim community, the ummah'. The chapter explores the intersection between Islamophobia and cultural racism, which she argues gives rise to a 'racialized Muslimness'. Such prejudices are a product of globalized cultural racism that labels all Muslims as dangerous others. The resulting hostilities affect Muslim communities worldwide (though mainly in Western societies), who often seek refuge in safe spaces (in this case the city of

Leicester in England). Still, as Zempi notes, the global pervasiveness of Islamophobia means that Muslims even here feel the collective pains that other Muslims experience internationally through their cultural and religious connectedness (ummah).

In Chapter 8 Duncan Breen, Ingrid Lynch, Juan Nel, and Iole Matthews examine hate crime through the lens of transitional societies, using South Africa as their reference point. Though the post-apartheid South African Constitution was, as they observe, considered 'exemplary' for its inclusive nature, prohibiting as it does discrimination based on grounds such as race, sex, gender, ethnic or social origin, and sexual orientation, South Africa continues to struggle to eradicate the culture of segregation and marginalization which characterized the institutionalized discrimination that epitomized the system of apartheid. The authors examine the particular and oftentimes brutal experiences of victims of hate crimes against non-nationals and lesbian, gay, bisexual, transgender, and intersex (LGBTI) persons, and conclude that in light of deeply held prejudices, sometimes held by political leaders, the much-celebrated equality guarantee in the Constitution exists only on paper.

Chapter 9 offers insight into a jurisdiction seldom written about in the context of hate crime. Bengi Bezirgan analyses the construction of the 'ideal citizen' in the creation of the Turkish State, observing that this process has informed the development of recently introduced so-called hate crime laws. These laws reflect, as the author observes, the recognition of 'legitimate victims' and omit to recognize either ethnicity or sexual orientation as protected characteristics. This selective understanding of victimhood, she argues, reflects the international approach to tackling hate crime, but also 'illustrates the power of a heteronormative socio-political system for the trivialization of violence against LGBTI individuals'. The Turkish example, she concludes, thus shows that the development of hate crime laws can act as a political and ideological tool which maintains pre-established forms of discrimination.

In Chapter 10 Amanda Haynes and Jennifer Schweppe examine a further obstacle to the internationalization of hate. As Ireland is one of the few countries in Europe without hate crime legislation of any form, they argue that a legislative permission to hate exists in that country, with the legal system largely blind to the hate element of crimes. Despite this position, the State remains resolute in its refusal to address this issue, despite increasing pressure from both internal civil society organizations, as well as international organizations such as the European Commission against Racism and Intolerance (ECRI), the Council of the European Union, the Committee on the Elimination of Racial Discrimination (CERD), and the Organization for Security and Co-operation in Europe (OSCE), as well as the UN Universal Periodic Review process. Having established robust evidence to contradict the response of the State to these international bodies, they ask whether, when these technical arguments are disposed of, legislation will be enacted, or if further ideological objections will be revealed.

In Chapter 11 Piotr Godzisz and Dorota Pudzianowska assess the development of hate crime laws in Poland. In particular, the authors examine why sexual orientation has been excluded from its legislation. They offer a thorough exploration of recent attempts to change the Polish Criminal Code and the reasons that have been proffered for the continued denial of sexual orientation as a protected characteristic.

Godzisz and Pudzianowska argue that hate crime in Poland must be understood in the context of its history as a Catholic and culturally conservative country. This history has prioritized racial and religious hatred over other forms of prejudice as a consequence of the narrative of cultural and ethnic identity that was formed after the Second World War. The authors illustrate how law makers remain steadfast in their refusal to acknowledge other 'Western' forms of hate crime. However, they conclude that the status quo may be about to change due to the influence of both domestic and international organizations that are lobbying hard within Poland to gain better protection against anti-LGB hate crimes.

Concluding Part II of the book, Paul Giannasi and Nathan Hall in Chapter 12 give an account of the legal, policy, and cultural changes in policing in England and Wales which took place following the murder of Stephen Lawrence. They consider the extent to which this experience is transferable to other jurisdictions seeking to address hate crime, noting that the political response to hate crime is crucial, in that even where there is a shift in the response of criminal justice agencies, without strong governmental support, hate crime will be potentially allowed to flourish. They conclude by observing that it is undoubtedly preferable to address the legal, policy, and cultural issues that exist as a pre-emptive measure, rather than in reaction to a tragic event such as that of the murder of Stephen Lawrence.

PART III

The final part of this book seeks to examine the different ways in which hate speech and hate crime are being challenged globally. International law, internet regulation, and the use of restorative practices are evaluated as methods of addressing hate-based conflict. The analyses found here draw from existing frameworks as well as exploring normative standards for future international efforts.

In Chapter 13 Michael Whine details the international monitoring mechanisms for hate crime which have developed in countries across Europe. Whine provides a detailed summary of the various institutions which are engaged in transnational monitoring of hate crime, noting that progress has been made over recent years in improving data collection. He notes that the development of more comprehensive policies at the international level has also played an important role in highlighting the problem of hate-motivated offences.

Chapter 14 continues with a European theme by discussing the role that the European Court of Human Rights should play in combating hate crime. Jasmina Mačkić outlines a number of cases which illustrate the Court's reluctance to address complaints of discriminatory violence within Europe. She argues that current responses by the Court have been unsatisfactory and that the Court ought to be playing a more active role in highlighting the problem of hate crime in Europe. She outlines four reasons why the Court must do more to tackle hate crime, including: its role as an 'alarm bell' warning that a Member State is 'going totalitarian'; the Council of Europe's growing concern with tackling discrimination generally; the so-called agenda-setting function of the Court; and finally that discriminatory violence claims deserve more attention by the Court given its increasing constitutional role.

In Chapter 15 Viera Pejchal and Kimberley Brayson examine the international legal framework for hate speech as it has developed since the Second World War. The chapter poses the key question of whether a universal law on hate speech is either possible or desirable. Pejchal and Brayson group the current laws chronologically through the lens of the three generations of human rights. They assert that the third generation of hate speech laws (those which focus on protection from discrimination and protecting human dignity) are most suited to stable democratic regimes as a means of balancing democratic freedoms with protecting vulnerable groups from persecution. Nevertheless, the authors stop short of recommending this approach be applied universally within a single legal instrument, instead concluding that all three generations remain purposeful in today's world in order to combat the different forms of hate speech that are expressed in countries with diverging political regimes.

In Chapter 16 Chara Bakalis has the vexing task of searching for an answer to the growing problem of regulating cyber-hate. Bakalis' chapter is distinct from others who have ventured into this discrete area of scholarship in that she attempts to unpick the distinct nature of online hate, including its more nuanced and complex forms of harms, compared with offline hate. Distinguishing between the more traditional personal/impersonal and public/private law distinctions, Bakalis notes that any new form of cyber-hate regulation must contend with the blurred lines between these distinctions in the virtual world. Not only this, but regulation must attempt to address the more pervasive pollutant qualities of cyber-hate, which can cause harms to large groups of people across the globe. Such is its reach, she argues, that a streamlined international response encompassing both legal instruments and private (internet service providers) forms of regulation must be co-ordinated.

In the penultimate chapter of the book (Chapter 17), Ruby Axelson assesses the position of international criminal law in relation to state-sponsored hate and hate speech as crimes against humanity. Focusing on the persecution of sexual minorities, Axelson offers insight into how the principles espoused in both universalism and post-colonialism may be reconciled in order to consider how universal protection of sexual minorities can be legitimized in the face of varying cultural contexts. In doing this Axelson explores how the protection of sexual minorities could be situated within the existing framework of persecution, either under 'gender' or within 'other grounds universally recognized'. However, she concludes that, faced with dominant heteronormative standards in interpreting international criminal law, it will be essential that further attempts be initiated to expand the Rome Statute to explicitly recognize sexual minorities.

The final chapter of the book (Chapter 18) asks whether a restorative approach to combating hate crime and hate-based conflicts can offer a more effective way of addressing the causes and consequences of hate. Mark Austin Walters questions the emerging orthodoxy that hate crimes should be tackled by enacting (international) laws that increase the punishments of individuals found guilty of hate-motivated offences. Instead, he argues that greater attention should be paid to dialogical processes that focus on inter-group communication centred on identity difference, hostility, and harm. One way this can be achieved is through the advancement of restorative justice practices that can be utilized for different levels of violence. These include: micro-levels incidents (inter-personal crimes between community members); meso-level conflicts (identity-based conflicts involving groups of people or entire communities); and macro-level violence (involving systemic abuse and state actors). Walters asserts that these dialogical practices are better positioned to address the causes of hate-based conflicts and thus are more likely to be effective at resolving the differing (though intersecting) manifestations of hate that affect communities globally.

REFERENCES

Al-Marashi, I. 2015. 'Why the caliphate survives', Al Jazeera.

BBC 2015. Copenhagen shootings: Police kill 'gunman' after two attacks, BBC News.

Chakraborti, N. and Garland, J. 2015. *Hate Crime: Impact, Causes and Responses*, London: Sage.

Citron, D.K. 2014. *Hate Crimes in Cyberspace*, Harvard University Press.

Community Security Trust 2015. *Antisemitic Incidents Report 2014*, Community Security Trust: London.

Copsey, N., Dack, J., Littler, M., and Feldman, M. 2013. *Anti-Muslim Hate Crime and the Far Right*, Middlesbrough: Teesside University.

de Vos, P. 2015. 'Mind the Gap: Imagining New Ways of Struggling towards the Emancipation of Sexual Minorities in Africa', *Agenda* 29(1): 1–15.

Duffy, N. 2015. 'This sick crowd gathered to watch ISIS murder three gay men', Pink News.

Duggan, M. 2015. 'Pride, Prejudice and Politics: Global Tensions in Effecting Sexual and Religious Rights', International Network for Hate Studies Blog: http://www.internationalhatestudies.com/pride-prejudice-politics-global-tensions-effecting-sexual-religious-rights/

European Agency for Fundamental Rights (FRA) 2012. *Making hate crime visible in the European Union: acknowledging victims' rights* http://fra.europa.eu/sites/default/files/fra-2012_hate-crime.pdf

European Agency for Fundamental Rights (FRA) 2013. *EU LGBT survey–European Union lesbian, gay, bisexual and transgender survey—Results at a glance* http://fra.europa.eu/en/publication/2013/eu-lgbt-survey-european-union-lesbian-gay-bisexual-and-transgender-survey-results

European Agency for Fundamental Rights (FRA) 2014. *Antisemitism Summary overview of the situation in the European Union 2003–2013* http://fra.europa.eu/en/publication/2014/antisemitism-summary-overview-situation-european-union-2003-2013

Findlay, M. 2008. *Governing through Globalised Crime: Futures for International Criminal Justice*, Cullompton: Willan Publishing.

Findlay, M. 2013. *Contemporary Challenges in Regulating Global Crises*, Palgrave Macmillan.

Hall, N. 2013. *Hate Crime* (2nd edn) London: Routledge.

Hall, N., Corb, A., Giannasi, P., and Grieve, J. (eds.) 2014. *The International Handbook on Hate Crime*, London: Routledge.

Hamm, M. (ed.) 1994. *Hate Crime: International Perspectives on Causes and Control*, Cincinnati, OH: Anderson Pub.

Held, D., McGrew, A., Goldblatt, D., and Perraton, J. 1999. *Global Transformations: Politics, Economics and Culture*, Cambridge: Polity Press.

Iganski, P. and Lagou, S. 2015. 'Hate Crimes Hurt Some More Than Others: Implications for the Just Sentencing of Offenders', *Journal of Interpersonal Violence*, 30(10): 1696–1718.

Iganski, P. and Levin, J. 2015. *Hate Crime: A Global Perspective*, Policy Press.

Kaplan, J. and Bjørgo, T. 1998. *Nation and Race: the Developing Euro-American Racist Subculture*, Boston: Northeastern University Press.

Kelly, R.J. and Maghan, J. (1998) *Hate Crime: The Global Politics of Polarization*, Carbondale and Edwardsville: Southern Illinois University Press.

Lawrence, F.M. 1999. *Punishing Hate: Bias Crimes under American Law*, London: Harvard University Press.

Martell, L. 2010. *The Sociology of Globalization*, Cambridge: Polity Press.

McDevitt, J., Balboni, J., Garcia, L., and Gu, J. 2001. 'Consequences for Victims: a Comparison of Bias- and Non-bias-motivated Assaults', *American Behavioral Scientist*, 45(4), pp. 697–713.

Organization for Security and Co-operation in Europe (OSCE) 2013. *Hate Crimes in the OSCE Region–Incidents and Responses: Annual Report for 2012*, Warsaw: OSCE. http://tandis.odihr.pl/hcr2012/pdf/Hate_Crime_Report_full_version.pdf

Organization for Security and Co-operation in Europe (OSCE) 2009. *Hate Crime Laws: A Practical Guide*, Warsaw: ODIHR, OSCE.

Perry, B. (2009) *Hate Crimes*, Westport, CT: Praeger Perspectives Greenwood Publishing Group, Incorporated.

Perry, B. 2015a. 'Intervening Globally: Confronting Hate Across the World', *Criminal Justice Policy Review* doi:10.1177/0887403415599643.

Perry, B., Perry, J., Schweppe, J., and Walters, M. 2015. Understanding Hate Crime: Research, Policy and Practice: *Special Edition, Criminal Justice Policy Review*, doi: 10.1177/0887403415599642.

Perry, J. 2015b. 'A Shared Global Perspective on Hate Crime?' *Criminal Justice Policy Review*, doi:10.1177/0887403415601473.

Ralston, N. 2014. 'Martin Place, Sydney siege gunman identified as Man Haron Monis', Sydney Morning Herald.

Schweppe, J. and Walters, M.A. 2015. 'Hate Crimes: Legislating to Enhance Punishment' in Tonry, M. (ed.), *Oxford Online Handbook of Crime and Criminal Justice*, Oxford: Oxford University Press.

Shaheen, K. and Black, I. 2015. 'Beheaded Syrian scholar refused to lead Isis to hidden Palmyra antiquities', The Guardian.

SOS homophobie 2014. *Rapport sur l'homophobie 2014*, SOS homophobie.

Vasilopoulou, S. and Halikiopoulou, D. 2015. *The Golden Dawn's 'Nationalist Solution': Explaining the Rise of the Far Right in Greece*, Palgrave.

Walters, M. 2014. *Hate Crime and Restorative Justice: Exploring Causes, Repairing Harms*, Oxford: Oxford University Press.

PART I

THE GLOBAL DIMENSIONS OF HATE CRIME

1

DEFINING HATE CRIME INTERNATIONALLY: ISSUES AND CONUNDRUMS

Jon Garland and Corinne Funnell

INTRODUCTION

The years following the financial crash of 2008 and the subsequent adoption of policies of fiscal austerity by governments across the globe have seen a rise in concern about levels and forms of hate crime. In the United Kingdom some of the hostile government and media rhetoric directed towards social security claimants has created a climate in which those on disability benefits have experienced harassment and abuse from members of the public (Chakraborti and Garland 2015). Other European countries have seen reactions to austerity take the form of increases in support for far-right parties (such as in Greece (Golden Dawn) and France (Front National)) or rises in antisemitic attacks (Denmark, Germany, the Netherlands, and France (BBC 2015)), assaults and harassment of Roma and Sinti (Hungary), or alarming increases in homophobic abuse and violence (as in the case of Russia—see, inter alia, European Union Agency for Fundamental Rights (FRA) 2013a, 2013b; Hall et al. 2014). At the same time, events in other countries, such as the terrorist attack in Sydney, Australia in 2014, the lethal assault upon an African American church congregation in Charleston, USA by a white supremacist in 2015, the murders of fifty-nine trans women in Brazil in 2014 (Kellaway 2014), and the global reach and impact of the ongoing Israel/Palestine conflict have all increased concern about the nature and forms of contemporary hate crime. In many cases, it has been the levels of violence involved in these incidents that commentators have interpreted as an indicator of a rise in hate crime, but in reality (as is acknowledged in the growing corpus of related literature) it is very difficult to discern accurately the actual levels of hate crime in any individual state (see Perry 2003).

This problem is compounded when we analyse the issue from a cross-national perspective. A casual observer would only have to look at interpretations of hate crime offered at state level in a handful of European countries, for example, to see how much they differ in terms of conceptualization, measurement, victim group recognition, types of legal intervention, and forms of crime included within it; global variations are even more striking. These disparities reflect the lack of a common understanding of the notion of hate crime, and even when the concept has been discussed it has often been conflated with racism (see, e.g., Framework Decision (2008/913/JHA)). Furthermore, the Office for Democratic Institutions and Human Rights (ODIHR) notes that the term 'hate crime' was first used officially by the Organization for Security and Co-operation in Europe (OSCE) only as recently as 2003 (ODIHR 2013).[1] At a time when hate crime appears to be a significant international issue there is a pressing need for states and statutory and voluntary organizations (both within and across nations) to grasp the complexities of the phenomenon of hate crime and develop comprehensive policies to counter it.

The aim of this chapter is therefore to consider the issues and conundrums raised by the different conceptualizations of hate crime evidenced worldwide and, in so doing, argue that the causes and consequences of the phenomenon are international as well as domestic. It will assess differing national interpretations of hate crime and implementations of legal interventions designed to counter it. Hate crime is, of course, a global phenomenon, played out in different (and damaging) ways across different continents. However, due to the limited space available here, and not least because many Western jurisdictions in particular have developed quite extensive policies and laws designed to combat hate crime, the chapter will focus primarily upon the situation in Europe, the United States, Canada, Australia, and New Zealand. It will reflect upon some local historical contexts, which flavour national responses to hate crime while also seeing where there are commonalities in approaches. It will assess the range of cross-national initiatives, often devised from a human rights perspective, that have been put in place to encourage and sometimes require nations to combat hate crime, and will examine how they play out at a local level. It will argue that this 'top-down' human rights-based approach to combating hate crime, endorsed by many cross-national institutions, has failed to tackle the problem as effectively as it might, resulting in the uneven protection of hate crime victim groups. By developing grassroots initiatives and policies locally, via a 'politics of justice' approach, it is suggested that the damaging nature and effect of such 'targeted victimization' upon hate crime victims can be better understood and addressed globally.

THEORETICAL CONCEPTUALIZATIONS OF HATE CRIME

Academic debates around hate crime have in many ways mirrored those in the practitioner sphere, as they have focused upon how we understand what constitutes a hate crime, what the motivations of the offender typically are, and what characteristics hate crime victim groups normally possess. Are hate crimes, for instance, solely motivated by hate? Are offenders influenced by feelings of frustration and anger borne from acute

---

[1] Some individual states have been referring to 'hate crime' since the early 1990s.

feelings of strain, as they struggle with socio-economic instability and precariousness (Walters 2011)? Or is it the fact that victims are targeted because of their actual or perceived membership of a social grouping, rather than the presence of any bias or hatred towards them, that is the most significant factor when defining hate crime?

The debates surrounding these issues have, over the past decade, engaged scholars from North America, Europe, and Australasia. However, much of the discussion in this field has revolved around the difficult issue of whether hate crime victimization is the sole preserve of minority 'outgroups' that have suffered a history of oppression and marginalization, or whether more 'privileged' social groups are also worthy of protection (see Hall 2013). Some authors have suggested that, generally speaking, victim groups should indeed be conceived of as those that have been historically marginalized and harassed, reflecting the origins of the concept of hate crime in the civil rights struggles in the 1960s, when it served as a way of uniting oppressed communities by recognizing the commonalities in their victimization (Perry 2001). Which of these disadvantaged groups is more 'deserving' of legal protection has also been the subject of much deliberation (see, inter alia, Iganski 2008; Turpin-Petrosino 2015).

Linked to this is the suggestion that perpetrators target potential victims due to their membership of despised 'outgroups', making hate crimes classic 'stranger-danger' forms of crime in which it is not the *individual* that is targeted per se, but rather their *identity*. However, this aspect of the concept has also been challenged, with Mason (2005, amongst others) arguing that often offenders actually know their victims, at least to a degree, or are familiar enough with them to know that they belong to a social group they despise.

Accompanying the act of hate is the inherent threat that further violence will be meted out upon any member of the targeted group if they continue to conduct themselves in ways that the perpetrator deems 'unacceptable'. Such acts have a 'cumulative impact' that extends beyond the individual to 'their families' and 'communities', with the 'domino effect' 'rippling across an extended group' (Feagin and Sikes 1994: 16; see also Weinstein 1992). In addition, as they target cultural, ethnic, religious, or sexual identity, for instance, these acts are more hurtful than 'everyday' crimes that lack the bias motive as they damage feelings of self-worth, personal security, and confidence (see for example Funnell 2014).

Perry (2001), meanwhile, suggests that hate crime is not a static problem but one which needs to be seen as a dynamic social process involving context, structure, and agency. The role of relevant actors in the process, namely the victim, perpetrator, and their respective communities, is therefore vital. Perpetrators, typically from powerful social groups, target 'subordinate' ones in order to maintain their privileged position within society while reinforcing the 'lower' position of the targeted group. Perry also suggests that hate crimes mirror dominant attitudes within society, meaning that mainstream media discourse around issues to do with sexual orientation, for example, is inherently heteronormative in nature, privileging heterosexuality over other forms of sexual identity and thus creating the backdrop for acts of homophobia by 'othering' homosexuality.

More recently, though, developments in hate crime theory have utilized aspects of Perry's influential theory in order to develop what is perhaps a simplified understanding of hate crime. Chakraborti, Garland, and Hardy (2014), for example, utilized a broader definition—as acts of violence, hostility, and intimidation directed towards people because of their identity or perceived 'difference'—as the conceptual framework for conducting a large-scale hate crime victimization study. This concise definition steps out of Perry's structural framework by acknowledging that some victims are targeted not just because they are part of a stigmatized outgroup but also because they are regarded as vulnerable, 'different' in a way that may be perceived as threatening (see the example of the targeting of those from alternative subcultures in Garland and Hodkinson 2014), or weak in the eyes of the perpetrator. A definition like this covers forms of targeted hostility and anti-social behaviour which might not be criminal acts in themselves but which can have just as significant an impact upon the victim, their family, and wider communities. Furthermore, the more lo-quacious definitions that academics are inclined to use sometimes feel too complex, ethereal, and detached from the everyday realities confronting those who deal with hate crime cases in the 'real world' (Chakraborti 2015). However, as we will see below, international understandings of hate crime, as reflected in policy and practice, include differing aspects of these theoretical arguments, and it is to a discussion of these, initially via the context of Europe, that this chapter now turns.

GLOBAL DIMENSIONS IN HATE CRIME POLICY AND PRACTICE

BACKGROUND: THE HUMAN RIGHTS FRAMEWORK

The European Court of Human Rights, via its landmark decision in the 2005 case of *Nachova and Others v Bulgaria*,[2] ruled that state organizations have an obligation to investigate the possible racist motivation behind crimes or crimes committed because of bias against the religious belief of the victim. Furthermore, any criminal justice system that overlooks a bias motivation may be in violation of Article 14 of the European Convention on Human Rights which states that:

The enjoyment of the rights and freedoms set forth in this European Convention on Human Rights shall be secured without discrimination on any ground such as sex, race, colour, language, religion, political or other opinion, national or social origin, association with a national minority, property, birth or other status.

Thus Article 14 provides a human rights framework not just for equal rights across all identity categories but also for the right to be protected from discrimination, including hate crime.

---

[2] *Nachova and Others v Bulgaria*, Judgment of the European Court of Human Rights (Grand Chamber), 6 July 2005, paragraphs 160–8. The Court ruled that the State authorities' failure to discern racist motivation in this case constituted a violation of the non-discrimination provision in Article 14 (Prohibition of Discrimination) of the European Convention on Human Rights—see http://www.echr.coe.int/Pages/home.aspx?p=caselaw/analysis&c=

In an EU context, a number of interventions within the statutory framework of the EU seek to further guarantee these rights. Article 13 of the Treaty of Amsterdam, for instance, aims to prevent discrimination on the grounds of certain identity characteristics (race and ethnic origin, religion and belief, gender, sexual orientation, age, and disability) while the Lisbon Treaty, along with the legally binding Charter of Fundamental Rights of the European Union, strengthens the framework of non-discrimination legislation. Resolutions and recommendations by the Council of Europe Committee of Ministers and the Parliamentary Assembly also reaffirm the EU's requirement to combat discrimination in its policy and practice (FRA 2012).

Impetus for the implementation of hate crime legislation internationally came from 'the emergence of identity politics, the rise of the victims' rights movement and the return of retributivism to penal policy and practice' (Mason 2014a: 77), following the lead shown by the United States in enacting such laws. However, while there are a number of commonalities in the way that such legislation has developed across nations (in that many operate by 'topping up' sentences that exist under already existing legislation by imposing harsher penalties for bias-motivated offences), a number of inconsistencies have appeared too. In recognition of this, the EU, in 2008, adopted a Framework Decision (2008/913/JHA) on combating racism and xenophobia through criminal law, which was designed to 'harmonize' relevant legislation and create a common approach to tackling hate crime across the EU (for further discussion, see Goodall 2013; Mason 2014a; Whine 2014). As well as containing provisions on genocide, crimes against humanity, and war crimes, the Decision required Member States to criminalize incitement to hatred directed at people 'defined by reference to race, colour, religion, descent or national or ethnic origin' (FRA 2012: 25). It also directed Member States to ensure that 'racist and xenophobic motivation is considered an aggravating circumstance' which should be considered when sentencing in such cases is passed (ibid). In addition, in late 2012 the EU adopted Directive 2012/29/EU which contained provisions for improving recognition of the specific support that victims of hate crime need by obliging states to introduce laws, regulations, and administrative procedures in order to comply with the Directive's deadline of 16 November 2015.[3] Furthermore, Article 22 sets out obligations on Member States to identify measures that need to be taken to 'protect' people from being victimized on the grounds of 'age, gender and gender identity or expression, ethnicity, race, religion, sexual orientation, health, disability, residence status, communication difficulties, relationship to or dependence on the offender and previous experience of crime'. Those victims with 'specific protection needs' and who would benefit from 'specific protection measures' should be identified and responded to following 'an individual assessment' (ODIHR 2013: 39—further details can be found in Article 22).[4]

This raft of initiatives therefore provides EU states with the impetus and opportunity to devise their own hate crime legislative framework which encapsulates

---

[3] Among other things, the Directive instructed Member States to make sure that employees throughout the criminal justice system were trained in recognizing and dealing with hate crime cases.

[4] For additional information, see European Commission (2014).

some of these universal ideas of human rights in ways that can protect a wide range of minority groups. However, the introduction of such legislation and other related initiatives across the EU has been problematic, with a number of barriers, such as budgetary considerations and the perception that victims' rights can somehow clash with the purpose of criminal justice systems, thwarting their implementation (Centre for European Constitutional Law/Institute for Advanced Legal Studies 2014).

For those nations outside of the EU, such as Russia, there has been even less incentive to develop laws and programmes designed to protect marginalized groups from abuse, something which may have contributed to the growing climate of hostility faced by gay communities there (Arnold 2015).

MONITORING LEVELS OF HATE CRIME

The first step in combating hate crime is to gain a clear statistical picture of its quantity. In 2009 the OSCE Ministerial Council enacted Decision 9/09, which states that OSCE participating states should 'collect, maintain and make public reliable data and statistics in sufficient detail on hate crimes and violent manifestations of intolerance' (ODIHR 2013: 92). Despite this requirement, as FRA (2012: 8) notes, fourteen EU states provide only 'limited', infrequently published data on hate crime on a narrow range of bias motivations, while nine 'generally' publish 'good' data on a broader range of such motivations. Only four—Finland, Sweden, the Netherlands, and the United Kingdom—'always' publish 'comprehensive' data on a broad range of motivations, types of crime, and incidents. This is, of course, both frustrating for ODIHR but also worrying for those concerned with monitoring levels of hate crime on a cross-national level, as a lack of statistics obviously renders any international comparisons difficult if not impossible. It also may well reveal a lack of commitment to tackling hate crime on behalf of these 'non-returning' states, whose efforts in this regard do very little to help scholars and practitioners develop even basic understandings of the situation in their countries. Furthermore, any suggestion that hate crimes are not being recorded properly in a country like Russia, in which minority ethnic and gay people have been harassed, abused, violently assaulted, and even murdered in recent years, gives more than cause for concern (Turpin-Petrosino 2015).[5]

As ODIHR (2013) also admits, different recording and reporting practices evident in OSCE countries create further problems with the undertaking of cross-national analyses. It may be, for example, that worryingly high recorded hate crime figures merely reflect the better recording practices that a nation has, or its recognition of more types of hate crime in its legislation, rather than a more severe problem of hate crime in that country. Table 1.1 details ODIHR's most recent statistics regarding the numbers of hate crime offences recorded and prosecuted in selected OSCE countries.

---

[5] The fact that Russia has returned no data to ODIHR regarding the number of hate crimes recorded by police, or the number prosecuted, for 2010–12 adds another layer to these concerns (ODIHR 2013: 29).

Table 1.1 Hate crime offences recorded and prosecuted by selected OSCE states 2012

	Cases Recorded by Police	Cases Prosecuted	Cases Sentenced
Belgium**	1,152	865	–*
Bosnia & Herzegovina**	15	–*	–*
Canada**	1,322	–*	–*
Croatia**	57	20	10
Germany	4,514	–*	–
Greece	–*	1	1**
Ireland	98	–*	–*
Italy	71	31	10
Serbia**	39	36	26
Sweden	5,518	347	–*
United Kingdom[1]	47,676	19,802**	12,651[2]
United States	7,254	–*	–*

Source: ODIHR 2013: 25–30.
* No data returned.
** Data is for 2011.
[1] Figures are for England & Wales, Northern Ireland, Scotland.
[2] Figures are for England & Wales, 2011.

The figure in Table 1.1 for the United Kingdom, for example, of over 47,000 recorded hate crimes for 2012, is the highest figure recorded in any state by quite some margin. On the surface, this extraordinary statistic for the UK would appear to indicate that it has a problem with hate crime that dwarfs that of any other nation, and that it is far behind others in its attempts to tackle that problem. However, this figure may merely reflect the UK's well-developed suite of hate crime legislation and the progress that has been made in recognizing, reporting, and recording hate crime following the publication of the Macpherson Report in 1999.[6]

The figure for the United States, a comparatively small 7,254, may be explained by the fact that of the 14,575 law enforcement agencies responsible for collecting hate crime data in 2011, 87 per cent reported that no hate crimes occurred in their jurisdiction in 2011 (FBI 2012), something that may be explained by a 'lack of participation, lax recording, and different hate crime practices' evident among them (Woods 2014: 158). The number of recorded hate crimes in 2011 for Canada, 1,322, is also surprisingly low, especially as Canada, like the US, had developed some of the earliest policy and legal interventions in the field of hate crime, although issues with the way

---

[6] The Macpherson Report (1999) contained the findings from an official enquiry into the flawed investigation of the racist murder of black Londoner Stephen Lawrence in 1993. The Report contained seventy recommendations for change in the police, including the adoption of a new, victim-oriented method of recording a racist incident (Macpherson 1999).

some of the legislation is framed (see below) may partly explain this small number. Perhaps even more surprising are the figures for Bosnia & Herzegovina, Croatia, and Serbia, post-conflict nations who all recorded less than sixty hate crimes during 2011 in a climate of high religious, ethnic, and nationalistic tensions. A dearth of 'protocols/instructions/guidelines on handling hate crime' in the region, coupled with a lack of knowledge and understanding of hate crime exacerbated by a lack of suitably trained criminal justice practitioners, may help to (partially) explain these figures (Lučić-Ćatić and Bajrić 2014: 54).

DIFFERING UNDERSTANDINGS OF HATE CRIME AND ASSOCIATED PROTECTED CHARACTERISTICS

ODIHR, the intergovernmental organization, has developed its own definition of hate crime that acts as guidance to all of the fifty-seven countries in OSCE. It has two key facets: first, a hate crime must constitute a criminal offence, and second, the victim of the offence must have been deliberately targeted 'because of [their] ethnicity, "race", religion or other status' (ODIHR 2013: 6). Reflecting academic suggestions that hate crimes commonly involve bias or prejudice (rather than hate), ODIHR uses the term 'bias' when defining the hate crime motivation, rather than the more extreme emotion of hate. Similarly, Sweden's National Council for Crime Prevention (Brå) includes 'fear', 'hostility' or 'hate' in its definition of motivations behind hate crimes (Brå 2013: 6), while in the UK the College of Policing's hate crime guidance, which applies to all forty-three police forces in England and Wales, similarly does not use 'hate' in its definition but rather the 'lesser' emotions of 'hostility or prejudice against an identifiable group of people', which only have to be a '*factor* in determining who is victimised' for the offence to be deemed a hate crime (2014: 3— our emphasis). This mirrors ODIHR's notion that 'bias' does not even have to be the primary motive for the offence: just being an element of it is enough for the offence to be considered a hate crime. By way of contrast, in Germany, an incident is only deemed a hate crime if either hate or bias are identified as the *primary* motive for the offence. Also, in that country the classification of the two main subcategories of hate crime (xenophobic and antisemitic) as 'politically motivated right-wing crimes' can result in a narrow understanding of hate crime viewed solely through the lens of far-right extremism. This can mean that the hate element of crimes which are not deemed to have been perpetrated by fascists or neo-Nazis are missed, something which places Germany at odds with countries that recognize that hate crimes are also, and indeed commonly, perpetrated by 'ordinary' members of the public (see Glet 2009; McDevitt et al. 2010).

Unsurprisingly, though, it is not just within Europe where there is a lack of consensus regarding the parameters of the concept of hate crime and hate crime victim groups. Of the fifty-seven Member States of OSCE (which includes nations from outside of that continent too), fifty-one collate hate crime data under a number of different bias categories (ODIHR 2013). The most widely used categories are those based around race, ethnicity, and religion, which are utilized by two-thirds of OSCE states for data collection. Interestingly, statistics are also compiled on gender and language in a significant minority of states, while thirteen gather them for categories such as right-wing extremism, wealth, health, and political beliefs, suggesting a broader understanding of hate crime victimization (Garland and Chakraborti 2012). These often reflect local social conditions and norms, with Poland, for example, including 'lack of religious affiliation' as a category in order to protect the small atheist community in what is an overwhelmingly Catholic country (Fingerle and Bonnes 2013). In the case of sexual orientation, ILGA-Europe asserts that of the forty-nine European states it monitors, just twenty-six have hate crimes laws relating to anti-lesbian, gay, bisexual, and transgender (LGBT) hate speech, while fifteen have similar laws relating to gender identity (ILGA-Europe 2015).

In the context of the UK, the 2012 Coalition Government Action Plan on hate crime made explicit reference to five monitored strands of 'disability, gender-identity, race, religion/faith and sexual orientation' (HM Government 2012: 6), suggesting perhaps that it is not just any form of prejudice or hostility that can form the basis of a hate crime, but rather that against particular groups of people with a history of marginalization and discrimination (see above). The College of Policing's guidance (2014) also lists these strands as those that police forces in England and Wales must monitor levels of hate crime, although it goes further by suggesting that individual forces *can* monitor other strands (such as sex workers (Merseyside) or alternative subcultures (Greater Manchester)) if they so wish.

In the US, the United States Federal Violent Crime Control and Law Enforcement Act 1994 list the following protected categories: race, colour, religion, national origin, ethnicity, gender, and sexual orientation (Schweppe 2012). As Woods (2014: 156) reports, as of May 2013 race/ethnicity/colour, religion, and national origin/ancestry are protected by hate crime laws in forty-four states and Washington DC, and disability and sexual orientation are covered in thirty-two and thirty-one states and Washington DC respectively, while sex/gender are included in twenty-eight states and Washington DC, age in fourteen states and Washington DC, gender identity/expression in thirteen states and Washington DC, and homelessness in five states and Washington DC. Others include characteristics such as age, class, family responsibility, personal appearance, and membership of a labour organization (Schweppe 2012). Meanwhile, in Australia, the Federal Criminal Code Act 1995 includes seditious incitement to violence on the grounds of race, religion, nationality, or public opinion, while in New Zealand, the Sentencing Act 2002 covers crimes committed partly or wholly because of hostility towards a group with 'enduring characteristics', such as race, colour, nationality, religion, gender identity, sexual orientation, age, or disability (Chakraborti and Garland 2012).

INTERNATIONAL VARIATIONS IN HATE CRIME LEGISLATION

Hate crime legislation has developed in a somewhat ad-hoc way in the United Kingdom over the past thirty years. Having said that, although there are a number of well-documented problems with these laws (see, for example, Law Commission

2014; Owusu-Bempah 2015) they do cover a broader range of characteristics—the so-called 'five strands' of 'race'/ethnicity, religion, sexual orientation, disability, and transgender status—than those present in many other nations. The international situation can be difficult to assess, though, due to the complexities of many laws. Mason (2014a: 77–8), however, suggests there are several discernible common characteristics to them: that they are concerned with types of crime in which 'hostility, bias, prejudice or hatred' towards an aspect (or presumed aspect) of a victim's identity informs, to a greater or lesser degree, the offender's actions. She also suggests that this prejudice or bias is directed towards certain specified victim attributes, and, also, that extant laws already cover much of the conduct that specific hate crime laws target. The imposition of more severe penalties for offences that have a bias element is therefore a common feature of the punishment of hate crime perpetrators, while the development of specific 'racially aggravated' and 'religiously aggravated' offences (such as in the UK) is relatively rare.[7] In contrast to these types of laws that require proof of motivation, in some states it is enough to secure conviction if a causal link is apparent between the offender's actions and the victim's characteristics, regardless of any evidence of bias on the part of the perpetrator.[8]

Another issue relates to how incidents are identified by law enforcers as hate crimes, with the victim-centred approach of the UK adopted following the publication of the 1999 Macpherson Report (Macpherson 1999)—that if a victim or any other person perceives that a crime was motivated by hostility or prejudice based on one of the five protected characteristics, then the police are obliged to record and investigate it as such—only replicated to a degree in twenty-six of the other fifty-six OSCE states (ODIHR 2013). Interestingly, twenty-nine OSCE states resemble the pre-Macpherson UK-based method of relying wholly or partially on 'law enforcement officers' to determine if there is a 'bias motivation' in a crime (ODIHR 2013), while the situation in the United States has developed differently still. The federal Hate Crime Statistics Act 1990 compels law enforcement agencies to gather data on crimes motivated by bias against a person's race, religion, disability, sexual orientation, or ethnicity, while the Hate Crimes Sentencing Enhancement Act 1994 allows for enhanced penalties on the grounds of race/ethnicity/colour, religion, national origin, gender, sexual orientation, or disability (see Woods 2014). The Matthew Shepard and James Byrd Jr. Hate Crimes Prevention Act 2009 followed, which (among other things) gives the US Justice Department jurisdiction to investigate and prosecute violent acts (but not speech) motivated by bias against the actual or perceived identity of an expanded range of groups, which now includes race, colour, religion, national origin, gender, sexual orientation, gender identity, and disability. Almost all states include ethnicity/race/nationality/religion/colour (or something similar), reflecting the importance of the historical legacy of the period of slavery, while just over half include disability, sexual orientation, and sex/gender; thirteen include gender

---

[7] Sections 29–32 of the UK's Crime and Disorder Act 1998, for example, or Article 196(2) of the Czech Republic's Criminal Code.

[8] See Article 132-76(1) of the French Penal Code or Section 81(vi) of Denmark's Criminal Code.

identity and five homelessness (Woods 2014: 156). Additionally, the federalized nature of legislation in the US adds layers of complexity to the picture, with an array of legislation across the country covering a number of characteristics, including (rather unusually) family responsibility, matriculation, personal appearance, and marital status (Schweppe 2012).

Section 718.2(a)(i) of the Criminal Code of Canada allows for sentence enhancement involving 'bias, prejudice or hate' based on race, national or ethnic origin, language, colour, religion, sex, age, mental or physical disability, and sexual orientation. In addition, sections 318–320 cover 'hate propaganda', advocating genocide and public incitement to hatred, although complications arising from how this legislation was framed—a police officer needs to obtain written consent from the Attorney General before s/he can proceed with charges for these offences, causing severe delays in many cases—may provide an explanation for the lack of recorded hate crime cases (Corb 2014). Interestingly, and by way of contrast, Germany has no specific hate crime legislation as such, although section 46 of the German Criminal Code provides the opportunity for courts to punish acts of hate more severely by taking into consideration 'the motives and aims of the perpetrator; the state of mind reflected in the act and the willfulness involved in its commission' (Fingerle and Bonnes 2013: 4).

These cross-national differences regarding which characteristics are protected and which are not are illustrative of a number of things: local conditions, history, and context; the ability or willingness of governments to see hate crime as a significant social problem and one broader than racism or faith hate; or even which social groups are most successful in their campaigns for recognition (Mason-Bish 2013). Meanwhile, in Australasia Asquith (2014) notes that a lack of high-profile successful campaigns around 'signal' hate crime cases, coupled with a dearth of politicians or senior criminal justice figures championing the cause of combating hate crime, have contributed to the lack of adoption of relevant legislation. In contrast to this, in the UK some of those who have been campaigning for the inclusion of other groups under the hate crime 'umbrella', such as the Sophie Lancaster Foundation which has been lobbying for the recognition of alternative subcultures as the sixth victim 'strand', have gained some success. Drawing support from the worlds of business, the arts, music, and academia, and linking in with the theoretical approach suggested by Chakraborti and Garland (2012)—which is based less on a structural, group-based understanding of hate crime victimization and more on the individual vulnerability and risk of those being abused or assaulted—the Foundation's work has prompted several police forces to recognize alternative subcultures as a new hate crime strand. Since its inception, though, the Foundation has also encountered a degree of opposition from those who feel that such groups are ephemeral in nature, lack a long history of oppression and an established human rights discourse, and are thus not 'worthy' of being recognized as a hate crime victim group (Garland and Hodkinson 2014).

This debate was brought sharply into focus by two cases tried under hate crime legislation in New South Wales, Australia, in the early part of the twenty-first century (see Mason 2014a). New South Wales is one of just three jurisdictions in Australia (the others

being Victoria and the Northern Territory) in which provisions in sentencing legislation allow the courts to consider hatred and prejudice as an aggravating factor where
appropriate (Asquith 2014). In that state, section 21A(2)(h) of the Crimes (Sentencing
Procedure) Act 1999 states that an aggravating factor at sentencing occurs if:

the offence was motivated by hatred for or prejudice against a group of people to which the
offender believed the victim belonged (such as people of a particular religion, racial or ethnic
origin, language, sexual orientation or age, or having a particular disability) (Mason 2014b: 167).

The wording of this section is crucial as it appears to suggest that hate crime victim
groups are those deemed to be 'deserving' of this status due to their history of facing oppression and discrimination, including race, faith, or sexual orientation,
that are most commonly recognized internationally. However, the words 'such as'
allow for other groups to be considered too, and in two cases in New South Wales in
the early 2000s this applied to a socially reviled and despised group: 'paedophiles'.

As Mason (2014b) outlines, the Supreme Court of New South Wales applied section
21A(2)(h) in two cases, *R v Robinson* in 2004 and *Dunn v The Queen* in 2007, where
the victims were attacked because their assailant assumed, or knew, that they were a
paedophile. In both cases the judges felt that section 21(A)2(h) *could* be applied due
to the fact that the offences were proven to have been motivated by hatred or hostility
based upon the victims' membership of a certain social group. These rulings suggest,
perhaps, that a more individualized understanding of hate crime based upon vulnerability and risk of being targeted (Chakraborti and Garland 2012), when stretched
to its logical conclusion, can result in cases such as these where those who belong to
groups that engage in activities that most in society are repulsed by, nevertheless find
themselves regarded as a hate crime victim group, even though hate crime itself is a
concept rooted in a totally different ethical and moral framework. Can hate crime, a
notion that developed from recognition of the suffering of historically marginalized
and oppressed groups, have any meaning if it also includes those whose actions most
find morally repugnant? To circumvent these issues, Mason (2014b: 176) suggests an
alternative approach centred around a 'politics of justice' in which hate crime laws are
based upon principles that embody ideas of social cohesion and justice which 'address
the vulnerability that flows from undeserving and unjustified intolerance, inequality,
disrespect or animosity towards forms of social differentiation between humans'.
Such an approach recognizes issues of individual vulnerability and the associated
risk of being targeted while also acknowledging that the roots of hate crime are bound
up with notions of addressing social justice and inequalities.

CONCLUSION: TOWARDS A 'POLITICS OF JUSTICE' FRAMEWORK?

Analysing understandings of the concept of hate crime and how these are reproduced in policy and practice is a difficult enough task at the national level, and
is therefore especially challenging in an international context. Nevertheless,

this chapter has attempted to undertake a brief assessment of the way that states monitor levels of hate crime, implement anti-hate legislation, and confer certain groups with the status of being hate crime victims. It has shown that while they have devised well-intentioned hate crime policies, organizations like ODIHR appear to have little influence over whether states actively seek to address and combat hate. Even directives from the European Union, international treaties, or the European Convention on Human Rights have failed to provide the necessary impetus for some states to act. Hate crime data is often haphazardly collated, which shows that there is a lack of commitment to tackling the problem, while poorly crafted legislation in some nations has failed to convict or even deter perpetrators of hate crime. Symbolically, it has had little value too. In many of these states social climates exist that are hostile to 'difference', on grounds of disability, faith, ethnicity, or sexual orientation, and thus victims are suffering while their plight goes unacknowledged.

In addition, the lack of an agreed definition of hate crime—and its susceptibility to reinterpretation based on political whim—has recently been starkly illustrated by the pro-Israeli Canadian Conservative government's apparent plans to make boycotting Israel a hate crime (Fisk 2015). Such an idea seems to (perhaps deliberately) misunderstand one of the core aspects of the concept—that it should be there to protect the marginalized and vulnerable—by equating criticism of the powerful State of Israel with antisemitism. Initiatives such as this can surely only further stir the already choppy waters surrounding the hate debate internationally.

Perhaps, then, pan-national human rights frameworks designed to combat hate crime need to be complemented, or even superseded, by 'bottom-up' initiatives developed at the local level that fully acknowledge the harms of hate crime. These would involve commitment from key statutory organizations such as the police and the courts, as well as voluntary sector organizations and academics, and could utilize, as their standpoint, the 'politics of justice' concept suggested by Mason (2014b) which offers the possibility of recognizing *all* groups as potential hate crime victim groups, including those that have thus far been marginalized from the hate debate, while at the same time acknowledging that the principle of social justice must inform such recognition. This would move hate crime away from the problematic field of identity group politics, which has seen some groups routinely accorded hate crime victim group status, while others with less political capital are not. By doing this, the 'victim hierarchy' evident in the uneven provision of legislative protection for victim groups evident in many OSCE states, outlined earlier, could be avoided.

REFERENCES

Arnold, R. 2015. 'Systematic Racist Violence in Russia between "Hate Crime" and "Ethnic Conflict"'. *Theoretical Criminology* 19(2): 239–56.

Asquith, N. 2014. 'A Governance of Denial: Hate Crime in Australia and New Zealand'. In *The Routledge International Handbook of Hate Crime* edited by N. Hall, A. Corb, P. Giannasi, and J. Grieve, pp. 174–89. London: Routledge.

BBC. 2015. 'Europe's Young Jews after Paris and Copenhagen Attacks'. *BBC News.* 25 February. http://www.bbc.co.uk/news/world-europe-31586890

Brå. 2013. *Hate Crime: A Summary of Report No. 2013:16.* Stockholm: Brå.

Centre for European Constitutional Law and the Institute for Advanced Legal Studies. 2014. *Protecting Victims' Rights in the EU: the Theory and Practice of Diversity of Treatment during the Criminal Trial: Comparative Report and Policy Recommendations* Athens: Centre for European Constitutional Law/Institute for Advanced Legal Studies.

Chakraborti, N. 2015. 'Introduction and Overview'. In *Hate Crime: the Case for Connecting Policy and Research* edited by N. Chakraborti and J. Garland, pp. 1–9. Bristol: Policy Press.

Chakraborti, N. and Garland, J. 2015. *Hate Crime: Impact, Causes and Responses (Second Edition).* London: Sage.

Chakraborti, N. and Garland, J. 2012. 'Reconceptualising Hate Crime Victimisation Through the Lens of Vulnerability and "Difference"'. *Theoretical Criminology* 16(4): 499–514.

Chakraborti, N., Garland, J., and Hardy, S. 2014. *The Leicester Hate Crime Project: Findings and Conclusions.* Leicester: University of Leicester.

College of Policing. 2014. *Hate Crime Operational Guidance.* Coventry: College of Policing.

Corb, A. 2014. 'Hate and Hate Crime in Canada'. In *The Routledge International Handbook of Hate Crime* edited by N. Hall, A. Corb, P. Giannasi, and J. Grieve, pp. 163–73. London: Routledge.

European Commission 2014. 'European Day for Victims of Crime: Commission Takes Action to Make Improved Victims' Rights a Reality'. 21 February. European Commission. http://europa.eu/rapid/press-release_IP-14-165_en.htm

European Union Agency for Fundamental Rights. (FRA) 2013a. *Discrimination and Hate Crime against Jews in EU Member States: Experiences and Perceptions of Antisemitism.* Vienna: FRA.

European Union Agency for Fundamental Rights. (FRA) 2013b. *Racism, Discrimination, Intolerance and Extremism: Learning from Experiences in Greece and Hungary.* Vienna: FRA.

European Union Agency for Fundamental Rights. (FRA) 2012. *Making Hate Crime Visible in the European Union: Acknowledging Victims' Rights.* Vienna: FRA.

Feagin, J. and Sikes, M. 1994. *Living with Racism.* Boston: Beacon Press.

Federal Bureau of Investigation (FBI). 2012. *2011 Hate Crime Statistics.* http://www.fbi.gov/about-us/cjis/ucr/hate-crime/2011/hate-crime

Fingerle, M. and Bonnes, C. 2013. *Hate Crime Survey Report: Perspectives of Victims, At-risk Groups and NGOs.* Frankfurt: Goethe Universitat.

Fisk, R. 2015. 'Canada's Plan to Make Boycotting Israel a "Hate Crime" is Stupid and Counterproductive'. *Independent.* 17 May. http://www.independent.co.uk/voices/comment/robert-fisk-canadas-support-of-israel-is-dangerous-10256597.html

Funnell, C. 2014. 'Racist Hate Crime and the Mortified Self: An Ethnographic Study of the Impact of Victimization'. *International Review of Victimology* 21(1): 71–83.

Garland, J. and Chakraborti, N. 2012. 'Divided By a Common Concept? Assessing the Implications of Different Conceptualisations of Hate Crime in the European Union'. *European Journal of Criminology* 9(1): 38–52.

Garland, J. and Hodkinson, P. 2014. '"F**king Freak! What the Hell Do You Think You Look Like?" Experiences of Targeted Victimisation Among Goths and Developing Notions of Hate Crime'. *British Journal of Criminology* 54(4): 613–31.

Glet, A. 2009. 'The German Hate Crime Concept: An Account of the Classification and Registration of Bias-Motivated Offences and the Implementation of the Hate Crime Model into Germany's Law Enforcement System'. *Internet Journal of Criminology* 1–20, http://www.internetjournalofcriminology.com

Goodall, K. 2013. 'Conceptualising "Racism" in Criminal Law'. *Legal Studies* 33(2): 215–38.

Hall, N. 2013. *Hate Crime (2nd edition)*. London: Routledge.

Hall, N., Corb, A., Giannasi, P., and Grieve, J. (eds). 2014. *The Routledge International Handbook of Hate Crime*. London: Routledge.

HM Government. 2012. *Challenge It, Report It, Stop It: The Government's Plan to Tackle Hate Crime*. London: HM Government.

Iganski, P. 2008. *Hate Crime and the City*. Bristol: The Policy Press.

ILGA-Europe 2015. *ILGA-Europe Rainbow Map* Brussels: ILGA-Europe.

Kellaway, M. 2014. 'Transgender Day of Remembrance: Those We've Lost in 2014'. *Advocate.com.* 24 November. http://www.advocate.com/politics/transgender/2014/11/20/transgender-day-remembrance-those-weve-lost-2014

Law Commission 2014. 'Hate Crime: Should the Current Offences be Extended? Summary for Non-Specialists'. *Law Commission Consultation Report No 348* London: The Law Commission.

Lučić-Ćatić, M. and Bajrić, A. 2014. *Prosecution of Hate Crimes in Bosnia and Herzegovina: The Prosecutors' Perspective*. Sarajevo: Analitika Centre for Social Research.

Macpherson, Sir W. 1999. *The Stephen Lawrence Inquiry: Report of an Inquiry by Sir William Macpherson of Cluny*. London: Stationery Office.

Mason, G. 2014a. 'The Symbolic Purpose of Hate Crime Law: Ideal Victims and Emotion'. *Theoretical Criminology* 18(1): 75–92.

Mason, G. 2014b. 'Victim Attributes in Hate Crime Law: Difference and the Politics of Justice'. *British Journal of Criminology* 54(2): 161–79.

Mason, G. 2005. 'Hate Crime and the Image of the Stranger'. *British Journal of Criminology* 45(6): 837–59.

Mason-Bish, H. 2013. 'Examining the Boundaries of Hate Crime Policy: Considering Age and Gender'. *Criminal Justice Policy Review* 24(3): 297–316.

McDevitt, J., Levin, J., Nolan, J., and Bennett, S. 2010. 'Hate Crime Offenders'. In *Hate Crime: Concepts, Policy, Future Directions* edited by N. Chakraborti, pp. 124–48. Cullompton: Willan.

Office for Democratic Institutions and Human Rights (ODIHR). 2013. *Hate Crimes in the OSCE Region: Incidents and Responses–Annual Report for 2012*. Warsaw: OSCE/ODIHR.

Owusu-Bempah, A. 2015. 'Prosecuting Hate Crime: Procedural Issues and the Future of the Aggravated Offences'. *Legal Studies* 35(3): 443–62.

Perry, B. 2003. 'Where Do We Go from Here? Researching Hate Crime'. *Internet Journal of Criminology*, 1–59. http://www.internetjournalofcriminology.com

Perry, B. 2001. *In the Name of Hate: Understanding Hate Crimes*. London: Routledge.

Schweppe, J. 2012. 'Defining Characteristics and Politicising Victims: a Legal Perspective'. *Journal of Hate Studies* 10(1): 173–98.

Turpin-Petrosino, C. 2015. *Understanding Hate Crimes: Acts, Motives, Offenders, Victims and Justice*. New York: Routledge.

Walters, M.A. 2011. 'A General *Theories* of Hate Crime? Strain, Doing Difference and Self Control'. *Critical Criminology* 19(4): 313–30.

Weinstein, J. 1992. 'First Amendment Challenges to Hate Crime Legislation: Where's the Speech?' *Criminal Justice Ethics* 11(2): 6–20.

Whine, M. 2014. 'Hate Crime in Europe'. In *The Routledge International Handbook of Hate Crime* edited by N. Hall, A. Corb, P. Giannasi, and J. Grieve, pp. 95–104. London: Routledge.

Woods, J.B. 2014. 'Hate Crime in the United States'. In *The Routledge International Handbook of Hate Crime* edited by N. Hall, A. Corb, P. Giannasi, and J. Grieve, pp. 153–62. London: Routledge.

2

CONCEPTUALIZING HATRED GLOBALLY: IS HATE CRIME A HUMAN RIGHTS VIOLATION?

Thomas Brudholm

Hate crime is, by nature a sustained and systematic violation of human rights.

Perry and Olsson (2009)

A hate crime cannot, by conceptual necessity, be a human rights violation.

Munthe (2011)

The combating of hate crime includes a struggle for recognition by states of a particularly intolerable kind of wrongdoing.[1] Arguably, and in spite of scholars' discontents, the word 'hate' has done well to signal this and to rally public support for the fighting of acts expressive of group prejudice. The aim of this chapter is to probe the significance of a more recent, yet comparably emphatic label, namely the categorization of hate crime as a human rights violation. Concerned, as we are in this book, with the internationalization and globalization of hate crime, the new tag craves attention. If hate crime is, or can be, a human rights violation, it immediately establishes the phenomenon as a global indignity and a legitimate international concern. The idea is expressed not only in political rhetoric or academic writings. In a series of judgments from within the past decade, the European Court of Human Rights has recognized specific occurrences of hate crime as human rights violations. For example, in *Stoica v. Romania* (ECtHR 2008) the court held that the racially motivated ill-treatment of a Roma minor by a police officer was a violation of the right not to be subjected to inhuman and degrading treatment (Article 3) in conjunction with a violation of the prohibition against discrimination (Article 14). The same pair of

---

[1] This chapter builds upon previous examinations of the topic in Brudholm 2011 and 2015. Thanks to David Brax, Antony Duff, Thomas Gammeltoft-Hansen, Birgitte S. Johansen, Darius Rejali, and the patient editors of this volume for helpful and critical comments. Thanks also for responses from participants in discussions of the original paper at the Danish Institute for Human Rights, the European Union Fundamental Rights Agency, and the editor-organized workshop at the University of Sussex.

articles was invoked in *Identoba and Others v. Georgia* (ECtHR 2015), in which case the court held that a hateful mob attack on individuals assembled to demonstrate against homophobia amounted to a violation of the victims' human rights.

Regardless of whether hate crime should, or should not, be considered a human rights violation, it is certainly an emergent issue on the international human rights agenda. In my opinion, there is no way of accounting for the internationalization of hate crime, at least in Europe, without attention to the role of human rights actors. Involved is not just the European Court of Human Rights, but also the Council of Europe, the European Commissioner for Human Rights, the European Union Agency for Fundamental Rights, and the Office for Democratic Institutions and Human Rights.[2] Add to this the employment of global human rights institutions (such as the UN Universal Periodic Review and the Human Rights Commission) and organizations (e.g., Human Rights First and Human Rights Watch). The actual force or effect, on the ground, of human rights law and advocacy can always be debated (cf. Haynes and Schweppe, this volume, on the case of Irish resistance to international critique). Nevertheless, for those who are struggling against hate locally or nationally, the mobilization of international human rights actors and mechanisms must be a reason for hope—not least in countries where governments are complicit in the perpetration of hate crime, averse to acknowledge their existence, or reluctant to comply with existing obligations. As mentioned above, the inclusion of hate crime as an issue on the human rights agenda establishes the public response to hate crime as a matter of international concern and activism. It offers an extra tier of accountability (cf. Mačkić, this volume) and a well-developed set of standards for anti-discrimination legislation (cf. Bezirgan, this volume, on the issue of insufficient and uneven protection of given groups).

Clearly, hate crime is a human rights *issue*. That is, the reality of such offences and the quality of state responses to them is a subject of concern and activism amongst human rights actors. The question is whether or why we should go along with the claim that hate crime is a human rights *violation*.[3] What can it mean and what does it presuppose (as to the concepts of hate crime and human rights)? Why should we acquiesce to it or perhaps deny it? Does the mobilization of the human rights machinery hinge on affirming it? The investigation begins with a clarification of the concept of hate crime, mainly for the purpose of delimiting the ensuing discussion. It continues with an elaboration of two contradictory answers to the initial question as to whether hate crime is a human rights violation: *no*, it is not, because the concept of the latter does not apply to the conduct of private individuals; *yes*, it is, in so far as it amounts to an affront to the human dignity that human rights are there to protect. As I intend to show, the opposite answers can be grounded in equally viable yet mutually conflicting conceptions of human rights and violations thereof

---

[2] The latter being the human rights branch of the Organization for Security and Co-operation in Europe (OSCE).

[3] For comparable attempts to hedge the concept of human rights violations in relation to various neighbouring concepts (infringe, abuse, interfere with rights), see Baehr (1994), Weissbrodt (1998), ODIHR (2014: 40).

(I will speak of power-regulative and dignitarian conceptions). This means that the decisive conceptual question is not whether hate crime is a human rights violation; it is on one conception, but not on the other. The real question is which conception to rely on. My argument that both conceptions are viable does not imply that they are incommensurable, or that the one cannot be said to provide a better approach to human rights or to the combating of hate crime than the other. I have previously argued that we should hesitate or even abstain from classifying hate crime as a human rights violation—and that doing so is compatible with taking both hate crimes and human rights seriously (cf. Brudholm 2015). The present examination maintains the basic position, but in a way that builds on a more nuanced appreciation of the complexities pertaining to the questions at hand. Sometimes I think that the claim (that hate crime is a human rights violation) makes good sense and that it is almost obscene to contest it. Other times—most times—I think it is expressive of a well intentioned but misleading understanding of what it requires for something to qualify as a human rights violation. Certainty is perhaps unavailable, but I would like to facilitate further discussion by bringing out for examination some of the reasons why I prefer the restrictive (power-regulative) conception of human rights, and—by implication—why one might think twice before endorsing the classification of hate crime as a human rights violation. The reader must be prepared for an interdisciplinary inquiry; philosophical (conceptual and normative) at its core, but made possible only by inclusion of perspectives from within law and social science. What concerns me is the maintenance of precision and clarity in our thinking about and response to wrongdoing. Hence, the inquiry will have met its aims if it contributes to the deliberation of anyone who cares to stop and think about the basis, point, and limits of classifying hate crimes as human rights violations.

HATE CRIME AND ITS LIMITS

According to Hannah Arendt, 'words can be relied on only if one is sure that their function is to reveal and not to conceal' (1969: 66). In that case, the pairing of the two words 'hate' and 'crime' is notoriously unreliable. There are crimes motivated by genuine hatreds that would never be prosecuted as hate crimes, and the term 'hate crime' can cover forms of bias that would never qualify as hateful on any conventional use of the term. However, the ambiguity of 'hate' is only one among several causes of confusion about the meaning of 'hate crime'. Defining it has been described as 'notoriously difficult' (Hall 2013: 1) and like entering a 'conceptual swamp' (Berk, Boyd, and Hammer 2003: 51). Definitions abound and consensus seems both improbable and to some degree undesirable. It is, however, possible to reconstruct a more basic conceptual framework that may help us delimit 'hate crime' and think more clearly about specific definitions of it, including its underlying structure and possible variations. I propose that definitions of hate crime characteristically feature four elements that, taken together, account for the concept of hate crime. More precisely, concrete conceptions of hate crime can be seen and analysed as specific combinations of different interpretations of four constitutive features.[4]

First, if there is no crime, there can be no hate crime, but conceptions differ with regard to the range of crimes eligible for hate crime status. In many jurisdictions, any offence under criminal law is a potential hate crime, but it is generally assumed that we are in the realm of *domestic* criminal law.

Second, any conception of hate crime involves some determination of what distinguishes this type of crime. There is general agreement that the proof of the hate crime lies in the answer to the question *why* the crime was committed, but different conceptions favour different definitions of the salient motive. Some emphasize prejudice or hate, others bias or discrimination. An emphasis on the latter (which is common among human rights actors) makes sentencing easier, since establishing that the victim was chosen because of his/her identity is easier than proving that the offender was motivated by hate, or that the offence was an enactment of hatred. Yet, risks may also pertain to the inclusion of hate crime in an anti-discrimination law perspective (cf. Malik 1999). In standard cases of discrimination, for example, the same act (e.g., hiring, grading, managing access, etc.) without the bias is not a wrong. If this model is hastily transposed to the context of hate crime, there is a risk that the struggle for recognition of the discriminatory element outshines recognition of the independent wrongness of the base offence. For example, media headlines like 'A hate crime—or simply a crime?'[5] (in a murder case) belittle the base offence, and that may be as misguided as neglecting the bias motivation: murder is murder whether or not it is committed with a discriminatory motive. At the same time, the socially embedded element of 'hate' (however interpreted) clearly does alter, sometimes in dramatic ways, the civic and political significance of the situation in which it is enacted. What could have been an isolated and interpersonal affair may take on the momentum of a message to and from entire groups.[6] Why? Because the enactment of socially embedded hatreds may effectively communicate a radical message from 'us' to 'them', that we cannot and will not tolerate you—any of you, at all. For the one who hates 'it is agony to breathe in the same world where the hated one breathes' (Kierkegaard 2013 [1847]: 308).

Third, any conception of hate crime implies a position on the requisite relation between the hate (however interpreted) and the crime. Specific definitions may require proof of causation connected to motivation (i.e. that the crime was motivated by prejudice or bias), or alternatively a demonstration of identity-based hostility before, during, or after the commission of the offence. When proof of causation is required there is also a need to decide on whether the crime must have been motivated in whole or only in part by hate.

Fourth, and I think finally, conceptions of hate crime imply a specification of a list of so-called protected characteristics, for example 'race' or 'sexual orientation'. In

---

[4] I am here relying on a well-known distinction between concepts and conceptions (cf. Forst 2013: 17). For a more detailed account of the concept of hate crime, see Brudholm 2015.

[5] The quote is taken from an Aljazeera reportage on the German response to the shocking murder (inside a courtroom) of a pregnant woman. Cf. https://www.youtube.com/watch?v=izPQFrr8_1k

[6] Cf. '[H]ate crime transcends the context of the individuals directly involved . . . Homophobic, just like racist and sexist, crimes happen between "us" and "them" rather than just between "me" and "you".' (FRA 2012: 22).

other words, the 'hate' in hate crimes must be directed towards categories of group identity (that polities find worthy of protection). Hence, specific conceptions of hate crime differ with regard to the range of characteristics to be included, and variation on this parameter is the most easily recognized among the four given root causes of diversity between conceptions. In sum, the four-tiered concept exposes the skeleton around which concrete conceptions of hate crime are moulded. It does not say which is the best interpretation in a particular context, but it facilitates distinction between constitutive and contingent aspects of hate crime and provides the basis for delimitations of discussions about its scope.

For the purposes of this examination there is a need for clarification and some delimitation with regard to the first dimension of the general concept (i.e. which crimes to admit as potential hate crimes). To begin with, *hate speech* will not be given specific attention, mainly because there is no space for discussion of the issues to which inclusion would give rise. Arguably, the conclusion of the present examination will be applicable also to discussions on whether hate speech is a human rights violation, but focused inclusion of hate speech would require additional discussion of the tension with human rights commitments to freedom of speech. More fundamentally, it would require sorting out whether hate speech can be treated as an instance of hate crime at all. Definitions of hate speech do *not* feature the hallmark of hate crime, that is, the combination of an independent base offence and a discriminatory motive (cf. ODIHR 2009: 25). In cases of hate speech, the expression of hate *is* the offence. Thus, the use of 'hate' in 'hate speech' and 'hate crime' typically refers to different things; a particular kind of expression versus a particular kind of motivation (cf. Waldron 2012: 35). Does this make it possible to treat hate speech as an instance of hate crime? That is, when an expression *of* hate is motivated *by* hate (which is probably often but not always or necessarily the case). Perhaps this is logically intelligible, but it also looks like double counting in so far as 'hate' both constitutes and aggravates the given offence.

The following examination will also omit consideration of crimes against humanity (including genocide) under the concept of hate crime. On the one hand, this is hardly an omission in need of justification at all. To the best of my knowledge, there is little reference to such crimes in public discourse on hate crime, and international criminal law contains no clause establishing bias motivation as an aggravating circumstance, or a reason for penalty enhancement, in relation to crimes against humanity. On the other hand, it could be argued that this delimitation stands in exceptional need of justification, because it may look like ad hoc exclusion of cases that threaten to falsify my thesis (that hate crime is not a human rights violation). Why? Because crimes against humanity count as human rights violations on any account of human rights. Hence, *if* crimes against humanity are instances of hate crime at least *some* hate crimes are appropriately seen as human rights violations. Accordingly, arguments that hate crimes should be seen as human rights violations feature ideas of a kinship or continuum between ordinary or everyday hate crimes and the extremity of crimes against humanity (cf. Goldberg 1995; Perry 2005; Perry and Olsson 2009). Besides, there is no need to discuss whether genocide—*if* seen as a hate crime—should count as a human rights violation. The issue in need of probing is whether it is justifiable or commendable to extend our use of the term 'hate crime' that far along its first dimension (i.e. with regard to the range of crimes eligible for hate crime status)? Will it support the combating of daily occurrences of bias-motivated violence in everyday contexts? Can it do so without trivializing the extreme horrors of mass murder? Also are we certain that rhetorical attempts to embed a European fighting of hate in appeals never to forget the ultimate hate crime, the Holocaust, will not—ironically—undermine our concerns with ordinary occurrences of hate crime—being after all extremely remote from anything like the Nazi mass atrocities. Most importantly, will a demonstration of a kinship between ordinary hate crimes and state-sponsored mass perpetration assure recognition of the former not just as distant relatives of genocide, but also as human rights violations? What may account for a kinship between ordinary hate crimes and crimes against humanity (e.g., a discriminatory and group targeting logic) is not necessarily what sustains recognition of the latter as human rights violations. Contrary to hate crimes, crimes against humanity must be part of a widespread or systematic attack on any civilian population, committed 'pursuant to or in furtherance of a State or organizational policy to commit such attack' (ICC Rome Statute 1998: art. 7).[7] Even where hate crimes are widespread or systematic, they are not part of a literal *attack* on an entire civil population. True, hate crimes are typically embedded in widespread patterns of prejudice, the targeting of vulnerable minorities might be quite systematic, and hate crimes are sometimes committed by or under the aegis of public authorities. In this latter case, hate crime becomes a matter of international human rights law because the state has become implicated in the targeting of their abuse. Still, and even if we should recognize a grey zone or an overlap, the reality of hate crimes—as bad as it is—is not the mayhem of crimes against humanity. Nevertheless, these are questions that should be given independent scrutiny on another occasion.[8] When I use the term 'hate crime', focus lies—in accordance with common usage—on offences under *domestic* criminal law.

Finally, few would contest that hate crimes committed by police or security forces can be categorized and treated as human rights violations. The same point applies to hate crimes committed by death squads or other agents operating de facto as state agents (cf. Rodley 1993: 298). As we shall see, according to one approach to human rights this concern with types of actors is essential, whereas according to another it is obsolete. In any case, the need for scrutiny of the claim that hate crime is a human rights violation emerges especially in relation to hate crimes perpetrated by a fourth type of actor (private individuals). Private individuals, whether acting alone or in the company of their peers, represent the almost exclusive focus in existing concerns with hate crime offenders. There are questions of their age, sex, relationship to their victims, secondary motivation (thrill, mission, etc.), and the like, but the status of the perpetrators as ordinary citizens is typically simply assumed and state agents are

---

[7] For discussions of the policy/state aspect of crimes against humanity, see Schabas 2008 and Hansen 2011.

[8] Card (2010) provides some discussion of the relation between hate crimes and crimes against humanity (including genocide).

almost absent from existing hate crime statistics. For instance, in a national Swedish survey, only 3.9 per cent of reported hate crimes were registered as committed by public agents (Roxell 2011). Studies of 'official' hate crimes would be interesting (not least from a human rights perspective), but their status as human rights violations is not contested. In sum, what needs probing is whether *ordinary* hate crimes (i.e. offences under domestic criminal law, committed by private individuals with a discriminatory motive) should be considered a species of human rights violations. Now we can move on to consider the concept of human rights (violations).

TWO CONCEPTIONS OF HUMAN RIGHTS (VIOLATIONS)

There is a quick way (or so it seems) to dismiss extended deliberation as to whether hate crimes committed by private individuals can be considered as human rights violations. It runs roughly like this: only states can violate human rights, because human rights are, by definition, among the kind of rights that we hold exclusively against such entities. The violence of a private individual A against another private individual B (whether enacted with a discriminatory motive or not) *cannot* (by conceptual necessity) count as a human rights violation. To characterize it as such is like insisting that a bachelor can be married. Knockdown argument? Only, it seems to me, if one somehow would have to accept (as conceptually necessary) the premise that human rights can be violated *only* by states. But such acceptance is not conceptually necessary. It is possible, that is, intelligible, to argue that what is, and should count as, a human rights violation depends on the nature of the harm, not on the identity of its perpetrator. That is, one may define human rights as the rights we hold simply in virtue of our human dignity and prior to eventual recognition (or disregard) by the laws of states. On this conception, 'the person of the duty-holder does not appear to be of particular importance' (Dembour 1996: 26), and there is no conceptual bar against applying the concept of violations to incidents far beyond the realm of state responsibility. Hence, arguing that hate crime can be a human rights violation is neither unintelligible nor self-defeating. The tie between human rights violations and state responsibility is internal to one specific conception of human rights, and the appeal to necessity—what I would call the *argumentum ad necessarium* (because it claims the inevitability of its conclusion)—hides the reality of a *petitio principii*. That is, the legitimacy of what needs to be brought out for examination and justification is unwittingly assumed (in this case that human rights *ought* to be restricted to claims against the state). In spite of appeals to nature and necessity, I think we should treat any idea of human rights as a proposition in need of explanation and justification. Human rights can be conceived of in several ways (Cruft et al. 2015; Dembour 2010) and different conceptions of human rights yield different responses to our main question. Therefore, the issue is not whether hate crimes can intelligibly be seen as human rights violations: they can. The issue is whether one should endorse a conception of human rights that excludes, or one that accommodates, the application of the term 'human rights violation' to what I have called ordinary hate crimes. To engage with this question is to enter debates that have developed over decades and on which there is an enormous, mainly legal, expert literature (e.g., Alston 2005; Clapham 1993, 2006; Cook 2012; Copelon 1994; McQuigg 2012; Rodley 1993, 2013). I will draw on this literature (eclectically and without pretensions of adding something new to given positions) with only one aim in mind, namely to clarify what is at stake in the choice between human rights conceptions that support versus undermine the claim that hate crimes are human rights violations.

THE POWER-REGULATIVE CONCEPTION

A *denial* of the claim that hate crime is a human rights violation can be grounded in a well-established conception of human rights. International human rights law developed as 'a means to set limits to the power of the state *vis-à-vis* its citizens' (Dembour 1996: 24). Today, this traditional view has been extended in at least two ways (cf. Rodley 2013: 523). First, by recognizing that human rights impose not only negative, but also positive obligations on states. That is, states can violate human rights not only by what they do, but also by not doing what they should have done. Second, by acknowledging, in quite varying and mainly theoretical ways, that some so-called non-state actors (including, e.g., multinational corporations, non-governmental organizations, armed opposition groups) should be seen and treated as human rights duty-holders and potential violators. Even in its extended version, this conception 'invariably stresses the limits of human rights' (Dembour 2010: 3). Human rights, on this view, are *not* for the whole of human life, but for the regulation of certain kinds of power. They set out what people 'can demand from those with power over them' (Wenar 2011). More precisely, 'Human rights are those rules that mediate the relationship between, on the one hand, governments or other entities exercising effective power analogous to that of governments and, on the other, those who are subject to that power.' (Rodley 1993: 300).

Accordingly, the main function of the human rights machinery is to shine its light on the failure of the powers that be (states primarily) in fulfilling or complying with their human rights obligations. The related concept of human rights violations is delimited to situations where responsibility can be imputed, directly or indirectly, to states or other entities exercising effective power. The limited mandate or perspective of the power-regulative conception is manifest, for example, in the rules of the European and the Inter-American human rights courts. In both cases, only States Parties can be held to account, and complaints *from* public authorities are inadmissible.[9] Hence, complaints that someone's human rights have been violated must be premised on claims about some breach of obligations on the part of states or other entities exercising effective power analogous to that of states. A similar logic distinguishes the UN *Convention against Torture* (CAT) as a traditional human rights instrument. As a matter of human rights, torture must be 'inflicted by or at the

---

[9] Cf. the admissibility guide of the European Court of Human Rights, available at www.echr.coe.int

instigation of or with the consent or acquiescence of a public official or other person acting in an official capacity' (CAT, art. 1). Of course, pain and suffering can be intentionally inflicted in circumstances that do not involve or compromise public officials or the governments behind them. Under such circumstances, the violence is not a human rights violation and not—in itself—the business of a human rights court. The torturous violence of a sadistic individual is a criminal offence (both under domestic and international criminal law) and it should be prosecuted and punished as such. Likewise, a group of teenagers who target and brutally murder a stranger, simply because he represents to them a group they hate, are murderers. They deserve to be held individually and criminally accountable, and their act deserves censure, not just as the reprehensible crime of murder, but indeed as a murder motivated by hate or bias. But the crime is not a human rights violation, the teenagers are not human rights violators, and the victim has not suffered a violation of his human rights. The group of teenagers are too far a cry from exercising the kind of power that human rights, on this conception, is intended to regulate. But the most important point is not the identity of the perpetrators, but rather the question of responsibility. A concrete case before a human rights court may well involve hate crimes committed by private individuals. But the basis for the human rights complaint, and the reason why a human rights court would admit it, will never be the crime as such or in itself. It is always some failure of the state in relation to the prevention, investigation, or punishment of the crime: 'the human rights violation would consist not in the actions of the private individuals or groups, but in the omission of the state in preventing their actions' (Rodley 1993: 309). On this conception, to allege a human rights violation (in relation to the given case) would require indications, for example, that the teenagers were acting under the instruction of the police or that the murder could have been prevented if relevant authorities had shown due diligence.[10] Claims about a human rights violation could also become pertinent in relation to the public response to the case. For example, if the investigation of the case proved itself biased or ineffective; if the hate motive was not acknowledged during trial and punishment, etc. Regardless, there is no human rights violation without some nexus to a breach of state responsibility. The human rights mandate, on this conception, is limited (cf. Baehr 1994), but its proponents can argue that the task of holding states to account is a full-time job, and that the restrictive conception of a human rights violation serves to uphold the edge and precision of human rights claims and language.

THE DIGNITARIAN CONCEPTION

Alternatively, an *affirmation* that 'ordinary' hate crimes should be recognized as human rights violations may be grounded in the view that human rights are the rights we hold as human beings; by nature or simply in virtue of our humanity.

---

[10] Cf.: 'The due diligence standard establishes that states are not responsible for purely private harm' (Shelton 1993: 272).

Philosophical elaborations of the view provide precise interpretations and add supplementary reasons (cf. Griffin 2008; Tasioulas 2015), but the key term is typically
dignity and it plays, as Massimo Renzo has observed, a double role:

Firstly, human dignity is the value that explains why all human beings can be said to have
human rights [...] Secondly, human dignity constitutes the ultimate value that human
rights are supposed to protect. These rights protect human dignity by placing limits on how
human beings can be treated. (Renzo 2012: 450)

The dignitarian conception, as I will call it (Dembour (2010) names it the 'natural
school'), has been and still is as central to the history of human rights as the power-
regulative alternative. The concurrent and continuous viability of both conceptions
is probably testimony of an enduring—and perhaps valuable—ambivalence at the
heart of the human rights discourse itself, namely the mobilization of human rights
both as claims against the state *and* as a more general moral baseline or vision of
justice and freedom (cf. Dembour 1996). The role of human rights, in the dignitarian
perspective, is not limited to 'a contract between individuals and the state' (Clapham
2006: 58). Human rights violations, at least the most basic among them, are characterized by their universality and pre-institutional nature; they represent breach of
norms that exist prior to their implementation in positive law. Defining human rights
as the rights we hold by virtue of our humanity 'does not say anything about who
the holder of the duty corresponding to the right(s) is' (Dembour 1996: 26).[11] Respect
for human dignity and rights involve duties of various kinds for everyone, not just
states or governors. Proponents of this conception (cf. Weissbrodt 1998) can point to
several human rights instruments, including the *Universal Declaration of Human
Rights* (UN 1948), where it is proclaimed that human rights represent our 'common
standard of achievement', for all peoples and 'every organ of society'. Although the
history and reality of the international human rights machinery is focused heavily
on States Parties, dignitarians may argue that they are better aligned with the vision
of a world where 'all forms of human rights violations—by state and non-state actors
alike—are eliminated and the perpetrators of the violations—whether state or non-
state actors—are liable to be held responsible for them' (Chirwa 2010: 410). Also, the
idea of a common standard for *every* organ of society can be taken to mean that any
sharp distinction between human rights law on the one hand and other realms of law
or justice is ultimately artificial. Criminal law and justice, indeed any legal institution and instrument, may be seen as a means of human rights protection.

In this perspective, it makes little sense to refuse recognizing a type of harm as a
human rights violation simply because responsibility cannot be imputed, whether
directly or indirectly, to a state. If there is a human right to be protected against x,
and if hate crimes subject their victims to x, then hate crime is a violation of the given
right. The dignitarian can also refer to actual practice, for example, at the European
Court of Human Rights. For example, in the already mentioned case, *Identoba and*

---

[11] In so far as the identity of anyone is salient, it is that of the rights-*holder*: only human beings can
suffer a human rights violation. Unsurprisingly, notions of the inhuman and the monstrous have played
an interesting limiting role in the Western history of natural rights and law (cf. Rorty 1994, Sharpe 2010).

Others v. Georgia, the applicants alleged that they had suffered a bias-motivated vio-lation of the right not to be subjected to inhuman or degrading treatment. What mattered—as the court considered the merits of the claim—was not the identity of the perpetrators, but the question whether the violence reached the requisite threshold of severity. That is, were the demonstrators treated in a way that was degrading and an affront to human dignity? In confirming this, the court argued that 'discrimin-atory treatment as such can in principle amount to degrading treatment', and it con-cluded that 'the treatment of the applicants must necessarily have aroused in them feelings of fear, anguish and insecurity [. . .] which were not compatible with respect for their human dignity and reached the threshold of severity within the meaning of Article 3 taken in conjunction with Article 14 of the Convention' (ECtHR 2015: § 71). Establishing some harm as a human rights violation, at least beyond the realm of legal practice, does not require such reference to specific articles. For example, phil-osopher James Griffin argues that torture is a human rights violation, because it has certain characteristic aims that attack the human dignity, namely 'normative agency' (cf. Griffin 2008: 52) of its victims. Likewise, hate crimes may be considered a matter of human rights because they 'deny the human dignity and individuality of the victim' (ODIHR 2014: 16). As scholars Perry and Olsson put it, hate crime deprives its victims of freedom and dignity and *thus* 'deprives them of their human rights'. Exemplifying the agent-indifferent logic of the dignitarian conception, they write: 'If we can agree that . . . human rights are characterized by the cardinal prin-ciples of human integrity, equality, and freedom, then we must also agree that hate crime constitutes an egregious violation of human rights' (2009: 188). *Must* we? Only, I would add, if one chooses to endorse a dignitarian conception of human rights.

DELIBERATION

If we want to find out whether to endorse or deny that hate crime is a human rights violation, it seems that we have to take sides in a comprehensive and bewildering dispute between proponents of mutually conflicting conceptions of human rights and violations thereof. In any event, there is a need to consider one's stand on the question of whether to restrict the concept of a human rights violation to conduct or situations the responsibility for which can ultimately be imputed to a state (or some other entity exercising effective power). Obviously, the deliberation required for jus-tifying an informed choice of one or another conception of human rights lies far be-yond the reach of this chapter. With the more limited purpose of instigating further discussion, I will bring out for examination some reasons for preferring the power-regulative conception of human rights, and—by implication—for *not* endorsing any general claims about hate crime being a human rights violation.

First, the power-regulative conception provides a more accurate fit with what is actually admissible and primarily at stake in existing human rights mechanisms of accountability (human rights courts, UN review and monitoring institutions). Admissible are cases involving some state failure to comply with given human rights obligations—negative or positive. At stake is *primarily*—and accordingly—whether allegations about the complicity of states in the commission of hate crimes can be sustained. Admittedly, at stake is also whether the crimes, as such, amount to violations of particular articles (cf. reference above to *Identoba*), but as a matter of human rights (rather than criminal law and justice), the trials as well as the reporting begin and end with determinations about the responsibility of states. Though the dignitarian conception may be supported theoretically, it is misleading in a practical sense in so far as it constructs a number of human rights violations that are strictly inadmissible within the international human rights apparatus. Discourse based on the dignitarian conception tells victims of hate crime that their human rights have been violated. Yet, should these 'human rights victims' seek recognition or compensation as such before a human rights court or review mechanism, their complaint would not be admitted and their case would not be reported. Why? Because, as the European Court of Human Rights has repeatedly put it, the obligations on the state 'cannot be interpreted as requiring the State to guarantee through its legal system that inhuman or degrading treatment is never inflicted by one individual on another' (ECtHR 2009: para. 71). As already demonstrated, a case of a human rights violation requires evidence 'that the domestic legal system, and in particular the criminal law applicable in the circumstances of the case, fails to provide practical and effective protection' (ibid). Therefore, if one is concerned about the legal force or accuracy of one's claims about what is a human rights violation, the power-regulative conception seems to offer a more accurate position: it reflects and appreciates what is actually required for something to be documented or tried as a violation of international human rights law, and this could be a reason to prefer this conception. Against this first point, it could be objected that our concept of human rights violations should not be determined simply with reference to which conception provides the best fit with the always debatable content of positive law or the changeable rules of its institutions. Left unsupported by other reasons, the first point could be nothing but a recipe for conservatism in our thinking about human rights; it does not explain whether or why we *should* maintain the power-regulative requirement of a nexus between the concept of a human rights violation and state responsibility.

Therefore, second, I would like to suggest that we *should* prefer the relatively 'limited mandate' (cf. Baehr 1994) of the power-regulative conception, because it might do a better job of maintaining the edge and function of human rights instruments and claims. Human rights, in my view, are first and foremost a weapon, not an ethics or a philosophical idea. Employing, freely, the language of Christine Van den Wyngaert, I would say that human rights are like a shield and a sword. For the protection, that is, of human dignity, but for the lashing out against whom? Anyone or primarily the state and other entities vested with tremendous powers, both to protect and to destroy the lives of individual human beings? My preference for the latter is premised in part on an appreciation of the challenges related to the very project of holding the powers that be to account. We have perhaps come to expect as a given the reality of an international court where cases hold titles like *Beganović v. Croatia*, or *Identoba v. Georgia*, but this institutionalization of a set-up where the individual can accuse a state is in fact amazing. The times are not that long gone when little helped to prevent Joseph Goebbels from saying that 'we will do what we want with our Socialists, our pacifists, our Jews; we will not accept the control of either humanity or the League of Nations' (Bettati 1996: 93). An instrument designed to regulate the use and abuse of power needs to be kept sharp and focused. Not just because the asymmetry of power between governors and the governed is radical and ripe with potentials for abuse and oppression, but also because 'the greatest violators', as Charles Taylor has put it, tend to try to 'hide behind a smoke screen of lies and special pleading' (1989: 9). I worry that the more encompassing and possibly ambiguous rhetoric allowed for by the dignitarian conception can be used by states as a smoke screen, making it possible to pose as actively engaged in the human rights combating of hate crime, but in a way where the critical gaze can be directed distractingly away from the specific responsibilities of the state and onto the culpability of individual perpetrators of hate crime. In contrast, the power-regulative conception allows no mistake as to the object and addressee of claims about violations.

A third reason for *preferring* the focused or limited mandate of the power-regulative conception proceeds from the perspective of the human rights victim. Offhand, to adopt this perspective could be thought to support the dignitarian conception. One might think that victims care little whether their tormentor wears a uniform or not, or whether the responsibility for their suffering can, ultimately, be relegated to the state or not. This is, however, precisely what can be contested. I would like to argue that it is desirable to maintain a restrictive conception of human rights violations, because there should be a distinct place in our moral and legal vocabulary for wrongs committed by official authorities, governors and those who act on their behalf or with their connivance. In order to explain why, let me first cite the words of an attorney for relatives of the victims of the National Socialist Underground (NSU) group from Germany.[12] According to the attorney, her or his clients were not deeply interested in trial and punishment of the single surviving murderer:

But the family desperately wants to see the death of their son and brother explained. They want answers to the question of why the government failed so blatantly, at all levels and for such a long time, and why some of the investigations were marked by such an unusual sense of restraint. (Friedrichsen 2013)

The normative expectations of this family brings to mind the point pressed by Nagel, that 'not only is it an evil for a person to be harmed in certain ways, but for it to be

---

[12] The NSU was responsible for a series of execution-style murders on immigrants in different parts of Germany. Their hate crimes were committed between 2000 and 2006, but due, not least, to ineffective and faulty policing, the group was only uncovered in 2011. The official German response to the scandal illustrates the confluence, in concrete political discourse and practice, of the two conceptions of human rights. That is, held to account before the UN, the German Commissioner for human rights referred to the series of murders as 'ganz ohne Zweifel eine der schlimmsten Menschenrechtsverletzungen in den letzten Jahrzehnten in Deutschland' ['without doubt one of the worst human rights violations in Germany in the last decades'] (*Die Zeit Online* 2013). At the same time, the official apologies, uttered both by the Commissioner and the Chancellor, were clearly—and appropriately—focused not on the murderous hate crimes, but on the failure of German authorities to discharge their positive obligations to deal responsibly with the violence ('law enforcement institutions failed to identify the motives and as a result to get hold of the murderers' (Federal Republic of Germany 2013: 3).

permissible to harm the person in those ways is an additional and independent evil' (2002: 38). That is, it is one thing to be wronged or injured by other individuals, act- ing on the basis of whatever powers or forces they can muster in their private cap- acity; it is something different, and arguably often something morally worse, to be wronged or abandoned by the very entities vested with the power 'to protect and to serve', to provide care or to maintain the legal frameworks and institutions through which much of our lives are structured. As John Gardner has put it, perpetrators 'in uniform' 'not only fail in their protective duty (bad enough); they not only turn that duty on its head (worse); if the rule of law prevails, they also leave those whom they are there to protect, with nowhere else to turn (the worst so far)' (Gardner 2013: 106). The power-regulative conception of human rights violations sustains a vocabulary designed to capture and express this particular offensiveness of official responsi- bility of wrongdoing and that seems to me another reason to prefer this conception.

These are some reasons for preferring the power-regulative conception or at least for not acquiescing without qualification in rhetoric that hate crime is a human rights violation. More should be done, I think, to clarify the eventual compatibility or func- tional complementarity of the two given conceptions of human rights. The power- regulative conception may give us the most precise idea of the practical purpose of human rights, and it may provide a necessary delimitation of what should be seen as international human rights violations. Yet, it tells us nothing about the content or basis of these rights. What are our most basic rights? Against which harms should we be able to expect protection? Answering such questions may well be the job of dig- nitarian conceptions, that is, conceptions of *what* human rights are there to protect.

CONCLUSION

We have come to the end of this chapter, not to the end of the issues in need of discus- sion in relation to the claims for and against seeing hate crime as a human rights vio- lation. I will not recapitulate the twists and turns of the investigation (there is no space for it), but let us finish by asking what is the value of the two conceptions in relation to a concern with the recognition of hate crime internationally and globally? Of course, human rights are not the sole means of addressing hate crimes beyond the domestic context (cf. chapters in the final section of this book). Paraphrasing what Habermas once said about the undertaking of dealing with the past, the task of conceptualizing and fighting hate 'is a multidimensional undertaking that also involves a division of labor' (1997: 20). Habermas' point was that the power of different approaches (dis- courses) was premised on not overburdening them through mutual confusion (e.g., through conflation of issues of individual guilt and collective responsibility). I think that the general point can be transferred to our concern with the fighting of hate internationally and globally. In other words, what matters is to pinpoint a specific and delimited role to be played by human rights language and instruments.

Dignitarian human rights advocates speak a language—a moral lingua franca— that is today understandable across borders and world regions. Hence, within the perspective of dignitarians, hate crime can be explained and condemned as a global wrong, qua an affront to our inherent dignity or common humanity. In this way, the role of human rights language (in addressing hate globally) could be a matter of sustaining an international mobilization of 'hearts and minds' or humanitarian sentiment (cf. Rorty 1993).[13] The anti-hate advocate may be attracted to the dignitarian position, to calling hate crime a human rights violation, and to zoom in on the similarities between hate crime and crimes against humanity, so as to draw attention to the gravity and seriousness of hate crime. This is a laudable intent. The question is whether it is a prudent long-term strategy. If every crime motivated by hate or bias (and, indeed, if every other wrong that can be seen to represent a violation of human dignity) was seen as a human rights violation, what purchase would calling something a human rights violation have? Also, what would be the implications as to the potential abuse of state power if every hate crime was a human rights violation? That is, if one thought that human rights duty-holders, states included, had failed on every occasion where degrading treatment was inflicted by one individual on another, and if states took preventing all such violations seriously, would it not—ironically—sustain the development of a justified fear of state intrusions in the name of a zero tolerance of all indignities?

Human rights advocates of the power-regulative school may say that this is all speculation. When it comes to the actual fighting of hate globally and internationally, that is, when it comes to the mobilization of existing human rights institutions (regional courts, universal periodic reviews, etc.), little will be gained by insisting that hate crime is a human rights violation in itself. Even if hate crimes were labelled as human rights violations, international and global human rights mechanisms would not mobilize without additional evidence of state failure or responsibility. But what about the implications of the power-regulative aversion against seeing and speaking about hate crime as a human rights violation—does it mean that all reference to human rights should be avoided when the problem of 'ordinary' hate crimes is addressed globally and internationally? Clearly not. If one chooses to align with the power-regulative conception of human rights violations, there will be plenty of reason to invoke human rights. Namely, in so far as there are reasons (and there will always be such reasons) to criticize, monitor, and put pressure on states and authorities due to their record and policy with regard to hate crime. But can we—on the power-regulative conception—*only* address the issue of hate crime if or when it involves state responsibility (or the responsibility of other comparably powerful entities)? Yes, but (recalling Habermas) the limited mandate is not a liability. It is the precondition of allowing human rights to do their specific part in the labour required for dealing with hate globally and internationally. All too ordinary, indeed terribly banal (recalling decades of debate on

---

[13] One may question whether it is the concept of human dignity or the concept of human rights that does the job? The two concepts may appear like a set of conjoined twins, but it could be interesting to ponder whether the concept of universal human dignity can be used—on its own—to explain the value of criminalizing 'hate' globally. Cf. Hörnle 2012 for a discussion of the use of dignity arguments in the context of criminal law and discussions on criminalization.

Arendt's idea of evil), hate crimes are not human rights violations, but they are an important human rights issue.

REFERENCES

Alston, Philip 2005. 'The "Not-a-Cat" Syndrome: Can the International Human Rights Regime Accommodate Non-State Actors?' in P. Alston (ed.), *Non-State Actors and Human Rights*, Oxford: Oxford University Press, pp. 3–36.

Arendt, Hannah 1969. *On Violence*, Orlando: Harcourt.

Baehr, Peter 1994. 'Amnesty International and its Self-Imposed Limited Mandate', 2 *Neth. Q. Hum. Rts.* p. 5.

Berk, R.A., E.A. Boyd, and K.M. Hammer 2003. 'Thinking More Clearly about Hate-motivated Crimes' in B. Perry (ed.), *Hate and Bias Crime: a Reader*, London: Routledge, pp. 49–60.

Bettati, Mario 1996. 'The International Community and Limitations of Sovereignty' in P. Ricoeur (ed.), *Tolerance Between Intolerance and the Intolerable*, Oxford: Berghahn, pp. 91–110.

Brudholm, Thomas 2011. 'Crimini dell'odio e diritti umani' in F. Sciacca (ed.), *Giustizia Globale: Problemi e Prospettive*, Rome: Rubbettino, pp. 89–110.

Brudholm, Thomas 2015. 'Hate Crimes and Human Rights Violations', *Journal of Applied Philosophy* 3 (1), pp. 82–97.

Card, Claudia 2010. *Confronting Evils: Terrorism, Torture, Genocide*, Cambridge: Cambridge University Press.

Chirwa, Danwood M. 2010. 'State Responsibility for Human Rights' in M. Baderin and M. Ssenyonjo (eds.), *International Human Rights Law Six Decades after the UDHR and Beyond*, Aldershot: Ashgate, pp. 397–410.

Clapham, Andrew 1993. *Human Rights in the Private Sphere*, Oxford: Oxford University Press.

Clapham, Andrew 2006. *Human Rights Obligations of Non-State Actors*, Oxford: Oxford University Press.

Cook, Rebecca J. (ed.) 2012. *Human Rights of Women: National and International Perspectives*, Philadelphia: University of Pennsylvania Press.

Copelon, Rhonda 1994. 'Recognizing the Egregious in the Everyday: Domestic Violence as Torture', *Columbia Human Rights Review* 25, 291–367.

Cruft, Rowan, S.M. Liao, and M. Renzo 2015. *Philosophical Foundations of Human Rights*, Oxford: Oxford University Press.

Dembour, Marie-Bénédicte 1996. 'Human Rights Talk' in O. Harris (ed.), *Inside and Outside the Law, Anthropological Studies of Authority and Ambiguity*, London: Routledge, pp. 19–40.

Dembour, Marie-Bénédicte 2010. 'What Are Human Rights? Four Schools of Thought', *Human Rights Quarterly* 32(1), pp. 1–20.

Die Zeit Online 2013. 'Deutschland entschuldigt sich vor UN für NSU-Fehler' (25 April), accessible at http://www.zeit.de/politik/ausland/2013-04/deutschland-un-menschenrechte

ECtHR 2008. *Stoica v. Romania*, available at www.echr.coe.int

ECtHR 2009. *Beganović v. Croatia*, available at www.echr.coe.int

ECtHR 2015. *Identoba and Others v. Georgia*, available at www.echr.coe.int

Federal Republic of Germany 2013. 'Opening Statement by Commissioner for Human Rights Policy and Humanitarian Aid at the Federal Foreign Office Mr. Markus Löning', retrieved 9 September 2015 from http://www.genf.diplo.de/contentblob/3871696/Daten/3224061/20130425UPR16Loening.pdf

Forst, Rainer 2013. *Toleration in Conflict: Past and Present*, Cambridge: Cambridge University Press.

FRA 2012. *Making Hate Crime Visible in the European Union: Acknowledging Victims' Rights*, Vienna: FRA—European Union Agency for Fundamental Rights.

Friedrichsen, Gisela 2013. 'Seeking Closure: Relatives Claim New Rights in Neo-Nazi Trial', *Spiegel Online International* (10.04).

Gardner, John 2013. 'Criminals in Uniform' in A. Duff et al. (eds.), *The Constitution of the Criminal Law*, Oxford University Press, pp. 97–118.

Goldberg, David Theo 1995. 'Afterword: Hate or Power?' in R.K. Whillock and D. Slayden (eds.), *Hate Speech*, Thousand Oaks, CA: Sage, pp. 267–75.

Griffin, James 2008. *On Human Rights*, Oxford: Oxford University Press.

Habermas, Jürgen 1997 [1995]. *A Berlin Republic: Writings on Germany*, Lincoln: University of Nebraska Press.

Hall, Nathan 2013. *Hate Crime*, Oxford: Routledge.

Hansen, Thomas O. 2011. 'The Policy Requirement in Crimes against Humanity: Lessons from and for the Case of Kenya', *George Washington International Law Review* 43(1), pp. 1–42.

Hörnle, Tatjana 2012. 'Criminalizing Behaviour to Protect Human Dignity', *Criminal Law and Philosophy* 6(3), pp. 307–25.

International Criminal Court, Rome Statute of the International Criminal Court, 17 July 1998.

Kierkegaard, Søren 2013 [1847]. *Kierkegaard's Writings, XVI: Works of Love*. Trans. by H. Hong and E. Hong, Princeton: Princeton University Press.

Malik, Maleiha 1999. '"Racist Crime": Racially Aggravated Offences in the Crime and Disorder Act 1998 Part II', *Modern Law Review*, 62(3), pp. 409–24.

McQuigg, Ronagh J.A. 2012. 'Domestic Violence and the Inter-American Commission on Human Rights: Jessica Lenahan (Gonzales) v United States', *Human Rights Law Review* 12(1), pp. 122–34.

Munthe, Christian 2011. 'Hate Crime and Human Rights: A Complicated Story', posted on author's blog *Philosophical Comment*, http://philosophicalcomment.blogspot.dk/2011/08/hate-crime-and-human-rights-complicated.html

Nagel, Thomas 2002. *Concealment and Exposure and Other Essays*, New York: Oxford University Press.

OSCE/ODIHR 2009. *Hate Crime Laws: A Practical Guide*, Warsaw: OSCE.

OSCE/ODIHR 2014. *Prosecuting Hate Crime: A Practical Guide*, Warsaw: OSCE.

Perry, Barbara 2005. 'A Crime by Any Other Name: The Semantics of "Hate"', *Journal of Hate Studies* 4(1), pp. 121–37.

Perry, Barbara and Olsson P. 2009. 'Hate Crime as a Human Rights Violation' in B. Perry (ed.), *Hate Crime*, Vol. 2 (Westport: Praeger).

Renzo, Massimo 2012. 'Crimes against Humanity and the Limits of International Criminal Law', *Law and Philosophy* 31, pp. 443–76.

Rodley, Nigel 1993. 'Can Armed Opposition Groups Violate Human Rights?' in K. Mahoney and P. Mahoney (eds.), *Human Rights in the Twenty-first Century: A Global Challenge*, Dordrecht: Nijhoff, pp. 297–318.

Rodley, Nigel 2013. 'Non-State Actors and Human Rights' in S. Sheeran and N. Rodley (eds.), *Routledge Handbook of International Human Rights Law*, London: Routledge, pp. 523–44.

Rorty, Richard 1993. 'Human Rights, Rationality and Sentimentality' in S. Shute and S. Hurley (eds.), *On Human Rights: The Oxford Amnesty Lectures 1993*, New York: Basic Books, pp. 111–34.

Roxell, Lena 2011. 'Hate, Threats, and Violence. A Register Study of Persons Suspected of Hate Crime', *Journal of Scandinavian Studies in Criminology and Crime Prevention* 12(2), pp. 198–215.

Schabas, William A. 2008. 'State Policy as an Element of International Crimes', *Journal of Criminal Law and Criminology* 98(3), pp. 953–82.

Sharpe, Andrew 2010. *Foucault's Monsters, the Challenge of Law*, Abingdon: Routledge.

Shelton, Dinah 1993. 'State Responsibility for Cover and Indirect Forms of Violence' in K. Mahoney and P. Mahoney (eds.), *Human Rights in the Twenty-first Century: A Global Challenge*, Dordrecht: Nijhoff, pp. 265–76.

Tasioulas, John 2015. 'On the Foundations of Human Rights' in R. Cruft, S.M. Liao, and M. Renzo (eds.), *Philosophical Foundations of Human Rights*, Oxford: Oxford University Press.

Taylor, Charles 1989. *Sources of the Self*, Cambridge: Cambridge University Press.

Waldron, Jeremy 2012. *The Harm in Hate Speech*, Cambridge, MA: Harvard University Press.

Weissbrodt, David 1998. 'Non-State Entities and Human Rights within the Context of the Nation-State in the 21st Century' in M. Castermans-Holleman, F. v. Hoof, and J. Smith (eds.), *The Role of the Nation-State in the 21st Century*, The Hague: Kluwer Law International, pp. 175–95.

Wenar, Leif 2011. 'Entry on "Rights"' in E.N. Zalta (ed.), *The Stanford Encyclopedia of Philosophy*, http://plato.stanford.edu/archives/fall2011/entries/rights/

3

HATE CRIME CONCEPTS AND THEIR MORAL FOUNDATIONS: A UNIVERSAL FRAMEWORK?

David Brax

INTRODUCTION

Approaching the topic of hate crime from the discipline of philosophy, two fundamental questions stand out as obvious starting points. These questions are not merely of philosophical interest, but play central roles in most other approaches to hate crime. The high level of generality and concern with principled argumentation that a philosophical approach brings should be able to contribute to the understanding of these aspects of hate crime, and inform hate crime law making, policy making, and scholarship. In order to address the hate crime problem effectively wherever it occurs in the world, we need to understand, first, what the term covers and, second, the reasons why governments, law makers, scholars, and others should be particularly concerned with these crimes, and why they should be dealing with them in a particular way. These matters are particularly important as hate crimes are increasingly being recognized as matters of concern across the globe. In this process, it is important that experiences and expertise can travel and be applied to new contexts and circumstances. The aim of this chapter is to address these two general questions about hate crime and to provide two frameworks with which to capture the hate crime domain. The first question is conceptual: What is a hate crime? What should count as a hate crime? While most substantial texts on hate crime include a short section on conceptual matters, and some recognize the existence of viable alternatives (Dillof 1997; OSCE-ODIHR 2009; see also Jenness and Grattet 2002; Lawrence 1994, 2002), very few give anything akin to a complete or systematic account of these alternatives, or make any claims or arguments based on the availability of such alternatives and the choices they afford. The first part of this chapter aims to provide such an account, and to do so in highly general terms. My preliminary understanding of hate crime is that of a crime that is, in a sense to be determined, distinguished by its connection to negative group-based attitudes. The second part concerns the normative considerations that apply to the hate crime domain. What makes hate crimes, understood in any of the ways suggested, a matter of particular interest? Why are they considered especially serious? The former question allows for answers having to do with the purely explanatory role of the hate element in these crimes. The latter concerns the justification for why and to what extent hate crimes call for particularly severe punishments, and why they may call for policy measures specifically targeting these crimes.

The main point of this chapter is to demonstrate that the two questions afford numerous answers, and to explicate why this matters. The answers are to some extent connected: certain normative grounds recommend the adoption of particular conceptions in particular domains and contexts. Some conceptions may be better at capturing real life phenomena. Some connect directly with reasonable grounds for moral concern, and for punishment. A conception suitable for employment in a criminological study need not be ideal for employment in criminal law. Yet using different conceptions in these fields is problematic, as the data on hate crime largely depends on criminal justice enforcement, which in turn depends on how the criminal law works and is interpreted. The existence of alternatives means that we will often face vagueness and meaning lost in translation. But greater precision can be reached if these alternatives are taken into consideration and careful arguments are given for the choices that are made. It would be useful to consider these conceptions during the legislative process,[1] in the education of criminal law practitioners, and in societal conversation about hate crime more generally.

I will present five distinct hate crime concepts (or conceptions) and demonstrate how distinguishing between them makes a difference in how we categorize and treat cases. All five are recognizable as conceptions of hate crime by virtue of tying criminal conducts to a set of negative attitudes. The conceptions differ mainly in how they interpret and connect the key constituents. Conceptual clarity is important in any policy, legislative process, legal procedure, or scientific study that aims to target these crimes efficiently. Clarity is important for precision, transparency, legitimacy, and accountability. The conception should neither be too broad (such as counting all crimes between members of distinct social groups), nor too narrow (limiting our attention to acts of extremist violence, while ignoring the much wider problem of bias-motivated crimes). There is a frequent need to translate between disciplines and actors: between scholarship and law; between law enforcement and non-governmental organizations (NGOs) etc. Hate crime studies is a cross-disciplinary field and conceptual clarity is essential in order to translate between disciplines. Conceptual clarity is also vital for facilitating international, national, and regional comparisons, and for

---

[1] Compare with the OSCE-ODIHR's 'Hate Crime Laws—a Practical Guide' (2009).

identifying trends and evaluating counter measures.[2] This is perhaps most obvious in the case of hate crime statistics. When Sweden reported roughly 4,000 hate crimes in 2013, were they counting the same thing and in the same way as Italy, reporting 473?[3]

In the second part of the chapter I deal with the normative considerations that apply to the treatment of hate crimes. There are a number of reasons why hate crimes are of particular interest, and why we should single them out for particular attention. In some domains, such as law, it is reasonable for the concept used to relate in a transparent manner to some normative ground. In many legal contexts around the globe hate crimes are recognized and considered as more serious than so-called 'parallel' crimes, and hate crime laws, where they exist, recommend penalty enhancements. In this domain and given this connection between specific legislation and the extent of punishment, at least, there must be a connection between the conceptual and the normative questions.[4] It may not be conceptually necessary that a crime of this type is morally worse than a crime lacking the hate element, but if it is not, an account of how crimes of this kind connect to features that are normatively/morally relevant is needed. Some uses, however, do not require such normative foundations, or allow for a looser normative basis of interest. Hate motivated criminality is clearly of scientific interest, as is criminality categorized by any type of motive, cause, and consequence. In this section, I explore the many reasons why hate crimes are of particular interest. As in the previous section, it is important to see that while these reasons are related, they are also distinct. Having a grasp of the reasons involved, whether one agrees with their status as reasons or not, is useful in understanding the debates and controversies surrounding hate crimes and hate crime laws.

Do we need a universal hate crime concept, or conceptual framework? Is it a problem that the way hate crimes are understood varies between governments, organizations, disciplines, scholars? Hate crime, understood broadly as crimes somehow connected to group enmity based on perceived difference, is clearly a global phenomenon and a problem wherever it occurs. International organizations like the Committee on the Elimination of Racial Discrimination (CERD), the Organization for Security and Co-operation in Europe (OSCE), and various institutions connected to the European Union aim to address problems of racism and xenophobia generally, and recommend that Member States monitor

---

[2] As Garland and Chakraborti (2012: 39) point out, '…it is very difficult to establish the precise levels of hate crime across the EU owing to the absence of a shared transnational understanding of what it actually is'.

[3] These numbers are from the OSCE-ODIHR collection of hate crime statistics available at www.hatecrime.osce.org

[4] Of course, criminal law is not limited to this, and may single out types of crimes for other reasons than to determine punishment. One notion that has been developed at length by Walters (2014) is the use of restorative justice in the hate crime context. Such responses may limit the harm done to the victim and the community, and lower the risk of re-offending.

hate-based violence and address it by means of criminal law (see OSCE-ODIHR 2009). Hate crime is generally recognized as a universal problem, but also as a problem in which local conditions play a crucial role; including specific histories of oppression and conflict. This means that local variations of measures to counter hate crime are likely to have greater precision and thus be more effective. It is nevertheless important for the international community to be able to have a common grasp of this sort of criminality. The most obvious reason why this is so is that there is clear interest in comparing data between countries, and this requires that the data is collected in a uniform manner (see Whine, this collection). Other reasons are political. Given our history as a political species, the risk that states ignore or even perpetrate violations against marginalized groups can never be ignored. It is important that the international community is able to correctly identify and condemn such developments when they appear. This means that we need both a common conceptual framework—allowing for local variations when it comes to certain variables—and a rich source of normative considerations in order to persuade states, or to help local organizations, to take action. The notion of a universal framework should, nevertheless, not make us blind to other related phenomena that may not fit with it. The conceptions listed below do not exhaust the possibilities, and the framework should be kept open for further development.

The approach in this chapter is philosophical, as distinct from sociological, legal, or historical. It is based on reflections of how the term hate crime is actually used and interpreted, and not primarily on how it was introduced into our discourse. The first uses of the term 'hate crime' and the first calls for special hate crime legislation were arguably based on the recognition of the extent of victimization experienced by certain social groups in the US (Jenness and Grattet 2002). In general, if crimes of a certain type are becoming more frequent, or if they are concentrated in certain areas, policy measures may be called for, and a distinct term for the phenomenon is likely to be coined. Crimes are, and they create, social problems. In their book *Making Hate a Crime* Jenness and Grattet argued that hate crime represented a 'social problem requiring a legal response', and that the criminal law in the form of penalty enhancement statutes became the weapon of choice. In recent years, however, the focus seems to have turned to matters of effective policing, victim support, and other alternative approaches available to the criminal justice system (FRA 2012; Walters 2014). In all these endeavours, it is worth keeping a clear view of the conceptual and normative aspects of hate crimes.

HATE CRIME CONCEPTS

What are the conditions that an act must satisfy in order to count as a hate crime? This question has no single plausible answer. There is no 'natural kind' that a definition of hate crime somehow should capture and get right. Rather, hate crime is a *social* kind, and there is a range of conceptions, corresponding to what aspects of these crimes we are most interested in (see also Brudholm 2015). Many hate crime laws, and policy documents describing such laws, are rather vague on which of the conceptions described below they are using.[5] As a result, those working with hate crime in the criminal justice setting (e.g., police officers, prosecutors, courts, etc.) have to do some interpretative guesswork, using not only the law as written, but legislative history, case law etc. as an imperfect guide. Given that hate crime laws are not only vague but also controversial, this is a risky procedure. Hate crime prosecutions may derail due to a lack of understanding between the actors involved. A person who does not approve of the law may set the bar too high if given the chance. Below I describe five distinct hate crime conceptions, corresponding to five different aspects of these crimes. There are cases that will fit with all or most of them. Such cases are *obvious* hate crimes. There is, though, a question about *why* they are hate crimes, and about what aspects of an incident *make* it a hate crime. If we use clear-cut cases as exemplars, we may be unclear on how to treat difficult cases, cases that only fit with one or two of the conceptions below. Given the difficulties of recording and proving the hate element on any conception, difficult cases will rarely be judged as hate crimes at all. And if they are not, the lack of guidance will continue.

The list of conceptions can be viewed as a set of conditions, one, several, or all of which must be satisfied in order for a crime to count as a hate crime. Legislation, monitoring agencies, and researchers may choose different conceptions as their main concern or target. Criminal law may, for instance, use a particularly demanding conception of hate crime, while recognizing that hate crime is a societal problem that covers a more wide-ranging set of incidents. We may recognize a wide array of incidents as hate crimes, but have a more narrow conception in mind when treating these incidents in a court of law. Legislation can of course often be vague, and leave interpretation to the higher courts. This is arguably how the conceptual development has played out in in the US, where most of the scholarly discussion regarding the interpretation of hate crime laws has taken place (Jenness and Grattet 2002; Lawrence 1999). The relative absence of such discussions in other countries is problematic, as it means the meaning of these laws remains unclear and the laws themselves remain rarely used in many countries.[6]

---

[5] This fact is noted by the OSCE-ODIHR in their practical guide to hate crime laws (2009).

[6] The EU is of considerable interest here, as it involves various criminal law traditions, while attempting to reach common guidelines for addressing expressions of racism and xenophobia by means of criminal law. Very few countries will record or monitor hate crime cases all the way through the criminal justice process (see the OSCE hate crime monitoring at http://hatecrime. osce.org).

LIST OF CONCEPTIONS

The hate crime concept can be understood in at least five different ways: motive; intention; discrimination; expression; and effect.

Motive

According to this conception hate crimes are crimes committed with a hate, or 'bias', motive. The reason, or one of the reasons, why the crime was committed, or why it was executed in that particular way, is some negative attitude that the perpetrator harbours towards a group with which he/she associates the target of the crime. The conception Frederick Lawrence calls the 'racial animus model' may be said to fall in this category.[7] This is the 'literal' interpretation of hate crime—as it directly connects hate to crime. One example of this is the EU Council Framework Decision 2008/913/JHA, which states that 'In all cases, racist or xenophobic motivation shall be considered to be an aggravating circumstance or, alternatively, the courts must be empowered to take such motivation into consideration when determining the penalties to be applied.' However, the concept of motive is not entirely transparent. Should we understand motives as reasons for actions? And, if so, are we talking about explanatory or justificatory reasons? A crime can be committed because of hate without hate being what justifies the crime in the eyes of the agent. Negative attitudes can make a person look for *other* reasons that then 'justifies' the crime. Can both kinds of reasons transform a crime into a hate crime? And what does 'hate' signify in this context? Is it an emotion, an attitude, a disposition, or something other? There are some reasons to prefer the terms 'bias' or 'prejudice' to 'hate'—they conceptually imply that the attitude is at fault, and they are attitudes connected to groups, not individuals.[8] The motive-oriented hate crime conception has been controversial in criminal law, which we will return to below, but less so in a criminological context. Indeed, if we are looking for an explanatory conception, the motive-interpretation seems ideal.

Intention

Another conception is based on intentions. It is based on what the agent intended to do. If motive is the answer to the question *why* the agent committed the crime, the intention is the answer to the question *what* the agent was trying to do. Was the intention to create fear in the targeted group, causing its members to withdraw from public life, thus making the crime akin to an act of terrorism? Was it aimed to cause particularly extensive harm, or remind members of the group of their status as potential victims? In legal contexts, intentions are fair game as they may determine culpability (Gellman 1991). The suggestion that hate crimes could be described as specific intent crimes has, however, been challenged by

---

[7] Lawrence famously distinguishes between the racial animus model and the discriminatory selection model (Lawrence 1999).
[8] See Perry (2005) for an account of the semantics of hate.

some influential commentators (Gellman 1991; Hurd and Moore 2004; Jacobs and Potter 1998). Motives and intentions, while clearly related, are distinct. Hate motive is often the reason why someone intended to cause an effect. But I may commit a crime against a person because of hatred for the group, but lack any particularly firm intentions regarding impact. And I may intend to harm a group in order to keep them out of the neighbourhood, for the non-biased reason that I want to keep property prices up (Dillof 1997; Lawrence 1999). On the intention-based conception, this would count as a hate crime.[9] On this conception, one may well ask whether it is only intentions that are capable of thus making a crime into a hate crime, or if other *mens rea*, such as knowingly or recklessly risking causing these effects, may suffice. It is certainly possible to make such a case; it would fit better with the 'effect' conception developed below. The hate crime penalty enhancement provision in Swedish criminal penal code comes close to the intention-based conception, but actually involves a blurring of the distinction between motive and intention. It states that when determining the 'penal value' of a crime, the court should consider 'whether a motive for the crime was to aggrieve a person, ethnic group or some other similar group of people by reason of race, colour, national or ethnic origin, religious belief or other similar circumstance' (Swedish Penal Code, Chapter 29 Section 2 § 7).[10]

Discrimination

What Lawrence describes as 'the discriminatory selection model' puts hate crime squarely in the realm of discrimination. On this conception, it may not matter why you discriminate, or what you are trying to accomplish by thus discriminating: the mere intentional selection of victims from a particular group would suffice. On this conception, if you choose victims from a protected group because you believe they are less likely to go to the police, or that the police is less likely to take them seriously, you are in effect committing a hate crime even absent any hate motive. This conception, note, is also congruent with the 'because of' locution used in many hate crime statutes and policy documents.[11] On this interpretation, the crime is committed because of the victims' group membership, but not necessarily because of any particular attitude towards that group. The connection between the group and the choice to target it can take any form. Again, hate motive may explain why a particular group was targeted, but the motive would not be necessary for the crime to count as a hate crime. If I target a group in order to stir up not hate, but rather support for that group, I could conceivably be committing a

---

[9] We may also say that it is the combination of hate motive and intention that makes a hate crime.

[10] Since the translation was made, sexual orientation has been included.

[11] According to Jenness and Grattet (2002) this is the interpretation that now dominates the US, at least since the Supreme Court upheld the Wisconsin hate crime statute, which increases penalties if a person intentionally selects the victim 'in whole or in part because of the actor's belief or perception regarding the race, religion, color, disability, sexual orientation, national origin or ancestry of that person or the owner or occupant of that property'. This is less clear in European countries.

hate crime on this conception. Indeed, a hate crime would be the means by which I intended to bring about that effect.

Expression—'Symbolic' Crimes

A hate crime could be a crime that constitutes, or is accompanied by, something akin to hate speech. It is not the hate that you 'feel', but rather the hate you express that matters. The content or meaning of the crime is in some sense hateful or demeaning, or it sends a threatening message to targeted groups. This conception has been widely debated, as it threatens to violate principles of free speech (Jenness and Grattet 2002; Lawrence 1999). Of course, we do not need to violate such principles in order to publicly condemn the expression of such attitudes, nor to pour resources into investigating and counteracting such expressions, their causes, and their impact. But in the context of punitive measures, the expressive account remains controversial.[12] If hate crime is understood as an *explanatory* concept, that is, a concept that captures some causal explanatory mechanism, symbolic content seems to be a central aspect and thus worthy of inclusion as a conceptual condition. The expression of hate is often *how* the crime causes, and is intended to cause, harm of a particular kind. Once again, this conception will not perfectly overlap with the others when it comes to classifying real and imagined cases. I may express hate that I do not feel, and I may do so in order to bring some other effect about. In such cases I need not intend to harm the group, nor harbour any hate motives. Should such cases count as hate crimes? While they may be unlikely, it is important to consider unlikely cases in order to tease out the specific conception we have in mind. A law, or ordinance, incorporating this sort of conception was struck down by the US Supreme Court in *R.A.V. v City of St. Paul* (1992).

Effect

Hate crimes may be understood as crimes causing, or prone to cause, a certain sort of effect. In particular: harm. The harm these crimes cause is often at the centre of political and scholarly attention (see below). Hate crimes tend to cause particularly extensive harm to the victim, but also to have a harmful impact on the targeted group, and on society in general. But, of course, we can hardly argue that any crime with a relatively heightened likelihood of causing harm to a victim is a hate crime. While it may work as the normative ground for treating hate crimes in a particular manner, it can hardly be their distinguishing marker. But having a particularly high probability of creating a certain sort of harm may be such a distinguishing feature. The probability, or risk, may be caused via the fear or terror the crime spreads in the targeted group. The harm could be to the group's 'social standing' or consist in worsening the relationship between different societal groups (see further Iganski 2008; Iganski and Lagou 2015; Kaupinnen 2015). According to this conception, a

---

[12] Here there is a considerable difference between the US and Europe, where hate speech laws are more common. See Bleich (2011).

crime that causes or is likely to cause harm to the 'normative standing' of a targeted group, for instance by causing them to be perceived as vulnerable, prone to victimization, etc., would by virtue of that fact alone be a hate crime. This conception would understand hate crime in terms of its typical and most worrying effects. It is unlikely to work as a stand-alone category, however. To the extent that we can identify crimes likely to have such effects, it will be by tying them to some of the other conceptions considered.

A 'FRAMEWORK' CONCEPT

These are five different conceptions. A hate crime can be said to be a crime that fits with any of them, with a subset of them, or with all of them. We get a 'framework' concept, which give us certain alternatives to choose from corresponding to various aspects of these crimes: their motives, intentions, content, victims, and consequences. As mentioned, crimes fitting with all of these conceptions are clear-cut hate crimes, they have been used as *exemplars* in the discourse on hate crime, and they play a big role in the popular imagination; thus influencing what is perceived as a normal, or *typical*, hate crime. But it is when dealing with the difficult cases that we need guidance from a carefully thought through and well-established conception. When we have a clear grasp of which conception we intend the term to cover, the other factors are still as important as they may point to what may be used as evidence, how to reduce harm, etc. Different hate crime conceptions may serve different functions, corresponding to the differing approaches of criminal law, criminology, monitoring, prevention, policy making etc. Even if we were only to reach convictions in a criminal court in relatively clear-cut cases of hate crimes, the presence of any of these aspects should arouse suspicions and open a hate crime investigation. The set of cases that gets recorded and investigated as such by the police should be broader than the cases certain to result in hate crime convictions. Because hate crimes are crimes even absent the hate element, there is no risk of over-reaching. While this would mean institutionalizing the practice of recording cases that will not and could not get all the way through the criminal justice system, it seems preferable to the alternative.

The conceptions thus delineated focus on different aspects of hate crimes, but it should be clear that they partly overlap and intersect, and, on some interpretations, may even coincide. Motives are sometimes interpreted as a species of intention, and discrimination may essentially involve the intentional selection of victims from a protected group in order to demean that group. Other connections are causal in nature. As mentioned, hate motive often explains the intention to harm, and the distinctive harm to the community probably requires that the hate element was somehow made known, that is, expressed. In this chapter, I have only scratched the surface on these connections and instead focused on what makes the conceptions distinct from each other.

MORAL FOUNDATIONS

What makes hate crimes, understood in any of the ways outlined above, a class of particular interest? Why is it useful to single them out? Given that we manage to distinguish the class of hate crimes in an informative way from other crimes, there is some obvious interest in keeping track of them. There is an interest in who commits such crimes, who is targeted by them, when and where they occur, whether they are becoming more or less frequent, etc. This requires no particular normative foundation, only general criminological curiosity. But when it comes to policy measures and punishment, the need for a normative theory becomes far more pressing. Why should these crimes be the target of specific, possibly costly, policy measures? Should they be made a matter of priority? Should they be punished more? When we turn to these questions, we may start to wonder whether any of the conceptions successfully tracks some moral reason or other. Are the distinguishing features normatively significant? Is the hate element reasonably construed as an aggravating factor, or is it a mere proxy for something else? When we talk about criminal law, we need to take into account the nature and limits of punishment. In the policy domain, we need to talk about legitimate state interests. Here, I offer a list of seven normative grounds for treating hate crimes in a particular way. Each of these grounds requires a chapter-length treatment, as each comes with a set of qualifications and controversies, but here we will have to limit it to rather schematic and brief descriptions.

HARM

In criminal law, the seriousness of a crime is often composed of two aspects: wrongdoing and culpability. The former concerns how bad the act itself is, and the latter concerns, more or less, the blameworthiness of the actor. Other ways to make the distinction are in terms of 'objective' and 'subjective' aspects of the crime. The most obvious case of wrongdoing is causing harm. We tend to penalize acts that cause harm. The most obvious way in which a hate crime may be morally distinct from a 'parallel' crime, then, is by causing particularly extensive harm, or harm of a particular sort. In the hate crime literature, and in hate crime policy, the claim that hate crimes hurt more plays a central role. In hate crime scholarship, two influential voices defending and qualifying this claim are Paul Iganski and Frederick Lawrence (Iganski 2008; Lawrence 1999). Lawrence argues that 'The unique harm caused by bias crimes not only justifies their enhanced punishment, but compels it' (1999: 175). Whereas the first studies in support of this claim were flawed, and justly criticized, more recent work has confirmed a more qualified claim regarding the relation between hate and harm: hate crimes at the very least *tend* to cause more harm. And some hate crimes tend to cause more harm than others (Iganski and Lagou 2015). While this is a matter that requires careful consideration, this is not the place for it. Suffice to say that if there is a robust tendency for crimes of this nature to cause especially extensive harm, hate crimes can be viewed as worse than other crimes. Not because they always lead to more harm than a parallel crime would have, but because they are of the *sort* that tend to do so. They involve a *risk* of causing that sort of harm.[13] If the tendency to cause particularly extensive harm can be shown to relate to the bias element by being explained by a mechanism tying it to the harm, we have a better case for treating hate crimes as particularly wrongful. Some of the typical effects of crime in general, and hate crime in particular, are withdrawal from social and public life, and feelings of fear (Iganski 2008).

The harm argument also covers the harm caused to the targeted group. Hate crimes remind members that they are targets, often for reasons that make the risk impossible to avoid, or avoidance of which is a form of harm in itself. Hate crimes threaten to make the lives of those already among the worse off in a society even worse. According to the view known as 'prioritarianism', harm done to those people worst off has particular moral weight (Arneson 2008; Rawls 1971). The fact that disadvantages 'cluster' in this way is generally recognized as a marker of poor quality in society. Finally, harm is done to society as a whole. Hate crime may also be thought to cause a particular kind of harm, that is, harm to a group's social standing. This suggestion is tied to the expressive aspect below, that the crime expresses a devaluing attitude, and that leaving it without response means that the group's standing is affected (see Kaupinnen 2015). To commit a hate crime, then, is to commit a crime that creates a particular risk of a particular type of harm.

BAD INTENTIONS

Hate crimes can be worse because they are committed with particularly heinous intentions. Intentions concern what the criminal is trying to do. Suppose a hate crime is committed with the intention to instil fear in the victim and his/her group and to cause them to withdraw from public life. Maybe the intention is to cause societal discord and worsen relations between groups that, according to the actor, should be kept apart. If this is the reason why we think of hate crimes as more serious, there is no problem with 'punishing thoughts'; intentions are paradigmatically relevant for culpability. If the intention is to create this sort of effect, we have a clear basis for penalty enhancement, even if the criminal does not succeed in this part of the plan. The problem is that it seems to fit with a rather small set of cases. We are unlikely to establish, or to be able to infer, such intentions on the typical evidence available in such cases. Intentions are connected with a number of the other grounds on this list of moral considerations; the intent to create a certain form of harm, the intent to express a certain standpoint, the intent to select a disadvantaged victim, etc. Intent is clearly morally relevant, and part of what makes (at least some) hate crimes worse than similar crimes absent this intent. Note, however, that hate crimes will not be uniquely connected to bad intentions. Other intentions, that have little or nothing to do with hate or group enmity, may be considered just as bad.

As mentioned previously, there is a question as to whether other *mens rea* may suffice to make a crime into a hate crime. This question translates into the moral domain as well, as *mens rea* relates to levels of culpability. If it is especially wrong to intend these

---

[13] An argument against using hate motivation as a proxy for harm is developed at length in Hurd and Moore (2004).

effects, is it not also morally relevant whether such effects were foreseen, or should have been? That case can certainly be made, but I will not pursue it further here.

BAD MOTIVES

According to the motive model, hate crimes are committed with hate/bias motives. These are bad motives. In other words, attacking a person because of his/her connection to a particular racial, ethnic, religious, etc. group amounts to acting on a bad reason. Given that we understand 'hate' in this context as something that involves the negative appraisal of people based on group membership, it is a bad reason in so far that it is morally wrong. It is morally wrong in two ways: it is morally incorrect and it is morally detrimental to act on such reasons. Acting on bias goes against the principle that all people are of equal dignity and worth, and it is something people tend to try to stop themselves and others from doing. It should be noted that morally bad hate/bias may be connected to a pragmatically good reason insofar that the attitude may be widely shared among one's peers. This pragmatic reason, if anything, would seem to increase blameworthiness. We generally try to rid ourselves and others of prejudices for reasons both moral and pragmatic. Introducing this notion into criminal law has been controversial, however. It has been controversial on mainly two grounds: it is not 'content neutral', and it punishes people for things that they are not responsible for (Hurd and Moore 2004). This is not the place to address this debate in detail, but I will offer two quick responses. Regarding the first objection; the equal worth of people is arguably as important and as settled a value as is the undesirableness of harm (see Kahan 2001). Second, motives are matters of choice if we understand them as the reasons we choose to act on. Whatever your take on the limits of the law, motives can be targeted by moral condemnation. Hate crimes may be made a priority because of this moral fact, even if legislators may opt for other grounds for punishment.

DISCRIMINATION

On the discriminatory selection model, what makes a crime a hate crime is that it involves the intentional selection of a victim from a protected group, no matter what the reason. This factor may also serve the moral role required. What makes these crimes especially serious may be the mere fact that they are discriminatory. Even when group membership is used as 'proxy' for 'easy targets', or the like, the fact that one chooses a victim from a particular group is what makes the act wrongful. This claim can be understood in a number of different ways. If we must offend, we should do so on an equal basis, at random, or according to what the victim 'deserves', or maybe on the basis of the victim's capability of coping. This relates to the debate regarding discrimination and affirmative action, and what makes discrimination wrong.[14] Discriminatory violence may, for instance, be wrong simply by being discriminatory, that is, for being unfair. Or it may be wrong because it disproportionally affects those already at an unfair disadvantage in society, which is the focus of

---

[14] For a description of the many accounts of what makes discrimination wrong, see Hellman (2011).

the account below. Should the relative standing of the victim and perpetrator matter morally? If I choose a member of a privileged group, is this as bad as if I target a member of a disadvantaged group? Hate crime laws tend to be neutrally formulated. They cover racial, ethnic, and religious groups, but do not single out the disadvantaged subset of those groups. While arguably designed to protect those at a disadvantage, they cover the privileged as well. The question, then, is whether the moral import of discrimination is limited to when it hits people in subordinate positions. If so, the discrimination account would only offer justification for hate crime laws and policy measures when it comes to hate crimes against the relatively disadvantaged.

VULNERABLE/DISADVANTAGED VICTIMS

Hate crimes may be particularly wrong because they target the vulnerable and socially disadvantaged. They target people that, say, have less trust for the authorities, have less access to social security, and are discriminated against in general (Al-Hakim 2015). The standing of such groups means that they receive less support from their social environment, and will have a harder time dealing with the aftermath of their victimization. The normative importance of this may also be because harm done to the already disadvantaged is itself a greater moral wrong than harm done to the well off. When hate crimes target these groups, they are worse than other crimes. Preying on the weak is particularly culpable.[15] A 'pure' version of this argument would say that harming the disadvantaged is particularly wrong, no matter what the reason, whether one did so intentionally or not, or even whether or not this would be likely to cause any particular harm. It may, of course, be worse still if connected to the intention of targeting the disadvantaged, or doing so because the victim is disadvantaged. While there is some plausibility in assigning moral significance to the worst off, and to particularly condemn crimes directed towards them, it would be a reason that is in no way unique to the hate crime category.

BAD MESSAGES

Hate crimes are often understood as symbolic, or as 'message' crimes. The message is, in essence, that the targeted group is of lesser human worth. This, of course, is counter to the equality principle. The message is, as mentioned above, morally wrong in two ways; it is demeaning and it gets the 'moral facts' wrong. Now, sending such a message can be seen as wrong in itself, or it can be wrong because it threatens to cause harm, or because it is intended to cause such harm. More can probably be said about the matter, but the expressive account is rarely given independent weight. A demonstrable relation to some sort of harm is normally required, at least if restrictions on freedom of speech are suggested. In a criminal law context, justifying hate crime laws based on content or expression is often taken as being in conflict with freedom of speech principles. While most legislators seem to have considered and accepted this tension, a number of countries have introduced hate speech laws in

---

[15] Note that whereas basing victimhood on immutable characteristic fixes which groups should be covered, the matter of disadvantage may very well differ over the time.

some form or other, and thus have no reason to reject it as a consideration in the justification and formulation of hate crime laws either.[16]

BAD CHARACTERS

In a civilized society, rational people tend to want to rid themselves and others of prejudices. This is partly for the reasons mentioned; that because they have an effect on our interactions with others and may be detrimental to them. But we also do so for our own sakes, as prejudices may cause us to miscalculate the worth of others and their potential contribution, and thus hinder us from achieving our goals. But it may also be that prejudice is no part of an ideal character. That could be a reason to target these crimes in particular, to stop people from having or acting out bad characters, and to punish them when they do act out. The rehabilitative approaches in the criminal justice system may very well have this as part of its mission: to be racist, for instance, is to exhibit prejudices in a systematic fashion. To rid people of such traits would make them better people. Their characters would improve, and they would pose less of a threat to society in general. While character may or may not be a suitable concern for rehabilitation, it has been considered problematic as a target of criminal law. One argument against a character-based account of culpability which relates to an objection to the motive account above is that it is not clear that we are in control of our characters in the sense that we are in control of our actions (Hurd and Moore 2004).[17]

CONCLUDING REMARKS—HOW THE MORAL AND CONCEPTUAL QUESTIONS CONNECT

The main point of this chapter is the availability of several distinct hate crime conceptions, and several distinct moral grounds for treating hate crimes in a particular manner. A problem with many hate crime laws, policies, international agreements, and guidelines for police, prosecutors, and NGOs is that it is often unclear which conception they are working with, and what moral foundations they rely upon. This is a challenge both in order for hate crime laws and policies to be effective, and for the transferral of information to run smoothly between the actors concerned with these matters. Ideally, we would have enough of a common understanding of what hate crime is to be able to compare data from monitoring agencies around the world. One reason why we would want to do this is that we want to establish what sort of measures may actually work to limit the prevalence of hate crimes.

Hate crime is primarily understood as a social problem. It is, in fact, the intersection of two different problems: crime in general, and hate/bias/prejudice in general. The combination of these factors, in some of the ways considered above, is arguably what sets this problem apart. There are reasons, especially when the notion

---

[16] For a recent philosophically sophisticated account of the expressive meaning of hate crimes and of hate crime laws and sentencing provisions, see Kaupinnen (2015).

[17] For an argument in favour of this approach, see Taslitz (1999).

is introduced into criminal law and policy, to have the concept 'track' the moral grounds for recognizing the special nature of the hate crime problem. Ideally, what makes a crime a hate crime should also be what justifies the enhanced penalty. Hate crime would then be a 'moral kind', that is, a kind distinguished by a factor that is always morally relevant. At the very least, there should be some reliable connection between the moral reasons to single these crimes out for special treatment in criminal law and in policy, and the concept itself.

Some moral foundations translate directly to specific concepts. If we conceive of hate crimes as particularly serious because of the 'badness' of hate motives it seems reasonable to adopt a motive-oriented conception of hate crime. The same can be said for the expressive, discriminatory, and intention-based concepts. But the connection can also be indirect. If, for instance, the moral status of these crimes is merely based on the harm principle, we need to establish a reliable mechanism that connects crimes of that nature to the harm in question. We could, for instance, say that hate-motivated crimes only create this harm when they are also expressive of hate. This expression would create harm no matter why it was committed, so there would be a closer fit between hate-expressive crimes and harm than between hate-motivated crimes and harm.

It is important to note that all the moral considerations above provide reasons to counteract hate crimes globally, however they are understood. But in certain contexts, such as criminal law and policy making, the fit between concept and moral grounds must be reasonably close, and the moral grounds must be recognized as proper for that domain. If we are reluctant to use motive as grounds for punishment, we need not adopt a motive-oriented concept in law. We may, notwithstanding, want to do so in a research setting. We want to keep track of, and counteract, crimes based on hate motive. This is true, even if we choose only to apply punishment enhancements for crimes committed with or expressive of certain intentions.

Precision and clarity in both the conceptual and normative regards are of the utmost importance in developing an international framework of hate crime legislation, policies, and scholarship. Hate crime legislation, now adopted in most western countries and mandated by pan-European organizations and agreements, remains controversial. We need to constantly remind ourselves on the normative grounds on which these measures rest.

REFERENCES

Al-Hakim, M. 2015. 'Making a Home for the Homeless in Hate Crime Legislation'. *Journal of Interpersonal Violence* 30(10): 1.

Arneson, R. 2008. 'Egalitarianism', *The Stanford Encyclopedia of Philosophy* (Fall 2008 Edition), Zalta, E. (ed.).

Bleich, E. 2011. *The Freedom to be Racist—How the United States and Europe Struggle to Preserve Freedom and Combat Racism*, Oxford: Oxford University Press.

Brudholm, T. 2015. 'Hate Crimes and Human Rights Violations'. *Journal of Applied Philosophy* 32(1): 82.

Chakraborti, N. and Garland, J. 2012. 'Reconceptualizing Hate Crime Victimization through the Lens of Vulnerability and "Difference"'. *Theoretical Criminology* 16(4): 499.

Council Framework Decision 2008/913/JHA of 28 November 2008 on combating certain forms and expressions of racism and xenophobia by means of criminal law. Retrieved 4 May 2015 http://eurlex.europa.eu/LexUriServ/LexUriServ.do?uri=CELEX:32008F0913:EN:NOT

Dillof, A. 1997. 'Punishing Bias: an Examination of the Theoretical Foundations of Bias Crime Statutes'. *Northwestern University Law Review* 91(4): 1015.

FRA. 2012. Making Hate Crime Visible in the European Union: Acknowledging Victims' Rights. European Union Agency for Fundamental Rights. Retrieved 4 May 2015 http://fra.europa.eu/en/publication/2012/making-hate-crime-visible-european-union-acknowledging-victims-rights

Garland, J. and Chakraborti, N. 2012. 'Divided by a Common Concept? Assessing the Implications of Different Conceptualizations of Hate Crime in the European Union'. *European Journal of Criminology* 9(1): 38.

Gellman, S. 1991. 'Sticks and Stones Can Put You in Jail, but Can Words Increase Your Sentence?'. *UCLA Law Review* 39(2): 333.

Hellman, D. 2011. *When is Discrimination Wrong?* Cambridge, MA: Harvard University Press.

Hurd, H. and Moore, M. 2004. 'Punishing Hatred and Prejudice'. *Stanford Law Review* 56(5): 1081.

Iganski, P. 2008. *Hate Crime and the City*, Bristol: The Policy Press.

Iganski, P. and Lagou, S. 2015. 'Hate Crimes Hurt Some More Than Others: Implications for the Just Sentencing of Offenders'. *Journal of Interpersonal Violence* 30(10): 1696.

Jacobs, J.B. and Potter, K. 1998. *Hate Crimes: Criminal Law and Identity Politics*, New York: Oxford University Press.

Jenness, V. and Grattet, R. 2002. *Making Hate a Crime*, New York: Russell Sage Foundation.

Kahan, D.M. 2001. 'Two Liberal Fallacies in the Hate Crimes Debate'. *Law and Philosophy* 20(2): 175.

Kaupinnen, A. 2015. 'Hate and Punishment'. *Journal of Interpersonal Violence* 30(10): 1719.

Lawrence, F.M. 1994. 'The Punishment of Hate: Toward a Normative Theory of Bias-Motivated Crimes'. *Michigan Law Review* 93(2): 320.

Lawrence, F.M. 1999. *Punishing Hate: Bias Crimes Under American Law*, Cambridge, MA: Harvard University Press.

Office for Democratic Institutions and Human Rights of the Organization for Security and Co-operation in Europe (2009) *Hate Crime Laws—A Practical Guide*, Warsaw, Retrieved 4 May 2015 http://www.osce.org/odihr/36426

Perry, B. 2005. 'A Crime by Any Other Name: The Semantics of Hate'. *Journal of Hate Studies* 4(1): 121.

R.A.V. v City of St. Paul, 505 U.S. 377 (1992).

Rawls, J. 1971. *A Theory of Justice*, Cambridge, MA: Belknap Press of Harvard University Press.

Swedish Penal Code, translation available at http://www.regeringen.se/rattsdokument/departementsserien-och-promemorior/1999/01/ds-199936/

Taslitz, A.E. 1999. 'Condemning the Racist Personality: Why the Critics of Hate Crimes Legislation Are Wrong'. *Boston College Law Review* 40(3): 739.

Wisconsin Statute 939.645, Retrieved 4 May 2015, https://docs.legis.wisconsin.gov/statutes/statutes/939/IV/645

Walters, M.A. 2014. *Hate Crime and Restorative Justice*, Oxford: Oxford University Press.

4

WHITE PRIDE WORLDWIDE: CONSTRUCTING GLOBAL IDENTITIES ONLINE

Barbara Perry and Ryan Scrivens

To see the Internet as only a 'tool' or 'resource' for disseminating ideas and products, as much of the literature has done (e.g., Bostdorf 2004; Duffy 2003), is to miss an even more significant aspect of online venues. The Internet is also a site of important 'identity work', in which collective identities can be accomplished interactively. What is central to the enhanced capacity of the Internet as a site for the shared construction of identity is its active and interactive nature. Traditional media forms allow only one-way communication of ideologies and strategies. They are largely passive conduits for propaganda. Digital media, on the other hand, allow for dialogue and the *exchange* of ideas. Chat rooms, discussion forums, blogs and Facebook pages engage members and potential members in conversations about their common identities. The 'virtual public sphere' that characterizes the Internet invites active participation whereby collectives 'attempt to interpret and understand crises, injustice, and adversities, and to envision alternatives and map strategies' (Langman 2005: 54). Activists' use of the Internet is not passive, as implied by analyses that suggest the web 'provides' or 'gives' meaning or identity to users. Rather, participants are actively and discursively constructing collective identities (Back 2002; Bowman-Grieve 2009). We aim in this chapter to explore how white supremacists, specifically, exploit the web as a venue for expressing 'white pride worldwide'. We draw upon social movement theory, which broadly explores groups of actors engaged in political or social action on the basis of shared identities or interests (Diani 1992). We use the frame to guide our analysis of the ways in which the 'universal white man' is constructed by right-wing extremists, through active exploitation of varied online media and social media sites. In particular, we explore the Internet not as a tool, but as a site for the active construction of collective white identity.

The capacity to build shared projects across global borders is unquestioningly enhanced by the use of the Internet (Bowman-Grieve 2009; Levin 2002). Indeed, the social movement literature has begun to theorize the enabling role of the Internet in this context. However, the tendency has been to focus on progressive political movements, rather than on reactionary and regressive actors like right-wing extremists. Yet Langman's (2005: 44) observations on social justice movements resonate with respect to white supremacists as well: 'the significant political struggles that resist and contest neoliberal globalization are mediated across electronic networks that allow unprecedented opportunities for the exchange of information outside of the control of the dominant media corporations'. He goes on to characterize the responses to contemporary crises of globalization as, inter alia, radical, progressive, humanistic, and liberal—the right wing does not fall within the vision of most social movement theorists (e.g., Hunt and Benford 1994; Melucci 1995). Nonetheless, it is apparent that both the left and right share an increasing reliance on the Internet to facilitate movement expansion, both numerically and geographically.

The Internet is an enabling cyber venue, putting users in a position of power, wherein they actively engage with the material and with the other users therein. Consequently, 'the level of agency between the user and the material...actually defines how cyber media creates cyber culture. Cyber media puts into the hands, or the keyboard, of the Internet user the power to transform her/his own destiny—or at least that is the selling point of the technology' (Crisafi 2005: 39). Crisafi's point is well taken. However, he does not take the trope of 'action' far enough. Users do not simply engage with the technology, or the propaganda. Increasingly, they engage with one another, across borders. It is in part through this activity that they construct their own identities, but more significantly, collective identities. It is this development of a global white racialist/nationalist identity—via cyberhate—that this chapter explores. In particular, drawing on social movement literature around the building of collective identities, we explore the online identity work of the 'globalizing' right-wing extremist movement through four key frames: alternative media/ alternative messaging; identity borders; shared identity; and mobilizing hate.

COLLECTIVE IDENTITY

The notion of 'collective identity' is at the heart of our attempt to understand the global dispersion of a white racialist 'movement'. The scholarship on this concept explicitly recognizes that collective identity is actively produced; it is constructed through 'interaction, negotiation and the opposition of different orientations' (Melucci 1995: 43). This resonates strongly with Perry's (2001) theoretical emphasis on 'doing difference' in the context of hate crime specifically. Perry (2001) argues that hate crime is a forceful illustration of what it is to engage in situated conduct. The interactions between groups provide a context in which they compete for the privilege to define difference in ways that either perpetuate or reconfigure hierarchies of social power. These same processes occur within cyberspace. Face-to-face identity work that might take place at white power music concerts, for example, is supplemented by the 'many-to-many' capacity of Internet communication (Crisafi 2005). Collective identities 'are produced and reproduced in ongoing interactions between allies, oppositional forces, and audiences who can be real or imagined. While providing a sense of we-ness and collective agency, collective identities also create a sense of Other via boundary identification, construction, and maintenance' (Hunt and Benford 1994: 450).

Furthermore, collective identities are rooted in and shaped by particular discourses, fluid and relational in nature. Identities emerge from interactions with a number of different audiences, from bystanders to allies to opponents, and from news media to state authorities, for example. Such interactions in turn channel words and actions. They provide the grounds on which individuals can delegitimize the claims of Others and categorize themselves and Others, all in the name of making sense of their social worlds and their place in those worlds (Polletta and Jasper 2001). The social construction of movement identities is a cultural representation, a set of shared meanings that are produced and reproduced, negotiated and renegotiated, in the interactions of individuals embedded in particular sociocultural contexts. Indeed, online venues are sites of important 'identity work'. Ackland and O'Neil (2011: 187) emphasize the importance of participation in informal networks and direct control over the means of communication, both of which favour the pre-eminence of expressive behaviour leading to the formation of collective identity.

The model suggests four key elements of collective identity formation, each of which is enhanced through the extended use of the Internet (Snow 2001). A collective identity provides an alternative frame for understanding and expressing grievances; it shapes the discursive 'other' along with the borders that separate 'us' from 'them'; it affirms and reaffirms identity formation and maintenance; and it provides the basis for strategic action. In what follows, we explore how each of these elements contributes to our understanding of the Internet as a venue for the construction of collective identity around whiteness. We aim to establish that hate groups attempt to position themselves as a global force through their inter/action in cyberspace.

ALTERNATIVE MEDIA, ALTERNATIVE MESSAGES

'We all should be using these social networking sites to reach new people and bring them here. They're huge and their Thought Police won't be able to keep up' (Donald Black, 14 May 2009, https://www.stormfront.org/forum/t600609/).[1]

As one of the pioneers of the use of the Internet among right-wing extremists, Donald Black highlights here the importance of the Internet as an 'alternative medium' that counters the mainstream 'Jews-media' that is so reviled by the right. The next generation of activists concurs, as is evident on the Canadian Unit 14 website:

We in the Unit like to take advantage of all that social media has to offer for promoting our cause our twitter account has grown to over 500 followers, we have also recently launched a Facebook page & have begun adding videos to Youtube with much more to come in the future. (Jon Doe, 5 February 2015, http://unit14canada.blogspot.ca)

---

[1] All online quotes will be quoted verbatim.

On the Internet, activists can carve out safe spaces, or 'free spaces where members communicate, reinforce, materialise and celebrate their ideology and collective identity' (Futrell and Simi 2004: 39). They are sites for important counter-narratives that challenge the 'liberal Jewish agenda' (Ackland and O'Neil 2011). For example, the 14 Words Network was explicitly established with the aim of 'producing a quality media product for YOU'. As such, it is:

devoted to bringing you news that the mainstream media feels isn't newsworthy. Today, many stories remain hidden only being reported in local areas, when they really deserve international attention. It is our duty to shine a light on these issues and let the mainstream media know that they cannot hide the facts (http://www.14words.net/p/about_01.html).

From the perspective of far-right extremists, the 'liberal' mainstream media are not to be trusted. They are little more than a platform for proselytizing the one world vision of ZOG—Zionist Occupied Government. It is the media that are held responsible for indoctrinating white nations with the false ideologies of globalization, and multiculturalism in particular. White racialist websites, in contrast, are a conduit for the 'truth':

I often go onto the Yahoo message boards to inform the uninformed about Israel and the Jews, and our racial situation. It's a great way to learn propaganda skills, such as sound-bite agitational propaganda. Most of the political and current event boards are loaded with Jews, but there are still many Whites who post and read posts. (Sunwheel, 14 November 2001, https://www.stormfront.org/forum/t5797/)

While it represents an 'alternative medium', the Internet also allows for the promotion of alternative messaging. The Internet has become a crucial conduit for the right to air their grievances and to bond around the 'common enemy' (Anahita 2006). For example, a message posted anonymously on the website of Golden Dawn, a far-right political party in Greece, offers 'Greetings from Germany & best of luck to Golden Dawn! The peoples of Greece and Germany should realize that we are fighting the same common enemy' (Anonymous, 14 February 2013, http://golden-dawn-international-newsroom.blogspot.ca/p/our-identity.html); and another, also anonymous: 'The real Europeans watch Golden Dawn with admiration and hope for all our people. May the Gods bless your fight and grant you victory over the evil that threatens us all' (9 November 2012, http://golden-dawn-international-newsroom. blogspot.ca/p/our-identity.html).

As noted above, in the current climate of hate, that enemy is globalization and its associated ills. For right-wing extremists, globalization exacerbates an array of traditional 'threats' to the rightful authority and even survival of the white race and white culture. The twin problems of global capital and multiculturalism are thought to enhance the ongoing threats to national and regional economies and to white Christian culture. William Pierce sums up this critique, arguing that:

Nationalists in Germany, in Europe, and also in America, are facing the common enemy of all people, international monopoly capital, that wants to deal the death blow to all historically grown nations in favor of a multicultural 'melting pot'. Our fight against the attempts for world domination and economic imperialism by multinational corporations will be hard and full of privations (cited in Grumke 2013: 14).

In an online discussion about international communism and globalist capitalism, countless users proclaim solidarity with Golden Dawn. For instance, one anonymous user declares:

You have the support not only Greeks from all around the world (like myself) but the support of all people of free will and thought who want only to see International Jewry and their interests wiped from the pages of history once and for all (19 January 2013, http://golden-dawn-international-newsroom.blogspot.ca/p/our-identity.html).

Another user went as far as to refer to their website as the 'international newsroom' and a 'beacon of hope in a beleaguered Europe' (Anonymous, 20 December 2012, http://golden-dawn-international-newsroom.blogspot.ca/p/our-identity.html).

The World Wide Web has become a key conduit for the shared expression of this strong opposition to globalization. On the Golden Dawn webpage, a user discussed the impact of transnationalism and globalization, especially with respect to the 'flood' of non-white migrants:

Look at the brainwashed Italians who were ordered by their government to weep for the African and Muslim invaders who sank to the bottom of the Mediterranean Sea. Those boats with parasites and enemies of Europe must be machine-gunned before they reach the coasts of Europe…(T)hey are sent by the international financial plutocracy to destroy Europe and its identity and pave the way for capitalist planned fusion of all countries and people of the world in order to turn the world into one country run by one government, with one language and one religion (Anonymous, 6 October 2013, http://golden-dawn-international-newsroom.blogspot.ca/p/our-identity.html).

In high-immigration countries such as Australia and Canada, right-wing extremists have displayed a strong disapproval towards transnational policy, primarily around the idea of 'multiculturalism'. For example, as one user noted:

I am sick of self hating whites, white guilt, and multiculturalism which is jost a codeword for antiwhite. Enough is enough…I can't a job because I speak English. I'm on welfare now (which i despise greatly) and I am so deppressed …All I want to do is get a job, save up, and move to a 'white' town (IrishPride1975, 6 November 2014, https://www.stormfront.org/forum/t1072627/).

The Internet represents a site for figurative collective hand wringing and gnashing of teeth in response to the 'dangerous' effects of globalization. It facilitates a shared airing of grievances, which white power activists would argue is not possible in mainstream venues. Online dialogues lend weight to individual 'injustices', turning them into collective injuries. While the primary focus of these contemporary harms is globalization, the further development of a collective identity is also grounded in the related construction of an 'us' versus 'them' binary, wherein right-wing extremists typically associate their losses, real or perceived, with the (illegitimate) gains of the Other. This critical alternative frame, then, 'make(s) a compelling case for the "injustice" of the condition and the likely effectiveness of collective "agency" in changing that condition. They also make clear the "identities" of the contenders, distinguishing "us" from "them"' (Polletta and Jasper 2001: 291).

SEPARATING 'US' FROM 'THEM'

The much-maligned policies of globalization—especially those that foster multiculturalism—have seemingly empowered those Others whom right-wing hate groups construct as threats to white homelands. Indeed, the establishment of a collective white identity resides in what Snow (2001: 212) describes as 'a shared sense of "one-ness" or "weness" anchored in real or imagined shared attributes and experiences among those who comprise the collectivity and in relation or contrast to one or more actual or imagined sets of "others"'.

The formation of 'us' is predicated on the corollary formation of 'them'. Perry (2001) argues that, in the context of hate crime generally, identity is shaped relationally. The self is typically created through reference to the other. Identity work involves 'constructing both a collective self and a collective other' (Hunt and Benford 1994: 442). Moreover, 'they' are shaped in ways that stress the dangers they represent with respect to the preservation of white identity and security. Thus, cultural or racial or gender differences, for example, are read as grounds for hostility if not outright fear. In support of this, one online user wrote: 'We in Australia are having the same problems as Europe with the migrants. Moslems want sharia law, they want halal meat, they don't mix and rape our women. Golden Dawn is the answer we need in Australia as well' (Anonymous, 6 July 2013, http://golden-dawn-international-newsroom.blogspot.ca/p/our-identity.html).

As this statement suggests, non-white immigrants, for example, are constructed as major contributors to the breakdown of morality, security, unity, and stability. 'Us' versus 'them' dichotomies are constructed and proliferated via global online platforms, wherein non-whites are said to carry with them customs, folkways, and language which make white native born citizens 'strangers in their own land'. Such perspectives illustrate the social boundaries that groups use to highlight moral, cognitive, affective, behavioural, and other qualifying differences between themselves and others. Thus: 'By virtue of constructing an elaborated sense of who they are, movement participants and adherents also construct a sense of who they are not. In other words, boundary work entails constructing both a collective self and a collective other, an "us" and a "them"' (Hunt and Benford 1994: 442).

Correspondingly, significant energy is devoted to creating defensive boundaries. Borders are especially important as markers of the distinct boundedness of racialized groups, setting the limits as to who belongs where. They symbolically (and often physically) determine and reinforce ethnic separation and segregation (Perry and Blazak 2010). Nevertheless, in both symbolic and material terms, borders are permeable and subject to ongoing tendencies to transgression (Webster 2003). Clearly, immigrants crossing porous international boundaries are particularly reviled by adherents of white supremacist ideologies. They represent threats, in that they are perceived to have violated the carefully crafted barriers intended to keep them in their respective boxes (Perry and Blazak 2010). It is these margins that online activists are at pains to defend. As one user so clearly pointed out: 'I have nothing against people of all races, but we have nations and borders for a reason. If we were naturally inclined to live in diversity, we would have naturally done it thousands of years ago without it being forced upon us' (Anonymous,

12 January 2013, http://golden-dawn-international-newsroom.blogspot.ca/p/the-truth-about-golden-dawn.html).

It is in this context that anti-immigrant mobilization also emerges. It becomes a territorial defence of cultural, often national 'space', and a means to reassert the marginality of the other who dares to transgress (Perry 2001). There are arguably no destination states that do not experience at least periodic eruptions of exclusionary sentiment and activities. The United States and Europe are host to sustained patterns of xenophobia, and home to visible and vocal hate groups targeting Others (Caiani and Kröll 2014).

The activities of vigilantes on the US-Mexico border are an especially disturbing example of the use of violence to turn back the threat. In response to what they claim to be failed efforts on the part of official border agencies, organizations like the American Border Patrol and the Minuteman Project have emerged as self-described enforcers, defending the borders against the 'invading hordes' of 'illegal aliens', through use of force where necessary. They come to the border heavily armed, and equipped with increasingly sophisticated technology that allows them to track the movements of migrants through the desert landscape. These groups are animated by their online exchanges. For example, one disgruntled user created an online thread, titled 'illegal aliens murder', noting: 'the carnage wrought by illegal alien murderers represents only a fraction of the pool of blood spilled by American citizens as a result of an open border and un-enforced immigration laws' (halley, 17 November 2007, http://www.renewamerica.com/bb/viewtopic.php?f=1&t=6872&p=98936&hilit=border#p98936).

Such sentiments are scattered across the Internet. These isolationists take it upon themselves to defend *their* borders from 'them', threatening to eradicate anyone who oversteps their boundaries, especially immigrants and radical Islamists or anyone perceived as such.

While there is no recognizable border defence movement in Europe, there is nonetheless widespread xenophobic sentiment across the region. The UK's English Defence League (EDL) has actively incited violence through their rhetoric and public demonstrations (Treadwell and Garland 2011). The EDL claim to be non-racist and non-violent, and go as far as to call their members 'peaceful protestors against militant Islam'. However, their long-winded mission statement associates segments of the Muslim population with 'the denigration and oppression of women, the molestation of young children, the committing of so-called honour killings, homophobia, anti-Semitism, and continued support for those responsible for terrorist atrocities' (EDL 2015).

The EDL and other similar groups exploit the frustrations of disengaged and disenfranchised 'British' youth, laying the blame for their plight at the feet of what are argued to be comparatively privileged immigrants and refugees. They demonize the Other, creating and recreating one-dimensional narratives around their imminently threatening identities. As one Canadian xenophobe proudly proclaims:

I am rabidly anti-multiculti, not because is weakens my race...but because, by definition, it weakens my culture. A culture I believe superior to those that would hack the genitals off young girls, sell their children into sex-slavery, force women to cover up, allow polygamous families, encourage a culture of taking from society and not giving, spread desease and filth...There is NOTHING from any other cultures that we, as western civilazation need to import...nothing! (Anonymous, 3 May 2013, http://golden-dawn-international-newsroom.blogspot.ca/p/our-identity.html).

Greece's Golden Dawn party has provided additional impetus for already embittered residents displaced by the devastating economic crisis in that country. On their website, they develop and promote biased news reports, construing stories to fit their own pro-nationalist agenda. For example, as one report goes:

A Pakistani sexually offends the wife of an Albanian outside the Athens University of Economics and Business. Her husband demands explanations, and anarchists, along with other illegal immigrants, proceed to beat them up and trash their car. The Pakis of course, later claim they saw a 'knife' and a 'Golden Dawn tattoo'. The Media reports half the story, and the truth is hosted only in a few news websites (http://golden-dawn-international-newsroom.blogspot.ca/p/the-truth-about-golden-dawn.html).

The online responses that accompany this post and others like it are also telling, in that they reflect widespread and enthusiastic concordance with such constructions of the dangerous Other. For example, supportive messages like the following are common: 'Golden Dawn are an inspiration to Aryans all over our occupied homelands! Keep believing and give all for your Fatherland!' and 'We the white nations need to unite and defeat the ZOG in our governments. I like the way how you provide your own public service for the Greeks' (http://golden-dawn-international-newsroom.blogspot.ca/p/the-truth-about-golden-dawn.html). Indeed, the fervent nationalism of the party has found a ready audience, willing and eager to engage in simultaneous vilification of 'them' and glorification of the collective 'us'. As a counter to the expansion of the non-white threat, these racists come together under a universal banner of 'white pride worldwide'.

CONSTRUCTING THE COMMON IDENTITY

The denigration of the Other is accompanied by its opposite within the hate movement. The posturing of adherents also contributes to identity building and solidarity maintenance, which are key to the establishment of a collective identity. Importantly:

the collective, shared 'sense of we' is animating and mobilizing cognitively, emotionally, and sometimes even morally. The shared perceptions and feelings of a common cause, threat, or fate that constitute the shared 'sense of we' motivate people to act together in the name of, or for the sake of, the interests of the collectivity, thus generating the previously mentioned sense of collective agency (Snow 2001: 4).

Much of the literature on online identity construction has focused on the fluidity and mutability of these 'selves' (e.g., Daniels 2009; Weinberg 1998). Some argue that ongoing engagement with 'cyber worlds' allows 'rapid alterations of identity' by which individuals cycle through different characters, genders, races, sexualities, and other assorted identities (Turkle 1995: 174; see also Poster 1996). From this perspective, users form and reform identities at random. Notwithstanding, it is important to consider the extent to which the opposite is also possible. The Internet can also be used—collectively—to attempt to fix identities, to create stable identities that span diverse contexts (Bowman-Grieve 2009). In contrast to the centrifugal forces suggested by the former accounts, these collectivist analyses point to centripetal tendencies which allow otherwise diasporic members to find a common space.

The collective identity at issue here—the universal white man—is one such illustration of a 'process that allows a disparate group of individuals to voice grievances and pursue a collective goal under the guise of a "unified empirical actor"' (Adams and Roscignio 2005: 760). What stands out about so many contemporary white supremacist groups is their allusion to a collective 'we' that transcends national boundaries (Back 2002; Caiani and Kröll 2014). In an effort to describe the collective identity shared by Stormfront's visitors, one user characterized the site as an expression of: 'the living awakening collective consciousness of the White Race Worldwide... The primary purpose of this awakened collective White Mind is to awaken other individual White Minds around the world -- and thus to grow in size and wisdom and potential strength' (Tenniel, 10 December 2014, https://www.stormfront.org/forum/t1077502-38/).

Just as the common threat is global in scope and nature, so too then must white identity formations cross those borders. This is accomplished, in part, through the mobilization of shared narratives and frames that are built through interaction and negotiation. Variously described as 'cultural resources', 'symbolic resources', or 'cultural materials', the building blocks of these narratives include 'names, narratives, symbols, verbal styles, rituals, clothing, and so on' (Polletta and Jasper 2001: 285). These symbolic resources represent key boundary markers of 'collective differentiation' that allow for enhanced 'awareness of in-group commonalities and connections' (Snow 2001: 8). The shared access to and use of white power music, symbols, cultural expressions, and naming are some of the tools used to construct a common story. The Internet enables this exchange. It facilitates the interactive negotiation of individual and collective identities.

But what identity is expressed in these discursive artefacts? Ironically, the right has responded to the perceived threats of globalization, noted above, with their own variant of globalism. Grumke (2013: 20) eloquently captures the crux of this apparent contradiction, observing that '[r]ight-wing anti-globalists "globalize"'—and to make it even more complicated, a unifying ideological element is the struggle against 'globalism'. The 'common enemies' of the white race—regardless of location—also provide common grounds for nationalist rallying. At first glance, it seems paradoxical that those coming together through the Internet should be characterized as white *nationalists*. They pledge allegiance to particular nation states: Sweden, Germany, or the United States, for example. Each refers to their imagined nation as the great white homeland. However, on the Web, otherwise diverse nationalists pledge a more profound allegiance to the mythic *white* nation, wherein nationality comes to be defined not by state, geography, or citizenship, but by race. More than pan-American, or pan-European, the appeal is to join the fraternity of pan-Aryanism, wherein online extremists assert a common lineage, traceable to white Aryan cultures of Western Europe. Examples of this sentiment can be found in online text. A Combat 18 adherent reminds the faithful that: 'Our National Socialist family now transcends national borders, we do not owe our allegiance to any nation, our only allegiance is to our race—The White Race. Our countries are just geographical areas in which we just happen to live, but our race knows no national boundaries in this eternal struggle' (http://www.skrewdriver.net/ao.html).

Interestingly, the latter statement is found in the 'comments' responding to an article posted on the website. Such dialogues reflect an active engagement in the process of constructing identity, in that they constitute expressive exchanges that affirm and reaffirm the stated position. Even the 'creator' of the original article is creating a foundation for further development of a shared, collective 'self'. That others are likewise able to then respond, react, and typically endorse the racialist/nationalist vision is what empowers each of the actors as individuals, but also as part of a group with a common cause. In short, such exchanges announce the collective agency of the adherents, uniting 'old world' whiteness with the 'white diaspora', whereby 'the rhetoric of whiteness becomes the means to combine profoundly local grammars of racial exclusion within a trans-local and international reach' (Back 2002: 633). The trans-national carrier of white nationalist culture is managed within cyber-culture. It provides like-minded individuals with a meeting place in which they can define themselves as belonging to a distinct national setting and position themselves within a shared racial lineage. It gives them a place to express and connect with others on the basis of national chauvinism. However, the shared framing of this global identity has limited meaning without corollary strategies for mobilizing to defend the collective against the perceived threats to white survival.

MOBILIZING HATE

The Internet is exploited by the extreme right as a mobilizing force. Site visitors and members are called upon to put words into action. A post on Stormfront's *Events* link urged fellow travellers to 'Get out from behind your computer, and go to the streets! Stand up for OUR people.' Gliding in and out of different spaces—real and virtual—members use their digital venues to mobilize for action. Alongside the grandiose calls for RAHOWA or other armed battles are more realistic incitements to collective action. Stormfront has dedicated threads for both *Events* and *Activism* that invite adherents to join in celebrations of white heritage, to engage in local white pride marches, or to attend upcoming white power concerts. Each of these activities encourages members to come together to express their racial pride and commitment.

By design, online dialogue spills over into real world action. Some of this is relatively benign, as on singles' sites that result in dates, even long-term relationships. Stormfront has an internal White Singles sub-forum, which has two main threads: Talk and Dating Advice. The banality of such sites should not overshadow their importance. The promotion of 'Aryan coupling' is intended to ensure endogamous relationships and the subsequent reproduction of the white race, in line with the 14 Words doctrine shared by so many white power activists: 'We must secure the existence of our people and a future for White children.' This credo—widely expressed in multiple ways online—provides the very foundation for mobilizing action around the protection of a global white identity. Indeed, the Internet is a useful venue for galvanizing action around the grievances noted above, by translating the rhetoric into real-world activism. For example, a number of online-offline campaigns have surfaced in recent years, including right-wing political campaigns to boycott Chinese and American products, the accession of Turkey to the European Union, and the combined threat of the Euro, immigrants, and multiculturalism (Caiani and Kröll 2014: 8). The intentions behind these mobilization techniques are very clear: protect white people from globalization, economic crisis, and integration.

Right-wing extremist websites also feature less benign calls to action. Here, the posturing of aggressive adherents revolves around the active expulsion of the 'common enemies' noted throughout. A Golden Dawn adherent is explicit about both the targets and strategies to be used against them:

People, fight against those criminal and ignominious plans and sleazy plans. Stop being cowards, rise as one man, shoulder to shoulder, fight them courageously. Go get the plutocrats and their subservient corrupt governments and organizations. Organize a wide front of military attack on them, get them, punish all of them, hang them, get the power in your hands, reorganize future economy according to other new principles. Kick all aliens from Europe and other similar countries back to their own continents. Europe is for Europeans. Crush the vermin. (Anonymous, 6 October 2013, http://golden-dawn-international-newsroom.blogspot.ca/p/our-identity.html).

The overlapping belief systems documented herein lead many hate groups to the conclusion that, through organized action, the white race can and must reverse the trends represented by the myriad forms of white racial 'suicide', 'homicide', and 'genocide'. Blood and Honour Poland, for example, eschew 'compromise' or 'complicity' with mainstream politics of any sort:

National Socialism is the only hope that the White Aryan Race has to survive the new Millennium. Forget the 'Patriots', the flag wavers and the grovellers to Kings and Princes. They are weak and stupid and worship the forces which are pledged to keep them in chains. Forget the politicians and the 'democrats', they exist only to dilute and divert our movement. Their Gods are their Egos and the Shekels that their Jew masters have bought them with. Forget the 'entrepreneurs' and money-makers who have become rich from selling trinkets within the movement. They have cast away their Aryan birthright and have become as the Jew. Forget the apologists who cry 'If only we show ourselves to be nice, respectable people then the Enemy will allow us everything we want'. They are weak and stupid and do not understand the Eternal Laws of Nature. The new Millennium must be one of struggle for if we do not destroy the Enemy then He will destroy us. The final battle is approaching, the last chance of the White Aryan Race. (http://www.bhpoland.org/strona/en_index2.htm).

Web communities such as Stormfront are magnets for the most aggrieved white people, and a medium in which to rally around far-right ideals, and to strategize around preserving them in the real world. Aggressive posturing around racial defence is common online. For example, as one user wrote:

If as a White man you are not by now an extremist, then you are quite simply nothing but a cowardly traitor. JEWS KILLING GERMANS, NOTHING IS EVER ACHIEVED BY BEING 'NICE.' KILL THE JEW OR HE KILLS YOU (vindicator06, 8 August 2014, http://vnnforum.com/showthread.php?t=201105).

As the ultimate testament to their racial loyalty, such extremists offer a fight to the death—theirs or the enemies.

Not all online rhetoric goes to this extreme, however. Indeed, while the goals of extremists' action—as given by the 14 Words noted above—are fairly consistent from group to group, the means by which to achieve those aims are diverse. For some, the first step is relatively simple: close the borders in order to halt the darkening of the 'white' lands. Another common theme is the idea of racial segregation, generally in geographical terms. According to this position, the white race can survive only if it is isolated from the biological and cultural influences of the non-Aryan races. Angry and apparently in fear of the changing demographics of the west, white supremacists call for a renewal of the great white homeland, preferably through a thorough purging of the 'dirt and filth', or, as a compromise, through a rigid separation of 'us' from 'them'. The most effective way to keep the bloodline pure is to establish autonomous racial nations. Lilith88, for example, proclaims that:

The world can be divided in several parts, and to each of them belongs a different human race. These races are characterized by particular cultures and those cultures are quite the same in each racial area. So North America and Europe, which are Aryan, have the same type of culture and traditions, even if they are variations from one country to the other ... Africa belongs to the Black race, North Africa and Near East to Arabic race, and so on, except for the Jewish race, but the Jewish plague is not my current subject (http://www.skrewdriver.net/wraces.html).

This rigid segregation is favoured among an array of white supremacists. It implies, obviously, deporting non-Europeans to their country or continent of origin. It is especially important to them, however, that whites regain 'a nation': 'We must have White schools, White residential neighborhoods and recreation areas, White workplaces, White farms and countryside. We must have no non-Whites in our living space, and we must have open space around us for expansion' (National Alliance, online, https://natall.com/about/what-is-the-national-alliance/).

The white supremacist mapping of the western world, in particular, brings to mind Oikawa's (2002: 74) discussion of the 'cartography of violence' which suggests that the processes of nation building are 'based upon systematic racial exclusions and other social divisions'. None so explicitly attend to this in crude and explicit terms than those within the white supremacist movement. For them the construction of 'white nations' is crucial to the salvation of the white race.

CONCLUDING REMARKS

Prior to the introduction of the World Wide Web, members of the far right recruited members and/or spread their message of intolerance through traditional means. Since then, right-wing extremists have become increasingly reliant on the Internet to facilitate movement expansion—both numerically and geographically—to publicize messages of hate and recruit and connect with like-minded others within and be-yond domestic borders. However, we argue that it is not only a 'tool' or 'resource' for disseminating ideas and products; it is also a site of important 'identity work', accomplished interactively through the *exchange* of ideas. White supremacists' use of the Internet is not passive; rather, participants actively and discursively construct collective identities. Moreover, the Internet allows this shared project to cross the global rather than simply the local or national landscape. It is readily acknowledged and exploited as a central node for extremists to exploit as they come together under the banner of 'white pride worldwide'.

This is part of a new racial project. As we noted above, regardless of location, right-wing extremists have traditionally associated with a local and insular vision of 'place', referring variously to 'the nation', or 'the homeland'. Groups in Germany spoke to their Aryan heritage, those in the UK emphasized Britishness, and those in the US talked of what it is to be American. Consequently, there has been a tendency to view the related movement(s) as largely national in focus. Yet, as with other contemporary cultural forms, these narrow representations have been broadened by the diverse impacts of globalization, and access to Internet media. To state it simply, globalization has provided renewed motivation for trans-national cooperation and a parallel increase in right-wing extremist movements, while the simultaneous evolution of the Internet has provided the vehicle by which to enhance connectivity and solidarity across the world. Paradoxically, then, right-wing extremists have framed their anti-globalist stance through efforts to globalize the movement.

REFERENCES

Ackland, R. and O'Neil, M. 2011. 'Online Collective Identity: The Case of the Environmental Movement'. *Social Networks*, 33(3), 177–90.

Adams, J. and Roscigno, V. 2005. 'White Supremacists, Oppositional Culture and the World Wide Web'. *Social Forces*, 84(2), 759–78.

Anahita, S. 2006. 'Blogging the Borders: Virtual Skinheads, Hypermasculinity, and Heteronormativity'. *Journal of Political and Military Sociology*, 32(1), 143–64.

Back, L. 2002. 'Aryans Reading Adorno: Cyber-Culture and Twenty-First Century Racism'. *Ethnic and Racial Studies*, 25(4), 628–51.

Bostdorf, D.M. 2004. 'The Internet Rhetoric of the Ku Klux Klan: A Case Study in Web Site Community Building Run Amok'. *Communication Studies*, 55(2), 340–61.

Bowman-Grieve, L. 2009. 'Exploring "Stormfront": A Virtual Community of the Radical Right'. *Studies in Conflict & Terrorism*, 32(11), 989–1007.

Caiani, M. and Kröll, P. 2014. 'The Transnationalization of the Extreme Right and the Use of the Internet'. *International Journal of Comparative and Applied Criminal Justice*, doi: 10.1080/01924036.2014.973050.

Crisafi, A. 2005. 'The Seduction of Evil: An Examination of the Media Culture of the Current White Supremacist Movement'. In S. Ni Fhlainn and W.A. Myers (eds.), *The Wicked Heart: Studies in the Phenomena of Evil* (pp. 29–44). Oxford: Inter-Disciplinary Press.

Daniels, J. 2009. *Cyber Racism: White Supremacy Online and the New Attack on Civil Rights*. Lanham, MD: Rowman & Littlefield Publishers.

Diani, M. 1992. 'The Concept of Social Movement'. *Sociological Review*, 40, 1–25.

Duffy, M.E. 2003. 'Web of Hate: A Fantasy Theme Analysis of the Rhetorical Vision of Hate Groups Online'. *Journal of Communication Inquiry*, 27(3), 291–312.

English Defence League. 2015. Mission Statement. Retrieved https://www.english defenceleague.org/?page_id=9

Futrell, R. and Simi, P. 2004. 'Free Spaces, Collective Identity, and the Persistence of U.S. White Power Activism'. *Social Problems*, 51, 16–42.

Grumke, T. 2013. 'Globalized Anti-Globalists: The Ideological Basis of the Internationalization of Right-Wing Extremism'. In S. Von Mering and T.W. McCarty (eds.), *Right-Wing Radicalism Today: Perspectives from Europe and the US* (pp. 13–22). London: Routledge.

Hunt, S.A. and Benford, R.D. 1994. 'Identity Talk in the Peace and Justice Movement'. *Journal of Contemporary Ethnography*, 22(4), 488–517.

Langman, L. 2005. 'From Virtual Public Spheres to Global Justice: A Critical Theory of Internetworked Social Movements'. *Sociological Theory*, 23(1), 42–74.

Levin, B. 2002. 'Cyberspace: A Legal and Historical Analysis of Extremists' Use of Computer Networks in America'. *American Behavioral Scientist*, 45(6), 958–88.

Melucci, A. 1995. 'The Process of Collective Identity'. In H. Johnston and B. Klandermans (eds.), *Social Movements and Culture* (pp. 41–63). Minneapolis: University of Minnesota Press.

Oikawa, M. 2002. 'Cartographies of Violence: Women, Memory, and the Subject(s) of the "Internment".' In S. Razack (ed.), *Race, Space and the Law: Unmapping a White Settler Society* (pp. 71–98). Toronto, ON: Between the Lines.

Perry, B. 2001. *In the Name of Hate: Understanding Hate Crimes*. New York, NY: Routledge.

Perry, B. and Blazak, R. 2010. 'Places for Races: The White Supremacist Movement Imagines U.S. Geography'. *Journal of Hate Studies*, 8(29), 29–51.

Polletta, F. and Jasper, J. (2001). 'Collective Identity and Social Movements'. *Annual Review of Sociology*, 27, 283–305.

Poster, M. 1996. 'Databases as Discourse, or, Electronic Interpellations'. In D. Lyon and E. Zureik (eds.), *Computers, Surveillance, and Privacy* (pp. 175–92). Minneapolis: University of Minnesota Press.

Snow, D. 2001. Collective Identity and Expressive Forms. *University of California, Irvine eScholarship Repository*, http://repositories.cdlib.org/csd/01-07

Treadwell, J. and Garland, J. 2011. 'Masculinity, Marginalization and Violence: A Case Study of the English Defence League'. *British Journal of Criminology*, 51(4), 621–34.

Turkle, S. 1995. *Life on the Screen*. New York, NY: Simon and Schuster.

Weinberg, L. 1998. 'An Overview of Right-Wing Extremism in the Western World: A Study of Convergence, Linkage and Identity'. In J. Kaplan and T. Bjørgo (eds.), *Nation and Race: The Developing Euro-American Racist Subculture* (pp. 3–33). Boston, MA: Northeastern University Press.

Webster, C. (2003). 'Race, Space and Fear: Imagined Geographies of Racism, Crime, Violence and Disorder in Northern England'. *Capital and Class*, 80, 95–122.

5

GLOBAL TERRORISM EVENTS AND ENSUING HATE INCIDENTS

Kathryn Benier

Hate crimes are often portrayed as being defensive in nature, and precipitated by an affront to one demographic group by another (Craig 1999). Thus they constitute a form of informal social control, sending a message to the targeted group that they are not welcome (King et al. 2009; Perry 2001). Given the increasing global attention to acts of terrorism following the turning point of September 11, 2001, scholars suggest there may be links between terrorist events in Western democracies and resulting hate crime incidents which may occur as an act of payback (Hanes and Machin 2014; King and Sutton 2013; McDevitt et al. 2002). Yet research into the temporal nature of hate crimes is in its infancy. What we know from the few studies that consider the timing of hate crime is that conflict against particular minority groups seems to increase after significant events (Jacobs and Wood 1999; Pinderhughes 1993). Hate crimes are more likely to occur when the group harbouring a grievance cannot turn to the law to rectify the conflict or to find closure, or when circumstances of an event preclude the possibility of justice through usual legal channels, such as a suicide bombing (King and Sutton 2013). This has led some to suggest that hate crime may become a form of retribution against those who share, or are perceived to share, a minority group status with the perpetrator (Lickel et al. 2006).

This chapter examines retaliatory hate crime following internationally recognized terror events. It includes a discussion of the research into the association between terrorism and hate crime in the United States, Europe, and Australia. It then examines the extent to which these global events transcend borders to effect retaliatory racial/ethnic hate crime in Australia, a country that has not yet faced a large-scale domestic act of terrorism. Although Australia does not have federal hate crime laws, the State of Victoria enacted a substantive offence model in the *Racial and Religious Vilification Act* in 2001 and sentence aggravation provisions in the 2009 amendment to the *Sentencing Act 1991*, making it an interesting site to investigate this relationship.

THE RELATIONSHIP BETWEEN TERRORISM AND HATE CRIME

Hate crime and terrorism have key differences which make them unique offences, but the constructs do overlap. Both hate crime and terrorism comprise acts that are designed to 'terrorize a broader social group' (Green et al. 2001: 483). They are also different manifestations of the same underlying concept—a symbolic action designed to send a message and intimidate members of society grouped by their identity rather than victimize a small number of individuals (Deloughery et al. 2012a; LaFree and Dugan 2004). For acts of terror or hate, the ultimate goal is to indirectly affect a large group of people (Krueger and Malečková 2002).

Despite their symbolic similarity, hate crime and terrorism are distinct constructs. Terrorism is predominantly an upward crime, involving a perpetrator of a lower social standing than the targeted group or victim (Deloughery et al. 2012b). In an act of terrorism, the aim of the perpetrator is to draw attention to a political or social cause through the publicity they may receive. Such events have more planning involved than a hate crime and are likely to be part of a sustained effort to draw attention to that political or social cause (LaFree and Dugan 2004). It is essential to note that many acts of terrorism in recent years aim to draw attention to conflict within the Middle East, such as the war in Iraq, the Israeli–Palestine conflict or the Islamic State campaign in Syria. Thus it could be argued that just as hate crimes may be inspired by international terrorism events, terrorism globally may also be inspired by war and conflict in specific regions of the world.

Another key difference is the law enforcement response, as terrorism often involves the mobilization of an entire response force such as the Federal Police, Army, or specialized police task forces. In contrast, hate crimes are handled by local authorities. These incidents are labelled as downward crimes as perpetrators are positioned within the powerful or dominant group in society and aim to reaffirm their perceived superiority to groups lower on the social hierarchy in the community (Grattet 2009; Green et al. 1998; Lyons 2007).

Recent studies suggest that hate crime is influenced in the short-term by singular events, such as widely publicized terrorist events (Hanes and Machin 2014; King and Sutton 2013; Legewie 2013; McDevitt et al. 2002). Terrorist attacks can trigger anger and prejudice, and can ignite a backlash by the victimized group against individuals who are visually similar in appearance to the alleged perpetrators (King and Sutton 2013). Vicarious, or *in terrorem*, victimization targets all members of the group who share an identification with the victim(s) (Perry and Alvi 2012). In a retaliatory hate crime, members of the group targeted by the terrorism event may seek retaliation for the incident, despite neither the perpetrator nor the victim of the hate crime being present at the initial act (Deloughery et al. 2012b; Lickel et al. 2006). The driving forces behind these hate crimes are two-fold: to 'restore order'; and/or to enhance group solidarity among the victimized group. Retaliatory hate crime therefore targets innocent members of the group *perceived* to be responsible for the initial act.

INTERNATIONAL RESPONSES TO SEPTEMBER 11, 2001

To date, the biggest threat to social order in many Western countries was the September 11 terrorist attack. The series of attacks that unfolded on this day substantially changed interactions between countries globally and led to the 'War on Terror'. This response disrupted everyday life within many communities around the world leading to an increased suspicion of the 'Arab Other' and reducing acceptance, tolerance, and cohesion within neighbourhoods in many Western nations (Poynting and Noble 2004). It also led to a significant increase in hate crime victimization within the immigrant Muslim population in the United States (Disha et al. 2011). For example, prior to September 11, the Jewish population reported the highest rates of hate crime victimization in the United States' Uniform Crime Reports, comprising 78–79 per cent of all religious hate crimes in the five years prior to 2001 (Rubenstein 2004). Following the attack, hate crime victimization against Jewish persons dropped (Rubenstein 2004), yet there was a notable increase in anti-Arab and anti-Islamic hate crimes (Disha et al. 2011, see also Deloughery et al. 2012a). Specifically, the FBI recorded 481 crimes in 2001, with 279 of these committed within a two-week period following the attack (King and Sutton 2013). Considering only twenty-eight hate crimes were recorded in 2000, this represents a 1,600 per cent increase in hate-related incidents (Disha et al. 2011). This increase is also reflected in Rubenstein's (2004) research, which notes that the annual anti-Arab hate crime figure in the United States was eighteen times higher in 2001 than the average annual rate from 2000.

While national hate crime numbers in the United States demonstrate a clear increase in crimes following September 11, these incidents were not randomly distributed. There is some evidence that hate crimes were clustered in particular geographic regions. Disha and colleagues (2011) found that increased anti-Arab and anti-Muslim hate crimes were more likely to be recorded in regions of the United States which had a high proportion of non-Hispanic white residents. As expected, increased hate crimes were also reported where the population of Arabic and Muslim residents was relatively high, as there are a greater number of potential victims. The authors conclude, however, that the individual risk to each resident of this background is actually lower where they constitute a greater proportion of total residents. This is in line with the defended neighbourhood theory of hate crime which argues that as the proportion of residents in a minority group increases, hate crime decreases (Green et al. 1998).

There was also a spike in unofficial victimization reports in the weeks following September 11, 2001. Again in the United States, the Arab Anti-Discrimination Committee reported over 700 violent incidents in the nine weeks following the September 11 terrorist attack (Hanes and Machin 2014; Kaplan 2006). In comparison, 165 reports were received between 1 January and 11 October 2002 (Kaplan 2006). Similarly, several studies observed an increase in the newspaper reports of violence and discrimination immediately following the events of September 11. A report by the South Asian American Leaders of Tomorrow (SAALT 2001) noted 645 incidents motivated by racial prejudice against residents of South Asian or Middle

Eastern descent in the week following September 11. These incidents were reported in over 400 media sources in the United States. Swahn and colleagues (2003) identified incidents of violent attacks against those from (or perceived to be from) the Middle East in the four weeks following September 11. These reports detailed the victimization of at least 128 people, with most attacks occurring within ten days of the terrorism events. However, it is essential to note that at this time media sources were focused on the Islamic terrorist network and may have selected these stories with a purpose to increase readership.

ONE INCIDENT, GLOBAL REACTIONS

The effects of September 11 were felt in communities beyond the United States. As well as increases in hate crime, evidence shows that the Muslim populations in both Europe and Australia noted increases in discrimination. A report on Islamophobia in the European Union after September 11, 2001 found that all European Member States reported victimization of Muslims or those associated with Islam, with many states reporting increases in the post-September 11 period (Allen and Nielsen 2002: 34). Verbal and physical assaults increased in Denmark, Italy, the Netherlands, Spain, Sweden, and the United Kingdom. Islamophobic verbal abuse increased in Austria, Belgium, Germany, and Ireland. Interestingly, Finland, Greece, France, Luxembourg, and Portugal reported no change in the frequency of incidents. Such variations may be a result of between-country differences in visible signs of Islamic association (such as wearing a hijab or niqab) or different proportions and clustering of people who identify as Muslim.

In the United Kingdom, Muslim groups also reported a significant increase in discriminatory experiences after September 11 (Sheridan and Gillett 2005). This measure involved participants assessing thirty-three items examining discrimination, negative media portrayal, hate speech, and hate-motivated violence on a five-point Likert scale ranging from 'a lot less than usual' to 'a lot more than usual'. In contrast, Hindus reported a slight increase in discrimination, though this was statistically non-significant. Jewish, Sikh, and Christian participants reported decreases in discrimination (Sheridan and Gillett 2005). This suggests that those of a Muslim background had become perceived as more as a threat than other ethnic groups.

Evidence from Australia shows similar patterns of retaliatory hate crime. The Australian Arabic Council reported a twenty-fold increase in the numbers of reports of vilification of Arab Australians following the September 11 terrorist attacks (Poynting 2002). Poynting and Noble (2004) explored racism experienced by the Arab and Muslim populations post-September 11 in Sydney and Melbourne—two cities with the greatest numbers and highest population density of people from a Middle-Eastern background. Surveys administered through ethnic and religious organizations showed that two-thirds of the 186 survey respondents noted an increase in racism against them personally, with women significantly more likely to report this increase. This gender difference may have been a result of the visibility of specific items of Muslim dress, or because they may have been more targeted in the community as they were perceived to be weaker and to not retaliate. Ninety-three per cent of respondents identified an increase in racism, abuse, and violence targeted towards their ethnic or religious community (Poynting and Noble 2004).

The above studies identify that the high-profile terrorism act on September 11 had consequences for race relations in many Western countries. As one of the most powerful countries in the world, an attack on United States soil was seen as a threat to world order, demonstrating that a major event in one country had repercussions for people internationally who shared the identity of the assailants (Sheridan and Gillett 2005). Globally, this attack increased a sense of fear and vulnerability in the general population, as evidenced by increased security measures in many aspects of our daily lives. In some instances, the attack also increased pre-existent prejudices and hatred of the would-be perpetrators of hate crime against groups perceived to share an ethnicity with the perpetrators of the terrorism act (Allen and Nielsen 2002). Indeed, some people believed that all Muslims constituted 'a possible menace' and threat to society (Sheridan and Gillett 2005: 196). Thus one terrorist event sparked major implications for social groups living in other countries.

As a result of one act on September 11, 2001, a number of people experienced targeted victimization based on their identity. This victimization transcended international borders, with most Western countries reporting an increase in victimization with an anti-Muslim sentiment despite the offence taking place in the United States. Yet these prejudices were not a recent phenomenon. Perceptions of ethnic minorities representing an underclass of the population have existed for centuries. Rather, September 11 offered perpetrators a new justification for xenophobia and a 'legitimate' target for their actions against certain groups in the community. Such hate crime targets included Muslims, residents from Arabic backgrounds, and in some cases of mistaken identity, Sikhs.

RETALIATORY HATE CRIME POST-2001

While the terrorist acts of September 11, 2001 were to date the most disruptive events in recent years, they are by no means the only act of terrorism which has affected hate crime rates. Since 2001, anti-Muslim sentiment has been a consistent presence in many Western countries and as such, this group remains one of the most targeted groups in hate-motivated crimes. However, these rates of victimization are heightened in the aftermath of a terrorist event. Deloughery and colleagues (2012b) identified a significant two per cent increase in the number of hate crimes reported in the FBI's Uniform Crime Reports in the one week following four major terrorism events. Yet hate crime levels decreased again after a two- to three-week period. This suggests the idea of retribution offences, where hate crime is enacted against someone who shares the perceived terrorism perpetrators' identity in the immediate aftermath of the terrorism event. In a similar study, King and Sutton (2013) find that anti-Arab and anti-Muslim hate crimes are increased for approximately one month following lethal terrorism attacks which involved Islamic fundamentalists as suspected perpetrators. Evidence suggests that hate crime levels escalate immediately after the terrorism event but also decay rapidly, indicating a spike rather than a plateau. Deloughery and colleagues (2012b) note that while terrorism is predictive of increased hate crime, there is no evidence of the reverse—that increasing hate crime may build to a point of a terrorist attack.

Retaliatory hate crime research in Europe shows that the terrorism–hate crime connection holds beyond the United States. Western European countries have recorded several terrorism incidents in the last decade, and these have had a direct effect on hate crime rates. In July 2005, four bombs were set off in central London during morning peak hour by extremist Islamic terrorists (CNN Library 2014). According to Allen and Nielsen (2002), religious-based hate crimes reported to police in the following four weeks increased to 269 incidents compared to forty incidents reported the previous year. In a further examination of the London bombings, Hanes and Machin (2014) identified a 26 per cent spike in anti-Arab and anti-Asian hate crime reported to police. This increase remains significant for the three months following the attacks. The authors also consider regional differences in hate crime reports, and identify that the strongest increase in hate crimes was in London. In Leicestershire, the West Midlands, and West Yorkshire increases were less severe; again giving rise to the idea that geographical distance plays a role in the way that terrorism events influence hate crime rates.

Further research shows spikes in hate crimes against British Muslims in response to both the Charlie Hebdo massacre in Paris in January 2015 and the Copenhagen murders in February 2015. Reports from Tell MAMA (Measuring anti-Muslim Attacks), a non-government reporting and victim support agency, demonstrate substantial increases in hate crime rates after these two terrorism events. Forty-five hate crimes were reported in the seven days following the Charlie Hebdo incident, an increase from twelve in the week before the incident (Littler and Feldman 2015). Similar patterns were seen in Copenhagen, with eighteen hate crimes reported before the murders and thirty reported the following week (Littler and Feldman 2015). Littler and Feldman (2015) note the role of the media coverage around the terrorism event as a key factor in the occurrence of retaliatory hate crimes. The effect of the media will be further explored at the end of this chapter.

Few studies of retaliatory hate crime have been conducted in continental Europe. However, research has considered the effect of terrorism on anti-Muslim or anti-immigrant sentiments. Such studies identify clear decreases in the favourability of ethnic diversity within Europe. Given that many recent terror attacks have been conducted by Islamic extremists, it is probable that ideas of anti-Muslim and anti-immigrant sentiment are conflated in the minds of the participants.

In 2004 when the Madrid bombings occurred, international public opinion surveys were in progress, allowing Legewie (2013) to consider the effect of the bombings on attitudes towards immigration in thirteen European countries. Perhaps not surprisingly, the 507 respondents in Spain rated immigration as one of the vital issues in their country. Residents of the Netherlands also rated immigration highly, while residents in Finland, Denmark, Portugal, and Greece did not see immigration as an important issue. In this study, Legewie (2013) also considers the Bali bombings in 2002 and compares the responses of those interviewed before the bombings and those interviewed thirty days afterwards. Here the author finds significantly less favourable attitudes towards immigration and multiculturalism in Portugal, Poland,

and Finland. Yet the increases in anti-immigrant sentiment associated with Bali are smaller than those in Madrid, suggesting that, as one may expect, the effects of terrorism are more severe when the event is geographically closer to home. Legewie (2013) also identifies regional differences within the countries, further suggesting that rates of unemployment have an additional effect on perceptions of immigrants. This notion ties in with resource-threat theories, which posit that discrimination and hate crime rates will be higher in areas with strong competition for the availability of economic resources (Grattet 2009).

Following the train bombings in Madrid in 2004, Echebarria-Echabe and Fernández-Guede (2006) conducted a survey of social attitudes in the Basque region in Spain. Comparing responses to the surveys they administered before the bombings, participants who completed the questionnaire after the attack demonstrated stronger anti-Arab and antisemitic prejudices and more conservative attitudes, suggesting that the decreased acceptance of these groups in society was a consequence of the incident. Similarly, the London bombings had a deleterious impact on religious acceptance. At this time, the Department for Communities and Local Government Citizenship Survey highlighted a rise in prejudices (Ratcliffe and von Hinke Kessler Scholder 2015). Respondents who completed the survey after the bombings occurred were more likely to agree with the statement that religious prejudices had increased within the past five years than those who completed it before the incident. These studies provide strong evidence that terrorist activities are detrimental to the acceptance of ethnic minorities within the community.

THE HATE CRIME—TERRORISM RELATIONSHIP IN AUSTRALIA

Evidence from the United States and Europe demonstrates that a terrorism event is often accompanied by a spike in hate crimes. These spikes are particularly substantial when the event occurs on domestic soil, or in a country which is in a close geographical proximity. Yet Australia has not experienced significant acts of terrorism in the post-September 11 environment. Australia is more geographically isolated than other Western countries. Thus there is little evidence to indicate whether the cultural proximity of international events transcend borders to increase retaliatory hate crime in Australia.

VICTORIA POLICE DATA

An empirical test of the hate crime—terrorism relationship was carried out using data provided by Victoria Police. Australia's second largest state behind New South Wales, Victoria has a population of 5.8 million and is one of Australia's fastest growing areas (Australian Bureau of Statistics 2015). Of these residents, approximately 75 per cent live in the capital city of Melbourne (Australian Bureau of Statistics 2012). Approximately

31.4 per cent of residents of Victoria were born outside of Australia (Australian Bureau of Statistics 2013).

Victoria is one of the few states in Australia in which police record hate crimes as a distinct offence type, using a check box on the crime report form to record the presence of a bias motivation and space to record the category of the motivation, such as race, religion, or disability. This research employs incident data of those identified by Victorian Police officers as prejudice-motivated crimes and recorded on the Law Enforcement Assistance Program (LEAP) database. The Victoria Police Prejudice Motivated Crime Strategy uses the definition: 'a criminal act which is motivated (wholly or partly) by hatred for or prejudice against a group of people with common characteristics with which the victim was associated with or with which the offender believed the victim was associated' (Victoria Police 2011: online).

The Victorian Police incident data reflect 2,899 prejudice-motivated offences reported between January 2001 and December 2013. These data were provided by Victoria Police as a monthly count of offences recorded in the LEAP database. Although previous studies use daily or weekly counts, these data are only available as a monthly count. This will still allow for observation of any post-terrorism spikes which may occur, but may not be able to detail the exact duration of the increase. In each month, the count of hate-motivated offences ranges from 0 to 63, with a mean of 18.5 reports made per month.

GLOBAL TERRORISM DATABASE

The hate crime data was accompanied by information obtained from the Global Terrorism Database. This is an open-source database containing over 125,000 incidents of terrorist events from 1970 to 2013 (National Consortium for the Study of Terrorism and Responses to Terrorism 2013).

Hypotheses presented three possible locations of terrorist attacks which may inspire retaliatory hate crime in Victoria, including terrorism which is domestic (Australia and New Zealand), geographically proximate (Asia-Pacific region), or culturally proximate (Western countries including Australia, Western Europe, and North America). A monthly count of incidents recorded in the database was created for events in each of these regions. Australia and New Zealand have limited experience of terrorism events in the region. Over the twelve years included in this analysis, this included seventeen small-scale incidents, including acts of property damage to shops and synagogues, pipe bombs, car explosions, and poison letters. According to the database, these incidents tally to three fatalities in total. The Asia-Pacific Region included South-East Asia, East Asia, and Australia and captured 5,179 incidents. This translates to a mean of thirty-three incidents per month. Examples include bombings and explosions, hostage taking, and armed assaults. Western countries included those in Western Europe, North America, and Australia. This tallied to 2,116 incidents over the twelve-year period symbolizing a greater experience with acts of terrorism in these countries, averaging thirteen per month. These incidents ranged from the Madrid and London bombings to small-scale car bombings and acts of property damage.

OUTCOMES

Time series graphs were created to visualize the relationship between terrorism in each of these regions with hate crime reports in Victoria. The graph of Australia and New Zealand is shown in Figure 5.1, and illustrates no visible relationship between terrorism acts and counts of hate crime. This pattern was also demonstrated in the graphs of terrorism in Western countries, and of terrorism acts in the Asia-Pacific region. Statistical analyses then revealed no significant correlation between terrorism events in each of the three regions with counts of hate crimes reported to Victoria Police. Finally, regression models were run to investigate the ability of terrorism events to predict hate crime, and of hate crime to predict terrorism events. Again these models were non-significant, demonstrating no relationship between the events.

These results are not suggesting that Australia does not have hate crime nor organized race riots. Certainly the events surrounding the Cronulla race riots of December 2005 demonstrate that such events occur in Australian society. This riot involved over 5,000 people and was organized through an SMS encouraging local residents to repel the Middle Eastern population, specifically the Lebanese groups, as a result of increasing tensions in the area (Jackson 2006). What these results do show is that hate crime which occurs in Melbourne does not appear to be clustered around terrorism events. This lack of association may be because Australia is yet to face an act of terrorism on a large scale. It may also be a result of Australia's geographic isolation. Perhaps there is less of a perceived threat associated with terrorism

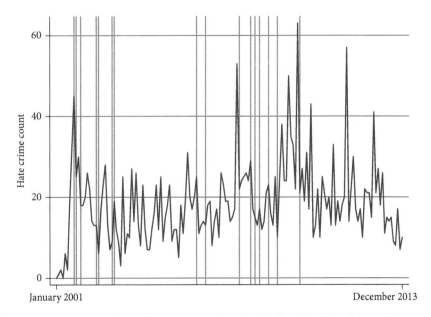

Figure 5.1 Graph of hate crime reported in Victoria showing the relationship with Australian terrorism events recorded in the Global Terrorism Database. Each vertical line represents an event in the database.

in other countries when surrounded by ocean. Certainly it is unlikely to be a result of a lack of information about events in other countries, as media and social media increase our knowledge and understanding of international events instantaneously.

The non-significant findings may also reflect the use of officially reported data. A number of scholars highlight the underreporting of hate crimes to the police, with Perry (2001) suggesting hate crimes may be reported in less than 20 per cent of incidences, whereas Levin (1999) estimates around 30 per cent of hate victimizations are taken to the police. A recent study in Australia found that 57 per cent of respondents who had experienced hate crimes motivated by race, religion, or sexuality did not report these incidents to any formal agency (VEOHRC 2010). While the hate crimes reported to Victoria Police may underestimate the figures of hate crime victimization, they provide the best measure to date to allow an examination of the incidents. Perhaps data from human rights organizations and anti-discrimination boards present different results. Alternatively, nationwide data may clarify this relationship. More recent data may also tell a different story, as the dataset used in this analysis ends in 2013. Arguably the closest action to terrorism that Australians have faced was the Sydney siege in December 2014.

'THE SYDNEY SIEGE'

On 15 December 2014, a 'lone-wolf' terrorist took eighteen hostages in a café in the central business district (CBD) of Sydney, Australia, stating that he was acting on behalf of the Islamic State. This was the first incident of its type to take place on Australian soil and had a resounding effect on Australian acceptance and inclusion. The siege lasted some sixteen hours, and during the incident many Australians expressed their concern that there was a potential for increased violence or intimidation towards the Islamic community as a result of the siege. By the end of the siege, derogatory and at times disturbing anti-Muslim sentiment was emerging on social and mainstream media against the Islamic community (Simmonds 2014). Yet this negativity was soon overwhelmed by an 'I'll ride with you' campaign on Twitter, aimed at supporting the Muslim community in society, particularly those travelling alone on public transport (ABC News 2014). The campaign was initiated by a Brisbane social media user who posted that she had witnessed a Muslim quietly removing her hijab on the train after details of the Sydney siege came to light. She told her to put the scarf back on, and they could ride together. The tweets took off, with users tweeting their transport paths along with the hashtag #illridewithyou. Over 120,000 tweets were recorded within a three-hour period on the evening of the siege, obtaining global media coverage and reaching as far as the White House with Barack Obama tweeting using the hashtag (ABC News 2014).

Despite this support, the Islamophobia Register Australia still received twenty-seven reports of anti-Muslim incidents in the six days after the attack (Islamophobia Register Australia 2014). The register has received 460 submissions since its foundation on 17 September 2014, suggesting that this rate of hate crime incidents is higher than the average rate of the last nine months of operation (Islamophobia Register Australia 2015). This Register is the first third-party agency specifically targeted towards recording anti-Muslim incidents, with previous reports being recorded by anti-discrimination boards if reported to them. Incidents following the Siege included online death threats or threats of violence, as well as physical actions such as Muslim women being intimidated, threatened, and verbally abused in public. Further discrimination was noted with several businesses reportedly displaying 'no Muslim' signs on their doors. Property damage was also involved, with mosques around Sydney reporting broken windows, vandalism, and graffiti (Islamophobia Register Australia 2014).

The Sydney siege was the first instance of Islamic extremism on Australian soil and while there was some reaction from the community, this was not to the strong scale noted in other countries after domestic terrorism. Indeed many social media users noted their pride in the Australian community in the way that they bound together to highlight that the views and actions of one extremist was not reflective of an entire religious group. Littler and Feldman (2015) argue that one contributing factor to the low number of retaliatory hate crimes may have been the speed in which the media highlighted the impaired mental status of the extremist. Many people labelled him as mentally ill, rather than labelling him a terrorist. This may have decreased the perceived threat felt by potential hate crime perpetrators.

THE ROLE OF THE MEDIA
IN RETALIATORY HATE CRIME

A consistent element of this exploration of retaliatory hate crime following terrorist events is the role of the media, and the international reaction which can be sparked post-terrorism. With the increase in the availability of news online, there is a global knowledge of major events as soon as they happen. This means that news of terrorism transcends international borders instantaneously. As such, the media has an extremely powerful role in the way in which events of terrorism are portrayed.

An act of terrorism is arguably the most effective way to obtain global publicity for a cause. Indeed, Sharma (2003: 225) suggests that 'terrorism has become a form of advertisement'. Yet the key element to ensuring the political message behind the act is conveyed to the public audience is the media. Without media coverage to draw attention to the cause and the demands of the group which claim ownership of the attack, the effects would remain confined to the immediate victims (Hoffman 2006). Thus terrorism has to be communicated to have an effect (Seib and Janbek 2011). As such, scholars highlight that democratic societies may be more susceptible to terrorism due to the notion of a free press reporting on incidents (Kydd and Walter 2006). Where the government has a tight control on the media, incidents may be suppressed and receive little to no coverage (Dershowitz 2003; Kydd and Walter 2006).

Consider, for example, the media response to September 11. Far from presenting the news coverage objectively, outlets communicated hysteria and hatred (Kellner 2005). The media called for government action and political revenge on Arab and Muslim countries. These views substantially changed the public's perceptions of the 'Arab Other' and the way that ethnic and religious minorities were now perceived as a threat within the community. The media replayed the footage of the events repeatedly for three days without so much as a commercial break, conveying the message that terrorists could take on a country as powerful as the United States and complete a number of attacks successfully (Kellner 2005). They highlighted that the United States and indeed any country in the Western world was 'vulnerable to terror attack, that terrorists could create great harm, and that anyone at anytime could be subject to a violent terror attack' (Kellner 2005: 4).

In comparison to the media coverage after September 11, coverage of the Sydney siege in 2014 showed a large difference in the style of reporting. From the first stories, the offender was portrayed as a lone wolf who had a history of mental illness and a substantial criminal record of serious offences (Aly 2014; Dolnik 2014; Wells 2015). Stories highlighted that his motives were egotistical and individually driven rather than being designed by or linked to terror groups (Aly 2014; Dolnik 2014). Such reports also reached the United States and United Kingdom (BBC News 2014; Holley 2014). Data from third-party reporting sites Tell MAMA and the Islamophobia Register in the UK and Australia respectively shows that while some increases in hate crime occurred following the siege, this does not appear to be to the same extent as after September 11. Thus hate crime appears to be less likely when the motivation of the attackers is downplayed in favour of alternative explanations, such as the mental instability of the gunman in the Sydney siege (Littler and Feldman 2015). An extreme individual acting alone is perceived as less of a threat than a terrorist acting on behalf of an organized terrorist network.

Research findings demonstrate that survey participants with a high exposure to news coverage of acts of terrorism have stronger anti-Muslim sentiments than those with a low exposure (Boomgaarden and de Vreese 2007; Das et al. 2009). The role of the media in depicting terrorism and conveying anti-immigrant sentiments is evidenced by the European Social Survey study conducted before and after the murder of Dutch film-maker Theodoor Van Gogh in 2004. Following the release of his short film, a criticism of the way women are treated in Islam, Van Gogh was shot and stabbed by an Islamic radical (Boomgaarden and de Vreese 2007). The murderer allegedly left a five-page note on the body, threatening Western governments (Finseraas et al. 2011). Although it is arguable if this constituted a hate crime, a terrorist attack, or perhaps simple 'payback', the media portrayal of the incident highlighted the event as an act of terrorism. Following the incident, violent attacks occurred near Islamic schools and mosques in the Netherlands and increased tensions were reported in neighbouring countries including Denmark, the United Kingdom, and Germany through the European Social Survey (Finseraas et al. 2011). The intolerances and prejudices were studied by Boomgaarden and de Vreese (2007), who identified that anti-immigrant sentiments were highest for respondents who had high exposure to news coverage immediately after the event (Boomgaarden and de Vreese 2007; Das et al. 2009). Those with low news exposure reported smaller increases in anti-immigrant sentiment.

CONCLUSION

Previous research shows that retaliatory hate crime is a widely recognized problem which transcends international borders. There is a plethora of research which considers how the events of September 11 detrimentally affected social cohesion and trust in the immediate aftermath globally. Research also shows that since this time, Muslim communities have been perceived to be more threatening to social order than other ethnic minority groups. Retaliatory hate crimes are also visible with other terrorism events such as the London and Madrid bombings. While some of this research focuses on anti-immigrant sentiments, perceptions of immigration policies, or intolerance of religious groups rather than hate crime outcomes, it is easy to imagine that these sentiments could lead to hate crime incidents given the right circumstances. These studies also highlight the role of the media in creating an international reaction against this act of terrorism which results in a series of attacks and heightened anti-immigration sentiment.

In Australia, data from Victoria Police appears to show no correlation to data provided in the Global Terrorism Database while exploring terrorism events recorded in Western countries, nor those in South-East Asia. There is also no pattern with terrorism recorded domestically; although there are a limited number of incidents reported in the country and in terms of fatalities recorded, the number is an extremely small percentage when compared to those in other regions. This could be a result of the limited experience of terrorism in Australia, or of Australia's geographic isolation from other Western countries. The findings could be a result of the monthly data counts diluting effects which may be observed in daily or weekly trends. The findings could also be a limitation of using official data, and a further examination of this issue will engage with reports recorded by human rights and anti-discrimination agencies to determine different patterns around terrorism events. These data would be useful for future research, particularly when different jurisdictions utilize different reporting mechanisms.

Retaliatory hate crimes are an important issue in many Western countries and research in the United States, United Kingdom, and Europe notes an increase in anti-immigrant or anti-Muslim hate crimes in the wake of terrorism. Further research could assess this relationship temporally to examine if retaliatory hate crime is decreasing with the consistent recurrence of terrorism events over the past decade as terrorism is accepted as a semi-regular occurrence. Alternatively, and more probably, the consistency of Islamic extremism positions the Muslim community as a strong threat to community ideals, and may be strengthening the will of hate crime perpetrators to act to restore 'order'. Previous research has also focused on police-reported data, and data from human rights or anti-discrimination commissions could paint a different picture in terms of the numbers of hate crimes reported in the aftermath of a terrorist event.

Terrorism poses a consistent and on-going threat to the Western world. While governments and intelligence agencies are quick to investigate the groups and ideals behind terrorism events, little attention has been drawn to the number of hate crimes documented in the aftermath. Yet in some events, the number of victims of retaliatory hate crime in an area outweighs the number of people affected by the initial terrorism act. A stronger understanding of the nature of retaliatory hate crimes seems prudent for police and law enforcement, to allow for preparedness when the next high-profile terrorism event inevitably occurs.

REFERENCES

ABC News. 2014. '#illridewithyou: support for Muslim Australians takes off following Sydney siege'. Retrieved from http://www.abc.net.au/news/2014-12-15/illridewithyou-hashtag-takes-off-following-siege/5969102

Allen, C. and J.S. Nielsen. 2002. 'Summary Report on Islamophobia in the EU after 11 September 2001'. Centre for the Study of Islam and Christian-Muslim Relations, Department of Theology, University of Birmingham, European Monitoring Centre on Racism and Xenophobia.

Aly, A. 2014. 'Sydney siege: don't call Man Haron Monis a "terrorist" – it only helps Isis'. Retrieved from http://www.theguardian.com/commentisfree/2014/dec/16/sydney-siege-dont-call-man-haron-monis-a-terrorist-it-only-helps-isis

Australian Bureau of Statistics. 2012. 'Population by Age and Sex, Regions of Australia, 2011'. Retrieved from http://www.abs.gov.au/AUSSTATS/abs@.nsf/allprimarymainfeatures/5470C6B9CB8DFA2ACA257D41001740ED?opendocument

Australian Bureau of Statistics. 2013. '2011 Census QuickStats: Victoria'. Retrieved from http://www.censusdata.abs.gov.au/census_services/getproduct/census/2011/quickstat/2?opendocument&navpos=220

Australian Bureau of Statistics. 2015. 'Australian Demographic Statistics: Sep 2014'. Retrieved from http://www.abs.gov.au/ausstats/abs@.nsf/mf/3101.0

BBC News. 2014. 'Man Haron Monis: "Damaged" and "unstable"'. Retrieved from http://www.bbc.com/news/world-australia-30484419

Boomgaarden, H.G. and C.H. de Vreese. 2007. 'Dramatic Real-world Events and Public Opinion Dynamics: Media Coverage and its Impact on Public Reactions to an Assassination'. *International Journal of Public Opinion Research* 19(3): 354–66.

CNN Library. 2014. 'July 7 2005 London Bombings Fast Facts'. Retrieved from http://edition.cnn.com/2013/11/06/world/europe/july-7-2005-london-bombings-fast-facts/

Craig, K.M. 1999. 'Retaliation, Fear, or Rage: An Investigation of African American and White Reactions to Racist Hate Crimes'. *Journal of Interpersonal Violence* 14(2): 138–51.

Das, E., B.J. Bushman, M.D. Bezemer, P. Kerkhof, and I.E. Vermeulen. 2009. 'How Terrorism News Reports Increase Prejudice Against Outgroups: A Terror Management Account'. *Journal of Experimental Social Psychology* 45(3): 453–9.

Deloughery, K., R.D. King, V. Asal, and R.K. Rethemeyer. 2012a. 'Analysis of Factors Related to Hate Crime and Terrorism'. Final Report to the National Consortium for the Study of Terrorism and Responses to Terrorism. College Park, MD, START.

Deloughery, K., R.D. King, and V. Asal. 2012b. 'Close Cousins or Distant Relatives? The Relationship between Terrorism and Hate Crime'. *Crime & Delinquency* 58(5): 663–88.

Dershowitz, A.M. 2003. *Why Terrorism Works: Understanding the Threat, Responding to the Challenge*. New Haven, USA: Yale University Press.

Disha, I., J.C. Cavendish, and R.D. King. 2011. 'Historical Events and Spaces of Hate: Hate Crimes against Arabs and Muslims in Post-September 11 America'. *Social Problems* 58(1): 21–46.

Dolnik, A. 2014. 'Siege hostage taker "mentally ill"'. Retrieved from http://media.smh.com.au/video-news/video-nsw-news/siege-hostage-taker-mentally-ill-6093933.html

Echebarria-Echabe, A. and E. Fernández-Guede. 2006. 'Effects of Terrorism on Attitudes and Ideological Orientation'. *European Journal of Social Psychology* 36(2): 259–65.

Finseraas, H., N. Jakobsson, and A. Kotsadam. 2011. 'Did the Murder of Theo van Gogh Change Europeans' Immigration Policy Preferences?'. *Kyklos* 64(3): 396–409.

Grattet, R. 2009. 'The Urban Ecology of Bias Crime: A Study of Disorganized and Defended Neighborhoods'. *Social Problems* 56(1): 132–50.

Green, D.P., L.H. McFalls, and J.K. Smith. 2001. 'Hate Crime: An Emergent Research Agenda'. *Annual Review of Sociology* 27(1): 479–504.

Green, D.P., D.Z. Strolovitch, and J.S. Wong. 1998. 'Defended Neighborhoods, Integration, and Racially Motivated Crime'. *American Journal of Sociology* 104(2): 372–403.

Hanes, E. and S. Machin. 2014. 'Hate Crime in the Wake of Terror Attacks: Evidence from 7/7 and September 11'. *Journal of Contemporary Criminal Justice* 30(3): 247–67.

Hoffman, P. 2006. *Inside Terrorism*. New York: Columbia University Press.

Holley, P. 2014. 'Before the Sydney siege, alleged gunman Man Haron Monis faced sexual assault, murder conspiracy charges'. Retrieved from https://www.washingtonpost.com/news/world/wp/2014/12/15/before-he-took-hostages-at-a-sydney-cafe-man-haron-monis-had-been-tied-to-alleged-murder-sexual-assaults-and-offensive-letters/

Islamophobia Register Australia. 2014. 'Press Release: 24/12/2014'. Retrieved from https://www.facebook.com/islamophobiaregisteraustralia/photos/pb.563697713753175.-2207520000.1427087451./613233185466294/?type=3&theater

Islamophobia Register Australia. 2015. 'Press Release: 07/06/2015'. Retrieved from https://www.facebook.com/islamophobiaregisteraustralia/photos/pcb.697057757083836/697057347083877/?type=1&theater

Jackson, L. 2006. 'Riot and Revenge: Program Transcript'. Retrieved from http://www.abc.net.au/4corners/content/2006/s1590953.htm

Jacobs, D. and K. Wood. 1999. 'Interracial Conflict and Interracial Homicide: Do Political and Economic Rivalries Explain White Killings of Blacks or Black Killings of Whites?'. *American Journal of Sociology* 105(1): 157–90.

Kaplan, J. 2006. 'Islamophobia in America?: September 11 and Islamophobic Hate Crime'. *Terrorism and Political Violence* 18(1): 1–33.

Kellner, D. 2005. *Media Spectacle and the Crisis of Democracy*. Boulder, USA: Paradigm.

King, R.D., F.S. Messner, and R.D. Baller. 2009. 'Contemporary Hate Crimes, Law Enforcement, and the Legacy of Racial Violence'. *American Sociological Review* 74: 291–315.

King, R.D. and G.M. Sutton. 2013. 'High Time for Hate Crimes: Explaining the Temporal Clustering of Hate-motivated Offending'. *Criminology* 51(4): 871–94.

Krueger, A.B. and J. Malečková. 2002. 'Does Poverty Cause Terrorism?'. *New Republic* 226(24): 27–33.

Kydd, A.H. and B.F. Walter. 2006. 'The Strategies of Terrorism'. *International Security* 31(1): 49–80.

LaFree, G. and L. Dugan. 2004. 'How Does Studying Terrorism Compare to Studying Crime'. *Terrorism and Counter-terrorism: Criminological Perspectives* 5: 53–74.

Legewie, J. 2013. 'Terrorist Events and Attitudes toward Immigrants: A Natural Experiment'. *American Journal of Sociology* 118(5): 1199–245.

Lickel, B., N. Miller, D.M. Stenstrom, T.F. Denson, and T. Schmader. 2006. 'Vicarious Retribution: The Role of Collective Blame in Intergroup Aggression'. *Personality and Social Psychology Review* 10(4): 372–90.

Littler, M. and M. Feldman. 2015. *Tell MAMA Reporting 2014/2015: Annual Monitoring, Cumulative Extremism, and Policy Implications*, Teesside University Centre for Fascist, Anti-Fascist and Post-Fascist Studies.

Lyons, C.J. 2007. 'Community (Dis)organization and Racially Motivated Crime'. *American Journal of Sociology* 113(3): 815–63.

McDevitt, J., J. Levin, and S. Bennett. 2002. 'Hate Crime Offenders: An Expanded Typology'. *Journal of Social Issues* 58(2): 303–17.

National Consortium for the Study of Terrorism and Responses to Terrorism. 2013. Global Terrorism Database. Retrieved from http://www.start.umd.edu/gtd/

Perry, B. 2001. *In the Name of Hate: Understanding Hate Crimes*. New York: Routledge.

Perry, B. and S. Alvi. 2012. '"We Are All Vulnerable": The *in terrorem* Effects of Hate Crimes'. *International Review of Victimology* 18(1): 57–71.

Pinderhughes, H. 1993. 'The Anatomy of Racially Motivated Violence in New York City: A Case Study of Youth in Southern Brooklyn'. *Social Problems* 40(4): 478–92.

Poynting, S. 2002. '"Bin Laden in the Suburbs": Attacks on Arab and Muslim Australians Before and After 11 September'. *Current Issues in Criminal Justice* 14(1): 43–64.

Poynting, S. and G. Noble. 2004. *Living with Racism: the experience and reporting by Arab and Muslim Australians of discrimination, abuse and violence since 11 September: report to the Human Rights and Equal Opportunity Commission*. New South Wales, Centre for Cultural Research, University of Western Sydney.

Ratcliffe, A. and S. von Hinke Kessler Scholder. 2015. 'The London Bombings and Racial Prejudice: Evidence from the Housing and Labour Market'. *Economic Inquiry* 53(1): 276–93.

Rubenstein, W.B. 2004. 'The Real Story of U.S. Hate Crimes Statistics: An Empirical Analysis'. *Tulane Law Review* 78: 1213–1246.

Seib, P. and D.M. Janbek. 2011. *Global Terrorism and New Media: The Post-Al Qaeda Generation*. Abingdon: Routledge.

Sharma, D.P. 2003. *Victims of Terrorism*. New Delhi, India, APH Publishing.

Sheridan, L.P. and R. Gillett. 2005. 'Major World Events and Discrimination'. *Asian Journal of Social Psychology* 8(2): 191–7.

Simmonds, K. (2014, 17 Dec). 'Sydney siege: Police respond to anti-Muslim sentiment in wake of Lindt cafe shootout'. Retrieved from http://www.abc.net.au/news/2014-12-17/anti-muslim-sentiment-sydney-siege-auburn-mosque-threat/5972784

South Asian American Leaders of Tomorrow (SAALT). 2001. *American Backlash: Terrorists bring war home in more ways than one*. Retrieved from http://saalt.org/wp-content/uploads/2012/09/American-Backlash-Terrorist-Bring-War-Home-in-More-Ways-Than-One.pdf

Swahn, M.H., R.R. Mahendra, L.J. Paulozzi, R.L. Winston, G.A. Shelley, J. Taliano, L. Frazier, and J.R. Saul. 2003. 'Violent Attacks on Middle Easterners in the United States during the Month Following the September 11, 2001 Terrorist Attacks'. *Injury Prevention* 9(2): 187–9.

Victorian Equal Opportunity and Human Rights Commission (VEOHRC). 2010. *Review of Identity-motivated Hate Crime*. Victoria: Victorian Equal Opportunity and Human Rights Commission.

Victoria Police. (2011). 'Prejudice Motivated Crime'. Retrieved from http://www.police.vic.gov.au/content.asp?Document_ID=32278

Wells, J. 2015. Sydney siege inquest: Man Haron Monis thought "people could read his mind", inquiry told. ABC news. Retrieved from http://www.abc.net.au/news/2015-05-28/sydney-siege-inquest-man-monis-thought-people-read-his-mind/6502890

6

HOW 'HATE' HURTS GLOBALLY

Paul Iganski and Abe Sweiry

INTRODUCTION: THE TERRORISTIC IMPACT OF HATE VIOLENCE

We sat down for dinner with three armed guards defending the restaurant door. That's when we first started mentally drafting this chapter. We weren't in the heat of a war zone. It was a cold March evening in Brussels. Our dinner companions were two dozen or so colleagues attending the *Facing Facts Forward* conference on a victim-centred approach to hate crime in Europe (CEJI 2015). Earlier in the day we were discussing how to improve the reporting of hate crime. Now, with the guards at the door, we were mindful that we were a potential target of hate violence ourselves. We pondered on what our chances of survival would be if what the restaurant owner feared actually came to pass. A former police officer, he insisted on arranging the guard when he heard that the dinner booking was made by a Jewish organization. On seeing that one of us wore a kippa, a Jewish head covering, he respectfully but forcefully insisted it not be worn in the city, so that we minimize our chances of becoming the victims of hate violence. Thankfully, we enjoyed our dinner in peace and left the restaurant and the Belgian capital without incident.

Others have not been so fortunate. In Brussels the previous year, in May 2014, a gunman shot dead two men and a woman and seriously wounded a fourth person in an attack on the Belgian capital's Jewish museum (BBC News 2014). More recently in Denmark, a couple of weeks before our dinner, a gunman killed one man and injured three others in an attack on a free speech debate in a café in Copenhagen in February 2015 (BBC News 2015a). In a second shooting near Copenhagen's main synagogue some hours later a Jewish man was killed and three police officers wounded (BBC News 2015b). Just over a month before the Copenhagen shootings, twelve people—eight journalists, two police officers, a caretaker, and a visitor— were shot to death in Paris in early January 2015 in an attack on the offices of the satirical magazine Charlie Hebdo. According to news reports, witnesses said they heard the gunmen shouting 'We have avenged the Prophet Muhammad' and 'God is Great' in Arabic (BBC News 2015c). Two days later, during a siege of a kosher supermarket at Porte de Vincennes in the east of Paris, four hostages—all Jewish— were killed (BBC News 2015d).

Occasional high profile incidents of extreme hate violence such as these in Europe have occurred against a backcloth of rather more frequent routine violence in which prejudice, hate, or bigotry plays some part. Elsewhere in the world, acts of hate violence resulting in many fatalities have had extreme consequences and profound impacts upon the communities of people afflicted. In this chapter we unfold the spatial and psycho-social consequences of hate violence—everyday and extreme, local, and global—which, we argue, when viewed from a global perspective provide evidence of a major global public health problem that requires a paradigm shift away from a narrow criminal justice focus on the problem of 'hate crime'. We argue that there needs to be a shift of thinking and focus towards a public health approach to the problem of 'hate violence'.[1]

THE SPATIAL IMPACT OF HATE VIOLENCE

To date, the spatial and behavioural consequences of hate violence in relatively socially stable nations have received sparse attention in the scholarly hate crimes literature. From the small amount of research that has been undertaken, analysis of data from the Crime Survey for England and Wales concerning defensive and avoidance measures taken by small numbers of crime victims following victimization, indicate similar but also different behavioural patterns between hate crime victims and victims of otherwise-motivated crime. In the case of victims of household crime, it is evident that hate crime victims are more likely to report moving home and being more alert and less trusting of other people, while victims of otherwise-motivated household crime are more likely to report increasing the security of their vehicles and valuables. In the case of victims of crimes against the person, hate crime victims are more likely than victims of otherwise-motivated crime to say that they have started to avoid walking in certain places (Iganski and Lagou 2014). However, much more research is needed of crime survey data internationally, to explore the particular behavioural impacts of hate violence beyond these very limited findings.

A small number of qualitative studies of the impacts of hate crime victimization offer some explanations for the behavioural impact of hate violence. Some participants in a small qualitative study of hate crime victims in Latvia published by the Latvian Center for Human Rights (Dzelme 2008) described how their spatial mobility, or their movements around town, were constrained as they sought to escape

---

[1] In this chapter we use the term 'hate violence' to refer to violence in which the denigration of a person's perceived identity such as their 'race', their ethnicity, nationality, gender, religion, sexual orientation, disability status, or sexual identity plays some role. We also conceive of 'violence' not only in terms of direct physical acts but also as 'violence of the word', such as threats, slurs, epithets and other forms of verbal denigration and hateful invective (Matsuda 1989: 2332). The term 'hate violence' is more inclusive and consistent than the term 'hate crime' as there is very uneven recognition in the criminal law across nations of prejudice, hate or bigotry as motivating forces for criminal acts when viewed from a global perspective. Parts of this chapter have been adapted and amended from the book *Hate Crime. A Global Perspective,* by Paul Iganski and Jack Levin (New York: Routledge, 2015).

potential further victimization by avoiding seemingly risky places. Given that many attacks occur in public places—on the street in residential neighbourhoods as well as downtown, in shopping malls, on public transportation, in places of leisure and recreation such as bars, sport arenas, cinema complexes—the confinement can be profoundly limiting.

The spatial impacts of hate crime do not only affect those who are direct victims. Others who share the same identity as the victim and who come to hear about the violence—perhaps family, friends, or other people in the neighbourhood, or even people elsewhere in the region or the country—can suffer the same intimidatory impact and likewise take avoidance measures. Members of targeted communities carry mental maps of 'no go areas' in their heads (Rai and Hesse 1992: 177). They will understand that hate crimes are not personal: victims are attacked not for the individuals they are, but for what their visible social group identity represents to the attacker. They realize that they could be next.

In some cases, a whole country can assume the complexion of a 'no go' area—as evidence about the recent migration of Jews out of France shows. The recent spate of high-profile attacks against Jews in Europe has occurred in a climate of an apparently increasing occurrence of rather more frequent and less dramatic instances of anti-Jewish violence. Whilst Jews comprise less than one per cent of the French population, data from the French Interior Ministry suggest that a disproportionate share of recorded racist attacks in the country have been carried out against Jews in recent years. In 2011, 31 per cent (389 of 1,256) of racist acts in France were perpetrated against Jews, rising to 40 per cent (614 of 1,539) in 2012, falling to 33 per cent (423 of 1,274) in 2013 and then increasing dramatically to 51 per cent (851 of 1,662) in 2014 (Service de Protection de la Communauté Juive 2013, 2015).

The frequency of everyday anti-Jewish incidents in France, along with more high-profile incidents such as the 2015 attack on the kosher supermarket in Paris, have been associated with an increasing number of Jews leaving the country in recent years. In 2012—a year when an Islamist extremist killed three children and a teacher at a Jewish school in Toulouse (BBC News 2012)—1,920 French Jews moved to Israel. In 2013, the year after the Toulouse attack, that number grew to 3,295. In the following year, 2014, the number of Jews leaving France for Israel more than doubled to 7,230. The Jewish Agency for Israel, the organization responsible for immigration to the country, forecast the number to continue to grow after the Charlie Hebdo shootings and the accompanying attack on a kosher supermarket. Based on the figures for the first half of the year, they have predicted 9,000 immigrants from France in 2015 (The Jewish Agency for Israel 2015). Should that estimate come to fruition, it would signify the emigration of almost 7 per cent of France's Jewish population to Israel in the space of just four years. At the same time, internal migration of French Jews within the EU is likewise thought to have increased significantly, with a quarter of the estimated 20,000 French Jews living in Britain in 2015 believed to have arrived in the last four years.

Britain, however, is not a safe haven for Jews fleeing violence elsewhere. It has also been the site of apparently increasing anti-Jewish violence—leading some Jews to also consider emigration. Data from a Jewish communal organization, the

Community Security Trust (CST), suggest that during the past decade and a half, antisemitic incidents in the UK have generally been on an upward trend, with particular spikes noted at times of conflict in the Middle East. In 2014, the organization recorded the highest number of annual hate incidents against Jews in Britain (1,168) since it began recording such data in the 1980s, with 542 of those incidents reported in July and August alone, the two months of conflict in Gaza (Community Security Trust 2015).

It is now well known that each time there is an upsurge in the Israel–Palestine conflict there is a rise in violent and other abusive incidents against Jews around the world (cf. Iganski 2009, 2013). The conflict between Israelis and Palestinians has become a global phenomenon, spreading from Gaza and the Occupied Territories of the West Bank into some of Europe's major cities and other cities around the world. Jews are seemingly targeted as representatives for the State of Israel and attacked as proxies for the Israel Defence Force. It is a crude form of political violence. Given the context of the Gaza war in July and August 2014, the year was one of the worst years on record for antisemitic incidents globally according to the Tel Aviv University Kantor Center Antisemitism Worldwide 2014 report (Kantor Center 2015).

As concern about increasing antisemitism in the UK has intensified, so a variety of statistics on those considering emigration due to fears about antisemitism have also arisen. An online survey carried out in January 2015 by an ad hoc communal organization, the Campaign Against Antisemitism (2015), suggested that 25 per cent of the 2,230 Jews surveyed had in the previous two years considered leaving Britain due to antisemitism, and 45 per cent were concerned that Jews may not have a long-term future in Britain. While controversial and criticized for its non-representative nature (Institute for Jewish Policy Research 2015), the findings of the survey were deemed sufficiently concerning for Communities Secretary Eric Pickles to release a response on behalf of the UK Government stating, 'Jews are an important part of the British community, and we would be diminished without them' (Department for Communities and Local Government 2015). A poll of British Jews carried out shortly afterwards on behalf of the *Jewish Chronicle*, a UK Jewish newspaper, focusing specifically on feelings in the aftermath of the shootings in Paris, suggested that the events had led 32 per cent to feel much more concerned about their safety, and 41 per cent slightly more concerned (Survation 2015). More specifically, 11 per cent of the sample of 500 British Jews polled suggested that the events had made them consider leaving Britain. A survey of Jews across Europe carried out by the European Fundamental Rights Agency (FRA) two years earlier had suggested that 18 per cent of those surveyed in Britain had considered emigrating in the previous five years because they did not feel safe as a Jew. The survey had also suggested other behavioural impacts of anti-Jewish hate crime in Britain, with 21 per cent of those surveyed stating that they always or frequently avoided wearing, carrying, or displaying things that might help people identify them as Jewish in public, with a further 37 per cent suggesting that they occasionally did so (FRA 2013). The adoption of steps to avoid identification as Jews was even more pronounced amongst those surveyed in other EU countries, with 60 per cent of Swedish, 51 per cent of French, 45 per cent of Belgian, 38 per cent of Hungarian, 31 per cent of German, and 30 per cent of Italian

Jewish respondents suggesting that they did so either all the time or frequently. The survey also found that fear had led many respondents to curtail 'the extent to which they take part in Jewish life' (ibid: 35), with almost a quarter (23 per cent) of respondents across the eight EU countries, and 42 per cent in Belgium, 41 per cent in Hungary, and 35 per cent in France, suggesting that they avoided visiting Jewish events or sites at least occasionally due to concerns about their safety.

Notably, close to one third (29 per cent) of Jews in the eight European countries covered by the FRA survey had considered emigrating because they did not feel safe as a Jew in the country they lived (FRA 2013). This was most pronounced in Hungary, France, and Belgium, where 48 per cent, 46 per cent, and 40 per cent respectively of those surveyed had thought about leaving their country in the past five years.

Elsewhere in the world beyond the relative social stability of European nations, hate violence has had even more profound spatial impacts and claimed many lives. The phenomenon has a long history. But even in recent years there have been numerous episodes of large-scale killings around the world in which denigration of the victims' identities and violent mobilization around ethnic and religious identity in particular has played a role in the violence. In looking globally beyond Europe, such violence has led to people fleeing en masse from the areas of victimization. And when hate violence is perpetrated in regions of conflict, the spatial impacts can occur on a massive scale. In all situations of mass conflict, in wars and civil wars, the impact of violence is not confined to the combatants. Civilian populations too suffer profoundly as human collateral damage. But in conflicts motivated by ethnic and religious hatred, or where such hatred plays a role in inter-communal conflicts, civilian populations are not only collateral damage: they are the deliberate target of violence—indiscriminately targeted because of their identity. And while numerous types of violence can constitute crimes against humanity, hatred has featured prominently in such crimes as testified by the violence in Rwanda, Bosnia, and more recently in Iraq and Syria. The targeting of women through sexual violence has also been characteristic of such conflicts, used to intimidate, inflict terror, and ethnically cleanse. Wars are often waged because of disputes involving land, markets, or other resources. Hatred may not be the primary cause of such conflicts, but it is an important aggravating factor that makes the impact even more egregious and keeps warfare from being resolved.

Most recently, the spotlight of the world's media has been on the consequences of the atrocities committed by so-called 'Islamic State' extremists in Iraq and Syria. In the summer of 2015 the flight of refugees into Europe, particularly from Syria and Iraq, has dominated the headlines. Many of the refugees from Syria and Iraq have fled sectarian violence with atrocities propelled by religious zealotry. In an early episode of the large-scale impact of hate violence in the region widely reported by the international news media in August 2014, Islamic State extremists allegedly slaughtered hundreds of Iraq's Yazidi ethnic and religious minority community in and around the village of Kocho in northern Iraq. The Islamic State fighters reportedly demanded that the Yazidis convert to Islam or face death. After refusing to convert, men were shot and women and children abducted. In the same month, in a gruesome hate murder, an Islamic State fighter, apparently speaking with an English accent, beheaded American journalist James Foley in an act which clearly belied extreme hatred of America. By the summer of 2014, fleeing from the advances of Islamic State in northern Iraq, hundreds of thousands of displaced Iraqis from minority communities were seeking refuge near the Turkish border. The international news media widely reported the humanitarian crisis facing tens of thousands of Yazidis trapped in harrowing conditions and exposed to a hostile climate of soaring temperatures after fleeing to Mount Sinjar. Air drops of humanitarian aid including water and shelter were made by US, UK, and Iraqi air forces.

Less well reported by the international news media has been the sectarian violence between ethnic Arakanese Buddhists and Rohingya Muslims in Arakan State, Myanmar, in June and October 2012 which claimed the lives of 211 people according to the Myanmar Government, although Human Rights Watch estimated many more (Human Rights Watch 2013). There is a long history of violence between Buddhists and Muslims in Arakan State stretching back over decades. And while both populations have faced past oppression by Myanmar governments, the Rohingya population, which is denied citizenship and considered by many to be an illegal immigrant community, has particularly faced routine persecution and forcible displacement. The outbreak of violence in June 2012 was triggered in late May by the rape and murder of an Arakanese woman in Ramri Township by three Muslim men. Arakanese villagers retaliated by stopping a bus southeast of Ramri and killing ten Muslim passengers. Communal violence then escalated between Arakanese Buddhists and Rohingya and other Muslims. Allegedly, state security forces initially stood by without intervening to halt the violence, and later joined Arakanese mobs in attacking and burning Muslim villages and neighbourhoods (Human Rights Watch 2013: 7). In further violence in October 2012, Muslim villages in nine townships across the Arakan State were attacked by Arakanese men armed with swords, machetes, home-made firearms, and Molotov cocktails. Again, security forces allegedly either stood by or participated in the violence. Further outbreaks of violence against Muslims in 2013, which spread beyond Arakan State to other parts of Myanmar, claimed more lives, with numerous homes burnt to the ground.

In the two years following the upsurge of intercommunal violence in Myanmar in 2012 the United Nations Commission for Human Rights estimated that 87,000 people had departed irregularly by sea from the Bangladesh–Myanmar border region heading for Thailand, Malaysia, Indonesia, and Australia (UNHCR 2014). Many were transported by smugglers in cramped conditions and subject to verbal and physical abuse. Hundreds reportedly died from the deprivations of the journey: illness, heat, lack of food and water, and violence by smugglers. Some drowned while trying to escape in desperation (UNHCR 2014). Bangladesh closed its borders, returning Rohingya asylum seekers to sea. Thailand also resisted the influx of asylum seekers (Human Rights Watch 2013: 16).

Elsewhere in South East Asia, in September 2013, communal violence between Hindu Jat and Muslim communities in the Muzaffarnagar and Shamli districts of Uttar Pradesh in India left at least sixty-five people dead and many injured. The violence was stoked by hate speech and incitement in print and social media escalating a number of trigger incidents. The violence occurred in the context of regular incidents of inter-communal violence and the sowing of communal hostilities by political parties (Hassan 2014). Numerous homes in villages were burnt to the ground and 50,000 people were reportedly displaced by the violence (Hassan 2014).

Overall, when viewed from a global perspective, it is obvious that the displacement of people by violence and conflict, whether in relatively settled regions or regions of conflict, results in multiple negative impacts for those persons affected. Among them, it is widely recognized that displaced persons are more prone to mental health and psychosocial problems (Meyer 2013). Nevertheless, the impacts for persons fleeing hate violence can be even more egregious, as such violence potentially inflicts significant psychosocial consequences irrespective of any spatial consequences.

THE PSYCHOSOCIAL IMPACT
OF HATE VIOLENCE

All violence is hurtful in terms of the emotional and psychological impact. But there is a reason why there is a particular concern about hate violence. Hate violence can be more harmful than other forms of violence. Recognition of the particular harms involved has prompted some nation states to enact hate crime laws which impose higher penalties for convicted offenders compared with non-hate motivated crimes.

Most victims of violence suffer some post-victimization impact. Sometimes there is physical injury. Sometimes, there are behavioural changes, as just discussed. More often, there are emotional and psychological consequences. In the case of hate violence, however, there is evidence to show specifically that the emotional and psychological harms inflicted can potentially be greater (cf. Ehrlich et al. 1994; Herek et al. 1999; Iganski 2008; Iganski and Lagou 2015, 2016; McDevitt et al. 2001).

While the pattern of difference is not consistent for every single victim, on average it is clear that hate violence hurts more when the emotional and psychological injuries are measured in crime surveys for hate crime victims as a group compared with victims of parallel crimes. Victims in incidents of hate violence are more likely to report having an emotional or a psychological reaction to the incident and with a greater intensity, compared with victims of otherwise-motivated violence. In terms of specific symptoms of distress, victims of hate violence are more likely, when compared with victims of other forms of violence, to report suffering higher levels of depression and withdrawal; anxiety and nervousness; loss of confidence; anger; increased sleep difficulties; difficulty concentrating; fear; and reduced feelings of safety. In short, victims of hate violence are more likely to suffer post-traumatic stress type symptoms. Interviews with victims of hate violence indicate that the aftermath of the victimization is characterized by a pervasive feeling of fear (McDevitt et al. 2001). Their fear may be based on threats by the offender or friends of the offender but often it is simply based on the random nature of the crime which, because it involves an attack targeted against the victim's social identity, bespeaks a risk of similar future victimization. Differences in reported post-victimization emotional and psychological impacts between victims of hate violence as a group and victims of other types of violence even hold when controlling for differences in type of crime experienced (Botcherby et al. 2011; Iganski and Lagou 2014).

The impact of hate violence can also extend well beyond the person who is on the immediate receiving end (although such consequences are methodologically more difficult to scientifically demonstrate compared with the consequences for individual victims). Hate violence sends a terroristic message to everyone who shares the victim's identity: this 'could be you'.

Understanding why greater hurts are potentially felt by victims of hate violence and those around them who share their social identity has been informed by a body of qualitative research which suggests that such injuries are due to the perception by victims of their victimization experience as an attack upon the core of their identity: the very essence of their being (Craig-Henderson and Sloan 2003). The victim carries around with them the reason for their victimization: their visible appearance and what it represents to others in the dominant culture. Hate violence can be seen as sending a message to the victim, and those who share the victim's identity, that they are devalued, unwelcome, denigrated, despised. As victims of hate violence are attacked because of their social identity, such crimes are not personal. Because of this they also convey the potential for further victimization and therefore have a terroristic impact. Some victims, and potential victims, where possible, will try to manage their visibility to avoid potential victimization (Mason 2001). This terroristic impact also accounts in part for the higher level of post-traumatic stress type symptoms reported by victims of hate violence.

The emotional and psychological impact of hate violence has also been illuminated in greater depth than can be achieved by survey research, but with necessarily smaller and generally purposive samples, by a number of qualitative studies which have focused solely on hate crime victims without comparison samples of victims of parallel crimes. The study of hate crime victims in Latvia mentioned earlier in this chapter drew out, in depth, the profound and long-lasting psychological impact that can be inflicted (Dzelme 2008). Participants in the research reported that the psychological trauma suffered by victims of hate violence surpassed any immediate physical injuries inflicted. Some victims felt that it was the very essence of their being that was attacked. But at the same time, because it is the victim's group identity that is attacked, hate crimes are not personal. Because of this they convey the potential for further victimization. Consequently, some victims in the Latvian study said that they felt powerless and a constant sense of insecurity and alertness to the potential for further attacks marked by suspicion of others, and made constant assessments of their immediate surroundings with calculations of safety and danger.

Victims of violence against women have to date not been incorporated into the research exploring the emotional and psychological injuries of violence explicitly framed as 'hate violence' or 'hate crime'. However, there is much available evidence. FRA in its recent EU-wide survey of violence against women (2014) assessed the short-term emotional responses and the long-term psychological consequences of violent victimization. Overall, the reported impact of sexual violence was seen to be greater than the impact of physical violence, and the long-term psychological impact was greater when the perpetrator was a partner. The survey indicates:

- Women who experience sexual violence are more likely to report feeling fearful, ashamed, embarrassed, and guilty. There seems to be little difference between women victims of partner and non-partner sexual violence in reporting these emotional reactions.
- Women victims of sexual violence by a partner are less likely to report feelings of shock—possibly because the violence is part of a continuum of abuse.
- While the emotional reactions of women victims of physical violence are less pronounced than victims of sexual violence, victims of physical violence by a partner are more likely to report feelings of fear, shame, and embarrassment, than victims of non-partner violence.
- A majority of victims of physical and sexual violence by partners and non-partners report long-term psychological consequences. For both physical and sexual violence, long-term psychological impacts are more likely to be reported by victims where the violence is perpetrated by a partner—possibly as a consequence of repeat victimization or the ongoing fear of further violence.
- The long-term psychological impact of sexual violence is also more pronounced than the impact of physical violence. Victims of sexual violence by partners and non-partners are more likely to report long-term psychological impacts and more likely to report experiencing a combination of impacts.

Studies of sexual violence used for 'ethnic cleansing' in conflict zones indicate the severe long-lasting mental trauma inflicted on women victims. For instance, a study of sixty-five women victims of systematic mass rapes during the 1992 to 1995 war in Croatia and Bosnia and Herzegovina conducted during the war and in the early post-war period (Lončar 2006) illuminates the profound and enduring mental health impacts inflicted. A third of the women were raped every day and by different rapists while held captive, and most were physically and sexually tortured in further ways. In a number of cases the rapists were neighbours. While none of the women had a history of psychiatric disorder before the rape, approximately a year after the violence a majority suffered from depression, a majority manifesting 'social phobia', and almost a third suffering post-traumatic stress disorder. Seventeen out of twenty-nine women who fell pregnant as a consequence of rape had an induced abortion, with the decision to abort their pregnancies precipitated by suicidal thoughts and impulses. Only one of the twelve women who gave birth kept their baby: the rest were given up for adoption.

DISCUSSION AND CONCLUSION: HATE VIOLENCE—A GLOBAL PUBLIC HEALTH PROBLEM

The harm of hate violence begins with the act: it is intrinsic to the doing of the violence (Perry and Olsen 2009). All instances of hate violence, whether they involve mass violence amounting to crimes against humanity—of the type of some of the instances discussed in this chapter—or isolated acts by individuals, whether they occur in conditions of social turmoil or relative calm, involve some form of violation. The immediate harm of hate violence fundamentally lies in this violation. While hate violence in relatively stable societies is a rather more routine and everyday occurrence compared with the episodic outbreaks of mass hate violence in areas of communal conflict or war, given the scale of the problem of hate violence in more peaceful societies the problem also involves numerous violations even in relatively calm nations. The violation lies in the message sent. Hate crimes are 'message crimes'. The message inherent to, and sent by, hate violence is that some persons because of their identity have a lesser or little worth, and are not entitled to dignity and respect. While all violence is an assault against a person's dignity, hate violence is particularly egregious in terms of violation as it is a discriminatory assault on dignity.

Beyond the initial violation, hate violence has the potential to inflict serious post-victimization impacts, as the discussion in this chapter of the spatial and psychosocial impacts of hate violence shows. When examined globally, given the scale of the problem—which we only partially document in this chapter—it is evident that hate violence amounts to a major public health problem.

A public health approach to hate violence lays emphasis on prevention, rather than solely trying to ameliorate the effects of the problem. Prevention involves educative efforts with potential perpetrators and rehabilitative efforts with actual perpetrators. More broadly, preventative work involves addressing the cultural and social conditions in which hate violence is nested. Educational and civil society organizations are best placed to undertake such work. Furthermore, in responding to violence, a public health approach lays emphasis on support for entire communities rather than just individual care. This involves strengthening resources for community resilience. Civil society organizations can be well-placed to help build community resilience against hate violence. A public health approach to any problem requires collective action (Dahlberg and Krug 2002: 3-4). This is certainly the case for hate violence, where cooperation between civil society, education, social service, health, and criminal justice sectors is needed for addressing what has largely up to now been articulated as a criminal justice problem. A public health approach therefore requires a shift in the balance of resources away from a narrow criminal justice response to the problem towards civil society and community action. Attaining recognition that hate violence is a global public health problem which demands public health intervention is the challenge that lies ahead.

REFERENCES

BBC News 2012. 'France shooting: Toulouse Jewish school attack kills four' 17 March 2012. http://www.bbc.co.uk/news/world-us-canada-17426313 (last accessed 9 September 2015).
BBC News 2014. 'Brussels fatal gun attack at Jewish museum'. 24 May 2014. http://www.bbc.co.uk/news/world-europe-27558918 (last accessed 8 September 2015).

BBC News 2015a. 'Copenhagen shooting: One dead in deadly seminar attack'. 14 February 2015. http://www.bbc.co.uk/news/world-europe-31472423 (last accessed 8 September 2015).

BBC News 2015b. 'Copenhagen synagogue shooting: Eyewitness hid in bar on police advice'. 15 February 2015. http://www.bbc.co.uk/news/world-europe-31476321 (last accessed 8 September 2015).

BBC News 2015c. 'Charlie Hebdo attack: Three days of terror'. 14 January 2015. http://www.bbc.co.uk/news/world-europe-30708237 (last accessed 8 September 2015).

BBC News 2015d. 'France attacks: Police storm Kosher supermarket'. 9 January 2015. http://www.bbc.co.uk/news/world-europe-30753200 (last accessed 8 September 2015).

Botcherby, S., Glenn, F., Iganski, P., Jochelson, K., and Lagou, S. 2011. *Equality Groups' Perceptions and Experiences of Crime*, Manchester: Equality and Human Rights Commission.

Campaign against Antisemitism 2015. *Annual Antisemitism Barometer 2015 Full Report*, London: Campaign against Antisemitism.

CEJI 2015. *Conference Report. Facing Facts Forward Conference for a Victim Centred Approach to Tackling Hate Crime*, Brussels: CEJI.

Community Security Trust 2015. *Antisemitic Incidents Report 2014*, London: Community Security Trust.

Craig-Henderson, K. and Sloan, L.R. 2003. 'After the Hate: Helping Psychologists Help Victims of Racist Hate Crime'. *Clinical Psychology: Science and Practice* 10(4): 481–90.

Dahlberg, L.L. and Krug, E.G. 2002. 'Violence—A Global Public Health Problem'. In *World Report on Violence and Health*, edited by E.G. Krug, L.L. Dahlberg, J.A. Mercy, A.B. Zwi, and R. Lozano, pp. 1–21, Geneva: World Health Organization.

Department for Communities and Local Government 2015. *Government Response: Campaign Against Antisemitism Survey*, retrieved from https://www.gov.uk/government/news/campaign-against-antisemitism-survey

Dzelme, I. 2008. *Psychological Effects of Hate Crime*, Riga: Latvian Center for Human Rights.

Ehrlich, H., Larcom, B.E.K., and Purvis, R.D. 1994. 'The Traumatic Effects of Ethnoviolence'. Reprinted in *Hate and Bias Crime. A Reader*, edited by B. Perry (2003). pp. 153–67. New York: Routledge.

European Union Agency for Fundamental Rights (FRA) 2013. *Discrimination and Hate Crime against Jews in EU Member States: Experience and Perceptions of Antisemitism*, Vienna: European Union Agency for Fundamental Rights.

European Union Agency for Fundamental Rights (FRA) 2014. *Violence against Women: an EU-wide Survey. Main Results*, Vienna: European Union Agency for Fundamental Rights.

Hassan, S. 2014. 'Understanding the Dynamic of Communal Riots against Muslims in Muzaffarnagar and Shamli Districts, Uttar Pradesh, India'. In *State of the World's Minorities and Indigenous Peoples 2014*, edited by P. Grant, pp. 121–4. London: Minority Rights Group International.

Herek, G.M., Gillis, J.R., and Cogan, J.C. 1999. 'Psychological Sequelae of Hate Crime Victimisation Among Lesbian, Gay, and Bisexual Adults'. *Journal of Consulting & Clinical Psychology* 67: 945–51.

Human Rights Watch. 2013. *'All you can do is Pray'. Crimes against Humanity and Ethnic Cleansing of Rohingya Muslims in Burma's Arakan State*. New York: Human Rights Watch.

Iganski, P. 2008. *Hate Crime and the City*. Bristol: Policy Press.

Iganski, P. 2009. 'Conceptualising Anti-Jewish Hate Crime'. In *Victims of Hate Crime*, edited by B. Perry, pp. 107–19. Westport, CT: Praeger.

Iganski, P. 2013. 'Antisemitism and Anti-Jewish Hatred. Conceptual, Political and Legal Challenges'. In *New Directions in Race, Ethnicity and Crime*, edited by C. Phillips and C. Webster, pp. 18–36. London: Routledge.

Iganski, P. and Lagou, S. 2014. 'The Personal Injuries of "Hate Crime"'. In *The Routledge International Handbook on Hate Crime*, edited by N. Hall, A. Corb, P. Giannasi, and J. Grieve, pp. 34–46. London: Routledge.

Iganski, P. and Lagou, S. 2015. 'Hate Crimes Hurt Some More than Others: Implications for the Just Sentencing of Offenders'. *Journal of Interpersonal Violence* 30(10): 1696–1718.

Iganski, P. and Lagou, S. 2016 forthcoming. 'The Psychological Impact of Hate Crime'. In *The Psychology of Hate Crimes as Domestic Terrorism: US and Global Issues* (Volume 2), edited by E. Dunbar. Santa Barbara, CA: Praeger.

Institute for Jewish Policy Research 2015. *Researching Antisemitism*, retrieved from http://www.jpr.org.uk/newsevents/article.1012

Kantor Center 2015. *Antisemitism Worldwide 2014*, Tel Aviv: Tel Aviv University, Kantor Center for the Study of Contemporary European Jewry.

Lončar, M., Medved, V., Jovanović, N., and Hotujac, L. 2006. 'Psychological Consequences of Rape on Women in 1991–1995 War in Croatia and Bosnia and Herzegovina'. *Croatian Medical Journal* 47: 67–75.

Mason, G. 2001. 'Body Maps: Envisaging Homophobia, Violence and Safety'. *Social & Legal Studies* 10(1): 23–44.

Matsuda, M. 1989. 'Public Responses to Racist Speech: Considering the Victim's Story'. *Michigan Law Review* 87: 2320–2381.

McDevitt, J., Balboni, J., Garcia, L., and Gu, J. 2001. 'Consequences for Victims: a Comparison of Bias and Non-bias Motivated Assaults'. *American Behavioral Scientist* 45(4): 697–713.

Meyer, S. 2013. *UNHCR's Mental Health and Psychosocial Support for Persons of Concern*, Geneva: United Nations High Commissioner for Refugees.

Perry, B. and Olsen, P. 2009. 'Hate Crime as a Human Rights Violation'. In *The Impacts of Hate Crime*, edited by P. Iganski, pp. 175–91, Santa Barbara, CA: Praeger.

Rai, D.K. and Hesse, B. 1992. 'Racial Victimisation: An Experiential Analysis'. In *Beneath the Surface: Racial Harassment*, edited by B. Hesse, D.K. Rai, C. Bennett, and P. McGilchrist, pp. 158–95. Aldershot: Avebury.

Service de Protection de la Communauté Juive 2013. *Report on Antisemitism in France in 2012*, Paris: SPCJ. Retrieved from http://www.antisemitisme.fr/dl/2012-EN.pdf

Service de Protection de la Communauté Juive 2015. *Report on Antisemitism in France 2014*, Paris: SPCJ. Retrieved from http://www.antisemitisme.fr/dl/2014-EN.pdf

Survation 2015. *Jewish Topical Issues Poll*, London: Survation. Retrieved from http://survation.com/wp-content/uploads/2015/01/Jewish-Topical-Issues-Poll-Final.pdf

The Jewish Agency for Israel 2015. *2014/2015 Performance Report*, Jerusalem: The Jewish Agency. Retrieved from http://www.jewishagency.org/sites/default/files/JA_2014_15_Annual_Report_Low_ENG_v5_Final.pdf

United Nations High Commissioner for Refugees (UNHCR) 2014. *South East Asia—Irregular Maritime Movements*, UNHCR Regional Office for South East Asia.

PART II

GLOBAL ISSUES, NATIONAL EXPERIENCES

7

COVERED IN STIGMA? EXPLORING THE IMPACTS OF ISLAMOPHOBIC HATE CRIME ON VEILED MUSLIM WOMEN GLOBALLY

Irene Zempi

INTRODUCTION

Hate crime is the umbrella concept used in its broadest sense to describe incidents motivated by hate, hostility, or prejudice towards an individual's identity (Chakraborti and Garland 2009). As Copsey, Dack, Littler, and Feldman (2013) point out, definitions of 'hate crime' vary from one country to the next, and even within countries (e.g., the United States). In Britain the central point of reference is the operational definition offered by the College of Policing (2014), which earmarks hate crime as offences that are motivated by hostility or prejudice on particular grounds—race, religion, sexual orientation, transgender status, and disability. From this perspective, Islamophobic hate crime is defined as any criminal offence which is perceived, by the victim or any other person, to be motivated wholly or partly by a hostility or prejudice based upon a person's religion or perceived religion, that is, their Muslim religion.

In a post-9/11 and 7/7 climate, Islam is stereotypically perceived as a dangerous religion and culture. Muslim communities are homogenized into one group and the characteristics associated with Muslims, namely violence, misogyny, terrorism, and incompatibility with Western values, are treated as if they are innate (Garner and Selod 2015). Physical markers of 'Muslimness', such as wearing religious clothing, render individuals vulnerable to manifestations of Islamophobic hate crime (Chakraborti and Zempi 2012). The wearing of the Muslim dress—including the hijab (headscarf) and the niqab (face covering)—has become a visual representation of 'Muslim difference' in the UK and elsewhere in the West. Specifically, the niqab is seen as a 'threat' on multiple levels, including notions of gender equality, integration, national security, and public safety.

Stereotypes about the multiple 'threats' of the niqab—as a visible symbol of women's lack of agency and their subordination to Islamic patriarchal norms, lack of integration, and 'threat' to public safety—promote a climate of Islamophobic hostility towards veiled Muslim women both nationally and internationally. As Chakraborti and Zempi (2013) point out, this Islamophobic climate legitimizes violence directed towards veiled Muslim women when they are seen in public. In essence, it justifies acts of hostility towards veiled Muslim women as a means of responding to the multiple 'threats' of the wearing of the veil in the West. However, despite their vulnerability to Islamophobic hate crime, veiled Muslim women are rarely included within studies of victimization—a factor which in itself exacerbates their marginalization from both academic discourses and mainstream society.

Indeed, there has been much discussion about the growth of Islamophobic hate crime in the West (see, e.g., Allen 2010; Esposito and Kalin 2011; Kumar 2012; Kundnani 2007; Poynting and Mason 2007; Sayyid and Vakil 2011). However, this discussion has not been accompanied by as much empirical analysis of Islamophobic hate crime as one might expect (Moosavi 2014). In particular, there is a dearth of studies examining the lived experiences of Muslim women who wear the niqab in public in the West. As a result, they remain a relatively 'invisible' population in research terms, despite their vulnerability to Islamophobic attacks. Drawing from qualitative data elicited through a UK-based study, this chapter sheds light on the lived experiences of veiled Muslim women as victims of Islamophobic hate crime in the UK and elsewhere. In particular, I examine the effects of this victimization upon veiled Muslim women and the wider Muslim community. Amongst the central themes are impacts associated with their sense of vulnerability and fear, levels of confidence, and sense of belonging, as well as the management of their safety in public. As we shall see, veiled Muslim women limit their use of public space and often isolate themselves from society in order to keep themselves safe. The individual and collective impacts associated with this victimization are explored through notions of a worldwide, transnational Muslim community, the ummah. Ultimately, this chapter demonstrates the global dynamic of Islamophobic hate crime and the vulnerability of veiled Muslim women as actual and potential victims to the violence to which it gives rise.

METHODOLOGY

The research took the form of a qualitative study based on semi-structured interviews[1] with veiled Muslim women in Leicester between 2011 and 2012. Participation in the study was voluntary. The study comprised sixty individual and twenty focus group interviews with veiled Muslim women who had been victims of Islamophobic hate crime. Individual, in-depth interviews allow for 'rich' data to be collected with detailed descriptions (Hennink, Hutter, and Bailey 2011). This approach is especially valuable for researching sensitive issues that require

[1] All interviews throughout the study were anonymized and the research participants were given pseudonyms to protect their confidentiality.

confidentiality and a more intimate setting for data collection, and this is particularly appropriate for 'hard to access' groups such as veiled Muslim women. Focus group interviews incorporate the strengths of qualitative research in terms of gathering 'rich' data whilst generating additional insights through group interactions (Curtis and Curtis 2011). In the context of this particular piece of research, the focus group method afforded the possibility of open discussion amongst veiled Muslim women with similar or different experiences of Islamophobic hate crime whilst, at the same time, highlighting collectively held beliefs and attitudes.

Prospective participants were identified through local Muslim organizations including mosques, Muslim schools, and Islamic centres, as well as local Muslim university student societies and Muslim women's groups. Participants unaffiliated to any local Muslim organizations or groups were also recruited through snowball sampling. I took steps to access as broad a range of veiled Muslim women as possible, ensuring diversity in terms of nationality, race and ethnicity, age, education, and social class.

At the time of the fieldwork, the veiled Muslim women who took part in the study were residents living in Leicester. In particular, the majority of participants (40) had lived in Leicester for five years or more. According to the most recent Census data, Leicester is a city located at the heart of the East Midlands of England and has a population of approximately 330,000 (Office for National Statistics 2011). Leicester residents hail from over fifty countries from across the globe, making the city one of the most ethnically and culturally diverse places in the UK. In view of its diverse mix of cultures and faiths, Leicester is commonly depicted as the UK's most ethnically harmonious city and as a successful model of multiculturalism both nationally and internationally. Moreover, Leicester has a large and rapidly expanding population of Muslims and veil-wearing women, making it an ideal site in which to conduct this particular study.

EXPERIENCES OF ISLAMOPHOBIC HATE CRIME

Islamophobic hate crime has been described by Chakraborti and Zempi (2012: 271) as 'a fear or hatred of Islam that translates into ideological and material forms of cultural racism against obvious markers of "Muslimness"'. Within this framework, Islamophobic hate crime can be interpreted through the lens of cultural racism whereby Islamic religion, tradition, and culture are seen as a 'threat' to 'national identity', whilst 'visible' Muslims are viewed as 'culturally dangerous' and threatening the 'British/Western way of life'. From this perspective, Islamophobic hate crime manifests itself as an expression of cultural racism towards individuals identified as Muslims on the basis of their 'visible' Muslim identity.

I never had any abuse before. It's definitely because of the way I dress. When I didn't wear the niqab, people were treating me like a normal human being and now they treat me like I am sub-human.

Lina, 42 years old

I've converted to Islam four years ago and within a week I started wearing the niqab. Prior to wearing the niqab, I've experienced no problems at all. It's only since I became identifiably Muslim that I got threats and abuse.

I've started wearing the niqab two years ago. I was not a practising Muslim before. I did not get any abuse at all before wearing the niqab.

Focus group participants

As indicated in the comments above, participants were convinced that it was their distinctive Muslim appearance that made them a target of Islamophobic hate crime. Indeed, it is well established in the literature that there is a significant relationship between being visible as a Muslim and experiencing Islamophobic hate crime (Allen 2010; Meer 2010). If the markers of Islam (e.g., a Muslim dress or a Muslim name) are absent, 'passing' as a non-Muslim is possible for those without conspicuous Muslim names or dress, and those who do not 'look like' a Muslim (Garner and Selod 2015). That stated, it is important to recognize the diversity of Muslims in the West. For example, in the USA Muslims are composed of South Asians, Arabs, and African-Americans. In France the majority are North African, while most Muslims in the UK are South Asian (of Pakistani, Indian, and Bangladeshi origin). Yet despite their diversity, Muslim communities have become racialized and in turn frequently experience a specific racism that targets their 'Muslimness' (Carr and Haynes 2015). In other words, despite their cultural, ethnic, national, and 'racial' diversity, Muslims are typically perceived as a single racialized group in the eyes of their abusers.

The stigmatization of Muslims and the ways in which they are targeted for abuse reflects a broader globalized cultural racism, which 'manifests itself in similar ways, albeit adapted to local situations' (Babacan, Gopalkrishnan, and Babacan 2009: 4; see further section below, Collective Impacts). As Carr and Haynes (2015) point out, Islamophobia and the racialization of Muslims is a transnational project; across Western nations, public and institutional discourses and practices are infused with strikingly similar motifs of Islam and the veil as a 'threat' to British/Western culture. In the wake of the shootings at the French satirical newspaper Charlie Hebdo, mosques in France, Sweden, Germany, UK, and elsewhere in Europe have been attacked by firebombs, gunfire, pig heads, and grenades, whilest 'visible' Muslims have been targeted with violence. From this perspective, Islamophobic hate crime illustrates the interconnectedness and transnationalism of anti-Muslim discourse and practice. Regardless of country of origin and ethnic background, individuals are identified as 'Muslim' due to visible physical markers and to this extent they suffer Islamophobic hate crime because of the visibility of their Muslim identity.

Participants reported that Islamophobic hate crime was manifested in terms of physical violence, although most was in the form of verbal abuse. They described incidents of physical abuse such as attempted and actual physical assaults (including taking the veil off), pushing, shoving, being spat at, and even incidents where passing vehicles had attempted to run them over.

Taking the veil off and getting slapped in the face; that was in Lincolnshire.

Iman, 37 years old

I was six months pregnant with my first baby and a white man elbowed me in the stomach when I was in the queue at Boots in Coventry.

Kalila, 29 years old

I was beaten up in the park [in Southampton]. Nobody stepped in to help me.

Salimah, 22 years old

Participants also described incidents where people on the street or from moving cars had thrown eggs, stones, alcohol, water bombs, bottles, take-away food, and rubbish at them. In addition, verbal abuse from strangers in public including streets, parks, shopping centres, and public transport was a common experience amongst participants. They also reported that they often experienced intimidation and harassment on social networking sites such as Facebook, Twitter, and MySpace, as well as blogs and chat rooms. Underlying these incidents of intimidation, violence, and abuse was a clear sense of Islamophobic sentiments, and this was made apparent through the language used by the perpetrators that signified their motivations for the attack. For example, participants had been called names such as 'Muslim terrorists', 'Muslim bombers', and 'Suicide bombers', which indicate the perpetrators' perceptions of veiled Muslim women as a security or terrorist 'threat'. Understanding the veil as a 'threat' to national safety reflects the association between Islam, past and recent international acts of terrorism, and the globalized cultural racism. Relatedly, the following comments demonstrate that the wearing of the veil was perceived as a camouflage for a terrorist:

Have you got a bomb under there?

Nisha, 28 years old

Are you carrying belts full of explosives?

Jahidah, 22 years old

Importantly, participants argued that even if they were not thought to be involved in a terrorist plot—because veiled Muslim women are supposedly too oppressed, uneducated, and incapable of autonomy—they were nevertheless perceived as the mothers of future home-grown terrorists; hence perpetrators often called them names such as 'Bin Laden's wife'. As fear of 'homegrown terrorism' has risen in the West in recent years, Muslims are in effect perceived as potential 'Muslim domestic terrorists' and veiling marks Muslim women as a visual representation of this 'threat' (Zimmerman 2015).

Furthermore, the research findings illustrate that there is intersectionality amongst race, ethnicity, and religion. Participants experienced incidents where the nature of the verbal abuse suggested both racist and Islamophobic hate crime. For example, some of the black Muslim women who took part in this study revealed that they had bananas thrown at them and heard monkey noises or comments such as 'Black terrorist' or 'Go home Muslim monkey' being made when they were walking on the street. As Sallah (2010) points out, bananas and monkey noises are known symbols of racism. The white British Muslim women who took part in the study felt that in some cases they have been attacked because they were white, British, and Muslim. In the eyes of their abusers, they had supposedly betrayed the British values and the British way of life, as the following comments indicate.

I lived in Croydon [London] and there were some guys making comments like 'You are a traitor going against the values of our country'. I'm English so I get more abuse because they see me as a traitor.

Zoe, 27 years old

They know I'm English. They can see my eye colour, it's blue. They can see the colour of my skin, it's white. They can hear my English accent. People think I've moved over to the dark side because I've converted to Islam.

Sarah, 31 years old

Additionally, some participants described examples of verbal abuse that illustrated the xenophobic sentiments of the perpetrators such as:

Go back to your country, you don't belong here!

Nadia, 29 years old

If you want Sharia go back to Iraq!

Nabeeha, 22 years old

In the eyes of their abusers, veiled Muslim women are seen as foreigners who are alien to 'our way of life' and thus 'don't belong'. Within this paradigm, the wearing of the veil marks an unwelcome religious, cultural, and racial presence (Grillo and Shah 2012). Crucially, this type of language can be linked to the alleged 'Islamification' of Europe. In the current climate of economic instability, Muslims are supposedly 'taking over' Europe and as a result the visibility of the veil poses a 'threat' to national identity in a globalized world. This discourse mirrors certain European government policies that are designed to 'domesticate' Islam. For example, the banning of the niqab in public in European countries such as France and Belgium are clear examples of assimilation policies that aim to eradicate the visibility of Islam in the West.

At one level, this discussion shows that the targeted victimization of veiled Muslim women can be attributed to Islamophobic attitudes as well as to racist sentiments by virtue of the fact that these elements are often inextricably intertwined. In this regard, Islamophobic hate crime and racism become mutually reinforcing phenomena, and hostility against veiled Muslim women should also be considered in the context of a more general climate of hostility towards 'otherness'. Notwithstanding, this is not to overlook the fact that veiled Muslim women have been victims of Islamophobic hate crime because their abusers have been motivated either solely or partially by other factors. For example, the sight of the veiled female Muslim body might provoke anger in some men who are used to 'seeing' women's bodies in the public space. This gives rise to a form of sexual harassment manifested by a male gaze that desires possession of women's bodies and 'wants to see' (Al-Saji 2010). This demonstrates the intersectionality between religion, gender, and physical appearance. From this perspective, Islamophobic hate crime is not just an expression of religious hostility, but admonition and prescription related to gender performance in public spaces.

We are very different to the average non-Muslim woman. We are doing everything that the media tells us we shouldn't be doing in terms of how women should dress.

Roukia, 27 years old

In Western societies men are used to seeing women in all their glory really, aren't they? I think men appreciate the fact that they can see a woman's face and that they can see her figure. They probably feel deprived of this opportunity because they can't assess a veiled Muslim woman in the same way that they can assess a Christian, Sikh, or Hindu woman.

Aleena, 28 years old

In this sense, the face and body of a woman is an object of sexual attraction and when these are covered it disrupts public expectations, common amongst most Western societies, of how women *should* behave and dress in public in order to visually 'please' men. This emphasizes the 'appropriate' feminine sexuality, which ensures that the behaviour and attire of women are strictly monitored (Dwyer 1999). As a solution to the 'problem' of being 'covered up', perpetrators often demanded that participants uncovered their face and body by shouting 'Take it off' and 'Show me your face'. Halima, one of the participants, was approached by a man who shouted: 'I want to cut that black thing off your face'. These findings lend weight to the view that there is a male desire to uncover the female Muslim body that is covered in public (Dwyer 1999), thereby illustrating the link between religion, gender, and physical appearance.

INDIVIDUAL IMPACTS

Being a victim of any kind of crime can have devastating and long-term impacts upon individuals, including emotional, psychological, behavioural, physical, and financial effects. But as a form of hate crime, Islamophobic abuse and violence can be particularly distressing and frightening for victims, their families, and wider communities. Empirical studies of targeted victimization emphasize the more severe impact for victims of hate crime when compared to non-hate victims (see also Chakraborti, Garland, and Hardy 2014; Hall 2005; Herek et al. 2002; McDevitt et al. 2001; Williams and Tregidga 2014).

In addition to potentially suffering physical injury, victims of Islamophobic hate crime can be seriously affected emotionally. In particular, there are distinct emotional harms associated with this victimization. Throughout interviews and focus group discussions participants highlighted that they had low confidence and low self-esteem as a result of the abuse they suffered in public. They also pointed out that they were made to feel 'worthless', 'unwanted', and that they 'didn't belong', as the following quotations show:

Everyone thinks we are the enemy. I feel that I don't have the right to be here. It crushes my self-esteem.

Parveen, 24 years old

We feel like social lepers that no one wants to engage with.

Maryam, 28 years old

We've been made to feel that we are totally unwanted. It's like we are a virus to the community.

Focus group participant

Participants also described feelings of shame, self-doubt, and guilt. They referred to Islamophobic incidents as 'humiliating' and 'embarrassing' while feeling powerless to do anything about it. The following comments help to convey the sense of humiliation and embarrassment that veiled Muslim women might feel when experiencing Islamophobic hate crime in public, often in view of people passing by who do not intervene to help them.

I feel humiliated and I feel totally alone even though there are so many people around. If somebody would speak up and say 'Leave her alone, it is up to her how she dresses' but nobody has ever come to my defence.

Kalila, 29 years old

I got on the bus and a woman with a pushchair called me a 'Dirty Muslim' and spat at me, and then other people started calling me names too. The bus driver did not intervene to protect me. I felt so embarrassed and humiliated.

Sabirah, 35 years old

Several participants felt angry, upset, and frustrated. Hate crime studies have established both specific and generalized frustration and anger on the part of victims—towards the perpetrator and towards a culture of bias and exclusion (see also Craig-Henderson 2009; Herek et al. 2002; McDevitt et al. 2001; Williams and Tregidga 2014).

I'm proud to be a British Muslim but I get upset when people say to me 'Go back to your country' because this is my home. I was born here.

Iffat, 25 years old

We are born and bred here. Where do they want us to go? Where is our future?
    It is frustrating because it seems we don't belong anywhere. We have no place. It's like we are not wanted anywhere.

Focus group participants

Furthermore, rarely did participants describe manifestations of Islamophobic hate crime as 'one-off' incidents; rather there was always the reality, the fear, the expectation for another attack. In other words, participants painted a picture of an everyday phenomenon, which can be better understood as a process rather than as 'one-off' or incidental occurrences. The fact that Islamophobic hate crime is an everyday phenomenon for veiled Muslim women means that they are repeat and persistent victims. Bowling (2009) stated that repeated or persistent victimization can undermine the security of actual and potential victims, and induce fear and anxiety. Indeed, the distressing nature of Islamophobic hate crime coupled with the frequency with which these acts were committed had created high levels of fear and anxiety amongst participants. In line with the apparent exclusionary intent and impact of this victimization, participants felt extremely wary in public with a great sense of danger, which is illustrated in the following comments:

Every day I step out of my house I fear that I might not return.

Iman, 37 years old

When people abuse me I feel intimidated because I don't know where to go and there's no one actually there to help me. It is so frightening because I'm on my own and there's a group of them.

Aliyah, 18 years old

I do feel fear depending on where I am. Here [in Leicester] I know who my enemies are, I know where they are, so it's easier. If I were to go somewhere else I'll have more fear because I don't know that area. For example, when I go up North I know there's a lot more abuse.

Rahimah, 44 years old

Participants feared for their safety; nevertheless, this sense of vulnerability depended upon certain geographical places and spaces. For example, participants felt safer in cities in the UK where the Muslim public presence was well established such as Leicester, Blackburn, Bradford, Luton, and Birmingham, by virtue of 'safety in numbers'. By contrast, in areas where the Muslim population was rather small, the sense of vulnerability as well as the risk of attack was perceived to be significantly higher. Importantly, many participants revealed that they had decided to move to Leicester from other parts of the UK and even from other parts of the world in the belief that Leicester would provide a better life for them and their families. For example, some participants were French Muslim women of Algerian origin who had moved to Leicester because of the veil ban in France, as they could no longer wear the niqab in France. Similarly, other participants had left their countries such as the Netherlands and the US because of the hostile climate towards 'practising' Muslims in these countries, and with the view that they would be safe to practise Islam in Leicester.

Leicester provides Muslims with an authentic Islamic lifestyle based on its extensive infrastructure: veils, mosques with minarets, madrasahs (Islamic educational institutions), halal shops, and Muslim cemeteries. In the words of Sallah (2010: 18), one can 'feel and breathe Islam' in Leicester by virtue of its vibrant and thriving Muslim community. In light of this, participants felt confident that they would be safe to wear the veil in a city such as Leicester because of its high population of Muslims and veil-wearing women. This ties in with the suggestions of Githens-Mazer and Lambert (2010), who found that Muslims are at less risk of attack when they are in areas with a high Muslim population. For participants, hostility was a regular feature of living in communities unfamiliar with 'otherness' and 'Muslim difference' in particular, but they soon realized that Islamophobic hate crime exists even within a multicultural city such as Leicester, albeit to a lesser degree than in other cities in the UK and elsewhere in the West. As the following comments illustrate in the context of a focus group interview, there were mixed feelings about notions of safety in Leicester:

We left France because people are against Islam. In schools the girls can't wear the hijab and there is no Muslim school, it is forbidden. Also, they made it illegal for us to wear the niqab. We couldn't stay there anymore.

My husband chose Leicester. We had to leave the Netherlands because my kids were growing up in an environment where people were shouting at me, pushing me. I'm sure it will happen here but not as often as it would happen there. We are a bit more sheltered here but no matter how diverse a place is, it's always going to happen.

Focus group participants

Participants argued that the UK was more tolerant in comparison to other European countries such as France, Italy, Germany, and Greece, as well as in comparison to certain Muslim-majority countries such as Egypt and Turkey. This ties in with the suggestions of Scott-Baumann (2011), who argued that the UK provides a more veil-friendly environment than many European countries such as France where the hijab is banned in schools and within the civil service, and the niqab is banned in public. Sallah (2010) found that Muslims felt more 'accepted' in Leicester in comparison to their experiences of living elsewhere before moving to Leicester. Similarly, participants in the current study reported feeling 'unwelcome' in countries such as Greece and Turkey, as the following quotations demonstrate:

When I went to Athens on holiday I did notice that I got a lot more stares there than I did in the UK. Nobody said anything but it was obvious that people were making a point of looking at me because of my niqab.

Maryam, 28 years old

In Turkey I was treated very badly, they don't like women wearing niqabs.

Sabah, 32 years old

Clearly, there exists a paradox in the sense that the globalized cultural racism leads many Muslim people to seek out safe spaces but in doing so participate in a globalized society characterized by mobility allowing them to move to places where they can express their religious beliefs more fully. However, spaces such as Leicester are still not considered as safe spaces to express Muslim identity compared to traditional Islamic States. For example, Saudi Arabia, Kuwait, Qatar, Bahrain, Oman, and Yemen were seen by many participants as the 'ideal' country for 'practising' Muslims to live in, as the following quotation shows:

I've had the experience of living in Saudi Arabia and I can see the difference. I felt so much at peace there. I felt 'This is where I belong'. As soon as I'm here [England], it feels like we are at war, psychological war, a war of ideas, a war of culture, a war of our way of life. After living in England for eight years and then going to Saudi it was strange walking down the street and no one abusing me, nobody staring at me, nobody thinking I am the enemy. There we blend in so easily.

Focus group participant

Furthermore, participants made reference to changing patterns of social interaction which often culminated in isolation and withdrawal from society. In particular, they tried to limit their use of public and commercial space in order to reduce vulnerability to attack. They mentioned 'no-go areas' where they would face an increased risk of abuse, whilst others restricted their public travel to a minimum. In this regard, Islamophobic hate crime impacts upon the daily movements and lifestyles of veiled Muslim women. Poynting and Noble (2004) note that the public sphere, within which Islamophobic hate crime is experienced, includes not just streets and parks, but also hospitals, school, and workplaces. This strategy holds the possibility of limiting not just movement through public space but engagement in the public sphere and consequently equal participation in society (Carr and Haynes 2015).

This discussion demonstrates how the enactment of physical geographical boundaries impacts upon 'emotional geographies' in relation to the way in which participants perceived the places inside and outside their 'comfort zones' (Hopkins 2007). Rather than risk the threat of being attacked, many actual and potential victims choose to retreat to their 'own' communities and as a result become reclusive. Unarguably, this limits the behavioural options and life choices of individuals as it determines the area of residence, their vocational pursuits and leisure activities, as well as their mode of transport. Ultimately, this reality might result in segregation in housing, transportation, education, employment, and leisure activities. However, as Perry and Alvi (2012) point out, this is not a voluntary choice; rather, it is the 'safe' choice. They explain that the potential for future abuse creates social and geographical yet 'invisible' boundaries, across which members of Muslim communities are not 'welcome' to step. From this perspective, Islamophobic hate crime acts as a form of emotional terrorism on the basis that it segregates and isolates Muslims, particularly in terms of restricting their freedom of movement in the public sphere and changing their patterns of social interaction.

COLLECTIVE IMPACTS

The impact of Islamophobic hate crime is not restricted to those individuals who might have been attacked; rather, the harm extends to the wider Muslim community on multiple levels: local, national, and international. The abuse that veiled Muslim women suffer is linked to the suffering of Muslims globally through reference to the ummah (Mythen, Walklate, and Khan 2009). The word ummah means 'community of believers', which is often used to denote the oneness of Muslims regardless of nationality, background, ethnicity, or any other social stratification (Sallah 2010). The very essence of the concept of ummah is global Muslim brotherhood. This illustrates how manifestations of Islamophobia as typified by Islamophobic hate crime affect not only the individual victim but also the collective victim. As such, the individual fear and vulnerability discussed above is accompanied by the collective fear and vulnerability of all Muslims, particularly those individuals who have a 'visible' Muslim identity within 'non-Muslim countries'. An appreciation of the concept of ummah and its implications has relevance for understanding the wider impacts of Islamophobic hate crime in a globalized world.

For Saunders (2008), the notion of ummah reframes the parameters of what defines national identity in Islam. He points to the development of a robust collective identity amongst Muslims worldwide—one which cannot be adequately explained within the framework of religious fellowship. In essence, the ummah functions as a 'nation' that supersedes national and ethnic identities. As such, the term conveys the notion of 'one community' beyond geopolitical bounds. As Mandaville (2003: 135) put it, 'Muslims living in diaspora—particularly in the West—are of varied and diverse ethnic origins. What links them together, however, is a shared sense of identity within their religion, an idea most clearly located within the concept of the ummah.' For Jacobson (1998), this identification is not necessarily connected to personal participation in distinctive religious practices in Islam. Even in cases where Muslims may not be practising Islam, they tend to emphasize their sense of belonging to the ummah. Saunders (2008) points out that ummah membership does not necessarily reject competing national identities (e.g., Arab or British), nor does this membership prevent internal divisions (e.g., Sunni versus Shia, moderate versus fundamentalist). Rather the ethnic, regional, and linguistic differences that would have created divisions in a Muslim country are overshadowed by the shared difficulties of living as ethnic and religious minorities in the West.

According to Perry's (2001) conceptualization of hate crime as a mechanism for doing difference, the intent of hate crime offenders is to send a message to multiple audiences: the victim, who needs to be punished for his/her inappropriate performance of identity; the victim's community, who need to learn that they too are vulnerable to the same fate; and the broader community, who are reminded of the appropriate alignment of 'us' and 'them'. Within the present study, several participants explicitly acknowledged the nature of their experiences of Islamophobic hate crime as 'message crimes'. As such, the 'message' was received loud and clear. Participants were conscious of the fact that fellow Muslims were liable to abuse and harassment because of their group identity as followers of Islam. Throughout interviews and focus group discussions the consensus view amongst participants was that the wider Muslim community is under attack by virtue of the fact that 'an attack on one Muslim is an attack on all'. For Muslims this is a crucial aspect of their faith; they are one body in Islam and 'when any part of the body suffers, the whole body feels the pain'. This is demonstrated in the following quotations:

You feel it as a whole. Whilst it is an attack on the individual, it's actually an attack on Islam as a whole. Therefore, it has an effect on everybody. We talk very much about the ummah, so any part of that which is attacked is felt across the whole community.

Layla, 38 years old

We feel we are all under attack. When it has happened to another sister or brother it does affect me. It affects all of us.

In our religion, we believe we are all one body. If one person is hurt, it's like a part of our body is hurt so we all have to be concerned when women in niqabs are at risk.

Focus group participants

The abuse that veiled Muslim women suffer is linked to the suffering of Muslims globally through the ummah. At the same time, though, it is important to challenge any notion of the essentialized Muslim community (Bolognani 2007). The reified notion of ummah as a homogeneous religious cluster simplifies the enormous levels of diversity and heterogeneity amongst its members, including variations around age, gender, race, ethnicity, language, sexual orientation, and socio-economic status (Alexander, Edwards, and Temple 2007). Clearly there are differences across Muslim communities; nevertheless, the concept of ummah demonstrates that despite these differences, Muslim people feel connected through their religious beliefs and therefore their collective Muslim identity globally keeps them connected.

CONCLUSION

Despite their diversity, veiled Muslim women are homogenized and stigmatized as oppressed, dangerous to public safety, and unwilling to integrate into society. Stereotypes regarding the multiple 'threats' of the niqab promote a climate of Islamophobic hostility throughout the world. Drawing from qualitative data elicited through a UK-based study, this chapter examined the effects of Islamophobic hate crime upon veiled Muslim women and the wider Muslim community. For example, psychological and emotional impacts included feelings of insecurity, vulnerability, and fear, as well as low self-esteem and low confidence. The majority of participants had altered their lifestyle with the aim to reduce the risk of future attacks. They mentioned 'no-go areas' where they would face an increased risk of abuse and often restricted their public travel to a minimum. The findings also illustrated that manifestations of Islamophobic hate crime towards veiled Muslim women were perceived as an attack upon the fabric of the Muslim community itself. Essentially, Islamophobic hate crime is unique in the consciousness of the wider Muslim community through notions of a worldwide, transnational Muslim community, the ummah, which connects Muslims in the UK with other Muslims throughout the world. Clearly, increased awareness of the individual and collective impacts of Islamophobic hate crime related to the targeted victimization of veiled Muslim women is crucial. Only by raising awareness about the nature, extent, and impact of this problem, and learning about veiled Muslim women's experiences of Islamophobic hate crime, can we begin to address the harmful consequences of this form of hate crime both in the UK and globally.

REFERENCES

Alexander, C., Edwards, R., and Temple, B. 2007. 'Contesting Cultural Communities: Language, Ethnicity and Citizenship in Britain' *Journal of Ethnic and Migration Studies* 33(5): 783–800.

Allen, C. 2010. *Islamophobia*, Farnham: Ashgate.

Al-Saji, A. 2010. 'The Racialisation of Muslim Veils: A Philosophical Analysis' *Philosophy and Social Criticism* 36(8): 875–902.

Babacan, H., Gopalkrishnan, N., and Babacan, A. 2009. *Situating Racism: The Local, National, and the Global*, Cambridge: Cambridge Scholars Press.

Bolognani, M. 2007. 'Islam, Ethnography and Politics: Methodological Issues in Researching amongst West Yorkshire Pakistanis in 2005' *International Journal of Social Research Methodology* 10(4): 279–93.

Bowling, B. 2009. 'Violent Racism: Victimisation, Policing and Social Context' in B. Williams and H. Goodman-Chong (eds.), *Victims and Victimisation: A Reader*, Maidenhead: Open University Press, pp. 58–77.

Carr, J. and Haynes, A. 2015. 'A Clash of Racializations: The Policing of "Race" and of Anti-Muslim Racism in Ireland' *Critical Sociology* 41(1): 21–40.

Chakraborti, N., Garland, J., and Hardy, S. 2014. *The Hate Crime Project*, Leicester: University of Leicester.

Chakraborti, N. and Garland, J. 2009. *Hate Crime*, Sage: London.

Chakraborti, N. and Zempi, I. 2013. 'Criminalising Oppression or Reinforcing Oppression? The Implications of Veil Ban Laws for Muslim Women in the West' *Northern Ireland Legal Quarterly* 64(1): 63–74.

Chakraborti, N. and Zempi, I. 2012. 'The Veil under Attack: Gendered Dimensions of Islamophobic Victimisation' *International Review of Victimology* 18(3): 269–84.

College of Policing 2014. *Hate Crime Strategy and Operational Guidance*, London: College of Policing.

Copsey, N., Dack, J., Littler, M., and Feldman, M. 2013. *Anti-Muslim Hate Crime and the Far Right*, Middlesbrough: Teesside University.

Craig-Henderson, K. 2009. 'The Psychological Harms of Hate: Implications and Interventions' in B. Perry and P. Iganski (eds.), *Hate Crimes: The Consequences of Hate Crime*, Westport, CT: Praeger Publishers, pp. 15–30.

Curtis, B. and Curtis, C. 2011. *Social Research*, London: Sage.

Dwyer, C. 1999. 'Veiled Meanings: Young British Muslim Women and the Negotiation of Difference' *Gender, Place and Culture* 6(1): 5–26.

Esposito, J.L. and Kalin, I. 2011. *Islamophobia: The Challenge of Pluralism in the 21st Century*, Oxford: Oxford University Press.

Garner, S. and Selod, S. 2015. 'The Racialization of Muslims: Empirical Studies of Islamophobia' *Critical Sociology* 41(1): 9–19.

Githens-Mazer, J. and Lambert, R. 2010. *Islamophobia and Anti-Muslim Hate Crime: A London Case Study*, London: European Muslim Research Centre.

Grillo, R. and Shah, P. 2012. *Reasons to Ban? The Anti-Burqa Movement in Western Europe*, Göttingen: Max Planck Institute.

Hall, N. 2005. *Hate Crime*, Cullompton: Willan.

Hennink, M., Hutter, I., and Bailey, A. 2011. *Qualitative Research Methods*, London: Sage.

Herek, G., Cogan, J., and Gillis, R. 2002. 'Victim Experiences in Hate Crimes Based on Sexual Orientation' *Journal of Social Issues* 58(2): 319–39.

Hopkins, P. 2007. 'Young Muslim Men's Experiences of Local Landscapes after 11th September 2001' in C. Atkinson, P. Hopkins, and M. Kwan (eds.), *Geographies of Muslim Identities: Diaspora, Gender and Belonging*, Aldershot: Ashgate, pp. 189–200.

Jacobson, J. 1998. *Islam in Transition: Religion and Identity among British Pakistani Youth*, London: Routledge.

Kumar, D. 2012. *Islamophobia and the Politics of Empire*, Chicago, IL: Haymarket Books.

Kundnani, A. 2007. 'Integrationism: The Politics of Anti-Muslim Racism' *Race and Class* 48(4): 24–44.

Mandaville, P. 2003. 'Communication and Diasporic Islam' in K.H. Karim (ed.), *The Media of Diaspora*, London: Routledge, pp. 135–47.

McDevitt, J., Balboni, J., Garcia, L., and Gu, J. 2001. 'Consequences for Victims: A Comparison of Bias-and Non-bias-motivated Assaults' in P. Gerstenfeld and D.R. Grant (eds.), *Crimes of Hate: Selected Readings*, London: Sage, pp. 45–57.

Meer, N. 2010. *Citizenship, Identity and the Politics of Multiculturalism: The Rise of Muslim Consciousness*, New York: Palgrave Macmillan.

Moosavi, L. 2014. 'The Racialization of Muslim Converts in Britain and Their Experiences of Islamophobia' *Critical Sociology* 41(1): 41–56.

Mythen, G., Walklate, S., and Khan, F. 2009. '"I'm a Muslim, but I'm not a Terrorist": Victimisation, Risky Identities and the Performance of Safety' *British Journal of Criminology* 49(6): 736–54.

Office for National Statistics 2011. *National Statistician's Review of Crime Statistics: England and Wales*, London: ONS.

Perry, B. and Alvi, S. 2012. '"We Are All Vulnerable": The *in terrorem* Effects of Hate Crimes' *International Review of Victimology* 18(1): 57–71.

Perry, B. 2001. *In the Name of Hate: Understanding Hate Crimes*, London: Routledge.

Poynting, S. and Mason, V. 2007. 'The Resistible Rise of Islamophobia: Anti-Muslim Racism in the UK and Australia before 11 September 2001' *Journal of Sociology* 43(1): 61–86.

Poynting, S. and Noble, G. 2004. *Living with Racism: The Experience and Reporting by Arab and Muslim Australians of Discrimination, Abuse and Violence since 11 September 2001*, http://www.humanrights.gov.au/publications/isma-listen-independent-research (accessed 14 January 2015).

Sallah, M. 2010. *The Ummah and Ethnicity: Listening to the Voices of African Heritage Muslims in Leicester*, Leicester: Leicester City Council.

Saunders, R.A. 2008. 'The Ummah as Nation: a Reappraisal in the Wake of the Cartoons Affair' *Nations and Nationalism* 14(2): 303–21.

Sayyid, S. and Vakil, A. 2011. *Thinking through Islamophobia: Global Perspectives*, London: Hurst and Co.

Scott-Baumann, A. 2011. 'Unveiling Orientalism in Reverse' in T. Gabriel and R. Hannan (eds.), *Islam and the Veil*, London: Continuum, pp. 20–35.

Williams, M. and Tregidga, J. 2014. 'Hate Crime Victimisation in Wales: Psychological and Physical Impacts Across Seven Hate Crime Victim-Types' *British Journal of Criminology* 54(4): 946–67.

Zimmerman, D.D. 2015. 'Young Muslim Women in the United States: Identities at the Intersection of Group Membership and Multiple Individualities' *Social Identities* DOI: 10.1080/13504630.2014.997202.

8

HATE CRIME IN TRANSITIONAL SOCIETIES: THE CASE OF SOUTH AFRICA

Duncan Breen, Ingrid Lynch,
Juan Nel, and Iole Matthews

INTRODUCTION

South Africa is internationally recognized for its progressive Constitution which guarantees fundamental human rights, freedom, and equality. In stark contrast, the country continues to struggle with endemic crime and violence, ongoing intentional unfair discrimination, hate speech, and hate crime. Post-apartheid South Africa also continues to wrestle with the challenge of nation-building and creating a shared sense of identity to overcome the entrenched divisions of the past. More than twenty years after South Africa's first democratic elections, government intervention to address social divisions remains uncertain and frequently undermined by statements from leaders across the political spectrum. It is against this background that South Africa provides an opportunity to examine how the legacy of a divisive violent past is reflected in various forms of hate crime that currently occur.

While hate crime is not currently a separate crime category in South African legislation, there is an increasing acknowledgement that such crimes are not reconcilable with democratic ideals and damage the international image of the country. Consequently, the government is developing policy and legislation on hate crime, hate speech, and intentional unfair discrimination.

In this chapter we examine the nature of hate crime within the context of a post-apartheid project of generating social cohesion and a sense of belonging for all. We provide an overview of current patterns of hate crime—in particular, due to availability of data, those targeting lesbian, gay, bisexual, transgender, and intersex (LGBTI) people and non-nationals. We also elucidate the challenges that survivors of hate crime face in accessing justice, as well as current government and civil society efforts to respond to and monitor hate crime. We conclude with a reflection on lessons learnt, some of which may be of use to other transitional societies.

NATION-BUILDING AND SOCIAL COHESION: A STRUGGLING POST-APARTHEID PROJECT

In the immediate aftermath of the formal dismantling of apartheid, South Africa was widely acclaimed for its political transformation and the expected accompanying social change. The Bill of Rights in the South African Constitution is considered exemplary for its explicit prohibition of discrimination based on, among others, race, sex, gender, ethnic or social origin, and sexual orientation (Republic of South Africa [RSA] 1996). Yet despite aspirations to make South Africa an accommodating place for all who live in it—as envisaged in the Preamble to the Constitution—the process of forging a national identity has been difficult as apartheid's legacy was one of entrenching social divisions (Harris 2004). In fact, it is the country's history of institutionalized discrimination under colonialism and apartheid that forms the backdrop for hate crime in South Africa, where racism and other oppressions were '…institutionalised, legalised and internalised' (Nel and Breen 2013: 242). In addition, staunchly conservative Christian values and nationalist ideals, often underpinned by state policy, shaped political and social identities. This fuelled widespread intolerance and the devaluing of other religious groups, and constructed gender and sexual minorities as not only sinful but also criminal (Potgieter 1997).

In current-day South Africa, traditional identity markers, such as nationality, race, gender, ethnicity, and sexual orientation, have so long served as central to power relations that they remain coercive anchoring-points both for the establishment and perpetuation of difference (Nel and Judge 2008). Unsurprisingly, therefore, the production of 'otherness' and 'abnormality' has remained a near-automated and inherent practice of identity construction in South African society (Harris 2004). Indeed, if hate crimes can be understood as extreme forms of discrimination borne from a culture of segregation and marginalization of people who are somehow 'different', the impact of South Africa's past is clear (Perry 2001).

The transition to a democratic political dispensation in 1994 brought with it an urgency to remedy the divisions of apartheid and '…to inculcate a sense of nationhood and forge a common identity' (Valji 2003: 18). Accordingly, in the early days of the post-apartheid state, conscious efforts were made to foster tolerance. New national symbols such as the national flag and the national anthem deliberately incorporated both aspects from the liberation movement as well as from the apartheid state, powerfully communicating this vision of inclusivity. In so doing, the process of nation-building resembled that of many other African states where unity '…was subliminally communicated through its ubiquitous flag, its currency, its postage stamps, its identity documents' (Young 2004: 12). While South Africa projected a sense of shared social solidarity externally, the challenge of fostering real and inclusive national unity internalized by all proved more difficult.

Shortcomings in developing national unity in South Africa can be seen not only in ongoing hate crimes against non-nationals and LGBTI people, but also in frequent allegations of racism against businesses or individuals, highly charged debates regarding the lack of transformation at higher education institutions, and hate campaigns targeting Jewish-owned businesses following the 2014 Gaza conflict (Matthews and Tabensky 2015; Nel and Breen 2013; South African Jewish Board of Deputies [SAJBD] 2014). In response, the South African government has engaged in a series of initiatives to address social divisions, albeit mostly in a piecemeal approach and at times at the expense of forging unity with other lines of difference. Nation-building relies on the ongoing inscribing of boundaries: '...an exclusionary process has come to be part of the idea of citizenship. It is informed by a conception of national belonging based on differentiation between groups and on potentially opposed interests, rather than on inclusivity' (Hayem 2013: 79). Ironically then, the process of nation-building is often pursued in ways that can further entrench exclusion, in that the construction of certain groups as 'other' is what makes it possible to mould a unified national identity in relation to such difference. Nationalism thus '...has consequences for the way in which those included in the project view those outside of it' (Valji 2003: 19).

In this regard, political leaders in South Africa have contributed to the scapegoating of minority groups when expressing personal views that are at odds with those their constitutional mandate requires them to espouse. For example, South African President Jacob Zuma's criticism of Malawi in 2010 for sentencing two gay men to fourteen years' imprisonment for gross indecency and unnatural acts after holding an engagement ceremony (Roelf 2010) was undermined by his earlier remarks at Heritage Day celebrations in his home province KwaZulu-Natal. At these celebrations President Zuma remarked how, when growing up, he would have 'knocked out' any gay man who stood before him. Likewise, when asked for his thoughts on same-sex marriage in an interview with the *Guardian* newspaper, President Zuma stated: 'We have a constitution that is very clear that we all respect, which I respect. It has a view on that one, that gay marriage is a constitutionally accepted thing in South Africa. So no matter what my views would be' (Smith 2012). Similarly, in 2011, the Chairperson of the Parliamentary Portfolio Committee on Home Affairs questioned how long South Africa would continue accepting 'floods and floods' of non-nationals, urging that they should be turned away rather than having the South African government hiding behind the Constitution, 'human rights laws' and 'all sorts of excuses' (News24, 2011).

The transition from a society marked by systemic and structural violence to one that is inclusive has proved challenging elsewhere too. Parallels can be drawn between South Africa and other transitional societies regarding the impact of historical violence on current forms of hate crime. For example, Steenkamp (2005) argues that in Northern Ireland, the effect of political conflict has been to entrench a 'culture of violence', with violence simply shifting targets. Accordingly, a Criminal Justice Inspectorate review of hate crime in Northern Ireland (cited in Duggan 2014: 7) states: 'There are worrying signs that groups such as ethnic minorities, homosexuals and the disabled are becoming the new scapegoats on whom those so inclined are now exercising their aggression.' Similarly, in South Africa, Sigsworth and Valji (2011: 117) note that 'a legacy of normalised violence, ongoing trauma..., feelings of threat, insecurity and loss of status may play out in acts of violence against marginalised or less powerful groups'. While political attention in both countries is generally on hate crimes that affect the majority—sectarianism in Northern Ireland and racism in South Africa—deliberate and sustained efforts to tackle other forms of hate crime are critical in transitional societies, if the legacy of the past is to be fully addressed.

However, in South Africa, violence, including hate crime, is at times condoned as an expression of citizens' frustrations. For example, in condemning widespread xenophobic violence in April 2015, rather than outlining plans to address pervasive unemployment and poor service delivery, or putting forth a strategy to bring an end to the violence and hold perpetrators accountable, the South African President foregrounded the '... issues that are being raised by citizens nationally, in particular complaints about illegal and undocumented migrants, the takeover of local shops and other businesses by foreign nationals as well as perceptions that foreign nationals perpetrate crime' (South African Government 2015).

In this manner the historical legacies that make such violence possible are maintained through the explanations offered for such violence, and prejudicial statements by political figures that serve to reinforce relative privilege are to some extent tolerated (Duggan 2010).

HATE CRIMES AND HATE SPEECH IN SOUTH AFRICA

Crime, in general, is a major concern in South Africa. It is, however, hate crimes—particularly those targeting especially marginalized groups such as LGBTI people and non-nationals—that have drawn international attention, due not necessarily to their pervasiveness, but rather to their impact on the sense of safety and belonging. This has prompted calls from a range of local and international groups for greater action by South African authorities to tackle the causes of violence and hold perpetrators accountable. These calls include the UN Committee on the Elimination of Racial Discrimination (CERD 2006), the UN Special Rapporteur on the Human Rights of Migrants (Bustamante 2011), the South African Human Rights Commission (SAHRC) (2003, 2010), as well as many local civil society structures (Consortium for Refugees and Migrants in South Africa [CoRMSA] 2010a; Hate Crimes Working Group [HCWG] 2010; Joint Working Group 2008).

Non-governmental organizations (NGOs) lobbying for hate crime legislation have done so for different reasons, one of which has been that such legislation will have symbolic value in conveying the message that hate crime will not be tolerated (HCWG 2010). While efforts to address hate crime need to go far beyond the realm of legislation, increasing accountability for hate crime can assist in tackling the existing culture of impunity and allow for other initiatives to engage in the long-term process of social change. Legislation would also be expected to require ongoing monitoring of patterns of hate crime against particular groups—a factor that could support strengthened standardized responses. Further to this, hate crime legislation is expected to contribute to improved coordination of efforts to prevent and respond to hate crime, rather than relying on ad hoc efforts by different government departments in response to media and public pressure in specific incidents, as has been the case.

Efforts to address hate crime in South Africa are also critical to addressing the country's long history of institutionalized discrimination. This is evidenced in the framing of the proposed policy response to the mentioned calls, namely the *Policy Framework on Combating Hate Crime, Hate Speech and Discrimination* (Department of Justice and Constitutional Development [DoJ&CD] 2012), which also includes the intention to criminalize certain forms of speech. The proposal to review existing legislative provisions on hate speech remains politically contentious, given the strength of the freedom of expression lobby group in South Africa, but also considering the tensions between the constitutional rhetoric of inclusivity and controversial populist statements by leadership figures discussed earlier in this chapter. In this regard, there have been several high-profile court challenges and complaints to the SAHRC on grounds of hate speech, often focused on statements made by political and traditional leaders. For instance, in 2011 Julius Malema—an African National Congress Youth League leader at the time—was found guilty of hate speech after being taken to the Equality Court by an Afrikaner minority rights civil society group, AfriForum, for singing a song from the anti-apartheid struggle at political rallies, which roughly translates as 'shoot the boer (farmer)'.

More recently, complaints were lodged with the SAHRC against King Goodwill Zwelithini (the reigning Zulu king under South Africa's Traditional Leadership clause) who, in a community address in KwaZulu-Natal in 2015, made statements widely regarded as inflammatory about non-nationals in South Africa. He is quoted as stating, 'As I speak, you find [non-nationals'] unsightly goods hanging all over our shops, they dirty our streets. We cannot even recognise which shop is which, there are foreigners everywhere...We ask foreign nationals to pack their belongings and go back to their countries' (De Vos 2015). His statements were followed by a wave of xenophobic attacks in KwaZulu-Natal, and flare-ups of violence in other provinces. In some cases the perpetrators of violence sang songs stating 'Foreigners should be beaten, King Goodwill Zwelithini has spoken' (Hans 2015).

South African activists and researchers working with issues related to hate crimes generally share the conviction that hateful speech (such as harassment, slurs, and other forms of verbal abuse) creates fertile ground for physical forms of hate-motivated victimization. These stakeholder groups understand hate crimes as representing the extreme side of a continuum that commences with the social acceptability of slurs and denigration of specific social groups (Breen and Nel 2011; HCWG 2010; Nel and Judge 2008). Yet, as indicated, it is anticipated that resistance to the pending finalization of hate crime legislation and policy guidelines of the South African government, will centre on the perceived curbing of freedom of expression.

HATE CRIMES AGAINST NON-NATIONALS
AND LGBTI PERSONS IN SOUTH AFRICA

When incidents of race-based hate crimes occur, there is usually political pressure for a rapid and effective criminal justice response. Furthermore, the SAJBD consistently monitors antisemitic incidents, although mostly limited to discrimination and hate speech, rather than hate crime, and has taken steps to call perpetrators to account. While other forms of hate crime undoubtedly occur (DoJ&CD 2012; Nel and Breen 2013), NGOs working on issues such as disability rights and other religious groups have as yet not taken active steps to consistently monitor hate crimes against those they serve. The extent of hate crime against, for instance, persons with disabilities and those motivated by Islamophobia are thus not well known.

In contrast, local civil society groups have, since as early as 1994, directed somewhat more focused efforts on the documentation of, and advocacy around, violence against LGBTI people (Holland-Muter 2012) and, since 1998, awareness campaigns targeting xenophobia as well as increased documentation of violent incidents against non-nationals (see, e.g., CoRMSA 2010b). Reasons for such heightened civil society attention include the apparent reluctance by many in government to address the plight of these marginalized and thus vulnerable sectors that lack a strong political constituency to force effective redress; more established and organized civil society networks for these sectors; and the awareness that some LGBTI people and non-nationals also face double marginalization because of their nationality and sexual orientation and/or gender identity and, accordingly, report being marginalized by other non-nationals for being LGBTI and by LGBTI people for being foreign (People Against Suffering, Oppression, and Poverty 2012).

Violence against non-nationals received particular prominence in May 2008 when mobs went door to door across parts of Gauteng (the province encompassing Johannesburg and Pretoria) beating and killing non-nationals as well as some South Africans from border regions perceived to be 'outsiders'. The violence then spread to other parts of the country, displacing over 100,000 people and leaving sixty-two people dead. The government was slow to respond to the violence and the subsequent humanitarian crisis. Three months after the violence, the government announced its intention to close the safety camps set up for those displaced. Despite renewed attacks on some returning to their former homes, there was minimal government assistance to enable people to leave the camps and rebuild their lives, and no plans to address the root causes of the violence or even monitor the safety of those returning. This prompted civil society to approach the Constitutional Court to prevent the closure in the absence of a more comprehensive reintegration plan (Misago, Monson, Polzer, and Landau 2010).

Research in areas where violence took place showed that the attacks were organized and led by individuals and local groups who, building on popular frustrations in order to mobilize people, used the violence '...as a means to appropriate localized state authority for personal political or economic benefit' (ibid: 10). In addition, factors such as a culture of impunity regarding public violence and in particular xenophobic attacks, a lack of trusted conflict resolution mechanisms contributing to mob justice, and competition for local political leadership enabled xenophobic attitudes to turn to violence.

Other examples of ongoing xenophobic violence in the country include:

- Mob attacks on non-nationals around Johannesburg in January 2015—after a non-national trader shot and killed a youth attempting to rob his shop—and in Durban in April 2015—following earlier-mentioned remarks by Zulu King Goodwill Zwelithini for non-nationals to leave the country—killed at least nine people and displaced thousands;
- Somali national, Abdi Nasir Mahmood Good, 25, was stoned to death by a mob including school children in Port Elizabeth, Eastern Cape, in May 2013 after he tried to protect his shop from looters; and
- Non-nationals in different parts of South Africa were told they must leave the country before the end of the South African-hosted FIFA World Cup or they would be targeted for xenophobic violence on a larger scale than occurred in 2008. Despite proactive action from police and security personnel following advocacy and media attention, at least twenty-six separate attacks on non-nationals and their property occurred that month. At least ten people were murdered, including two Somali nationals who were burnt to death in their shop and a Malawian national who was killed and his genitals cut off.

Attacks on non-nationals remain a frequent occurrence, despite violence on the same scale as 2008 not having been repeated nationally since then. In 2011, civil society monitors reported at least 120 non-nationals killed and in 2012 at least 140 were killed, with another 250 seriously injured (Landau 2013).

Violence against LGBTI people has similarly attracted concern domestically and abroad. Despite progressive constitutional protections, LGBTI persons remain targets of discrimination and homophobic attacks. While a comprehensive evidence-base is lacking, early suggestions are that, in comparison to contexts such as the United States, LGBTI persons in South Africa are less likely to report hate speech and threats of violence than their American counterparts, but are more vulnerable to physical assault and much more prone to sexual assault (Nel and Judge 2008). While further research is needed, South Africa has deeply entrenched heteronormative beliefs around gender, with concomitant endemic sexual and gender-based violence. In such a context, LGBTI hate crimes are a continuation of generally high levels of violent regulation of normative beliefs around gender and sexuality (Lee, Lynch, and Clayton 2013). This gendered nature of homophobic victimization is demonstrated in research findings indicating that gender-nonconforming black lesbian women in townships and informal settlements are most affected (although hate crimes targeting transgender persons and gender-nonconforming gay men are increasingly reported, further suggesting that divergence from gendered norms appears to increase vulnerability) (Nel and Judge 2008).

Furthermore, attacks on LGBTI persons are often marked by extreme brutality—an aspect typical of hate crimes in general (Iganski 2001), demonstrating that the aim, informed by entrenched heteronormativity and patriarchal mind-sets, is not merely to harm the person(s) involved, but also to destroy their bodies and what these bodies represent. These common aspects are reflected in the following cases (Lee et al. 2013):

Duduzile Zozo (26), a lesbian woman, was raped and killed in 2013 in Thokoza, Gauteng. Her body was found in her next-door neighbour's yard with a toilet brush pushed up her vagina;

Thapelo Makhutle, a 24-year-old gay man who identified as transgender, was killed in Kuruman in the Northern Cape in 2012. His throat was slit to the point where he was virtually beheaded, his genitals were mutilated and his severed testicles were forced into his mouth. A former LGBTI pageant winner, Thapelo was reportedly killed after being interrogated about his sexuality by the alleged perpetrator at a tavern;

In 2006, Zoliswa Nkonyana, a 19-year-old lesbian woman, was with her friend at a tavern in Khayelitsha in the Western Cape, where they were called 'tomboys' and taunted for 'acting like men'. They were followed outside by a group of young men and while her friend managed to break away, Zoliswa was stabbed and stoned to death in the street; and

Ivan Johannes, a 30-year-old gay man from Elsies River, Cape Town, was murdered by a group of men in 2001. He was taken to a derelict building where his attackers pushed him down a flight of stairs, kicked him and assaulted him with a belt. When he fell to the floor below, two of the attackers repeatedly dropped cement blocks on his head and chest. A third attacker then set his body alight while he was still alive.

Further contributing to the vulnerability of hate crime victims are challenges in accessing justice. Secondary victimization at the hands of the police and other service providers, who often share the prejudice of wider society, is common and results in discrimination being replicated even within state institutions meant to provide protection and support (Human Rights Watch 2011; Lee et al. 2013). Such treatment fuels under-reporting of LGBTI-related violence and hate crimes. In research conducted among survivors of homophobic hate crimes in the Western Cape, 66 per cent of women said they did not report their attack because they would not be taken seriously. Of these, 25 per cent said they feared exposing their sexual orientation to the police and 22 per cent said they were afraid of being subjected to further abuse (Triangle Project & University of South Africa [Unisa] Centre for Applied Psychology 2006). Similarly, non-nationals have long complained to local NGOs of police refusing to open a case to assist them and sometimes telling them to go back to their own countries (see, e.g., the Commission of Inquiry 2014). As such, strengthening police responses and improving the quality of services provided to victims are essential parts of a comprehensive approach to addressing hate crimes.

A further challenge in holding hate crime perpetrators accountable is the politicization of some forms of hate crime. Following attacks on non-nationals, a number of politicians have been quick to rule out xenophobia as a motivating factor and instead blame 'criminality'—suggesting the two are mutually exclusive (see, e.g., Sosibo, De Wet, and Zwane 2015). This has encouraged local police officers to not recognize a hate motive regardless of what the evidence points to, contrasting with practice in the UK and other countries where the perception of the victim or the victim's community is a key factor in determining whether or not the incident should be investigated as a hate crime (see, e.g., Crown Prosecution Service n.d.).

In addition to secondary victimization and failures in investigation and arrest at police level, hate crime-related cases that do make it into the court system are generally characterized by lengthy trials and have low conviction rates (Lee et al. 2013). For example, in a homophobic assault on a gay man in Gauteng, it was only after intervention by a local LGBTI NGO that arrests were made and the matter prosecuted, despite witnesses being able to identify the three perpetrators (Williams 2012). After delays of nearly two years, the accused were convicted of assault with intent to do grievous bodily harm and the NGO supporting the case sought to be admitted as *amicus curiae* to establish the hate-based motive as an aggravating factor to be considered during sentencing. Expert witness testimony regarding the impact of hate crimes on victims and their broader community was rejected by the judge who held that '... any form of crime has a negative impact on the community' (Williams 2012: 43). Similarly, the trial of Zoliswa Nkonyana, referred to above, was marked by more than forty postponements; charges against most of the accused were dropped due to improper gathering of evidence; and the remaining accused were only sentenced six years after Zoliswa's murder.

What differentiates Zoliswa's case, however, is that it was the first case of LGBTI-related violence in South Africa in which prejudice was acknowledged as motive, based on testimony provided by a local LGBTI NGO and thus setting an important precedent (Lynch and Van Zyl 2013). To date two other cases of LGBTI-related hate crime have followed suit—the first being that of Duduzile Zozo referred to above and the second being the murder of a lesbian woman, Disebo 'Gift' Makau. Duduzile and Disebo's cases were the first to be taken up by the government-led task team aimed at addressing LGBTI-related violence (The National Task Team), established by the DoJ&CD in 2011 in response to domestic and international appeals for the government to address hate crimes against lesbian women, in particular. The National Task Team has a mandate to, among other matters, identify and urgently attend to LGBTI-related pending cases as received from civil society organizations (CSOs), and reported cases in the criminal justice system. As part of this mandate, Duduzile and Disebo's murders received specific attention and both cases saw guilty verdicts in which the hate element was recognized as an aggravating factor, with enhanced sentences being imposed (Germaner 2014). It remains to be seen if these small but significant successes will translate into more widespread improved outcomes in cases that do not necessarily benefit from targeted intervention by state or civil society actors.

Given the marginal status of non-nationals, as well as the widespread denial of xenophobia, cases of hate crimes against non-nationals have also faced numerous obstacles in obtaining successful convictions. As a result, civil society has argued that the State has sent the message that perpetrators can attack non-nationals with impunity (Misago et al. 2010). Following the xenophobic violence of 2008, the DoJ&CD, the South African Police Services (SAPS), and the National Prosecuting Authority (NPA) pledged to expedite investigations, fast-track prosecutions, and dedicate specific courts to deal with xenophobia-related cases (SAHRC 2010). Despite this, by October 2009—seventeen months later—only 159 out of 597 cases were finalized, with ninety-eight cases returning a guilty verdict, and sixty-one cases resulting in a not guilty verdict. A further 218 cases had been withdrawn—a figure observed by SAHRC researchers as being four times higher than for non-xenophobia-related cases of violent crime (SAHRC 2010). Nearly all convictions were for less serious offences, such as assault or theft, than the range of crimes committed, which includes at least sixty-two murders, a number of rapes, and numerous attempted murders, and most had the option to pay a fine rather than face jail time (Sosibo et al. 2015). Perhaps the most iconic image of the 2008 violence was that of thirty-five-year-old Mozambican Ernesto Nhamuave being burnt alive before police and a crowd of onlookers. In October 2010, police closed his case with his file simply containing a note stating, 'Suspects still unknown and no witnesses' (Tromp 2015). Yet in 2015, an eyewitness pointed out two suspects to reporters visiting the area—raising questions about the previous investigation and commitment to justice for all.

Since the 2008 violence the NPA has stated that it is tracking what it considers to be xenophobia-related cases (SAHRC 2010). Yet NPA data for such cases in the Western Cape—the province around Cape Town—from March 2009 to April 2012 show that of 190 cases that went before Western Cape courts, only seven resulted in convictions—a success rate of 3.68 per cent—lower than non-xenophobia-related cases of aggravated robbery. Of the eighty-three cases that went before courts in Cape Town, none resulted in convictions. Most of the cases related to business robberies but others included public violence, murder, and arson (Gastrow and Amit 2012).

While various efforts have been made to respond to particular types of hate crimes, often in a reactive manner following domestic and international pressure, South Africa has not yet implemented a coordinated strategy and interventions to strengthen social cohesion have not explicitly recognized the importance of tackling all forms of hate crime. Some of the projects include the DoJ&CD-led National Task Team with the Deputy Minister of Justice, John Jeffery, as champion (DoJ&CD 2014); the National Action Plan against Racism and Xenophobia being developed by the DoJ&CD; the work on social cohesion being led by the Department of Arts and Culture (DAC); the work of Home Affairs' Counter-Xenophobia Unit; and efforts to develop early warning systems for xenophobic and other civic violence by the National Visible Policing Unit of the SAPS and the National Disaster Management Centre (see CoRMSA 2010a).

MONITORING HATE CRIME

Civil society has recently taken steps to strengthen the monitoring of hate crimes in the absence of a consistent government monitoring mechanism. Existing state initiatives aimed at responding to hate crimes, such as the DoJ&CD-led National Task Team, have highlighted that the absence of hate crime legislation or a separate related crime category means that LGBTI-related cases cannot easily be identified in the criminal justice system and that government has to largely rely on CSOs to provide case information. Members of the HCWG—a multi-sectoral network of CSOs that cover a cross-section of vulnerable sectors and people at risk for hate crimes, including non-nationals and LGBTI persons—have developed their own mechanism to record data on the pervasiveness and impact of hate crime in South Africa. This—along with strengthening joint efforts to lobby for measures to combat hate crimes—was a primary aim of the network when founded in 2009.

Guided by the objective of contributing to the full enactment of hate crimes law once legislated, the Unisa Department of Psychology, as a founding member of the HCWG, initiated a project in 2010 aimed at strengthening the advocacy efforts of the HCWG. This Hate Crimes Monitoring Project aims to determine and describe the nature as well as psychological and societal impact of hate crimes in South Africa. The HCWG Hate and Bias Crime Monitoring Form and its accompanying User Guide (Nel, van Wyk, and Mbatha 2013) is a rigorous research instrument developed in consultation with the member organizations of the HCWG, and piloted across sectors in different settings. The Monitoring Form is currently being implemented by the HCWG in partnership with key CSOs in five provinces (Eastern Cape/Gauteng/KwaZulu-Natal/Limpopo/Western Cape) to provide a baseline record for a five-year longitudinal study (2013–2017). The Monitoring Form was also recently developed into an online system (see www.hcwg.org.za).

Early findings suggest that there is limited and inconsistent documentation of all forms of hate crimes across the country. Despite various advocacy efforts by CSOs, accurate knowledge, expertise, and documentation in addressing hate crimes is lacking across all sectors in all provinces. Monitoring efforts are severely affected by levels of organizing and resources; the extent to which related organizations are involved in service delivery to victims, rather than only advocacy; and their research literacy. Victims report a primarily emotional impact following victimization that affects various levels of their daily functioning (Nel et al. 2013). This research aims to complement and strengthen other important monitoring efforts, including that of the Joint Working Group (Nel and Judge 2008; Triangle Project & UCAP 2006) and other local organizations such as Iranti-org, working to strengthen the monitoring capacity of LGBTI CSOs in three provinces (see www.iranti-org.co.za), as well as the work initiated by the UN Refugee Agency with police to monitor and respond to xenophobic violence.

LESSONS LEARNED FOR THE GLOBALIZATION OF HATE CRIME

The experience of South African civil society in seeking greater actions to combat hate crimes offers some lessons for those in countries facing similar challenges. First, South Africa is fortunate to have a strong civil society. To complement local expertise, NGOs have also been able to draw on international experiences of addressing hate crimes shared by groups such as Amnesty International, Human Rights Watch, and Human Rights First. The positive impact of the involvement of international groups has been undisputable. Amnesty International, in particular, was instrumental in supporting hate crimes advocacy by facilitating the visit of a British hate crimes expert to the country in 2009 to share knowledge about British policing approaches to address hate crimes. In addition, Amnesty International has been campaigning since 2012 for justice for a lesbian woman, twenty-four-year-old Noxolo Nogwaza, who was raped and murdered in KwaThema, Gauteng in April 2011. Also, international pressure in the form of an online petition that was signed by more than 170,000 people contributed to encouraging the South African government to take more action to address violence against LGBTI people.

In response to domestic and international pressure, South Africa not only developed a National Intervention Strategy on Gender and Sexual Orientation-based Violence (DoJ&CD 2014), but since 2011 also demonstrated leadership at the United Nations Human Rights Council (UNHRC) towards ensuring the rights of LGBTI citizens worldwide. Despite the positive impact overall, there have also been instances where the involvement of international groups has contributed to defensiveness and reservations on the part of the South African government, at times hampering full engagement with civil society.

Second, the South African experience demonstrates the value of strengthening measures to document hate crimes in the absence of official monitoring. For example, when in May 2009, a year after the major xenophobic violence, the Presidential spokesperson claimed that attacks since then were rare and measures were in place to stop reoccurrence, civil society was able to cite numerous recent incidents of xenophobic violence to highlight the need for further actions. Third, the HCWG's Monitoring Form provides a template that can be replicated elsewhere and can thus be considered an example of how good practice domestically might be translated across borders. Finally, South Africa shows the value of CSOs working on different aspects of hate crime to jointly lobby and share expertise with government to build its capacity on the subject. Members of the HCWG as well as members of the government-led LGBTI-related National Task Team have held numerous meetings with those responsible for developing legislation, monitoring prosecutions as well as political leaders responsible for overseeing such efforts, to strengthen their knowledge of hate crimes.

CONCLUSION

Since 1994, South Africa has faced many challenges, such as inequality, lack of access to essential services, and unemployment, and—as a society in rapid transition—there are additional obstacles such as endemic crime and violence, a lack of social cohesion and sense of belonging for all, and many related competing priorities. Like other transitional societies, South Africa's history of institutionalized divisions makes nation-building a priority and addressing hate crimes and hate speech important—particularly given their negative impact on social cohesion. In the absence of coordinated efforts by government to build social cohesion and tackle hate crimes, interventions remain piecemeal and lack a common strategy to address all forms of intolerance on an equal basis. This has resulted in attention being devoted to addressing violence against LGBTI people or non-nationals at particular times, as political pressures dictate. Deeply held prejudices, including by senior leaders in government, also contribute to an environment where equality and human rights for all often exist only on paper and 'outsiders' are routinely blamed for social ills. While South Africa has taken on a leadership role at the UNHRC in its efforts to address violence against LGBTI people, the credibility of such efforts will depend largely on whether domestic measures to address hate crimes against LGBTI people and other marginalized groups are backed by the necessary political support to ensure their successful implementation. Work to introduce policy and legislation on hate crimes continues, but effective implementation may largely depend on whether government leaders consistently recognize the impact of all types of hate crimes on social cohesion and show the commitment to making South Africa the home for all it aspires to be.

REFERENCES

Breen, D. and Nel, J.A., 2011. 'South Africa—A Home for all? The Need for Hate Crime Legislation'. *South African Crime Quarterly*, 38 (December), 33–43.

Bustamante, J., 2011. *Report of the Special Rapporteur on the human rights of migrants: Mission to South Africa.* A/HRC/17/33/Add.4. Available at http://www2. ohchr.org/english/bodies/hrcouncil/docs/17session/A-HRC-17-33-Add4.pdf

Commission of Inquiry into Allegations of Police Inefficiency and a Breakdown in Relations between SAPS and the Community in Khayelitsha (Commission of Inquiry) 2014. 'Towards a Safer Khayelitsha'. Available at http://www.khayelit-shacommission.org.za/images/towards_khaye_docs/Khayelitsha_Commission_Report_WEB_FULL_TEXT_C.pdf

Consortium for Refugees and Migrants in South Africa (CoRMSA), 2010a. 'Taking Action on Threats of Xenophobic Violence: Recommendations for the Inter-Ministerial Committee'. Available at http://www.cormsa.org.za/wp-content/uploads/2010/06/recommendations-to-the-imc-on-xenophobic-violence-june-2010.pdf

CoRMSA, 2010b. 'Database of Violence against Foreign Nationals', September 2010. Available at http://www.cormsa.org.za/wp-content/uploads/2009/05/cormsa-data-base-of- violence-against-foreign-nationals.pdf

Crown Prosecution Service, n.d. 'Hate Crime, What is it?' Available at http://www.cps.gov. uk/northeast/victims_and_witnesses/hate_crime/

Department of Justice and Constitutional Development (DoJ&CD), 2012. *Policy Framework on Combating Hate Crime, Hate Speech and Discrimination. Executive Summary.* June 2012. Pretoria: Department of Justice and Constitutional Development.

Department of Justice and Constitutional Development (DoJ&CD), 2014. *National Intervention Strategy for Lesbian, Gay, Bisexual, Transgender and Intersex (LGBTI) Sector.* Pretoria: Department of Justice and Constitutional Development.

De Vos, P., 2015. 'The King of Hate Speech?', in *the Daily Maverick.* Available at http://www.dailymaverick.co.za/opinionista/2015-04-15-the-king-of-hate-speech/#.VT3kmiGqqkp

Duggan, M., 2014. 'Sectarianism and Hate Crime in Northern Ireland', in *The International Handbook on Hate Crime*, edited by N. Hall, A. Corb, P. Giannasi, and J. Grieve, pp. 117–28. Abingdon: Routledge.

Gastrow, V. and Amit, R., 2012. *Elusive Justice: Somali traders' access to formal and informal justice mechanisms in the Western Cape*. African Centre for Migration and Society. Available at http://www.migration.org.za/uploads/docs/report-38.pdf

Germaner, S., 2014. 'Respect gay rights, judge tells killer', in *IOL News*. Available at http://www.iol.co.za/news/crime-courts/respect-gay-rights-judge-tells-killer-1.1786344#.VT3xrSGqqkq

Hans, B., 2015. 'Xenophobic attacks: Extortion claims', in *IOL News*. Available at http://www.iol.co.za/news/crime-courts/xenophobic-attacks-extortion-claims-1.1843133#.VT3kIiGqqkp

Harris, B., 2004. *Arranging Prejudice: Exploring hate crime in post-apartheid South Africa*. Race and citizenship in transition series. Available at: http://www.csvr.org.za

Hate Crimes Working Group (HCWG), 2010. *Memo for the Department of Justice and Constitutional Development on Hate Crimes in South Africa*. June 2010. Johannesburg: Hate Crimes Working Group.

Hayem, J., 2013. 'From May 2008 to 2011: Xenophobic Violence and National Subjectivity in South Africa'. *Journal of Southern African Studies*, 39(1), 77–97.

Holland-Muter, S., 2012. *Outside the Safety Zone: An Agenda for Research on Gender-based Violence Targeting Lesbian and Bisexual Women in South Africa*. Johannesburg: MaThoko's Books.

Human Rights Watch, 2011. *'We'll Show You You're a Woman': Violence and Discrimination against Black Lesbians and Transgender Men in South Africa*. New York, NY: Human Rights Watch.

Iganski, P., 2001. 'Hate Crimes Hurt More'. *American Behavioral Scientist*, 45(4), 626–38.

Joint Working Group, 2008. 'Universal Periodic Review Submission'. Available at http://lib.ohchr.org/HRBodies/UPR/Documents/Session1/ZA/JWG_ZAF_UPR_S1_2008_JointWorkingGroup_uprsubmission.pdf

Landau, L., 2013. 'Xenophobic Demons Linger in South Africa', in *Mail and Guardian*. Available at http://mg.co.za/article/2013-05-17-00-xenophobic-demons-linger-in-sa

Lee, P.W.Y., Lynch, I., and Clayton, M., 2013. *Your Hate Won't Change Us! Resisting Homophobic and Transphobic Violence as Forms of Patriarchal Social Control*. Cape Town: Triangle Project.

Lynch, I. and Van Zyl, M., 2013. *Justice Delayed: Activist Engagement in the Zoliswa Nkonyana Murder Trial*. Cape Town: Triangle Project.

Matthews, S. and Tabensky, P. (2015). *Being at Home: Race, Institutional Culture and Transformation at South African Higher Education Institutions*. Durban: UKZN Press.

Misago, J.P., Monson, T., Polzer, T., and Landau, L., 2010. *May 2008 violence against foreign nationals in South Africa: understanding causes and evaluating responses*. Forced Migration Studies Programme. Available at http://www.cormsa.org.za/wp-content/uploads/2009/05/may-2008-violence-against-foreign-nationals-in-south-africa.pdf

Nel, J.A. and Breen, D., 2013. 'Victims of Hate Crime', in *Victimology in South Africa*. Second edition, edited by Robert Peacock, pp. 239–53. Pretoria: J.L. van Schaik.

Nel, J.A. and Judge, M., 2008. 'Exploring Homophobic Victimisation in Gauteng, South Africa: Issues, Impacts and Responses'. *Acta Criminologica*, 21(3), 19–36.

Nel, J.A., van Wyk, H., and Mbatha, K., 2013. *User Guide: Hate & Bias Crime Monitoring Form*. Johannesburg: Hate Crimes Working Group. DOI: 10.13140/2.1.4548.2563.

News24, 2011. 'ANC MP apologises for "xenophobic" comment'. Available at http://www. news24.com/SouthAfrica/Politics/ANC-MP-apologises-for-xenophobic-comment-20110703

People against Suffering, Oppression, and Poverty, 2012. *A Dream Deferred*. Available at http://www.passop.co.za/wp-content/uploads/2012/06/1.-PASSOP-LGBTI-REPORT-A-Dream-Deferred-2.pdf

Perry, B., 2001. *In the Name of Hate: Understanding Hate Crimes*. New York: Routledge.

Potgieter, C., 1997. 'From Apartheid to Mandela's Constitution. Black South African Lesbians in the Nineties', in *Ethnic and Cultural Diversity among Lesbians and Gay Men*, edited by B. Greene, pp. 88–116. Thousand Oaks, CA: Sage Publications.

Republic of South Africa (RSA), 1996. *Constitution of the Republic of South Africa*. Act 108 of 1996. Pretoria: Government Gazette.

Roelf, W., 2010. 'South Africa's Zuma condemns arrests of gays in Malawi'. *Reuters*. Available at http://uk.reuters.com/article/2010/05/27/uk-malawi-gays-zuma-idUKTRE64Q45K2010 0527?feedType=RSS&feedName=worldNews&utm_source=feedburner&utm_medium= feed&utm_campaign=Feed%3A+Reuters%2FUKWorldNews+(News+%2F+UK+%2F+ World+News)

Sigsworth, R. and Valji, N., 2011. 'Continuities of Violence against Women in South Africa: The Limitations of Transitional Justice', in *Gender in Transitional Justice*, edited by S. Buckley-Zistel and R. Stanley, pp. 115–35. London: Palgrave.

Smith, D., 2012. 'Jacob Zuma says Marikana killings a wake-up call on workers' conditions', in *The Guardian*. Available at http://www.theguardian.com/world/2012/dec/13/ jacob-zuma-marikana-wake-up-call

Sosibo, K., De Wet, P., and Zwane, T., 2015. 'Township politics fuel the attacks on "outsiders"', in *Mail & Guardian online*. Available at http://mg.co.za/article/ 2015-01-29-township-politics-fuel-the-attacks-on-outsiders

South African Government, 2015. 'President Jacob Zuma sends ministers to attend to incidents of violence in Durban'. Media statement available at http://www.gov.za/ speeches/president-jacob-zuma-sends-ministers-attend-incidents-violence-durban-12-apr-2015-0000-0

South African Human Rights Commission (SAHRC), 2003. *Hate Crimes and Hate Speech in South Africa*. Available at http://www.sahrc.org.za/hate_crimes_paper.pdf

South African Human Rights Commission (SAHRC), 2010. *Report on the SAHRC Investigation into Issues of Rule of Law, Justice and Impunity Arising out of the 2008 Public Violence against Non-Nationals*. Available at http://www.sahrc.org.za/home/21/ files/Reports/Non%20Nationals%20Attacks%20Report_1-50_2008.pdf

South African Jewish Board of Deputies (SAJBD), 2014. *Antisemitic Incidents in South Africa, January to August 2014*. Unpublished report.

Steenkamp, C.K., 2005. 'The Legacy of War: Conceptualizing a Culture of Violence to Explain Violence after Peace Accords', *The Round Table*, 94(2): 253–68.

Triangle Project and University of South Africa (Unisa) Centre for Applied Psychology UCAP, 2006. *Levels of Empowerment among LGBT People in the Western Cape, South Africa*. Commissioned by the Joint Working Group. Available at https://thetriangle-projectsite.files.wordpress.com/2014/02/levels-of-empowerment-among-lgbt-people-in-the-western-cape-south-africa.pdf

Tromp, B., 2015. 'SA's xenophobia shame: "burning man" case shut', in *TimesLive*. Available at http://www.timeslive.co.za/local/2015/02/19/sa-s-xenophobia-shame-burning-man-case-shut

United Nations Committee on the Elimination of Racial Discrimination (CERD), 2006. *Report: Concluding Observations of the Committee on the Elimination of Racial Discrimination.* Sixty-ninth session, 31 July–18 August 2006.

Valji, N., 2003. 'Creating the nation: The rise of violent xenophobia in South Africa'. Unpublished Master's thesis, York University. Available at http://cormsa.org.za/wp-content/uploads/Research/Xeno/riseofviolent.pdf

Williams, K., 2012. '"Dip Me in Chocolate and Throw Me to the Lesbians": Homophobic Hate Crimes, the State and Civil Society'. *South African Crime Quarterly*, 42 (December), 39–46.

Young, M., 2004. 'Revisiting Nationalism and Ethnicity in Africa'. James S. Coleman Memorial Lecture Series. UCLA. Available at https://escholarship.org/uc/item/28hor4sr

9

THE PROBLEMATIZATION OF HATE CRIME LEGISLATION IN TURKEY: THE RE-EMERGENCE OF LEGITIMATE VICTIMS

Bengi Bezirgan

The passage of so-called hate crime legislation within the Turkish criminal justice system is relatively new despite a long history of hate-motivated violence targeting individuals with different ethnic and religious backgrounds and sexual identities in Turkey. Regardless of the globalization of hate and the internationalization of the concept of 'hate crime', there are distinct national patterns (such as the role of state or civil society groups in the definition of collective memory, different citizenship laws, and the distinct nature of the political system and political culture) that have clearly shaped the Turkish response to the phenomenon of hate-motivated violence. These factors have also affected the ways in which national memories of hate have become institutionalized in laws and in law enforcement (Savelsberg and King 2005: 581–8). Considering these perspectives, this chapter critically deals with the problematical aspect of hate crime legislation in Turkey. It also situates the specific discussion of the Turkish case within the global context of the criminalization of hate-motivated violence.

Before addressing the legislative response to hate crime in Turkey it is significant to clarify the conceptualization of the notion of 'hate crime'. This chapter thus adopts Perry's (2001: 10) definition of hate crime as 'acts of violence and intimidation, usually directed towards already stigmatized and marginalized groups'. Perry's framework portrays hate crime within the process of 'doing difference' as 'a mechanism through which violence is used to sustain both the hegemonic identity of the perpetrator and to reinforce the boundaries between dominant and subordinate groups' (Chakraborti 2015: 15–16). The effects of wider power relations and established hierarchies of identity on the emergence of hate crime also intersect with the understanding of hate crime as an outcome of 'political culture which allocates rights, privileges and prestige according to biological and social factors' (Sheffield 1995: 438). When considered from this point of view, the Turkish case provides fertile ground for exploring the exclusion of 'already stigmatized' groups from hate crime legislation. The historical marginalization of these groups mainly derives from discriminatory state policies that intended to suppress non-Turkish and non-Muslim identities during the Turkish nation-state building process. This state-led discrimination still affects the penalization of prejudice-motivated crimes against members of these groups due to their 'incompatible' identities. The availability and the scope of legal remedies for these groups are accordingly controlled by the prevailing socio-political context in Turkey.

I begin this chapter by examining how the construction of the Turkish nation-state and national identity has led to the creation of the ideal citizen. I then focus on recent developments, namely the effects of the integration process to the European Union (EU) on the protection of minority rights in Turkey. The chapter then briefly explains the response of the Turkish legislative system to the phenomenon of hate crime. This is followed by an analysis of the exclusion of particular victim attributes, particularly those relating to ethnic and sexual minority status, from hate crime legislation, accompanied by the causes and implications of this legislative exclusion. Finally I conclude with an overview of the importance of the Turkish case for an international approach to combating hate crime. In particular, this chapter highlights how hate crime legislation in Turkey is based on the understanding of selective victimhood that fails to include the members of particular communities. By indicating the connection between past and present state-sponsored violence I argue that the idea of the 'legitimate victim' overshadows the vulnerability of specific groups in hate crime legislation.

THE CREATION OF THE IDEAL CITIZEN

In order to situate my discussion of the construction and perpetuation of the notion of the legitimate victim through hate crime legislation, it is first important to explore the contextual background with respect to the treatment of different social/identity groups by the Turkish State. As the heir of the multicultural and multi-ethnic Ottoman Empire, the Turkish State's approach towards various ethnic and religious minority groups has been persistently problematical. The attitude and approach of the political authorities towards non-Muslim and non-Turkish groups in their efforts to establish and consolidate Turkish nationhood have threatened the protection of minority rights. Since the foundation of the Turkish Republic in 1923 the nation-building process, similar to many other nation states, has been mainly built on the 'cultural standardization and homogenization within national borders, and differentiation from the rest of the world' (Olsen 1996: 257). The idealized image of the Turkish national identity accordingly corresponds to a Turkish Muslim, even Sunni, heterosexual man (Human Rights Association and Human Rights Foundation of Turkey 2007: 25; Kaya 2013: 201). This means that minority ethnic and religious belonging and non-heteronormative gender identities are regarded as risk factors for national unity and solidarity. The construction and reproduction of the national 'we' in the dominant national ideology and discourse are thus in a constant conflict with different ethnic, religious and gender identities; those that have gained legislative protection from hate crime in jurisdictions across the world.

In line with the process of Turkish nation-state formation identified as 'state-led nationalism' (Tilly 1994: 133) or as 'state-building nationalism' (Hechter et al. 2006: 89), the understanding of Turkish citizenship is also predicated on an inherent inconsistency between the legal definition and actual practices of the State. For the purpose of achieving a civic and territorially based formulation of Turkish nationalism, in 1924 the Turkish Parliament adopted Article 88 of the Constitution that defines 'the people of Turkey regardless of their religion and race were, in terms of citizenship, to be Turkish' (Kirişçi 2000: 1). Nevertheless, in contrast to the official discourse that identifies the Turkish national identity and citizenship in civic-territorial terms, actual state practices reflect an ethnic nationalist view (Aslan 2007: 249). This contention is substantiated by the state-sponsored discriminatory policies against minority groups along with 'direct and indirect discrimination by state and society' against LGBTI[1] individuals who are 'perceived and treated as less than citizens' (Ataman 2011: 128). In terms of the recognition and definition of minority groups and their rights, the foundational legal framework of the Treaty of Lausanne (1923)[2] shapes Turkey's current minority regime which is characterized by the gap between legal rights and their enforcement (Toktaş and Aras 2009: 699). This incompatibility mainly derives from the narrow identification of minority groups in the Treaty. More remarkably, the denial of the Turkish State to legally recognize any minorities beyond Armenians, Greeks, and Jews who had been protected groups in the Treaty resulted in the deprivation of rights by both Muslim minorities (Kurds, Alevis, Arabs, Laz, Circassians, Bosnians, Albanians, Roma) and other non-Muslim minorities (Assyrians, Protestants, Catholics) (Grigoriadis 2008: 31–2). Although the officially acknowledged groups seemed to enjoy privileged rights, a cursory glance at the history of the State demonstrates how these communities experience political, social, and economic types of discrimination in sequence.

First of all, as a part of the Turkification process, members of minority groups were asked to disperse their 'own community structures' and 'their religious/ethnic identities into the new national Turkish identity' so as to become 'Turks of Jewish or Christian faith, indistinguishable from Muslim Turks' (White 2013: 29). Thus the integration of those non-Muslim citizens depended on the number of criteria they met for Turkification and the survival and the protection of their rights could be guaranteed within the Turkish State. However, the strategies adopted by the State to assimilate non-Muslim minorities were multi-directional. For instance, the 'Citizen, Speak Turkish!' campaign of the 1930s was a typical example of the unification of language in the course of the nation-state formation. It compelled non-Turkish speakers to speak Turkish particularly in the public sphere and hindered their right to use their own language (Aslan 2007). The problematical relationship between the Turkish nation-building process and minority rights was also affected by the Second World War. Regarding the militaristic measures, national security concerns controlled the policies of the Turkish government. In order to preserve the

---

[1] Lesbian, Gay, Bisexual, Transgender, and Intersex.

[2] Treaty of Peace with Turkey Signed at Lausanne, 24 July 1923, The Treaties of Peace 1919–1923, Vol. II, Carnegie Endowment for International Peace, New York, 1924.

national security by detaching 'society's "untrustworthy" elements' from military camps, non-Muslim men aged between 26 and 45 were enrolled to the special recruitment 'known as the Incident of Reserves' (İçduygu et al. 2008: 367). In economic terms these unequal measures reached their peak when the Wealth or Capital Tax was implemented in 1942[3] which came into force in order to grant supplementary resources for wartime expenses. However, non-Muslims and Converts were charged five to ten times higher than Muslims, so they were forced to sell their properties to pay their taxes (Ökte 1978: 24). It was claimed that the underlying reason for this tax was the elimination of minorities from the economy and the replacement of the non-Muslim bourgeoisie by its Muslim counterpart (Akar 1999: 75). Moreover, the tense relationship between Turkey and Greece over the issue of Cyprus was the catalyst for the 6–7 September riots in 1955 targeting Greek and other non-Muslim citizens. These catastrophic acts of violence against non-Muslim minorities as 'the designated "others" of Turkish nationalism constitute an important episode in the ethnonational homogenisation (i.e. unmixing) of Turkey' (Kuyucu 2005: 364). These riots also demonstrated the means in which nationalist projects marginalized minority groups by creating an invented enemy. Despite the inclusionary narrative of the State, non-Muslim minorities became radicalized through the image of potential threat.

As this brief historical overview of repressive state policies indicates, the creation of the Turkish nation-state and national identity also resulted in the formation of ethnic, racial, and religious hierarchies among citizens. The power of this sociopolitical setting lies in its capacity to normalize vulnerability and victimization of particular community members. More importantly, 'the distinction between deserving and undeserving victims and how it impacts upon people's experiences of the criminal justice process' (Walklate 2007: 28) shows how the understanding of an ideal citizen has repercussions for the establishment of a legitimate victim in legal terms. For the purposes of any hate crime legislation a 'hierarchy of victimisation' (Carrabine et al. 2004: 115) becomes an issue since there emerges a necessity to struggle for the legitimacy of victimhood of distinctive groups. The paradoxical nature of policies on prosecuting cases of hate crime also sheds light on asymmetrical relationships between the motives behind the legislation and law enforcement.

On the one hand the main intentions behind hate crime laws are claimed 'to resist or nullify, not reinforce, the established power relations that infuse categories of identity' (Mason 2014b: 297) and 'to fight racism, heterosexism, anti-Semitism, and other prejudices' (Franklin 2002: 166). They are thus expected to challenge the second-class position of historically oppressed groups and provide a new legal ground for these groups to resist any acts of violence motivated by ethnic, racial, religious, or gender prejudices. It is also alleged that the extra penalty for hate crime offenders implies that any attack against vulnerable groups will no longer occur with impunity (Lawrence 1999). In spite of the portrayal of 'hate crime legislation as a form of rights based protection for vulnerable groups' (Ray and Smith 2001: 213), it can on the other hand fail to transform the legitimate victim status of particular

---

[3] The Wealth or Capital Tax Law (Türk Varlık Vergisi Kanunu), Law No. 4305, 11 November 1942.

citizens with different ethnic and religious backgrounds and sexual identities. These laws instead 'engage in a form of moral training' that composes 'the very norms and subject positions they regulate' (e.g., legitimate victim or racist offender) (Mason 2014b: 296). Given the pivotal role of activists and campaigners in reviving the issue of hate crime in political agendas, their support for 'certain strands of hate crime victim' also has an effect on 'who receives protection from hate crime laws' (Chakraborti 2015: 15–16). In other words, within hate crime policy itself another hierarchy becomes visible: that 'some identity groups seem to receive preferential treatment in criminal justice responses to hate crime' (Mason-Bish 2010: 62).

In light of this discussion it might be argued that a historically formed understanding of an ideal citizen throughout the nation-building process in Turkey also lays the groundwork for the present idea of the legitimate victim. The inherent conflicting aspects of hate crime legislation seem to intersect with the construction and reproduction of a homogeneous Turkish national identity that excludes different ethnic, religious, and sexual identities. Although this legislation is intended for the protection of non-Turkish, non-Muslim, and non-heterosexual individuals from hate-motivated violence and penalization of this type of offence, Turkey's own national history still shapes the purview of law. Consequently, the issue of the prioritization of particular citizens within the criminal justice system in Turkey once again is brought to the agenda through the criminalization of hate. Rather than rights-based protection and the improvement of rights, the law in its current form may instead contribute to the institutionalization of discrimination in Turkey.

THE EFFECTS OF THE EUROPEAN UNION INTEGRATION PROCESS

From the 1990s onwards the integration process to the European Union added a new dimension to the continuous policy of repression and discrimination against minority groups and the recognition of their rights in Turkey. In particular, one of three formal criteria defined by the European Council in 1993 with respect to the EU membership compels Turkey to achieve 'stability of institutions guaranteeing democracy, the rule of law, human rights, and respect for and protection of minorities' (Council of the European Union 1993: 13). These standards might be also interpreted as compulsory conditions for Turkey to move beyond the legal framework of the Treaty of Lausanne and make reforms with respect to the status and rights of minority groups. In order to comply with the Copenhagen criteria, the Turkish State primarily addresses three topics, namely 'eliminating discrimination, improving cultural rights, and improving religious freedom' (Toktaş and Aras 2009: 712).

In terms of eliminating discrimination, for instance, in 2003 the Labour Code[4] was amended to prohibit discrimination on the grounds of language, race, religion,

---

[4] Labour Act of Turkey, Law No. 4857, 22 May 2003.

and membership of a religious group, and the new criminal code implemented in 2004 contained some provisions focused on fighting racism, prohibiting genocide and crimes against humanity, as well as penalizing discrimination based on language, race, colour, religion, or sect in employment and access to services. Second, the issue of cultural rights is chiefly connected to the rights to be granted to Kurds such as establishing associations, permitting the learning of Kurdish, and using it in broadcasting. Yet the State does not abandon its restrictive attitude towards the use of these freedoms as the expansion of the cultural rights of Kurds is perceived as a threat to national unity and security. Third, as part of improving religious freedom, for example, foundations run by non-Muslim minorities were allowed to acquire and dispose of property through the introduction of constitutional amendments in 2002 and the restrictions in minority school enrolment for non-Muslim groups were lifted (ibid: 712–15).

These developments are just a few instances among many other efforts by Turkey to fulfil the EU's accession conditions. However, different progress reports issued by the European Commission criticized Turkey for not recognizing its non-Lausanne minorities, violations of the constitutional rights of Kurds and their political parties, and not allowing usage of the languages of groups other than officially recognized Lausanne minorities in mass media (Tasch 2010: 35–6). Regarding the Europeanization of minority policies and legislative changes, the constitutional amendments have failed to meet 'the standards of the international legal instruments providing the protection of minorities' (Kızılkan-Kısacık 2010: 26). More remarkably, the main structure of the official stance and policies towards minorities still fails to '[grant] cultural rights to any non-Muslim group' (ibid). In a similar vein, the Turkish State still interprets the Copenhagen criteria within the wider framework of universal human rights and liberties and denies the peculiarity of minority rights and problems (ibid: 26; Toktaş and Aras 2009: 718). Despite the steps taken by the Turkish State in terms of the change of its minority regime, it is still unwilling to widen its viewpoint to acknowledge the problems and rights of minority communities.

In addition to the EU integration process, the effects of globalization on the understanding and protection of minority rights in Turkey should also be taken into consideration. In particular, the efforts of civil society actors and the increasing visibility of identity claims of different ethnic and religious communities have affected the approach of the Turkish State towards members of minority groups who fall outside the scope of ideal citizen typology. Despite the positive assessments that underline the current climate of democratization which allows non-Muslim and non-Turkish societal actors to speak up for their demands (Ulusoy 2011: 421), the ongoing acts of hate-motivated violence against these actors, and the lack of legal protection, signify important deficiencies concerning the existing status of minorities in Turkey. For instance, the killing of Father Andrea Santoro of the Catholic Church in Trabzon in 2006; the assassination of Hrant Dink, an Armenian journalist in 2007; the killing of three Christians in Zirve Publishing House in 2007; and the murder of Sevag Şahin Balıkçı, an Armenian soldier in 2011, are only a few cases among many incidents against members of minority groups during recent years.

For all these cases it is very difficult to claim that thorough investigations were conducted. Indeed, the negligence of the State along with the security forces has been revealed in a number of cases.[5] This is why the official recognition of these offences targeting discriminated communities as hate crime and legislative amendments with respect to this particular type of crime have become important developments for the deterrence and punishment of various forms of hate crime in Turkey.

THE LEGISLATIVE RESPONSE TO
THE HATE CRIME PHENOMENON IN TURKEY

As I have attempted to point out in previous sections, the experiences of minority groups in Turkey in relation to hate-motivated violence have enduring presence and multi-faceted implications for the target groups. Notwithstanding this, it took a long time before the government and legal authorities took the first major step towards outlawing hate-motivated crimes. Thanks to the efforts of almost seventy non-governmental organizations (NGOs), the Hate Crime Legislation Campaign Platform was established in 2012, and in the same year a draft law was submitted to the Grand National Assembly of Turkey. Under the leadership of the steering committee of the Association for Social Change, different types of NGOs, such as Istanbul LGBTT Solidarity Association, Lambdaistanbul LGBTI Solidarity Association, The Alevi-Bektashi Federation, the Circassian Initiative for Democracy, the Dersim Armenians Belief and Social Aid Association, Hrant Dink Foundation, Human Rights Association, Disabled People Foundation, and Amnesty International in Turkey supported this campaign. Thus LGBTI groups, ethnic and religious minorities, and disabled people as well as refugees were represented via the platform. The impetus required for law making and policy enforcement was created by activists and campaigners through reviving public debates about bias and intolerance of difference (Lancaster 2014 and Perry 2014, cited in Chakraborti 2015: 16). This campaign was essentially set up to raise awareness amongst the public with regard to hate crimes and to compel the Government to enact law on this particular type of crime. A working group composed of legal experts prepared the draft law which provides for amendments in twenty-one Articles of the Turkish Penal Code.

In the preamble of this law hate crime is described as acts of violence resulting from prejudice against a victim or a group to which the victim belongs. A number

[5] Çetin, Fethiye and Tuna, Deniz (2010), 'Report for the 3rd Anniversary of Hrant Dink's Murder', Retrieved from: http://www.hrantdink.org/img/Hrant_Dink_Murder_Case-Three_Years_After.pdf

Karaca, Ekin (2013), 'No Verdict Yet in Sevag Balıkçı Murder Trial', *Bianet*, Retrieved from: http://bianet.org/english/youth/143899-no-verdict-yet-in-sevag-balikci-murder-trial

Önderoğlu, Erol (2007), 'In Malatya not Murders but "Missionary Activity" on Trial', *Bianet*, Retrieved from: http://bianet.org/english/minorities/103032-in-malatya-not-murders-but-missionary-activity-on-trial

Önderoğlu, Erol (2008), 'Police Marked Murdered Priest as "Separatist"', *Bianet*, Retrieved from: http://bianet.org/english/minorities/105044-police-marked-murdered-priest-as-separatist

of immutable characteristics were highlighted as being commonly targeted, such as race, ethnic identity, nationality, religion, language, colour, gender, sexual orientation, sexual identity, age, physical or mental disability. Furthermore it is stated that impunity for such crimes that endanger the respect for 'difference' and the culture of dialogue and tolerance required in a democratic society leads to an increase in social tensions and to the deterioration of societal security. Thus the legal necessity for the imposition of an additional punishment for the motive of hate and a separate legal definition of hate crime is emphasized. In line with this purpose, the draft law includes proposed amendments to certain Articles in the Turkish Penal Code. By considering the motive of hate as an aggravating circumstance, this draft recommends an imposition of extra penalties for particular clauses focusing on wilful murder, intentional injury, torture, persecution, sexual assault, child abuse, intimidation, deprivation of freedom, prevention of freedom of belief and opinion, violation of the immunity of residence, unlawful search, damage to property, and damage to places of worship and cemeteries (Hate Crime Legislation Campaign Platform 2012).[6] With the intention of criminalizing hate, this Bill suggests a comprehensive list of protected characteristics and major changes and inclusions in the Turkish Penal Code.

Following the submission of this draft in 2012, the issue of hate crime became a part of the 'democratization package' which comprised proposed legislative amendments announced by the Justice and Development Party (AKP) Government in 2013.[7] Through this package, hate crime was inserted under the Turkish Penal Code for the first time throughout the history of the Turkish Republic. While the draft prepared by the Working Group was broad in its scope and represented what would be commonly accepted as proper 'hate crime laws', the manner in which the Turkish government responded to the proposals is best described as 'minimal'. Since the position of non-Muslim minorities has turned into a testing ground for 'the government's commitments to contemporary standards of democracy and human rights' due to the role of the EU (Soner 2010: 25), the criminalization of hate, along with other series of reform Bills as components of the democratization process in Turkey, seem to serve the ideological interests of the AKP Government. The transformation process of Turkey is also claimed to be contradictory under the rule of the AKP government. On the one hand, in the wake of Turkey's attempts to realize its EU candidacy status, significant institutional reforms were implemented between 1999 and 2004, and during this period formerly taboo topics such as the suppression of the Armenian, Kurdish, and Alevi communities started to be discussed in the public domain. On the other hand, it is argued that the standpoint of AKP is in agreement with the Turkish State tradition of suppression and mass violence as persecutions, killings, displacements, and brute force against non-Turkish, non-Muslim, non-Sunni subjects as regular state practices continue to happen in Turkey (Ayata and Hakyemez 2013: 132).

---

[6] Retrieved from: http://www.sosyaldegisim.org/wp-content/uploads/2012/11/yasa-taslagi.pdf
[7] Turkish Criminal Code, Law No. 5237, 26 September 2004, Retrieved from: http://www.resmigazete.gov.tr/eskiler/2014/03/20140313-15.htm

In this context the ratification of the law on hate crime is noteworthy in terms of its potential capability to transform entrenched prejudices and acts of violence against minority communities and LGBTI in Turkey. On 13 March 2014 it was published in the official gazette (Law No. 6529 on Amending Some Laws for the Development of the Fundamental Rights and Liberties) that the title of Article 122 of the Turkish Penal Code numbered 5237 was to be amended to 'hate and discrimination', and this article was revised as follows:

(1) Any person who discriminates between individuals because of their language, race, nationality, skin colour, gender, disability, political opinion, philosophical belief, religion or sect and therefore;
   a) Prevents sale, transfer of movable or immovable property, or performance of a service, or benefiting from a service;
   b) Refuses to deliver nutriments or to render a public service;
   c) or bounds employment or unemployment of a person;
   d) Prevents a person to perform an ordinary economic activity,
   is sentenced to imprisonment from six months to one year or imposed a punitive fine.[8]

In spite of these amendments Article 122 mainly deals with the proscription of discrimination relating to service provision and employment rather than the criminalization of hate-motivated violence. As such, it is questionable whether these offences can accurately be described as hate crimes, at least as they have been defined by organizations such as the Organization for Security and Co-operation in Europe (OSCE) (OSCE 2009). From the viewpoint of the OSCE this law might be better identified as one of the instances of anti-discrimination laws which 'usually relate to workplace discrimination, or discrimination in the provision of goods and services' (OSCE 2009: 25). Nonetheless, in the absence of other hate crime legislation in Turkey, this is now considered the central regulation in Turkish law proscribing hate-motivated conduct. It is, however, ineffective hate crime-related legislation in the sense it does not protect individuals from targeted violence. Although 'the laws for the prevention of hate crimes differ from laws against discrimination' (Ataman and Cengiz 2009: 11), the discourse of the law in Turkey centres around discrimination whilst using the language of 'hate'. It should be also noted that prior to the adjustments introduced by the 'democratization package' there have been no convictions under this so-called hate crime law according to the criminal records of Turkish Criminal Justice System (Ataman and Cengiz 2009: 5; Cömert et al. 2013: 91). Therefore it is questionable whether the current form of Article 122 will bring about a change in the manner in which the law has been utilized until now.

In comparison to the proposal of the Hate Crime Legislation Campaign Platform, the legislation is a weakened version of recommended legal arrangements regarding hate crime. It is ambiguous as to how hate crime is a particular type of offence and characteristics such as 'race', 'political opinion', or 'philosophical belief' are not

---

[8] Turkish Criminal Code, Law No. 5237, 26 September 2004, Article 122, Retrieved from: http://www.resmigazete.gov.tr/eskiler/2014/03/20140313-15.htm

defined in the Article. It is equally interesting to observe that the Article concentrates on the enjoyment and protection of the rights of public service, employment, and economic activities. In contrast to the petitions of the Platform there is no reference to cases which might include acts of violence such as wilful murder, intentional injury, torture, or assault against vulnerable groups. It might thus be argued that the Turkish State has failed to pass comprehensive hate crime legislation and has instead equated acts of discrimination with criminal offences committed with bias motives. Furthermore, ethnicity and sexual orientation are excluded from defined protected characteristics in the legislation. In the next section I will deal with this central shortcoming of the legislation.

SELECTIVE VICTIMHOOD

While 'hate crime' is defined in the Turkish legal system as acts of discrimination based on someone's or some group's language, race, nationality, skin colour, gender, disability, political views, philosophical beliefs, or religion, it fails to address ethnic identity and sexual orientation as protected characteristics. More interestingly, the exclusion of ethnicity from the Bill means that discrimination against ethnic minorities in Turkey which are officially recognized or unrecognized by the Treaty of Lausanne are not assessed within the scope of this tenuous hate crime law. Article 122 creates new specific offences of discrimination and the notion of ethnicity is thus detached from the imposition of penalty for these offences under the legislation. In a similar vein the lack of legal protection of LGBTI individuals, as one of the most commonly targeted groups of hate crimes in Turkey, indicates how heteronormative legal arrangements neglect to protect these communities from hate crimes committed against them.

This selective understanding of victimhood in law enforcement in Turkey also corresponds to the international approach for tackling hate crime. By identifying particular groups as hate crime victims the legislature sends 'a clear message that these groups are deserving of more protection than others'; thus, depending how worthy they are deemed of legal protection, distinct victim types are categorized by the legislature (Schweppe 2012: 178). In this regard the Turkish context unveils the ideological setting for picking out ethnic identities as non-vulnerable subjects and leaving out the sexual orientation aspect altogether. Moreover, the refusal to recognize sexual minorities along with ethnic minorities in hate crime law illustrates the power of a heteronormative socio-political system for the trivialization of violence against LGBTI individuals. When considered from this point of view, deep-seated patriarchy and institutional discrimination towards different sexual orientations become mobilized and legitimized in the eyes of the criminal law. However, it should be noted that in an international context the absence of sexual orientation in hate crime laws is not unusual. For instance, of the thirty-seven countries within the OSCE that have some type of hate crime law, almost all of them contain 'race' and 'religion' as protected characteristics (OSCE 2009: 38). Yet only eleven countries take account of 'sexual orientation' in their hate crime laws and thus it is viewed as one of the 'frequently protected characteristics' (ibid: 43). In addition, according to a report by the European Union Agency for Fundamental Rights in 2010, only eight of twenty-seven EU Member States provided information about sexual orientation hate crime in their official data (Moran 2015: 267). Hate crime legislation in the Turkish case therefore seems to follow a similar path by ruling out the inclusion of sexual orientation.

On the contrary, the exclusion of ethnicity from hate crime legislation exemplifies a more unusual situation, as ethnicity is one of the most frequently protected characteristics, together with race, national origin, and religion (OSCE 2009: 40). Turkey's specific historical experiences and dominant official standpoint concerning different ethnicities evidently influence the perception of ethnicity in legal reforms. This might be also interpreted as one of the instances in which the creation of an ideal citizen based on certain features defines the boundaries of a legitimate victim in a nation state. Ethnicity by itself appears as insufficient to meet the expectations of a legitimate victim. Its inclusion in the legislation may be regarded as a threat both to the national and international image of Turkey concerning minority rights, for the reason that ethnic minority groups are one of the most targeted groups of hate-motivated violence.

In addition to these limitations to the legislation, it is important not to fall into the trap of adopting 'the totalizing logic of either/or' (Moran and Sharpe 2004: 400) that runs the risk of the prioritization of a single characteristic of a victim's identity. To be more precise, for the Turkish context it implies the ignorance of the existence and complexity of the experiences of a homosexual Kurdish individual. Instead intersectionality as a 'conceptual tool' provides an appropriate ground for the efforts to 'resist the simple either/or of a politics of "racialisation", "sexualisation", "feminisation" or transgenderization in relation to violence' (ibid). Obviously the intersectional approach to criminalization of hate crime appears to be overarching and opposed to 'the overlooking of specificities and intersectionalities of victimisation' (Chakraborti 2010: 21). The question then arises: 'Can we ever have policy that truly takes account of each individual's experiences of oppression?' and, yet again, 'the group-based approach to hate crime' (Mason-Bish 2015: 31) comes into prominence especially for developing countries, such as Turkey, that fail to encounter forms of 'difference' in their judicial systems. Nevertheless, the notions of vulnerability and 'difference' rather than identity and group membership need to have a more central position within hate crime scholarship, as they play determining roles for the intersectionality of victimization (Chakraborti and Garland 2012).

On the subject of the emergence of a judgemental hierarchy of victimization, Mason (2014a: 79) maintains that the inclusion of victim attributes in hate crime law depends on 'a political and symbolic contestation' that is affected by 'the capacity of different groups to contribute to the symbolic purpose of these laws by convincing the public that they do not deserve to be the targets of racism, homophobia, ethnocentrism and the like'. Thus the interconnection between the category of the ideal victim and compassionate emotion/thinking shapes the public perception of deserved and undeserved sufferers of violence. More importantly, the ability of 'legitimate' victims to convince members of the public concerning their vulnerability and to achieve a 'sympathetic image' explains the variability between protected attributes in terms of being included/excluded in hate crime laws (Mason 2014a: 82–3). Following Mason's argument it might be claimed that ethnic and sexual minorities which challenge the representations of Turkishness, Islam, and heterosexuality in Turkey also lack satisfactory 'empirical credibility' to provoke compassionate thinking among the public for the experiences of vulnerable groups.

The findings of surveys conducted in Turkey also substantiate prevailing prejudice towards those groups. In the World Values Survey carried out in 2011, 1,605 participants in fifty-four provinces were asked 'who do you not want as a neighbour?' and homosexuals were ranked number one with 84 per cent (Esmer 2011). Other research completed by Hakan Yılmaz based on forty in-depth interviews in 2009, as well as a nationwide opinion poll with a sample of around 1,800 respondents in 2010, attempted to explore processes of othering and discrimination in Turkey. One of the main questions was 'who cannot freely reveal their identities?', and sexual orientation and gender identity had the highest score (72 per cent). Furthermore, the respondents positioned non-Muslims with 28 per cent in the third rank and individuals with different ethnic origins (19 per cent) ranked sixth (cited in Ataman 2011: 137).[9] Consequently, it is possible to observe strong public consensus with respect to the need for those particular minority groups to conceal their identities. From this point of view the current form of hate crime (related) law in Turkey gives the impression that it is situated at the intersection between dominant moral codes in the society and ideological preferences of the current government. The legal absence of hate-motivated victimization of particular ethnic and sexual minorities and the absence of intersectional visibility of target groups, even in the context of such limited provisions, also come to mean the political struggle of those groups for their rights is neglected once more at the official level.

CONCLUSION

In this chapter I first attempted to demonstrate the creation of an ideal citizen during the nation-building process in Turkey and discriminatory state policies against non-Turkish and non-Muslim communities in the following years of the Republic. I then briefly examined the developments in the European Union integration process in relation to the status of minority groups. This was followed by an overview of the draft law prepared by the Hate Crime Legislation Campaign Platform and the ultimate form of the legislation that was enacted in 2014. Finally I explored the exclusion of ethnicity and sexual orientation from the legislation that raises the issue of selective victimhood supported by the idea of the legitimate victim.

---

[9] In this survey the other identities were atheist persons (59 per cent), persons who have a discredited job in society (23 per cent), Muslim people being members of different sects (21 per cent), poor people (18 per cent), Muslims who are religious (11 per cent), and persons who are secularist (7 per cent).

This analysis has also illustrated the power of compassionate thinking/emotion from the public towards target groups for the legitimization of their victimhood.

Despite the expanding academic literature on hate crime in different contexts across the globe and the proliferation of legal measures proscribing acts of hate-motivated violence at the international level, Turkey has yet to be swayed into implementing hate crime legislation that adequately protects historically oppressed groups from targeted violence. The Turkish context provides fertile ground for an international approach to combating hate crime. Indeed, the current approach in Turkey epitomizes the ways in which the ideas of ideal citizens and legitimate victims have become manifest in the legislative response to hate crime, irrespective of the growing international pressures to legislate to protect certain marginalized groups. In fact, as this chapter has highlighted, there is good reason to believe current 'hate crime' laws operate as a political and ideological tool that maintains pre-established types of discrimination and violence depending on the interests of those in power.

REFERENCES

Akar, Rıdvan 1999. *Aşkale Yolcuları: Varlık Vergisi ve Çalısma Kampları (Passengers to Aşkale: Wealth Tax and Work Camps)*. Istanbul: Belge.

Aslan, Senem 2007. 'Citizen, Speak Turkish!: A Nation in the Making'. *Nationalism and Ethnic Politics*, 13(2): 245–72.

Ataman, Hakan 2011. 'Less Than Citizens: The Lesbian, Gay, Bisexual and Transgender Question in Turkey'. In *Societal Peace and Ideal Citizenship for Turkey* edited by Rasim Özgur Dönmez and Pınar Enneli, pp. 125–57. Lanham, Maryland: Lexington Books.

Ataman, Hakan and Cengiz, Orhan Kemal 2009. *Hate Crimes in Turkey*. Ankara: Human Rights Agenda Association.

Ayata, Bilgin and Hakyemez, Serra 2013. 'The AKP's Engagement with Turkey's Past Crimes: An Analysis of PM Erdogan's "Dersim Apology"'. *Dialectical Anthropology*, 37(1): 131–43.

Carrabine, Eamonn, Iganski, Paul, Lee, Maggy, Plummer, Ken, and South, Nigel 2004. *Criminology: A Sociological Introduction*. London: Routledge.

Chakraborti, Neil 2010. 'Crimes against the "Other": Conceptual, Operational and Empirical Challenges for Hate Studies'. *Journal of Hate Studies*, 8(1): 9–28.

Chakraborti, Neil 2015. 'Framing the Boundaries of Hate Crime'. In *The Routledge International Handbook on Hate Crime* edited by Nathan Hall, Abbee Corb, Paul Giannnasi, and John G.D. Grieve, pp. 13–23. London and New York: Routledge.

Chakraborti, Neil and Garland, Jon 2012. 'Reconceptualizing Hate Crime Victimization Through the Lens of Vulnerability and "Difference"'. *Theoretical Criminology*, 16(4): 499–514.

Cömert, Itır Tarı, Yükseloğlu, Emel Hülya, Erkan, Itır, Kostek Mehmet, Emekli Ahmed Serkan, and Ozar, Melek Özlem Kolusayın 2013. 'A General Outlook on Hate Crimes in Turkey'. *European Journal of Research on Education, Special Issue: Contemporary Studies in Social Science*, 85–93.

Council of the European Union 1993. *European Council in Copenhagen, 21–22 June 1993, Conclusions of the Presidency*. Copenhagen: Council of the European Union. Retrieved at: http://europa.eu/rapid/press-release_DOC-93-3_en.htm

Esmer, Yılmaz 2011. *'Türkiye Değerler Araştırması'* (Turkey Value Survey). Retrieved at: http://smgconnected.com/2011-turkiye-degerler-arastirmasi

Franklin, Karen 2002. 'Good Intentions: The Enforcement of Hate Crime Penalty-Enhancement Statutes'. *American Behavioural Scientist*, 46(1): 154–72.

Grigoriadis, Ioannis N. 2008. 'On the Europeanization of Minority Rights Protection: Comparing the Cases of Greece and Turkey'. *Mediterranean Politics*, 13(1): 23–41.

Hate Crime Legislation Campaign Platform 2012. 'Nefret Suçları Yasa Taslağı' (Draft Law on Hate Crime). Retrieved at: http://www.sosyaldegisim.org/wp-content/uploads/2012/11/yasa-taslagi.pdf

Hechter, Michael, Kuyucu, Tuna, and Sacks, Audrey 2006. 'Nationalism and Direct Rule'. In *The SAGE Handbook of Nations and Nationalism* edited by Gerard Delanty and Krishan Kumar, pp. 84–93. London: Sage.

Human Rights Association and Human Rights Foundation of Turkey 2007. *'Türkiye İnsan Hakları Hareketi Konferansı (Turkey Human Rights Movement Conference): Nihai Rapor ve Sonuç Bildirgesi: Hrant'tan Sonra Türkiye'de İnsan Hakları (Final Report and Final Declaration: Human Rights in Turkey after Hrant)'*. İzmir: Human Rights Association & Human Rights Foundation of Turkey. Retrieved at: http://www.ihd.org.tr/images/pdf/insan_haklari_hareketi_konferansi_bildirileri_2007.pdf

İçduygu, Ahmet, Toktaş Şule, and Soner, Ali B. 2008. 'The Politics of Population in a Nation-building Process: Emigration of Non-Muslims from Turkey'. *Ethnic and Racial Studies*, 31(2): 358–89.

Kaya, Ayhan 2013. *Europeanisation and Tolerance in Turkey: The Myth of Toleration*. Houndmills, Basingstoke; New York: Palgrave Macmillan.

Kirişci, Kemal 2000. 'Disaggregating Turkish Citizenship and Immigration Practices'. *Middle Eastern Studies*, 36(3): 1–22.

Kızılkan-Kısacık, Zelal 2010. 'Europeanization of Minority Rights: Discourse, Practice and Change in Turkey'. *European Diversity and Autonomy Papers*–EDAP, 2010(1): 1–43.

Kuyucu, Ali Tuna 2005. 'Ethno-religious "Unmixing" of "Turkey": 6–7 September Riots as a Case in Turkish Nationalism'. *Nations and Nationalism*, 11(3): 361–80.

Lawrence, Frederick M. 1999. *Punishing Hate: Bias Crimes under American Law*. Cambridge, MA: Harvard University Press.

Mason, Gail 2014a. 'The Hate Threshold: Emotion, Causation and Difference in the Construction of Prejudice-motivated Crime'. *Social and Legal Studies*, 23(3): 293–314.

Mason, Gail 2014b. 'The Symbolic Purpose of Hate Crime Law: Ideal Victims and Emotion'. *Theoretical Criminology*, 18(1): 75–92.

Mason-Bish, Hannah 2010. 'Future Challenges for Hate Crime Policy: Lessons from the Past'. In *Hate Crime: Concepts, Policy, Future Directions* edited by Neil Chakraborti, pp. 58–77. Cullompton: Willan.

Mason-Bish, Hannah 2015. 'Beyond the Silo: Rethinking Hate Crime and Intersectionality'. In *The Routledge International Handbook on Hate Crime* edited by Nathan Hall, Abbee Corb, Paul Giannnasi, and John G.D. Grieve, pp. 24–43. London and New York: Routledge.

Moran, Leslie J. 2015. 'LGBT Hate Crime'. In *The Routledge International Handbook on Hate Crime* edited by Nathan Hall, Abbee Corb, Paul Giannnasi, and John G.D. Grieve, pp. 266–77. London and New York: Routledge.

Moran, Leslie J. and Sharpe, Andrew N. 2004. 'Violence, Identity and Policing: The Case of Violence against Transgender People'. *Criminal Justice*, 4(4): 395–417.

Ökte, Faik 1978. *The Tragedy of the Turkish Capital Tax*. London and Dover, NH: Croom Helm.

Olsen, Johan P. 1996. 'Europeanization and Nations State Dynamics'. In *The Future of the Nation State: Essays on Cultural Pluralism and Political Integration* edited by Sverker Gustavsson and Leif Lewin, pp. 245–85. New York: Routledge.

Organization for Security and Co-operation in Europe 2009. *Hate Crime Laws: A Practical Guide*. Warsaw: the OSCE Office for Democratic Institutions and Human Rights.

Perry, Barbara 2001. *In the Name of Hate: Understanding Hate Crimes*. New York: Routledge.

Ray, Larry and Smith, David 2001. 'Racist Offenders and the Politics of "Hate Crime"'. *Law and Critique*, 12(3): 203–21.

Savelsberg, Joachim J. and King, Ryan D. 2005. 'Institutionalizing Collective Memories of Hate: Law and Law Enforcement in Germany and the United States'. *American Journal of Sociology*, 111(2): 579–616.

Schweppe, Jennifer 2012. 'Defining Characteristics and Politicising Victims: A Legal Perspective'. *Journal of Hate Studies*, 10(1): 173–98.

Sheffield, Carole 1995. 'Hate Violence'. In *Race, Class and Gender in the United States* edited by Paula S. Rothenberg, pp. 432–41. New York: St Martin's.

Soner, Ali B. 2010. 'The Justice and Development Party's Policies towards Non-Muslim Minorities in Turkey'. *Journal of Balkan and Near Eastern Studies*, 12(1): 23–40.

Tasch, Laman 2010. 'The EU Enlargement Policy and National Majority-Minority Dynamics in Potential European Union Members: The Example of Turkey'. *Mediterranean Quarterly*, 21(2): 18–46.

Tilly, Charles 1994. 'States and Nationalism in Europe 1492–1992'. *Theory and Society*, 23(1): 131–46.

Toktaş, Şule and Aras, Bülent 2009. 'The EU and Minority Rights in Turkey'. *Political Science Quarterly*, 124(4): 697–720.

Ulusoy, Kıvanç 2011. 'The European Impact on State–Religion Relations in Turkey: Political Islam, Alevis and Non-Muslim Minorities'. *Australian Journal of Political Science*, 46(3): 407–23.

Walklate, Sandra 2007. *Imagining the Victim of Crime*. Maidenhead; New York: Open University Press.

White, Jenny 2013. *Muslim Nationalism and the New Turks*. Princeton, NJ: Princeton University Press.

10

INTERNATIONALIZING HATE CRIME AND THE PROBLEM OF THE INTRACTABLE STATE: THE CASE OF IRELAND

Amanda Haynes and Jennifer Schweppe

INTRODUCTION

The law can, 'by its silences', exclude groups from protection afforded to others, such as through the failure to include characteristics like sexual orientation or gender in hate crime legislation, leaving the unnamed groups vulnerable to hate crime and to the 'ideological effect of indicating that they are unworthy of protection, and therefore legitimate victims' (Perry 2001: 198). In legislating for those who are recognized as a 'legitimate' victim, the state, Perry argues, 'tells a story' with the moral that it is 'acceptable to assault the legislatively unnamed victim' (2001: 207). She suggests that this approach creates a legislative justification for the 'violent marginalization' of excluded groups, and in the context of the exclusion of gender, sends the message that women are seen as 'individual rather than collective victims' (2001: 210). This exclusion then permeates the organs of the state, leaving those who are isolated by hate crime legislation unprotected by those tasked with defending them (Perry 2001). Certainly, such exclusions can be understood to construct some victims and some communities as less worthy of protection than others.

What then of a system where there is no hate crime legislation? In Ireland, the only relevant legislation prohibits hate speech, is drawn narrowly, and has limited (if any) effect (ECRI 2002, 2007). Nonetheless, the Irish State has thus far rejected calls from both domestic and international sources to introduce legislation which would recognize the hate element of other offences. From the perspective of victims and commonly targeted communities, we argue, this absence of hate crime legislation can also be understood as a legislative 'permission to hate'.

This chapter will examine the character, effectiveness, and interrelationship of international and national critiques of Ireland's legislative 'permission to hate'. Ireland has been intractable in its position that the system is fully capable of addressing hate crime, while lacking a statutory provision requiring it to do so. Research recently completed by the authors of this chapter dispatches this notion, finding that the hate element of crime is effectively 'disappeared' at multiple points in the criminal justice process (Haynes et al. 2015). Nonetheless, we will show that neither internal nor international pressure to address the legislative lacuna have been successful, raising questions regarding the possibility of globalizing responses to hate crime in the face of seemingly impassive state intransigence.

METHODOLOGY

The analysis presented here is informed by original research conducted by the Hate and Hostility Research Group (HHRG) at the University of Limerick, funded by the Irish Council for Civil Liberties and supported by a consortium of civil society organizations[1] (Haynes et al. 2015). This year-long project on the need for, and potential form of, hate crime legislation in Ireland incorporated a comparative analysis of the form and operation of legislation in a number of common law jurisdictions, the analysis of hate crime reports received by leading civil society actors—the European Network Against Racism (ENAR) Ireland; the Gay and Lesbian Equality Network (GLEN); and Transgender Equality Network Ireland (TENI); and (by the time of writing) seventy-seven qualitative interviews with twelve victims of hate crime, representatives of twenty-two civil society organizations, twenty-two criminal justice practitioners, eleven members of An Garda Síochána (the Irish police service), probation officers, and a number of other relevant experts. A postal survey was also completed by thirty-six barristers receiving significant legal aid payments from the state. The information provided by survey respondents was helpful in identifying current practice as well as in developing questions for the qualitative phase of the research. At the time of writing, the research had resulted in the drafting of Heads of Bill[2] for hate crime legislation, launched in July 2015 and a report presenting preliminary findings (Haynes et al. 2015).

CURRENT LEGAL POSITION

In Ireland, the only legislative recognition of 'hate' is through the Prohibition of Incitement to Hatred Act 1989. This Act prohibits expressions, including the dissemination of graphic or textual materials, which have the intention of provoking hatred against '... a group of persons in the State or elsewhere on account of their

---

[1] The organizations involved were: Doras Luimní, the European Network Against Racism Ireland, the Gay and Lesbian Equality Network, the Immigrant Council of Ireland, Inclusion Ireland, the Irish Council for Civil Liberties, the Irish Refugee Council, the Irish Traveller Movement, NASC, Pavee Point, the Public Interest Law Alliance, Sport Against Racism Ireland, and Transgender Equality Network Ireland.

[2] Heads of Bill contain the basic framework and are often published prior to the publication of the Bill proper, in an effort to engage in a consultative process with stakeholders.

race, colour, nationality, religion, ethnic or national origins, membership of the travelling community or sexual orientation'. At the time of its enactment, it was relatively progressive, including sexual orientation as a protected characteristic prior to the decriminalization of homosexuality in 1993 (Schweppe et al. 2014). However, it has proved utterly ineffective at combating hate crime, with only a small number of convictions secured under the Act (ECRI 2007: 11). This is to be expected, given its context and purpose, but Taylor observes what he calls '..."an expectations gap" and "a frustration gap" between community aspirations from this [the 1989] legislation and the reality of its limited application and implementation to date...[which he argues potentially]...undermines social cohesion, and a sense of the system working for all' (Taylor 2011: para 5.2.21). This is reflected in the findings of Schweppe et al. (2014: 24–5), which found civil society organizations explicitly referencing the inadequacy of the 1989 Act in combating hate crime. Members of the Gardaí (the national police service) recognized the limitations of the Act:

Sure you can see from the amount of prosecutions taken, is it successful? No it's not. Has it been of benefit? Not really, like, you know? It takes a lot to get a charge out of it...It isn't strong enough in relation to individual issues and problems, and you know, we're just leaning back on other acts that were there that don't probably encompass the actual ingredients of the crime that was done. (Haynes et al. 2015: 51)

Thus, the only legislative recognition of 'hate' in Irish criminal law is through the limited 1989 Act.

Hate crime, that is, '...criminal offences committed with a bias motive' (OSCE 2009: 1), is not specifically proscribed in any way in Irish criminal law. The sentencing system in Ireland is an absolutely discretionary one, with few limitations and even less guidance given either by the legislature or the appellate courts on sentencing issues. Courts are fiercely protective of their discretion, and have traditionally been slow to impose any structure or guidance on sentencing practices in lower courts. There are currently no guidelines in the context of hate-motivated offences, and the Irish Sentencing Information System offers no advice as to how such offences have been sentenced in the past. Irish courts have yet to issue a guideline judgment to the effect that where an attack appears to have been motivated or aggravated by hate, that fact should be treated as an aggravating factor. Indeed, it was only very recently that the Irish courts addressed the sentencing of racist crime in a way which is compatible which its obligations under international human rights law (which will be outlined in the following sections). In *Director of Public Prosecutions v Elders* (2014) Birmingham J observed:

Among the very many aggravating factors present were that there was a racist dimension, an aspect that was very properly highlighted by the Circuit Court judge. It may be that as counsel for the appellant said that this was not the case where someone was attacked because of their race, but that there was a racist dimension is nonetheless clear and that is an aggravated fact.[3]

[3] Ibid para 11.

Despite this indication from the courts that a hate motivation should be treated seriously, there is no *obligation* on a sentencing judge to treat a hate motivation as an aggravating factor, nor indeed is the language of hate crime used in a formal sense throughout the criminal justice system. As we will see, this absence means that the criminal justice system is, for all intents and purposes, blind to hate motivation and unsure as to how to address it when it is exposed. This failure to explicitly address hate crime through legislation has not gone unnoticed by the international community. It has been discussed and critiqued internally by a number of civil society organizations for a number of years.

INTERNAL CHALLENGES TO
THE LEGISLATIVE LACUNA

Internal pressure to introduce hate crime legislation in Ireland has been mounting since the late 2000s with a variety of civil society organizations campaigning and lobbying for change. This work occurred in silos, by organizations representing particular community groups such as the European Network Against Racism Ireland, Johnny (gay peer action group), Transgender Equality Network Ireland, and NASC (the Irish Immigrant Support Centre). These groups engage in both research and lobbying to highlight the legislative lacuna. They published reports on, for example, the prevalence of racist incidents and the capacity of existing legislation to address racist crime (NASC 2012) and the prevalence and impact of homophobic hate crime (Johnny 2006). When the National Consultative Committee on Racism and Interculturalism (NCCRI) closed as a result of budget cuts, civil society organizations introduced online hate crime monitoring systems to replace the one previously run by the NCCRI (ENAR Ireland, GLEN, TENI). Since 2013, the establishment of these third-party reporting mechanisms and regular research reports based on this data have also been key to the gathering momentum for change (see for example O'Curry 2015).[4]

In critiquing the position of the Irish State, supranational bodies draw upon national level actors' outputs. In turn, national organizations use the outputs of supranational actors to bolster their own arguments for reform. More fundamentally, many national civil society organizations depend upon international funding streams to finance work in the area of hate crime.[5] The newness of research on hate crime in the Irish jurisdiction means that lobbyists must also draw on transferable findings from other countries to support their arguments, for example Ireland has not engaged in a national-level research on crime victimization survey since 2006 (National Crime Council 2015). More generally, Irish civil society organizations and

---

[4] In 2011 Ireland's Equality Authority also published an issues paper entitled 'Responding to Racist Incidents and Racist Crimes in Ireland', authored by Séamus Taylor, and referenced earlier in this chapter as raising important questions regarding the adequacy of current legislation to addressing hate crime.

[5] See, e.g., ENAR Ireland 2012 and TENI 2012.

researchers have drawn upon an international language of hate crime, a language which, we argue, has been effective in facilitating advocates for a diverse range of identity groups to recognize and express common cause, creating a cross-sectoral platform for reform. The international critique of the Irish position will now be addressed.

INTERNATIONAL CHALLENGES TO THE LEGISLATIVE LACUNA

Ireland's failure to legislate against hate crime has repeatedly brought the State to the attention of a number of international organizations charged, inter alia, with ensuring the protection of minority groups. These bodies have in turn raised the omission with the Irish State in the context of its international obligations, and have, time and again, recommended legislative reform. One might have expected that the concerns raised by the international community would have provided the impetus required to ensure the Irish State act to protect victims of hate crime. This, unfortunately, has not been the case. The Irish example, as we will see, shows that in the absence of strong internal leadership on the issue, international pressure to act in the context of hate crime can be essentially ignored.

In its 2002 Report, the European Commission against Racism and Intolerance (ECRI) criticized Ireland's only existing piece of criminal legislation to specifically focus on hate—the Prohibition of Incitement to Hatred Act 1989—on the basis that it had resulted in very few prosecutions. Further, the Report referred to the manner in which racist offences were prosecuted under generic legislation such as the Public Order Act 1994 and noted the lack of specific criminal law provisions for hate offences. ECRI's criticism of the position of the Irish State took the form of encouragement to: '... introduce provisions specifically defining offences of a racist or xenophobic nature as racist acts and to introduce the possibility for courts to take into account racist motivation as an aggravating circumstance when sentencing' (ECRI 2002: 9).

In 2007, ECRI's report on Ireland again highlighted deficiencies in its criminal law provisions addressing racism and xenophobia, noting that the '... [1989] Act (as well as other relevant criminal legislation) need to be strengthened in order to provide for effective, proportionate and dissuasive sanctions' (ECRI 2007: 10). Addressing the issue of the treatment of racist and xenophobic motivations at sentencing, ECRI (ibid: 11) noted as problematic the discretionary manner in which judges in Ireland decide on taking racist aggravation into account and suggested that this process be put on a legislative footing in order to ensure racist crimes are treated differently to parallel offences. Again ECRI (ibid: 12) repeated a recommendation that the Irish State 'include in the criminal legislation provisions which allow for the racist motivation of a crime to be considered as an aggravating circumstance at sentencing and that they envisage providing that racist offences be defined as specific offences'.

In 2008, the EU introduced its Council Framework Decision on combating certain forms and expressions of racism and xenophobia by means of criminal law. The Framework Decision requires Member States, under Article 4, to 'take the necessary measures to ensure that racist and xenophobic motivation is considered an aggravating circumstance, or, alternatively that such motivation may be taken into consideration by the courts in the determination of the penalties' (Council of the European Union 2008: art. 4). The deadline for transposition was 28 November 2010. As we have observed (Haynes et al. 2015; Schweppe et al. 2014), Ireland is currently in breach of its obligations under the Framework Decision, and has been for nearly five years at the time of writing. The EU has not yet intervened to ensure its appropriate implementation.

In its 2006 Report, the Committee on the Elimination of Racial Discrimination (CERD) expressed concern that extant legislative measures were insufficient to meet the standards of the International Convention on the Elimination of All Forms of Racial Discrimination. A year following the transposition deadline for the Framework Decision, the United Nations Committee on the Elimination of Racial Discrimination (CERD 2011: point 19) highlighted its ongoing concern that 'the legislative framework in the State party does not cover all the elements of Article 4 of the Convention, and that racist motivation is not consistently taken into account by judges in sentencing for crime (Arts. 2 and 4)'. The actions commended to the Irish State included that a racist motivation be 'consistently taken into account as an aggravating factor in sentencing practice for criminal offences'. The Report twice highlights the importance of ensuring that where offenders are convicted of racist crimes they are 'punished with appropriate penalties' (CERD 2011: point 21 and 23).

Also in 2011, as part of the United Nations Human Rights Council's Universal Periodic Review (UPR) process, observers recommended that Irish authorities take steps to challenge racism, xenophobia, religious intolerance, and racial profiling through the introduction of legislation (United Nations Human Rights Council 2011). The UN Human Rights Council (2013) also examined Ireland's compliance with the International Covenant on Civil and Political Rights. In response to the advance list of issues raised by the Human Rights Committee, Ireland communicated that the 1989 Act and Ireland's compliance with the Framework Decision was scrutinized on an ongoing basis by the Council of the European Union and the European Commission and as such, Ireland would '... consider any proposals made by the Commission that would enhance the existing protections in the 1989 legislation' if it were required (UN Human Rights Committee 2014: 32).

Finally, the Organization for Security and Co-operation for Europe (OSCE) Office for Democratic Institutions and Human Rights (ODIHR) has been publishing reports on Member States' practices and legislation in relation to hate crime for almost a decade. During this time ODIHR has noted various instances of hate crime in the Irish context, including those of a racist, anti-Jewish, and homophobic character. ODIHR has criticized the potential in Ireland for inconsistency in enhanced sentencing for hate crime offences, given the discretionary manner in which this can be applied by judges. Reference is also made to the restrictive manner in which Ireland collects data on hate crime. In order to increase its utility, the need for sensitive data collection in relation to hate crime that details the situation of a diverse range of vulnerable communities is stressed. In relation to legislative measures, ODIHR has consistently underscored the need for specific legislation and enhanced punitive sentences if hate crime is to be challenged effectively (OSCE 2013). The OSCE Ministerial Decision No.9/09 made in 2009 is particularly relevant in this regard. It explicitly encourages Member States, in addition to ensuring thorough investigative practices and comprehensive data collection, to '[e]nact, where appropriate, specific, tailored legislation to combat hate crimes, providing for effective penalties that take into account the gravity of such crimes' (Organization for Security and Co-operation in Europe Ministerial Council 2009: 2).

THE RESPONSE OF THE IRISH STATE

Although, in 2007, the Irish State's response to international scrutiny of its legislative framework in relation to hate crime indicated an acknowledgement of shortfalls in its criminal law provisions, by the early years of the economic downturn this stance had changed to one of defensiveness and intransigence. The State refuses to accept the problematic nature of Ireland's current legislative position, arguing that the legal system is currently addressing hate crime appropriately. These assertions are made without supporting evidence, and show that, in the absence of enforcement mechanisms at an international level, a country can simply ignore international pressure to address hate crime in any meaningful way.

In its 2009 *Combined Third and Fourth Reports by Ireland*, the Irish State responded to CERD's criticisms of the sufficiency of its legislative provisions in regards to racist crime by noting that it was not required to transpose the Convention into domestic law and argued that, in any case, its existing provisions were adequate (Office of the Minister for Integration 2009: 18). The Irish State also drew on the conclusions of a Report co-authored by one of the writers of this chapter to argue that as educative and other flanking measures would also be necessary to address racism, the criminal law should not be reformed. Schweppe and Walsh's report had in fact highlighted a concern '... that judges are at present *not* considering racism as an aggravating factor and indeed some feel it *cannot* be considered as an aggravating factor under present law' (Schweppe and Walsh 2008: 4, emphasis in original) and recommended civil society measures as part of a larger, holistic approach to combating racism and xenophobia. It is worth noting that by 2011, CERD found it necessary to lament the impact of the Irish government's budgetary choices upon the State's equality infrastructure (refuted by the State; see CERD 2012). The State has not funded a National Action Plan Against Racism since 2008 (Holland 2015). Although Schweppe and Walsh (2008) recommended the introduction of legislation which would require a hate element to be treated as an aggravating circumstance at sentencing, the State argued that even this minimal reform would have ramifications for broader criminal law and as such stated that no plans were being made for the introduction of statutory provisions on aggravated sentencing (Office for the Promotion of Migrant

Integration 2014). Further, in its follow-up observations to the UNCERD Report, Ireland stated that 'the introduction of racially aggravated sentencing would involve a restructuring of penalties for basic criminal offences (assault or criminal damage, for example) to increase sentences and have wider implications for the criminal law' (CERD 2012: 3). This assertion is patently untrue: requiring a court to treat a hate motivation as an aggravating factor in sentencing does not necessitate any restructuring of penalties.

In its fourth and most recent report on Ireland in 2013, ECRI attributes statements to the Department of Justice, Equality and Law Reform which are ostensibly more defensive than in 2007. ECRI (2013: 12) notes that the Department, having conducted a review of the 1989 Act, characterized the jurisdiction's incitement to hatred provisions as 'sufficiently robust'. More significantly, the Report notes the Department's assertion that '...Ireland was in compliance with the Framework Decision 2008/913/JHA on combating certain forms and expressions of racism and xenophobia by means of criminal law by virtue of the provisions in its existing criminal law—Prohibition of Incitement to Hatred Act 1989 and public order legislation'. Clearly disagreeing with this assessment, ECRI again highlights Ireland's failure to introduce aggravated offences or place aggravated sentencing on a legislative footing. The Commission reiterates the point that leaving the aggravation of sentences on the basis of racist motivation entirely at the discretion of the judiciary is insufficient. Citing a CERD report from 2011, ECRI adds the finding that '...according to various sources, the racist motivation was not consistently taken into account by judges when sentencing' (ECRI 2013: 13), a conclusion which HHRG research also supports (Haynes, Schweppe, Carr, Carmody, and Enright 2015).

In March 2014, in response to the United Nations Human Rights Council's UPR, the Irish State published an interim report, which again argued that existing legislation (the 1989 Act) was fit for purpose and that the established generic criminal law is sufficient to the task at hand. Furthermore, the State argued that the judiciary do consider racist or xenophobic motivations at sentencing, as robust measures were already in place in Ireland to challenge hate crime (Government of Ireland 2014). No evidence was presented to support these conclusions regarding sentencing practices. Equally, Ireland's response to OSCE criticisms has been to argue that Ireland is fully compliant with its international obligations.

In responding to its obligations under Article 4 of the EU framework decision of 2008, Ireland has simply stated that 'motivation can always be considered by the courts' (European Commission 2014: 7). It remains to be seen whether infringement proceedings will be taken against Ireland in this context, though this dismissive attitude by the State to its international obligations is now part of an established pattern.

In summary, the response of Ireland has been to argue:

Generic criminal offences are sufficient to combat hate crime and the courts do consider racist or xenophobic motivations at sentencing (though they have provided no evidence that this is the case);

The criminal law alone would be insufficient to challenge hate crime which requires a broader educative measure to combat it;

Introducing aggravated sentencing provisions would have broader ramifications for the criminal law, including a restructuring of penalties for basic offences.

The approach of the Irish State in respect of international pressure to, at the very least, *recognize* hate crime is lamentable. The State's position seems to suggest that the Irish legal system, and the Irish criminal law, are so peculiar that it is not possible to introduce hate crime legislation: not only that, but so particular is the system that it is capable of recognizing hate, protecting victims, and punishing offenders without specific hate crime laws. This position is clearly untenable. Our closest neighbours, Northern Ireland and England and Wales, who have similar legal systems, clearly recognize and demonstrate the need for legislation to address hate in its many manifestations. In the context of the globalization of hate, the Irish case demonstrates a significant barrier to internationalizing responses to combating hate: where a state erroneously insists that its legislative position is in compliance with international law and is utterly intractable in this position, there is very little that can be done to rectify the situation.

REFUTING THE POSITION OF THE IRISH STATE (1): CONFLICT BETWEEN OFFICIAL AND CENTRAL STATISTICS OFFICE (CSO) DATA

In the absence of legislative provisions to address hate crime there is no incentive or need for the Irish criminal justice system to record hate crime. Nonetheless, the Irish police service has incorporated a number of markers into its crime recording software, which permit the flagging of hate crime. These markers, selected from a wide-ranging menu of motivations, consist of racism and xenophobia, antisemitism, sectarianism, and homophobia (Haynes et al. 2015).

Official statistics based on police recorded data and supplied by Ireland's CSO show that in 2013 there were 113 hate crimes recorded: ninety-four of which were manifestations of racism and xenophobia; two of which were antisemitic; and seventeen of which were homophobic. The total figure for police recorded hate crime drops to fifty-three for 2014 (CSO 2015). It is widely accepted, including by Garda interviewees, that these figures are in no way representative of the true levels of criminality in this context. For example, if we look at civil society reporting mechanisms, and even excluding incitement to hatred offences, the European Network Against Racism Ireland recorded 137 racist or religiously aggravated crimes in 2014 (including forty assaults); the Gay and Lesbian Equality Network recorded a further nineteen homophobic/transphobic crimes for a seven-month period from December 2014 to June 2015 (including eleven assaults); and Transgender Equality Network Ireland recorded an additional twenty-two transphobic crimes in 2014 (including six assaults, three sexual assaults and one aggravated sexual assault).

In a Report published in 2014, Ireland's Garda (Police) Inspectorate (2014: 45) notes: 'During inspection visits, the Inspectorate asked gardaí of all ranks about investigating racist and homophobic crimes and not one garda reported that they had ever recorded such a crime or investigated an offence.'

Thus, at the first stage in the criminal process, that is, the recording and reporting of hate crime, the statistics show that there is a clear disconnect between the experiences of victims on the one hand, and the official position of the state in terms of levels of hate crime.

REFUTING THE POSITION OF THE IRISH STATE (2): BRINGING HATE CRIME 'OUT OF THE SHADOWS'

As we have seen, internal pressure to introduce hate crime legislation in Ireland has been mounting since the late 2000s, with a variety of civil society organizations campaigning and lobbying for change. These groups were brought together in an 'NGO Working Group on Hate Crime' by Aodhán Ó Ríordáin TD,[6] then a backbench politician in the Labour Party, in an effort to consolidate the position of a number of civil society organizations and determine a strategy for addressing hate crime. Concurrently, research was being carried out which sought to establish the views of civil society organizations on the need for hate crime legislation (Schweppe et al. 2014). A month following the publication of this Report, the Irish Council for Civil Liberties brought together PILA (the Public Interest Law Alliance), TENI, NASC (the Irish Immigrant Support Centre), ENAR Ireland, GLEN, the Irish Traveller Movement, Pavee Point, Inclusion Ireland, the Immigrant Council of Ireland, Doras Luimní, Sports Against Racism Ireland, and the Irish Refugee Council for a roundtable discussion, hosted by the HHRG at the University of Limerick to develop a strategy for consolidating views and moving the agenda forwards. This roundtable was chaired by Aodhán Ó Ríordáin TD, who had by that time been appointed Minister of State with special responsibility for Equality, New Communities and Culture. With full support from all the civil society organizations present, the Irish Council for Civil Liberties funded the HHRG to conduct research investigating the need for reform and the form of legislation which would be best suited to the Irish criminal law.

As we have seen, hate crime as commonly understood (a criminal act committed with a hate element) is not specifically proscribed in Irish criminal law. In our research, the HHRG sought to unpick the claims of the State that the legal system was fully capable of addressing a hate crime in the absence of legislation. In this context, the primary claim we sought to address was that 'generic criminal offences are sufficient to combat hate crime and the courts do consider racist or xenophobic motivations at sentencing'. In this context, we examined the manner in which the legal

---

[6] TD stands for Teachta Dála, which translates as Member of Parliament.

system as a whole defined and understood hate crime at three key stages: recording of the hate element by An Garda Síochána; the prosecution of the hate element; and the sentencing of the hate element. The following sections detail the findings of the research, showing how the hate element is hidden in the shadows of the Irish criminal justice system.

RECORDING THE HATE ELEMENT

Despite protestations by the State to the contrary, our research found that the failure, in Ireland, to criminalize the hate element of a crime means that the term 'hate crime' is not part of the language of the Irish police service. Few members of the police service have any training in hate crime or its recording, investigation, or prosecution. In terms of policy and directives, members of the police service have access to one formal directive on the definition of a racist incident (dating from 2006): The Garda Inspectorate Report *Crime Investigation* (2014: Part 6, 45) observes that the Garda definition of a racist or homophobic incident is that which is used in the United Kingdom—often known as the 'Macpherson definition' and is: 'any incident which is perceived to be racist by the victim or any other person' (Macpherson 1999: section 45.17). There is no access to specific policy or directives relating to homophobic, transphobic, or disablist hate crime among other manifestations. While it is possible to flag a racist, xenophobic, sectarian, antisemitic, or homophobic motivation on the police national crime database, this is not carried out consistently. We found that even the ethnic liaison and LGBT liaison officers to whom we spoke had not always assimilated an accurate understanding of the Macpherson test into their policing practice (Haynes et al. 2015).

One police officer succinctly summarized the myriad of issues which might impact on this first task of the system in recognizing the hate element—that is, recording a hate crime appropriately:

You're relying on three groups of people to have it recorded. So those three groups of people: ... the victim ... may not be aware [it's a hate crime]; the gard probably won't have it in their head, they'll just see this as a crime, they'll look for criminal evidence; and then you have the person who records it on the system ... who probably isn't aware of what a hate crime is anyway ... They'll have even less of an understanding. Then you come to the fourth group of people which is at management level, and is there a management understanding this is even a thing? So when you don't have management constantly reviewing, like they do in the UK, the hate crimes that happen in an area, looking for [those] crimes, following them up, making sure something's done about them ... we're back to what's measured is done. This stuff isn't measured, it's not done.

Thus, the language of hate crime is absent even from this initial stage in the process, and oftentimes the hate element will be lost or 'disappeared' even at the initial point of recording.

INVESTIGATION AND PROSECUTION OF THE HATE ELEMENT

Police officers to whom we spoke differed as to whether the hate element of a crime is investigated if it is recognized by the investigating officer. Some held that it would attract the attention of management, others held that officers prioritize those aspects of the crime which must be proven for the prosecution to be successful; because standard charges are employed, this does not automatically include the hate element of the crime. Indeed, even in regard to public order charges to which language demonstrating bias might be central, the specifics of the offender's demonstration of bias might be summarized and 'disappeared' as 'abusive' (Haynes et al. 2015).

In the absence of effective substantive offences addressing hate crime, the base offences which members of Ireland's police service commonly use to address crimes involving a bias-related motivation include:

Assault
Harassment
Criminal Damage
Public Order Offences
Threats to Life

Using standard offences means that the hate element of the crime is not named in, or otherwise apparent from, the charge. In other jurisdictions this is addressed through proactively flagging possible hate motivations or demonstrations of hate (College of Policing 2014) and through the provision of guidance to police officers and prosecutors as to the responsibilities and tools which accrue to them in processing a hate crime (see, e.g., Crown Prosecution Service 2015).

Given that there will be cases in which the hate element of a crime will not be apparent either from the charge brought nor in the evidence gathered, the hate-related aspects of a crime may never reach court. Interviews with legal professionals demonstrated that even where the hate element of a crime has been investigated it may still be excluded from proceedings; first, where it is pleaded out; second, where it is deemed inadmissible because it is held to be prejudicial to the case; and finally, where the hate element is 'coded' during the course of the trial—for example professionals spoke of euphemizing the act as an 'egregious' offence, rather than naming it as a hate crime (Haynes et al. 2015).

SENTENCING THE HATE ELEMENT

Members of the judiciary can only sentence on what is before them, and as we have shown, the hate element of crimes is often disappeared before and during the court process. Where it is successfully raised in court, there is no obligation on members of the judiciary to enhance a sentence due to the presence of a hate motivation during the course of the commission of an offence (Schweppe et al. 2014). Again, the position of the Irish State is that though there is no requirement for judges to aggravate a sentence where a hate element is present, this is done routinely and as a matter of course. Our research found that this is not the case.

Both our survey of barristers and our interviews with criminal justice practitioners reflect a lack of clarity amongst, and considerable inconsistency between, criminal justice professionals regarding the response of the judiciary to hate crime. It is clear that some judges treat the hate element of a crime very seriously and will consistently and appropriately aggravate the sentence when it is present.

Well it's straight away an aggravating factor. There is…like what I'd say about this bringing in hate crime legislation and things like that it's obviously an aggravating factor and it's already treated by the courts as an aggravating factor.

A minority of interviewees and respondents held that a hate motivation will not typically be seen as an aggravating factor at sentencing with this interviewee being adamant in their position:

Interviewer: Do you think that hate is currently treated as an aggravating factor? Interviewee: No. It is not. It certainly is not. (Solicitor)

A significant number of interviewees perceived the hate element to be treated as an aggravating factor but said that it was not always stated clearly by the judge to be such an aggravating factor. Thus, in the same way that the hate element can be 'coded', the aggravating element of the penalty can also be coded:

That it may be that even as an aggravating factor it will be unspoken and you know, that will be a feature.

In the absence of legislation, we argue that the Irish criminal justice system lacks the internal impetus to introduce the measures required to ensure that the hate element of crimes are adequately addressed. The consequence of an absence of legislation and the internal structures it would provide is the progressive 'disappearing' of the hate element of the crime. It is important to note that no one organization or policy is at fault in this process. It is a system-wide failure to recognize the harms of hate: this systematic blindness results in the 'disappearing' of the hate element of crimes at multiple points in the criminal justice process, and consequently a failure to provide victims with appropriate protection under the law. The position of the State that the system is capable of addressing hate crime in the absence of statutory provisions is now simply untenable.

IMPACT ON VICTIMS AND THEIR COMMUNITIES

Asides from the impact of the absence of hate crime legislation on the criminal justice system, we also sought to assess the effect of a legislative permission to hate on victims and their communities. International research tells us that hate crime is a message crime. The targeting of victims on the basis of their social group member-ship communicates to all members of that group that they are equally at risk and that they do not belong (Perry 2003). Indeed, the targeted community must be counted as secondary victims of the offender (Lawrence 1999; McDevitt, Balboni, Garcia, and Gu 2001; Perry and Alvi 2012).

Whether the intention is there or not they are perceived to be message crimes…I can just talk about a work shop I was giving last week with the South Circular Road Mosque and we were talking about the impacts. Individuals' behaviours have changed. Nine years after an incident people's behaviours are still different. People still live in fear and the whole community hears about it and starts to behave differently. I mean this is the stuff that mar-ginalises communities….I would actually argue that this is the key difference between hate crime and common garden [offences] is the impact on community relations. (Shane O'Curry, Director, ENAR Ireland)

Our research found that the consequences of unmitigated risk for commonly tar-geted communities include an inability to participate equally and fully in society, as danger is managed through self-segregation, self-censorship, and assimilation (Haynes et al. 2015). Permission to target difference without criminal censure is therefore a mechanism through which the privilege of the majority is maintained:

…when you expect that something is going to happen to you—when it does it's obviously horrific—but it doesn't perhaps have the same impact as it would to somebody who didn't expect it. Cos somebody who doesn't expect it would then go 'Absolutely, that's unaccept-able and I shouldn't have had to deal with that'…Whereas I think for a lot of trans people, and there are exceptions of course, but for a lot of trans people 'Ah well, it was just a matter of time really'. And that's totally unacceptable. (Broden Giambrone, TENI)

If hate crimes are 'symbolic crimes' (Perry 2003) that operate as an exclusionary practice, what message is conveyed by the decision on the part of a state not to crim-inalize the targeting of people on the basis of their difference? While hate crime has the potential to disseminate a message of unbelonging to a community, we argue that it is society's response to that communities' victimization that determines whether or not that message is believed and internalized:

…we have a history of treating ethnic minorities so badly in this country…one of the consequences of that is that there is then a disengagement by those ethnic minority groups from playing a full and active role in this society…(Solicitor)

Ireland's legislative permission to hate is deserving of the national and international criticism it has drawn; it could perhaps be understood as an additional harm to the hate crime it refuses to address:

…The thing people get most upset about is that this is continuing. I experience this but my children and grandchildren will also experience it. It's often times to protect the future generation. Upset obviously, anger…disappointment. Frustration, the people who worked in the area of lobbying for rights and equality all their lives, given their whole lives to it and then you see that happening. And you see people getting away with it. I think you can get very disappointed and very disillusioned. (Solicitor)

CONCLUSION

It would appear that the Irish State has yet to fully accept the case for the introduction of hate crime legislation in Ireland. Nonetheless, the evidence base in support of hate crime legislation is reaching critical mass. Certainly, it is now incredibly
difficult for the State to argue either that hate crime is not a problem in Ireland or
that existing criminal law is adequate to the task of addressing it. Combined with
mutually supportive national and international pressure to address the shortfall in
Ireland's legislative protections for victims of hate crime, it is difficult to see how the
State might maintain a position of intransigence. The Irish State has never proposed
an ideological opposition to the introduction of hate crimes laws. Rather it has always relied on technical arguments against its introduction. It will be interesting to
see if, when technical arguments are disposed of, legislation is enacted or ideological
objections are revealed.

The Irish Immigrant Support Centre, NASC, has argued that '...the robustness
nor otherwise of a state's policy and legislation in this sphere serves as a barometer
of a state's "concern" with racist crime' (NASC 2012: 12). Extending this argument
to hate crime more generally, we argue that the current refusal of the Irish State to
address hate crime legislatively (and one could argue in any fashion) is revealing
of the position of commonly targeted groups in Irish society generally and in the
mind-set of those parliamentarians and civil servants who argue that better legal
protection for victims of hate crime is unnecessary.

Despite strenuous efforts from both the international community and internal
civil society organizations, successive Irish governments have refused to even engage in a conversation about the problem of hate crime in Ireland. In the context
of a globalized effort to combat hate, the Irish example is cautionary: without clear
enforcement mechanisms and strong oversight, recalcitrant states like Ireland can
avoid introducing measures by simply stating that the domestic situation is compatible with international law. We hope that, given the provision of evidence to the
contrary, Ireland will no longer be in a position to make this assertion.

REFERENCES

Attride-Stirling, J. 2001. 'Thematic Networks: an Analytic Tool for Qualitative Research',
    Qualitative Research, 1(3), 385–405.
Central Statistics Office (CSO) 2015. Email communication.
CERD 2012. *Concluding observations of the Committee on the Elimination of
    Racial Discrimination—Ireland: Addendum: Information received from the
    Government of Ireland on the implementation of the concluding observations*
    (CERD/C/IRL/CO/3-4), 24 May 2012 available at http://tbinternet.ohchr.org/_
    layouts/treatybodyexternal/Download.aspx?symbolno=CERD%2fC%2fIRL%2
    fCO%2f3-4%2fAdd.1&Lang=en accessed: 21July 2015.

Committee on the Elimination of Racial Discrimination 2006. *Report: Visit of co-ordinator on follow-up to Ireland (21–23 June 2006)*, CERD/C/69//Misc.9

Committee on the Elimination of Racial Discrimination 2011. *Concluding observations of the Committee on the Elimination of Racial Discrimination: Ireland*, CERD/C/IRL/CO/3-4

Crown Prosecution Service 2015. http://www.cps.gov.uk/publications/equality/hate_crime/index.html

Director of Public Prosecutions v Elders [2014] IECA 6.

ENAR Ireland 2012. ENAR Shadow Report 2011–2012: Racism and Related discriminatory practices in Ireland, available at http://enarireland.org/wp-content/uploads/2013/06/ENAR-Ireland-Shadow-Report-2011-12.pdf accessed 22 July 2015.

European Commission 2014. *Report from the Commission to the European Parliament and the Council on the implementation of Council Framework Decision 2008/913/JHA on combating certain forms and expressions of racism and xenophobia by means of criminal law*, COM(2014) 27 final, Brussels: European Commission.

European Commission against Racism and Intolerance (ECRI) 2002. *Second Report on Ireland*, Strasbourg: Council of Europe.

European Commission against Racism and Intolerance (ECRI) 2007. *Third Report on Ireland*, Strasbourg: Council of Europe.

European Commission against Racism and Intolerance (ECRI) 2013. *Fourth Report on Ireland*, Strasbourg: Council of Europe.

Garda Inspectorate 2014. *Crime Investigation*, Dublin: Garda Inspectorate.

Government of Ireland 2014. *Universal Periodic Review—Ireland: National Interim Report*, Dublin: Department of Justice and Equality.

Hall, N. 2013. *Hate Crime*, 2nd ed. London: Routledge.

Haynes, A., Schweppe, J., Carr, J., Carmody, N., and Enright, S. 2015. *Out of the Shadows: Legislating for Hate Crime in Ireland*, Dublin: Irish Council for Civil Liberties.

Holland, K. 2015. 'Government "In Denial" over Reality of Racism in Ireland', *The Irish Times*, 21 March. http://www.independent.ie/lifestyle/attitudes-may-have-changed-but-gaybashing-still-happens-29358960.html

Irish Times 1983. 'Manslaughter Sentence Suspended on Five Youths', 9 March, p. 9

Johnny 2006. *2006 LGBT Hate Crime Report: Stop Hate Crimes in Ireland Campaign*, Dublin: Johnny available at http://www.glen.ie/attachments/Johnny_Report.PDF

Macpherson, W. 1999. *Inquiry into the Matters arising from the Death of Stephen Lawrence*, London: UK Home Office.

McDevitt, J., Balboni, J., Garcia, L., and Gu, J. 2001. 'Consequences for Victims: a Comparison of Bias and Non-bias Motivated Assaults', *American Behavioural Scientist*, 45(4), 697–713.

NASC 2012. Stop the Silence: A snapshot of racism in Cork, available at http://www.nascireland.org/wp-content/uploads/2012/02/NASC-Report.pdf accessed 22 July 2015.

National Crime Council 2015. *Crime and Victimisation Surveys*, available at http://www.crimecouncil.gov.ie/statistics_cri_victim.html accessed 22 July 2015.

O'Curry, S. 2015. 'Fight against Hate Crime Must Continue', *Irish Examiner*, 22 July 2015.

Office for the Promotion of Migrant Integration 2014. *Information on Ireland's follow-up to recommendations contained in the Concluding Observations of the United Nations Committee on the Elimination of Racial Discrimination (UNCERD) following examination of Ireland's combined 3rd and 4th periodic report by UNCERD*, available at http://www.integration.ie/website/omi/omiwebv6.nsf/page/AXBN-8VMK3F15323926-en/$File/Concluding%20Observations%20Recommendations%20Response.pdf accessed 21 July 2015.

Office of the Minister for Integration 2009. *United Nations International Convention on the Elimination of All Forms of Racial Discrimination: Combined Third and Fourth Reports by Ireland*, Dublin: Stationery Office.

Organization for Security and Co-operation in Europe 2013. *Hate Crimes in the OSCE Region: Incidents and Responses—Annual Report for 2012*, available at http://www.osce.org/odihr/108395 accessed 21 July 2015.

Organization for Security and Co-operation in Europe Ministerial Council 2009. *Decision No.9/09 Combating Hate Crimes*, available at http://www.osce.org/cio/40695?download-true accessed 21 July 2015.

Perry, B. 2003. 'Where Do We Go From Here? Researching Hate Crime', *Internet Journal of Criminology*, 3, 45–7.

Perry, B. and Alvi, S. 2012. '"We Are All Vulnerable": the *in terrorem* Effects of Hate Crimes' *International Review of Victimology*, 18(1), 57–71.

PILA 2014. 'Case Studies: Legal reform working group – hate crime legislation', available: http://www.pila.ie/case-studies/, accessed 22 July 2015.

Schweppe, J., Haynes, A., and Carr, J. 2014. *A Life Free from Fear. Legislating for Hate Crime in Ireland: An NGO Perspective*, Hate and Hostility Research Group, Limerick: HHRG/University of Limerick.

Taylor, S. 2011. *Responding to Racist Incidents and Crime: An Issues Paper for the Equality Authority*, Dublin: Equality Authority.

TENI 2012. Looking Forward to 2013, available at http://forum.transgender.ie/teni-f16/looking-forward-2013-t437.html accessed 22 July 2015.

TENI 2013. TENI Annual Report 2012–2013, Dublin: TENI.

United Nations Human Rights Committee 2013. *List of issues in relation to the fourth periodic report of Ireland*, CCPR/C/IRL/Q/4, available at http://www.rightsnow.ie/go/iccpr_4th_periodic_report/list_of_issues accessed 21 July 2015.

United Nations Human Rights Committee 2014. *List of Issues in relation to the fourth periodic report of Ireland, Addendum, Replies of Ireland to the list of issues*, CCPR/C/IRL/Q/4/Add.1, available at http://tbinternet.ohchr.org/_layouts/treaty bodyexternal/Download.aspx?symbolno=CCPR%2fC%2fIRL%2fQ%2f4%2fAdd.1&Lang=en accessed 21 July 2015.

United Nations Human Rights Council 2011. *Report of the Working Group on the Universal Periodic Review, Ireland*, A/HRC/19/9, available at http://www.upr-info.org/sites/default/files/document/ireland/session_12_-_october_2011/ahrc199ire-lande.pdf accessed: 21 July 2015.

11

DO SOME IDENTITIES DESERVE MORE PROTECTION THAN OTHERS? THE CASE OF ANTI-LGB HATE CRIME LAWS IN POLAND

Piotr Godzisz and Dorota Pudzianowska

INTRODUCTION

Across Europe, there is a vast disparity in the catalogues of characteristics protected by hate crime laws. While the need to combat violence based on racial, ethnic, and religious grounds (so-called hate crimes) has been recognized almost universally in Europe, there is a considerable difference in the response to crimes based on sexual orientation. Out of forty-nine European countries, twenty-six have hate crime legislation that includes sexual orientation as a protected characteristic (ILGA-Europe 2014). The fact that only some jurisdictions seek to legislate against hate crimes targeting lesbians, gay men, and bisexual (LGB) people gives rise to the question: what determines which characteristics are deserving of special protection in any given jurisdiction?

This question cannot be answered by simply evoking the East/West divide on the rights of LGB people in Europe (Godzisz 2015). In fact, the majority of societies in Central and Eastern Europe (CEE) include sexual orientation in their legislation, yet Poland does not, despite the high level of reported victimization of LGB people there (EU FRA 2013). The level of prejudice towards various minority groups does not answer the question either. Poland, whose population is suspicious of a range of Others (Antosz 2012; Bilewicz et al. 2014), protects people from racist, xenophobic, and religious violence. The aim of this chapter is, therefore, to examine how victim groups are, or might be, selected for protection. In doing so, the chapter seeks to critique the applicability of Western hate crime models in a post-Communist, CEE country, and highlight how exclusionary discourses in Poland are different from those in the United States (US) and the United Kingdom (UK).[1]

---

[1] We would like to thank representatives of Campaign against Homophobia, Polish Association of Antidiscrimination Law, Association 'The Diversity Workshop', Robert Biedroń and Adam Bodnar for the information that they provided in the course of preparing this chapter.

While acknowledging that some anti-LGB narratives in Poland are similar to those in the US/UK, we argue that there are important differences which can help explain why adding sexual orientation to hate crime law in this country has proven so difficult. In particular, we argue that, next to high levels of societal homophobia,[2] these difficulties can be linked to the historicism of the legislation on targeted violence; as well as the fact that adding sexual orientation to the hate crime law is seen through the lens of Europeanization, thus imposing foreign norms on Poland.

This chapter is divided into four sections. In the first part, we briefly review the current academic debate on (not) protecting LGB people. Next, we analyse the construction of homosexuality in Poland as a threat. In the third part, we analyse how this construction feeds into the debate on the expansion of existing legislation,[3] showing the resistance to internationalization of hate crime. In the last part, we provide a discussion on the specific understanding of hate crimes in Poland, focusing on how legitimate categories of protection are constructed and why implementing the international model has not been successful so far.

CATEGORIES OF PROTECTION

While laws aimed at protecting racial, ethnic, and religious minorities have a long history in the US and parts of Europe, what we know today as the anti-hate crime movement emerged in the 1980s and 1990s in the US (Jenness 2002: 18), following the convergence of the civil rights and victim rights movement (Maroney 1998: 564), as well as the identity politics of minority groups (Jacobs and Potter 1998). The rapid proliferation of the concept was possible thanks, inter alia, to the strong symbolic function of hate crime laws, which expresses the official condemnation of prejudice-motivated violence (see, e.g., Gerstenfeld 2004; Iganski 2008; Jenness and Grattet 2001; Mason 2014a). In addition, a range of other variables, such as high-profile hate crime cases, highlighted the seriousness of the problem (for a recent discussion, see Mason 2014a, 2014b).

In the US (and, subsequently, in the UK and other countries), thanks to the expansion of policy and scholarly activities, violence targeting minorities was put high on the political agenda. Race and ethnic origin, followed closely by religion, became the first grounds to be protected. After the institutionalization of hate crime laws, some jurisdictions further expanded the catalogue of protected grounds to punish more bias motives. As a result, increasingly from the end of the 1990s, a second tier of categories, including sexual orientation, gender identity, and disability have been recognized by policymakers as 'axes along which hate-motivated violence, and thus hate crime, occur' (Jenness 2002: 28). More recently, a number of jurisdictions have started to recognize crimes based on other bias motives, such as hostilities demonstrated towards alternative subcultures (Garland and Hodkinson 2015).

[2] Throughout this chapter, the terms 'homophobia' and 'homophobic' are used to describe the negative sentiment against both homo- and bisexual people.

[3] We present and analyze the debate that took place in Poland before parliamentary elections in October 2015.

The political and historical justifications for how victim groups have been selected for protection in the US and the UK have been well analysed (see, e.g., Chakraborti and Garland 2012; Jacobs and Potter 1998; Jenness and Grattet 2001). In principle, the protected categories relate to groups which (1) can be identified as a 'community'; and (2) have a history of oppression, usually supported by identity politics. Even though LGB rights advocates have been among the strongest supporters of introducing hate crime laws across the globe since the beginning of the hate crime movement (Jenness 2002: 28), the inclusion of sexual orientation has rarely been straightforward. Mason expounds upon this by saying that LGB people 'fall short of the image of the *ideal victim* capable of contributing to the symbolic function of these laws and, hence, deserving of the legal protection they purportedly offer' (2014a: 77, our emphasis). There are many reasons why LGB people, unlike racial or religious minorities, fail to pass as ideal victims. Opposition to the inclusion of sexual orientation in hate crime laws can be seen as part of the general anti-LGB (or homophobic) discourse, which vilifies homosexuality as (1) being against nature, religion, and social norms (Boswell 1981; Mosse 1985); (2) being a threat to the hegemonic masculinity (Connell 1987, [1995] 2005; Nagel 1998); and (3) being an 'improper' way of doing gender (Perry 2001; West and Zimmerman 1987). For these reasons, throughout history, sexual minorities in Europe (and often elsewhere) were constructed as deviant and threats to the 'normal', Christian, and heterosexual community (see, e.g., Boswell 1981: 15–16).

Consequently, the moral panic connected with 'legitimizing' homosexuality could be observed when initial attempts were made to add sexual orientation to hate crime laws in the US (Perry 2001: 207–8) and in the UK (Law Commission 2013: 56). For example, during the debate on the Hate Crime Statistics Act (1990) in the US Congress, one of the senators wanted to add an amendment which 'condemned homosexuality, rejected it as a lifestyle, condemned government support for extending civil rights to homosexuals, and called for strict enforcement of state sodomy laws' (Jacobs and Potter 1998: 71). Debates in the UK echoed those in the US, with additional critique that 'the very idea of a hate crime was ridiculous and misleading, and tended to the importation of a transatlantic idea of group rights' (Law Commission 2013: 56).

Another argument that has been used to resist the inclusion of sexual orientation is that it limits the freedom of expression of those critical of homosexuality. In fact, some critics in the US challenged the entire idea of hate crime laws as unconstitutional (Jacobs and Potter 1998: 121). This argument is countered by advocates such as Lieberman and Freeman, who argue that well-written laws criminalize conduct, not thought (2009: 2). In Europe, however, the situation is more cumbersome, as hate crime provisions are often conflated with prohibition of hate speech. Nevertheless, proponents argue that even criminalization of the latter does not restrict freedom of speech (Iganski 2014).

POLITICAL HOMOPHOBIA IN POLAND

Despite increased acceptance of homosexuality in the Western world over the past few decades, some European nations have taken longer to 'accept' sexual orientation as a characteristic deserving of legislative protection. In particular, this is the case in countries where the Catholic Church remains dominant, social diversity is low, and where there remains a national perception of an 'ethnic collective', rather than a political community. Poland, even though it was quite early in decriminalizing homosexuality (President of the Republic of Poland 1932), is an example of such a country.[4]

LGB people, at least as an interest group with specific demands, have been largely invisible to the heterosexual majority in Poland until quite recently. In the 1990s the issue that divided the 'moral Poles' from the 'immoral West' was abortion (Graff 2006). Sexual minorities and their rights became an important topic of public debate only around 2003, following the establishment of the first advocacy groups. The beginning of their identity politics, coupled with the decline of acceptance of antisemitism, correlates with the emergence of political discourse vilifying sexual minorities as major 'threatening Others' (Ostolski 2007).

Some of the most prevalent themes and tropes in Polish political discourse are similar to those in other countries and can be seen both in the parliamentary discussions and at anti-LGB events (such as that during the 2013 Equality Parade in Warsaw, pictured in Figure 11.1 below). For instance, LGB people are ostracized for blurring the gender dichotomy. At the same time, same-sex relationships are portrayed as 'inferior' to heterosexual unions. For example, during the parliamentary debate on registered partnerships on 24 January 2013, Krystyna Pawłowicz, prominent MP of the Law and Justice party (PiS), asserted that Polish society 'cannot fund a sweet life to unstable, barren unions' of LGB people.[5]

What is more specific to CEE is the vilification of homosexuality, which is seen as a Western (European) 'import', incompatible with national norms (Graff 2010: 597). O'Dwyer and Schwartz (2010), who analysed Polish political homophobia in the context of Europeanization, point to the weakness of what they call 'EU conditionality' (in terms of rights of sexual minorities), which was unable to overcome 'resonance', 'weakly institutionalised party systems', and the understanding of national identity (ibid: 220). In this sense, what they call the 'anti-gay mobilisation' of the 2000s can be explained as a failure of the process of Europeanization of values.

With regard to national identity, authors observe that accepting Otherness in Poland is particularly difficult because the Polish national identity is conflated with Catholicism (Krzemiński 2001; for discussion see, e.g., Zubrzycki 2007). As a result, being gay (or bisexual) is viewed by many as antithetical to being Polish.[6] In this sense, LGB people, seen as sinful, are systematically excluded from mainstream society. Research indicates that this type of narrative is present in a number of CEE countries (Mole 2011), but is not typically present in nations which see themselves in political rather than ethnic

---

[4] Poland is a country with an almost homogenous population, where the vast majority of people are white, ethnically Polish, and Catholic. According to the recent census, about 99.7 per cent of the residents of the country hold Polish citizenship, 94.8 per cent declare Polish national belonging, and about 87.2 per cent declare Catholic faith (GUS 2013). See the work of Schöpflin (1995) for discussion on the civic and ethnic understanding of nationality.

[5] All translations in this chapter are ours. All official documents related to the legislative procedure mentioned in this chapter are available (in Polish) at http://www.sejm.gov.pl/

[6] Similarly to being Polish as well as Jewish: openly gay politician Robert Biedroń said, recalling his mayoral campaign: 'A woman on the street began to shout that a gay man cannot be the mayor. Then she shouted that a Jew, too, cannot be the mayor. I asked: "Why?" She said: "Because only a Pole can be the mayor." As if a gay man or a Jew could not be a Pole' (Stolarska 2014).

Figure 11.1 Anti-LGB protest during the 2013 Warsaw Equality Parade. The black slogan reads 'Not red, not rainbow, but national Poland'. The white slogan on the right says 'We want men, not poofs' (with a spelling mistake in Polish). On the bottom, the graph is known as 'ban of faggoting'. The protesters chanted 'A real family—a man and a woman'.

© Piotr Godzisz.

terms (Stychin 1997). At the same time, it is a regional variation of the argument about the 'foreignness' of homosexuality and denial of citizenship to sexual minorities (see, e.g., Richardson 1998: 91). The above themes, centred on the 'deviant' character of homosexuality, continue to be visible in the debates surrounding LGB rights in Poland, including the debate on the expansion of the hate crime provisions, analysed below.

HATE CRIME LAWS IN POLAND

The Polish Criminal Code 1997 (CC) criminalizes both hate crime and hate speech. The origin of these provisions is of historical nature. Their creation was mainly a result of the experience of the Second World War, particularly mass murder, which was an extreme consequence of the politics of discrimination by the Nazis against certain groups of people according to racial, ethnic, national, and religious criteria (Bachmat 2011: 707). As early as 1945 a decree was issued which criminalized publicly expressing contempt for a group of people or a particular person based on ethnic-national, racial, or denominational belonging. The same decree provided for criminalizing a special hate-based violent act against a group of persons or a particular person when such acts resulted in death, serious bodily harm, or disrupting public order. The provisions were later developed in 1946 and 1949 decrees and were repealed only when the Criminal Code of 1969 entered into force (Woiński 2014: 156–7). There is no doubt that the provisions in force today, however, implement in Poland international human rights standards formulated after the experience of atrocities of the Second World War; mainly in the International Covenant on Civil and Political Rights (ICCPR; United Nations 1966).[7]

As to the hate speech provisions, promoting a fascist or other totalitarian system of state or inciting hatred based on national, ethnic, racial, or religious differences, or for reason of the lack of any religious denomination, is prohibited (Art. 256§1 CC).[8] In addition, Art. 257 CC criminalizes publicly insulting a group or a particular person because of national, ethnic, racial, or religious affiliation, or because of the lack of any religious denomination. Article 119 CC also penalizes unlawful threats on grounds of nationality, ethnicity, race, religion (or lack thereof), and political views.

Regarding the hate-motivated violence provisions, Art. 257 criminalizes physical assault of a group or a particular person because of national, ethnic, racial, or religious affiliation, or because of the lack of any religious denomination. Article 119 penalizes the use of violence on grounds of nationality, ethnicity, race, religion (or lack thereof), and political views. Article 118 CC stipulates that 'whoever, with the intent to destroy in whole or in part, a national, ethnical, racial, political or religious groups or belief, commits homicide or causes serious bodily harm of a person belonging to such groups' should be punished.

There is no special provision in the CC mentioning sexual orientation as part of a specific crime. Instead sexual orientation bias motivation *may* only be considered by the courts as an aggravating circumstance when making a determination of punishment on the basis of general sentencing principles (see Art. 53§2 of the CC). However, in reality it has been very rare for the homophobic motivation of a crime to be taken into consideration by the courts as an aggravating circumstance (Jabłońska and Knut 2012: 140). Moreover, the main advantage of special hate crime provisions referred to above is that these offences are prosecuted ex officio (the victim does not have to make an official complaint), and, in case of hate speech provisions, there does not have to be an individual or an identified victim for proceedings to be initiated because groups are also protected. The argument is not theoretical. The fact that there is no special provision concerning incitement to hatred based on sexual orientation means that many such acts will not be prosecuted at all. In 2011, the problem

---

[7] This aspect is underlined in commentaries to the Criminal Code (see, e.g., Gruszecka 2014; Marek 2010).

[8] Art. 256§2 provides for liability for preparatory acts of dissemination ranging from producing, recording, importing, buying, holding in stock, presenting, transporting, and sending any medium containing the criminal content specified in art. 256§1, as well as any object that is a capable of conveying fascist, communist, or otherwise totalitarian meanings.

was discussed in the media as Bas Tajpan, a Polish rapper, published a song titled 'Weeds' (*Chwasty*). The lyrics read:

Among these beautiful flowers grow weeds, popularly called faggots and lame women. The words of my caste are: burn them, burn them, burn them! Shooting with words, kill the degenerates!

Until 2015, there were three Bills in the parliament proposing significant amendments to current legislation governing the issue of hate crimes and hate speech. Two of these Bills,[9] sponsored respectively by the Your Movement party (TR) (hereinafter 'draft amendment no 340') and Alliance of Democratic Left party (SLD) (hereinafter 'draft amendment no 383/2357'), originated from one Bill prepared by an alliance of non-governmental organizations (NGOs).[10] The origin of the Bill is linked with the mobilization and professionalization of sexual minority rights organizations in Poland. In 2005, Campaign against Homophobia (KPH) issued a letter to the Minister of Justice (MoJ) enquiring whether the amendment of the CC provisions could include sexual orientation in Arts. 256 and 257 CC (KPH 2005). The reply of the MoJ was that he did not see it necessary to include sexual orientation in the CC. In January 2008 during the first meeting of sexual minority, transgender, and queer rights organizations, the idea to amend the CC to include sexual orientation (as well as gender identity) found its way to the final list of demands (Liszka 2008). During the second meeting of these organizations in September the same year, the proposition of a Bill was discussed and approved. Apart from sexual orientation and gender identity, it included other grounds such as age, gender, and disability. The reason to include other grounds was pragmatic: it was judged that the more universal the character of the Bill, and the wider the support for it, the greater the chances of its adoption.[11] The choice of the grounds, however, was not subject to discussion and followed the suggestion of one of the participants.[12] A special group, which continued working on the Bill, was created. The Bill was officially announced during the seminar on 3 March 2011, and subsequently presented in the Parliament as a Bill sponsored by SLD. After the first reading (13 July 2011), the work on the Bill was discontinued due to the end of the Parliament's term. From this point, though, the support for the Bill was wider, as mainstream human rights organizations also started to lobby for its adoption.[13] In the new term of the Sejm, TR and SLD submitted draft amendments no. 340 and 383, almost identical to the original Bill.[14] It is not clear why both parties did not cooperate on the issue.

---

[9] Draft amendment no 340 (7 March 2012) and draft amendment no 2357 (7 July 2014), which is a repeat of the Bill no 383 (20 April 2012), withdrawn due to procedural issues, in February 2014.

[10] Draft amendment no 4253 (18 April 2011).

[11] This tendency to make a claim under more universal terms is also visible on other occasions; for example there is no gay pride in Warsaw per se, but an Equality Parade, and each year organizers want to include other discriminated groups in the event.

[12] Personal communication with representative of Association 'The Diversity Workshop' on 23–24 June 2015.

[13] One of the co-authors of this chapter has been engaged in public discussion, works of parliamentary commission, and lobbying for the Bill since 2011 on behalf of the Helsinki Foundation for Human Rights.

[14] Draft amendment 383 presented by SLD additionally included changes to the provisions governing freedom of religion or belief.

When it comes to the Bill's purpose, its main aim was to add sexual orientation, gender identity, gender, age, and disability to already protected grounds. In the Bills' explanatory memoranda, Poland's international obligations are firmly underlined. For example, the 2010 Human Rights Committee recommendations for Poland are cited, according to which Poland should '(. . .) amend the Penal Code to define hate speech and hate crimes based on sexual orientation or gender identity among the categories of punishable offences (. . .)' (HRC 2010). The Bill also refers to the recommendations of the Committee against Torture, which recommended that Poland amend the CC to include sexual orientation, disability, and age in the list of protected grounds (CAT 2007). These are arguments that legitimize the claim to add additional grounds to hate crime and hate speech legislation. However, another important factor was that human rights activists became more conscious of the problems that LGB people experience in daily life. Important mobilization took place in 2005–2006, when a case concerning local representatives of PiS in Poznań, who in 2004 compared homosexuality to zoophilia, paedophilia, and necrophilia, was litigated. Four gay women sued two local representatives on the basis of the general provision of CC penalizing slander.[15] The case triggered a public discussion on hate speech against LGB people. Moreover, research on the social condition of LGB persons, which was carried out from the beginning of the 2000s (on a smaller scale), and important research results which were published in 2007, showed that many LGB persons in Poland have experienced being victims of different acts of violence (Abramowicz 2007).

The official government stance towards Bills 340 and 383/2357, explained in the written opinions provided for Parliament, was initially rather negative. According to the MoJ, there was no need for such an amendment. In justifying this view, the Government invoked the rationale underpinning the introduction of Arts. 119, 256, and 257, which is to criminalize 'behaviours threatening specified general interests'. In reflection of the 'preventive' nature of the provisions, Art. 119 has been placed in a section of the CC listing crimes against peace and humanity as well as war crimes, and the two others in a section on public order. According to the Government, adding new grounds (even if they are aimed at protecting the groups most at risk of victimization) is not justified because they do not fulfil the requirement of being of 'general interest'. In this sense, only acts that could lead to the escalation of inter-group conflict should be criminalized. As a result, sexual orientation (or other proposed grounds) should not be protected in the same way as the existing grounds.[16]

The Government has made further attempts to make a case against adding sexual orientation by arguing that special provisions as provided by the proposals

[15] The case ended on 9 September 2006 with the court settlement which obliged the two representatives of PiS to apologize during a press conference for their statements. More information on this case can be found on the webpage of the Helsinki Foundation for Human Rights which litigated the case: http://www.hfhr.org.pl/dyskryminacja/litygacja/dyskryminacja-ze-wzgledu-na-orientacje-seksualna/sprawa-poznanska

[16] A similar opinion is shared by the Supreme Court, which believes that adding new ground would interfere with the axiological cohesion of the CC (Supreme Court 2015).

would lead to narrowing down the protection accorded by the law.[17] This argument undermines the very idea of special provisions concerning bias-motivated crimes as requiring special protection to groups identified as most at risk of targeted victimization. Second, the Government submitted that adding new protected grounds would work to the detriment of the victims because anti-LGB hate crimes would be prosecuted ex officio. This is because the obligation to prosecute would force the victim to disclose his or her sexual orientation, and because current provisions provide for harsher sentences than the proposed one. In making the case against sexual orientation, the Government engages in a paternalistic argumentation that LGB people are better off without sexual orientation being treated as a protected ground, due to the possibility of being 'outed'. Finally, it is argued that the terms 'sexual orientation', 'gender identity', and 'gender' are too vague to be added, *because* they originate from international law instruments (NB: to which Poland is a party). According to the Government, it would be too difficult to ensure that these characteristics be understood universally by criminal justice personnel.

The Government's reluctant stance has slightly changed recently. In the beginning of 2015, the MoJ declared his support for work on the amendments to the CC concerning the penalization of hate speech and violence based on sexual orientation and other grounds (Ministry of Justice 2015). However, the move has not been followed by any action on the side of the Government. Also, the previous negative opinions have not been retracted. It is to be assumed, therefore, that the support does not extend beyond initiating drafting.

Unlike the Government, the Prosecutor General sees gender and sexual orientation as 'natural, primary attributes of a human being' and therefore fulfilling the same conditions as race or ethnicity. However, he has doubts as to whether gender identity, age, and disability meet these criteria (Prosecutor General 2012). In his opinion, introducing 'arbitrarily' selected grounds would be unjust for other vulnerable groups, such as people living with HIV or homeless people. This view is shared by the Supreme Court, which fears that the change will lead to amending the law 'in infinity' and suggests finding 'the lowest common denominator' instead of listing grounds (Supreme Court 2015).

While official documents are usually free from bigoted remarks, statements made by politicians (and even civil servants) often highlight the pervasive homophobia amongst the political establishment. For instance, the then-deputy MoJ, when asked about his lack of support for the Bills, said:

We do not need any additional solution here. The problem is different. It is the fact that some group of persons feel disadvantaged because they are homosexual and want to have it directly written down that they are discriminated against because of this reason. Why would we introduce a Trojan horse to the Criminal Code? (Debate 2014)

---

[17] The Government submitted that the special provision (i.e. the proposed Article 256 CC proscribing hate speech) would derogate special punishment provided for aggravated manslaughter under Article 148.2 CC. The argument would thus suggest that aggravated manslaughter, for example, does not cover manslaughter motivated by racial, ethnic or national hatred, and other grounds enumerated in Article 256 CC because racial, ethnic and national hatred, etc. is only proscribed by the CC to the extent those words are spelled out in specific provisions of the code. Therefore in the Government's view such biases cannot be considered as criminal motivation deserving special condemnation as under Article 148.2 CC.

In the Deputy Minister's words, one can see the fear that introduction of anti-LGB hate crime laws paves the way for further advancement of sexual minorities. One Polish scholar rightly described this line of reasoning as the 'rhetoric of war' (Wyrzykowski 2015).

Similarly, Bills no. 340 and 383/2357 were criticized in Parliament during debates on 24 May 2012, 22 February 2013, and 9 June 2014. One of the most vocal MPs was Stanisław Pięta from PiS. His speech from 24 May 2012 is a salient example as to how the themes and tropes introduced in the previous sections (on homophobia and on controversies about hate crime) are often conflated. Arguing against the Bills, Pięta claimed that homosexuality is a sexual disorder similar to paedophilia or zoophilia. In his view, it is propagated by gay activists and supported by enemies of the traditional values of Catholic Poles (Obama and the EU are the external enemies, while *Gazeta Wyborcza*, the liberal Polish daily, is the enemy domestically). Furthermore, by outlawing anti-LGB hate speech, the Bills are criticized for attempting to curb the freedom of speech and introduce dreaded political correctness.

The third Bill currently under discussion ('draft amendment no. 1078'),[18] sponsored by members of the ruling Civic Platform party (PO), was a reaction to the above-mentioned Bills inspired by NGOs. It introduces significant changes in current legislation governing the issue of hate crimes. The Bill adds such general categories as 'political, social affiliation' and 'natural or acquired personal qualities or beliefs' to the catalogue of protected characteristics under current legislation. It does not mention any specific grounds such as sexual orientation or disability, as the two other Bills do. Whilst, on the face of it, this seems to be an effective and generous instrument, the Bill was widely criticized by lawyers and Polish NGOs. One concern is rather symbolic and pertains to the ruling party's obstinate refusal to use the 'sexual orientation' vocabulary. A more serious concern is practical: the proposed grounds of 'social affiliation' and 'natural or acquired personal qualities or beliefs' are vague, and thus in conflict with legislators' obligation to lay down criminal provisions that are clear and precise (Helsinki Foundation for Human Rights 2012). Negative opinions, criticizing the vagueness of the proposed solutions, were also expressed by constitutional bodies, such as the National Council of the Judiciary of Poland (14 February 2013), the Supreme Court (29 January 2013), and—interestingly—the Government (29 April 2013), in which PO is the senior coalition partner.

THE POLISH MODEL
OF UNDERSTANDING HATE CRIME

As discussed above, the rationale behind the provisions that we now call 'hate crime laws' in the Polish CC is historicized and emphasizes the need to protect peace and prevent mass inter-group conflict in the future. This dual focus on the history, on the

---

[18] Draft amendment no 1078 (27 November 2012).

one hand, and future, on the other, differentiates Poland from the US and the UK, and is an important obstacle in expanding the protection to add new grounds.

The historicism of the law is visible in the justification of the catalogue of protected grounds. In Poland, individuals are protected by virtue of having a characteristic that is considered a 'greater good' and which was used as a justification for mass killings in the Second World War. In effect, only ethnic or religious grounds, which were used as a justification for wars and ethnic cleansing, are considered 'worthy' of protection. This historicism of the law, enacted to prevent genocide and threats to international security, is also visible in Germany (Savelsberg and King 2005: 580). At the same time, it sets Poland apart from the US and the UK. There, the debates about targeted violence focused mostly on the domestic rather than international level. The changes (in both policy and legislation) were introduced as a response to *ongoing* acts of (not necessarily mass) violence targeting minorities.[19]

Unlike race, ethnicity, or religion, sexual orientation is not considered a 'greater good' by the Polish lawmakers. Even though gay men were also killed in the Nazi camps, they are 'forgotten victims', whose suffering does not exist in the collective memory. As anti-LGB violence did not threaten international peace, it is often overlooked (or even trivialized) by lawmakers. The historicized origins of the law mean that they are not an effect (at least not directly) of the identity politics of minority groups. In fact, at the time when the laws were enacted, NGOs did not exist (under the Communist rule), or, in 1997, they were not as active in the area of hate crime laws as they are now. This historicism of the law makes it largely immune to the work of local advocacy groups looking to expand the protection to other commonly victimized groups. It does not, nevertheless, mean that various interest groups do not influence the legislation in Poland at all; rather, this process is more indirect and filtered through international organizations. This point is worth expanding upon in the context of the internationalization of hate crime.

The suffering of ethnic and religious minorities during the Second World War gave rise to international instruments such as the ICCPR, which, in turn, influenced the level of protection for minorities in Poland. Therefore, while the laws are influenced by historical trauma, they are also an effect of Poland's belonging to international organizations. Moreover, after the collapse of Communism, the minimum standards of protection for ethnic and religious minorities became a condition that Poland had to fulfil in order to join the European Union (so-called 'hard multiculturalism'; Auer 2004: 70).

While, for the moment, there are no hard laws obliging Poland to specifically address anti-LGB violence, actors such as CAT and HRC and also, recently, the European Commission against Racism and Intolerance (ECRI) have started to put pressure on Poland to include sexual orientation in the hate crime provisions. It is here that we begin to observe a more contemporary influence of globalization, including the internationalization of hate crime, on Poland. These intergovernmental

---

[19] For example, in the US the federal Hate Crimes Prevention Act (2009) was a response to the murders of Matthew Shepard and James Byrd, Jr. In the UK, the Stephen Lawrence inquiry (Macpherson 1999) helped spawn the debate about 'institutional racism' in the police.

institutions are cross-jurisdictional and increasingly influenced by Polish advocacy groups. For example, the most recent ECRI report on Poland repeats in large part the recommendations submitted to it by a group of Polish NGOs (ECRI 2015).

While the laws in Poland have not yet changed, the developments on the policy level show a surprisingly positive picture. Here, the influence of internationaliza-tion is particularly visible. For example, over 77,000 police officers have undergone hate crime training based on the curriculum developed by the Office for Democratic Institutions and Human Rights of the Organization for Security and Co-operation in Europe (ODIHR; see ECRI 2015: 46). In 2013 Poland started monitoring and report-ing to ODIHR on hate crimes based on sexual orientation, gender identity, and dis-ability (Ministry of the Interior 2014). The impacts of internationalization are also visible in the increased cooperation between various national and supranational stakeholders. For example, representatives of the Polish Ministry of Interior partici-pate in the works of the EU Fundamental Rights Agency Hate Crime Working Party, which brings together a number of intergovernmental organizations and European governments. The aim of the Working Party is to improve the response to hate crime in the EU through the development of effective national instruments (EU FRA 2014).

CONCLUSIONS

The understanding of the role of hate crime legislation in Poland is limited to vio-lence based on race, ethnicity, and religion—grounds seen as 'greater goods' and known to be causes of wars and mass murders. This narrow understanding of hate-based violence is of course one that is grounded in the devastation inflicted on certain groups globally during the Second World War. As such, the laws on hate crime in Poland are a product of a historicized and globalized understanding of hate. However, this has left other groups—even those with a history of persecution, such as LGB people—without enhanced protection. The unwillingness of the Polish authorities to protect LGB people from targeted violence in the same way as victims of racially or religiously motivated crimes also reflects high levels of societal homo-phobia. Yet this too can be partly explained by global influences, the most stark of which is the expression of opposition towards the degeneration of national norms by Western influences.

The Polish model, which has focused on history and prevention of conflicts (similarly to the German model), is significantly different from those developed by other, internationally dominant, nations such as the US and the UK. These coun-tries have focused on addressing hate crime via an expanding list of vulnerable mi-nority groups. In the case of the US and the UK, the passing of hate crime laws has been driven mostly by numerous policy, legislative, and scholarly activities at the national level. These domestic laws and policies have, however, clearly influenced international bodies now tasked with combating hate crime (such as ODIHR). While such policies have yet to fully influence Poland's approach to addressing hate crime, the issue of hate-based violence currently on the Government agenda can be attributed to NGOs in Poland that are allied to international human rights organizations. If and when Parliament finally decides to amend its hate crime laws, cooperation between the Government, civil society, and these international organizations will help ensure that the laws are not only enacted, but also implemented.

REFERENCES

Abramowicz, M. (ed.) 2007. *Situation of Bisexual and Homosexual Persons in Poland. 2005 and 2006 Report.* Warsaw: Kampania Przeciwko Homofobii, Lambda Warszawa.

Antosz, P. 2012. *Równe Traktowanie Standardem Dobrego Rządzenia. Raport z badań sondażowych [Equal Treatment as a Standard of Good Governance. Report of the survey].* (J. Górniak, ed.). Kraków.

Auer, S. 2004. *Liberal Nationalism in Central Europe.* London, New York: RoutledgeCurzon.

Bachmat, P. 2011. 'Przestępstwo publicznego propagowania faszystowskiego lub innego totalitarnego ustroju państwa lub nawoływania do nienawiści (art. 156 § 1 k.k.) [The Crime of Advocating Fascist and Other Totalitarian System of Government and of Incitement to Hatred]'. In: Siemaszko A. (ed.), *Stosowanie praw. Księga jubileuszowa z okazji XX-lecia Instytutu Wymiaru Sprawiedliwości [Application of Statutes. A Volume Commemorating the 20th Anniversary of the Administration of Justice Institute],* Warsaw.

Bilewicz, M., Marchlewska, M., Soral, W., and Winiewski, M. 2014. *Mowa nienawiści. Raport z badań sondażowych [Hate Speech. Report from Survey].* Warsaw: Fundacja im. Stefana Batorego.

Boswell, J. 1981. *Christianity, Social Tolerance, and Homosexuality: Gay People in Western Europe from the Beginning of the Christian Era to the Fourteenth Century.* Chicago: University of Chicago Press.

CAT 2007. Conclusions and Recommendations of the CAT, Poland, Thirty-eighth session, Geneva 30 April–18 May 2007, CAT/C/POL/CO/4.

Chakraborti, N. and Garland, J. 2012. 'Reconceptualizing Hate Crime Victimization through the Lens of Vulnerability and "Difference"'. *Theoretical Criminology,* 16/4: 499–514. DOI: 10.1177/1362480612439432.

Connell, R.W. 1987. *Gender and Power: Society, the Person, and Sexual Politics.* Stanford, California: Stanford University Press.

Connell, R.W. 2005. *Masculinities,* 2nd ed. Berkeley and Los Angeles: University of California Press.

Criminal Code. 1969, OJ 1969 No 13 Item 94.

Criminal Code. 1997, OJ 1997 No 88 Item 553.

Debate 2014. Adam Bodnar, Michał Królikowski, Sebastian Duda, Zbigniew Nosowski, 'Prawa człowieka – łączą czy dzielą? dyskusja [Do human rights connect or divide? debate]', *Kwartalnik Więź,* no 3/2014, pp. 16–30.

ECRI 2015. ECRI Report on Poland (fifth monitoring cycle). Available at: https://www.coe.int/t/dghl/monitoring/ecri/Country-by-country/Poland/POL-CbC-V-2015-20-ENG.pdf [Accessed 9 June 2015].

EU FRA 2013. Survey data explorer: LGBT Survey 2012. EU FRA.

EU FRA 2014. Working Party Improving Reporting and Recording of Hate Crime in the EU Inaugural Meeting Report. EU FRA.

Garland, J. and Hodkinson, P. 2015. 'Alternative Subcultures and Hate Crime'. In: Hall N., Corb A., Giannassi P., and Grieve J.G.D. (eds.), *The Routledge International Handbook on Hate Crime*, pp. 226–36. London: Routledge.

Gerstenfeld, P.B. 2004. *Hate Crimes: Causes, Controls, and Controversies*. Thousand Oaks, London, New Delhi: Sage Publications.

Godzisz, P. 2015. Eastern Crimes, Western Theories: Conceptualising the Hate Crime Model in Central and Eastern Europe. The International Network for Hate Studies. Retrieved 22 January 2015, from <http://www.internationalhatestudies.com/eastern-crimes-western-theories-conceptualising-hate-crime-model-central-eastern-europe/>

Graff, A. 2006. 'We Are (Not All) Homophobes: A Report from Poland'. *Feminist Studies*, 32/2: 434–449. DOI: 10.2307/20459096.

Graff, A. 2010. 'Looking at Pictures of Gay Men: Political Uses of Homophobia in Contemporary Poland'. *Public Culture*, 22/3: 583–603. DOI: 10.1215/08992363-2010-010.

Gruszecka, D. 2014. 'Komentarz do art. 256, pkt. 2 [Commentary to Art. 256, Item 2]'. In: Giezek J. (ed.), *Kodeks karny. Część szczególna. Komentarz [Criminal Code Annotated with Commentaries]*, LEX.

GUS 2013. *Ludność. Stan i struktura demograficzno-społeczna. Narodowy Spis Powszechny Ludności i Mieszkań 2011 [Population. Status and Socio-demographic Structure. National Census of Population and Housing 2011]*. Warsaw: GUS.

Helsinki Foundation for Human Rights. 2012. Letter of 21 December 2012 to the President of the Civic Platform Parliamentary Club, no. 3192/2012.

HRC 2010. Concluding observations of the Human Rights Committee of the HRC, Poland, 100th session, Geneva, 11–29 October 2010, CCPR/C/POL/CO/6.

Iganski, P. 2008. *Hate Crime and the City*. Bristol: Policy Press.

Iganski, P. 2014. Using the law to challenge cultures of hate. Presented at the Stepping up the fight against hate crimes, 13 December Brussels.

ILGA-Europe 2014. ILGA-Europe Rainbow Map May 2014. ILGA-Europe.

Jabłońska, Z. and Knut, P. (eds.) 2014. *Prawa osób LGBT w Polsce, Raport z badań nad wdrażaniem Zalecenia CM/Rec (2010)5 Komitetu Ministrów Rady Europy dla Państw Członkowskich w zakresie środków zwalczania dyskryminacji opartej na orientacji seksualnej lub tożsamości płciowej [The Rights of LGBT People in Poland: An Implementation Report concerning Recommendation of the Committee of Ministers to member states on measures to combat discrimination on grounds of sexual orientation or gender identity (CM/Rec (2010)5)]*, Warsaw.

Jacobs, J.B. and Potter, K. 1998. *Hate Crimes: Criminal Law & Identity Politics*. New York, Oxford: Oxford University Press.

Jenness, V. 2002. 'Contours of Hate Crime Politics and Law in the United States'. In: Iganski P. (ed.), *The Hate Debate: Should Hate be Punished as a Crime?*, pp. 15–35. Profile Books Ltd. in association with the Institute for Jewish Policy Research: London.

Jenness, V. and Grattet, R. 2001. *Making Hate a Crime: From Social Movement to Law Enforcement*. New York: Russell Sage.

KPH 2005. Letter of 25 July 2005 to the Minister of Justice.

Krzemiński, I. 2001. 'The National Identity and European Consciousness of Poles'. In: Drulák P. (ed.), *National and European Identities in EU Enlargement: Views from Central and Eastern Europe*, pp. 57–68. Prague: Institute of International Relations.

Law Commission 2013. Consultation Paper No 213. Hate Crime: The Case for Extending the Existing Offences. Appendix B: History of Hate Crime Legislation. Law Commission.

Lieberman, M. and Freeman, S.M. 2009. 'Confronting Violent Bigotry: Hate Crime Laws and Legislation'. In: Lawrence F.M. (ed.), *Hate Crimes. Volume 5: Responding Hate Crime*, Praeger perspectives, pp. 1–30. Westport, Connecticut, London: Praeger.

Liszka, S. 2008. I Ogólnopolskie Spotkanie Organizacji LGBTQ. Sprawozdanie z obrad w Krakowie [1st Meeting of LGBTQ Organizations. Summary of the discussion in Cracow] Available at: http://queer.pl/news/190672/i-ogolnopolskie-spotkanie-organizacji-lgbtq [Accessed 8 July 2015].

Macpherson, W. 1999. The Stephen Lawrence Inquiry Report of an Inquiry by Sir William Macpherson of Cluny Advised by Tom Cook, The Right Reverend Dr John Sentamu, Dr Richard Stone Presented to Parliament by The Secretary of State for The Home Department by Command of Her Majesty.

Marek, A. 2010. *Kodeks karny. Komentarz [Criminal Code Annotated with Commentaries], Komentarz do art. 256 kk, pkt. 1. [Commentary to Art. 256 CC; Item 1], 5th edition*, LEX.

Maroney, T.A. 1998. 'The Struggle against Hate Crime: Movement at a Crossroads'. *New York University Law Review*, 73: 564–620.

Mason, G. 2014a. 'The Symbolic Purpose of Hate Crime Law: Ideal Victims and Emotion'. *Theoretical Criminology*, 18/1: 75–92. DOI: 10.1177/1362480613499792.

Mason, G. 2014b. 'Victim Attributes in Hate Crime Law'. *British Journal of Criminology*, 54/2: 161–79.

Ministry of Justice. 2015. 'Letter to the Plenipotentiary of the Government on Equal Treatment'. Retrieved (http://www.rownetraktowanie.gov.pl/aktualnosci/wystapienie-do-ministra-sprawiedliwosci-w-sprawie-penalizacji-mowy-nienawisci-ze-wzgledu).

Ministry of the Interior. 2014. Pismo [Letter] DKSiW-ZPC-078-10/14.

Mole, R. 2011. 'Nationality and Sexuality: Homophobic Discourse and the "National Threat" in Contemporary Latvia'. *Nations and Nationalism* 17(3): 540–60.

Mosse, G.L. 1985. *Nationalism and Sexuality: Respectability and Abnormal Sexuality in Modern Europe*. New York: Howard Fertig.

Nagel, J. 1998. 'Masculinity and Nationalism: Gender and Sexuality in the Making of Nations'. *Ethnic and Racial Studies*, 21/2: 242–69. DOI: 10.1080/014198798330007.

O'Dwyer, C. and Schwartz, K.Z.S. 2010. 'Minority Rights after EU Enlargement: A Comparison of Antigay Politics in Poland and Latvia'. *Comparative European Politics*, 8/2: 220–43. DOI: 10.1057/cep.2008.31.

Ostolski, A. 2007. 'Spiskowcy i gorszyciele. Judaizowanie gejów w polskim dyskursie prawicowym [Conspirators and Shockers: Judaizing Gays in the Right-wing Discourse in Polish]'. In: Głowacka-Grajper M. and Nowicka E. (eds.), *Jak się dzielimy i co nas łączy: przemiany wartości i więzi we współczesnym społeczeństwie polskim [How we are Divided and what we Have in Common: The Transformation of Values and Relationships in Contemporary Polish Society]*. Kraków and Warszawa: Nomos and Instytut Socjologii Uniwersytetu Warszawskiego.

Perry, B. 2001. *In the Name of Hate: Understanding Hate Crimes*. London: Routledge.

President of the Republic of Poland 1932. Rozporządzenie Prezydenta Rzeczypospolitej z dnia 11 lipca 1932 r.—Kodeks karny. [Ordinance of the President of the Republic—Criminal Code], p. OJ no 60 it 571.

Prosecutor General 2012. Opinion to the bill 340 of 23 April 2012.

Richardson, D. 1998. 'Sexuality and Citizenship'. *Sociology* 32(1): 83–100.

Savelsberg, J. and King, R. 2005. 'Institutionalizing Collective Memories of Hate: Law and Law Enforcement in Germany and the United States'. *American Journal of Sociology*, 111/ 2: 579–616. DOI: 10.1086/432779.

Schöpflin, G. 1995. 'Nationalism and Ethnicity in Europe, East and West'. In: Kupchan C. (ed.), *Nationalism and Nationalities in the New Europe*, pp. 37–65. Ithaca, London: Cornell University Press.

Stolarska, W. 2014. Robert Biedroń dla tvn24.pl: Marzę o ślubie w słupskim ratuszu [Robert Biedroń for tvn24: I dream about getting married in the Słupsk town hall]. TVN24. pl. Retrieved 7 January 2015, from <http://www.tvn24.pl/pomorze,42/slupsk-robert-biedron-w-rozmowie-z-tvn24-pl-o-tym-jak-slupsk-zmienil-jego-zycie-i-jak-sie-czuje-w-nowej-roli,499546.html>

Stychin, C. 1997. 'Queer Nations: Nationalism, Sexuality and the Discourse of Rights in Quebec'. *Feminist Legal Studies*, 5/1. DOI: 10.1007/BF02684854.

Supreme Court 2015. Opinion of the Supreme Court on the bill 2357 of 25 April 2015.

United Nations 1966. International Covenant on Civil and Political Rights Adopted and opened for signature, ratification and accession by General Assembly resolution 2200A (XXI) of 16 December 1966 entry into force 23 March 1976, in accordance with Article 49.

West, C. and Zimmerman, D.H. 1987. 'Doing Gender'. *Gender and Society*, 1/2: 125–51.

Woiński, M. 2014. *Prawnokarne aspekty zwalczania mowy nienawiści [Criminal Law Aspects of Combating Hate Speech]*, Warsaw.

Wyrzykowski, M. 2015. Lecture by Prof. M. Wyrzykowski, former justice of the Constitutional Court, during the 70th birthday of Prof. W. Osiatyński, 12 March 2015, Warsaw.

Zubrzycki, G. 2007. 'The Cross, the Madonna and the Jew: Persistent Symbolic Representations of the Nation in Poland'. In: Young M., Zuelow E., and Sturm A. (eds.), *Nationalism in a Global Era: The Persistence of Nations*, pp. 131–55. New York: Routledge.

12

POLICING HATE CRIME: TRANSFERABLE STRATEGIES FOR IMPROVING SERVICE PROVISION TO VICTIMS AND COMMUNITIES INTERNATIONALLY

Paul Giannasi and Nathan Hall

Undoubtedly, state responses to hate crime vary considerably both between, and indeed within, different countries. The relevant available literature, and the collective experience of the authors in working in the international field, leaves little doubt that the extent, nature, and quality of responses to the hate crime 'problem' around the world represent something of a patchwork quilt. Despite many states undertaking and subscribing to various pledges, commitments, and obligations (OSCE 2014), it is clear that the reality of formal responses to hate crime differs widely both in theory and in practice, notably in terms of the creation and enforcement of law, the level of political and cultural will to accept and address the problem, and the provision of services to those whose lives are blighted by hate and hate crime. Rather than attempt an overview of the various state responses to hate crime around the world (readers seeking this are advised to see the annual reports of the Organization for Security and Co-operation in Europe (OSCE)), this chapter will instead consider the 'journey' undertaken within England and Wales to improve its own responses to hate crime, with a particular focus on policing issues, and consider the extent to which this learning is transferrable and thus the extent to which it might benefit other states seeking to improve their own responses to the hate crime 'problem'. In so doing, we will identify and discuss what we believe to be the key issues that are central to improving state responses to hate and hate crime and highlight some of the strategies and actions that can help implement change.

UNDERSTANDING CHANGE

If we are going to understand and measure progress in any era, or any country, we first need to establish where we are—*our starting point*—and where we would want to be—*our aspiration*. In recent years, some countries, perhaps most notably but not exclusively those within the United Kingdom (UK) (see the annual OSCE reports for an outline of the various developments in different countries), have made significant advancements in their responses to hate crime, particularly in terms of criminal justice responses. So by examining some examples, as we will in due course, we can begin to understand the models and actions that might lead to an improved response. We can also see, in those states that provide transparent data (this data can also be found in the annual reports of the OSCE), some tentative indicators that demonstrate the current level of hate crime suffered by victims. As such, the availability and accuracy of data is central to framing both our starting point and identifying our aspiration.

If we are to measure progress it is also important to identify our strategic goals, as this provides us with something of a yardstick with which to measure progress. The 'utopian option' would clearly be that we live in a society that is free from hostility and bigotry and where every individual is protected from targeted abuse. However, history would tell us that this is unlikely to happen and it is perhaps impossible to envisage how any state could achieve this (see Hall 2013 for a discussion of the history of hate crime and its emergence as a contemporary social problem). That should not stop us trying, but perhaps it is more valuable to see progress in the context of 'the journey' and to measure success in terms of a roadmap for improvement, and in particular how far we have travelled along that route. It is perhaps more realistic to set goals that are achievable, but that show evidence of improvement. Examples of this might be, for example, transparent data, improved reporting, greater victim satisfaction, and effective rehabilitation programmes for perpetrators (College of Policing 2014; Hall 2013; Hall, Grieve, and Savage 2009).

We could consider the starting point for our deliberations at many points in history, but perhaps the foundations of modern global policy lie in the Universal Declaration of Human Rights, adopted by the General Assembly of the United Nations in 1948. This was agreed in the wake of one of the most horrific events in modern human history—the state-controlled murders of over twelve million people during the Holocaust in Europe—crimes that were, of course, fuelled by a hatred of victims' ethnicity, race, religious beliefs, sexuality, and disability, amongst other characteristics.

The Declaration set out a range of underpinning rights and recognized that: 'All human beings are born free and equal in dignity and rights. They are endowed with reason and conscience and should act towards one another in a spirit of brotherhood.'

Article 2 of the Declaration goes on to state that: 'Everyone is entitled to all the rights and freedoms set forth in this Declaration, without distinction of any kind, such as race, colour, sex, language, religion, political or other opinion, national or social origin, property, birth or other status.'

These basic rights have underpinned many international declarations since this time, including the UN's International Convention on the Elimination of All Forms of Racial Discrimination adopted in 1965, as well as the policy of both the European Union and the Council of Europe.

STATE RESPONSES—IDENTIFYING
THE STARTING POINT

The starting point for change is an essential factor in deciding the model for effectively bringing around change. The situation in different countries, both in terms of the extent and nature of the hate crime 'problem' and the sophistication of the response, varies enormously as a consequence of factors such as history, conflict, demographics, culture, politics, religion, and leadership, to name but a few. It is too simple to see this in the context of the juxtaposition between totalitarian regimes and democratic societies, though the obstacles to change in the former would appear to be significantly greater. In order to segregate states and the degree of protection they offer to their citizens, particularly minority communities, we have listed below five broad categories to try and identify the challenges they face. In reality, these categories are not mutually exclusive, and states are likely to have overlapping characteristics of more than one. In addition, the situation may be different dependent on the characteristics of the victims (OSCE 2013).

OPPRESSIVE REGIMES

There are some states that actively repress the rights of their citizens and visitors. This oppression might include, for example, capital punishment for homosexuality, the demonization of sections of a community, or the creation of two-tier citizen's rights.

PASSIVE CONDONING OF HOSTILITY

Some regimes and authorities would claim to support the principles of the Universal Declaration of Human Rights, but in practice would turn a 'blind eye' to attacks on minority communities, particularly where there is hostility towards them from large proportions of the population. Often political leaders will fuel the hostility towards communities through the demonization of minorities, producing a narrative which links them, for example, to criminality or disease, or that they are the cause of economic strife and reduced opportunity for the majority. We can often see examples of this attitude in the treatment of Roma communities across Europe or in communities where refugees from conflict have sought a place of safety.

LEGAL EQUALITY BUT PRACTICAL INEQUALITY

Some states have implemented legislation that provides equality to all citizens regardless of their personal characteristics. Whilst this is important in the development of a fair society, it is not necessarily the complete solution. The effective deployment of that legislation and the changing of negative cultures in agencies to help ensure effective service provision is a significantly greater challenge.

COMPREHENSIVE STATE COMMITMENT
TO DELIVER EQUALITY

In this context, the regime will coordinate criminal justice activities across the state and will include the views and experiences of victims at the heart of policy and legislative responses. This effective response will entail activity in a broad range of sectors including education, law enforcement, and the punishment and rehabilitation of offenders, but will also require inclusive communities, a responsible free media, and political moderation.

EQUAL LIFE EXPERIENCES FOR ALL

In this regime, individuals are treated differently but, equally, according to their needs, and are similarly to be protected from all forms of discrimination, including targeted violence. As mentioned above this 'utopian situation' is probably beyond the reach of any modern state, though, as we have already suggested, it serves as an aspirational target.

TRIGGERS FOR CHANGE: A CASE STUDY
OF ENGLAND AND WALES FROM 1993 TO 2015

For any country to implement effective change there needs to be a strong motivation, an effective shared strategy, and the political courage to stand up and defend the rights of groups who may face hostility from sections of the electorate. In practice, experience in England and Wales tells us that there often needs to be a 'trigger' event to bring around change. This trigger can come from a change of political leadership or the scrutiny of international government organizations, but, sadly for most, it is the response to a tragedy, to civil unrest, or to prolonged suffering in affected communities.

The UK, for example, has seen significant changes in its population demographics, particularly since the end of the Second World War. A combination of the contraction of the British Empire and the need to rebuild the country in the wake of the war led to large-scale immigration in the decades that followed. This has led to a strong multicultural identity, particularly in the larger urban areas. In the 1980s, and again in 2001, parts of England experienced significant public disorder, which was largely brought about in disaffected minority communities who felt that they were living in disadvantaged circumstances, were facing hostility from the majority community, and were being unfairly treated by the police and other public authorities (Hall 2005; Scarman 1981).

Whilst these issues have played their part in the evolution of policing in this field, we have decided to examine the response in England and Wales from 1993 because this was the year of the tragic murder of Stephen Lawrence, a young black man who was killed in an unprovoked racist attack in London. This seminal moment in the

UK's history has had a profound impact on race relations, both in terms of policy and the law. Whilst the response in Scotland and Northern Ireland has followed a similar path, we have concentrated on England and Wales to prevent confusion over the differences in the paths taken.

We have written extensively about the legacy of the Stephen Lawrence murder (Hall 2005; Hall et al. 2009; Hall et al. 2014) and whilst the impact it would have was not immediately obvious, the tireless campaigning of Stephen's family and other supporters brought around arguably the most significant changes to policing in modern times. The catalyst for this change was the Public Inquiry that reported in February 1999 (Macpherson 1999). It found that there had been significant failings in the way Stephen's murder was investigated and made seventy recommendations designed to improve the response to such crimes and to begin to rebuild the confidence in the police from within minority communities.

We have argued elsewhere (Hall et al. 2009; Hall et al. 2014) that England and Wales has been amongst the most responsive of states in its efforts to address hate crime and, whilst we would not argue that this response is perfect or complete, nor that it provides a 'one-size fits all' solution to the challenges faced by other states, it would be reasonable to cite England and Wales as a good practice example to others, not least because of the variety of changes that have occurred, some of which at least might prove transferrable. In short, and in relative terms, England and Wales has developed a robust legislative framework, transparent data of recorded crime, and the estimate of actual crime suffered by communities through the use of victim surveys (College of Policing 2014; Smith et al. 2012; True Vision 2015). It has also done more than most, if not all other states, to encourage the reporting and recording of hate crime through, for example, the adoption of a broad, victim-centred operational definition of hate crime, and the development and use of third-party reporting systems, both of which are directly related to the recommendations of the Stephen Lawrence Inquiry (Macpherson 1999; True Vision 2015). A good indicator of these is the annual report of the OSCE. The OSCE measures hate crime across the fifty-seven participating states and the UK stands out as recording significantly more hate crimes than any other state (see, e.g., http://hatecrime.osce.org).

Whilst it is possible to make a case that England and Wales is among the world leaders in how it deals with hate crime, it would be equally straightforward to make an argument that it is significantly falling short of its stated objectives. Successive governments and criminal justice leaders have committed to reducing the harm caused by hate crime (HM Government 2012). Indeed, it is probably fair to say there would be very few politicians who would not want to put an end to targeted hostility and provide circumstances where all sections of the community feel safe. With a few extremist individuals as exceptions, all parties in UK mainstream politics have committed to improving responses to hate crime. Despite these commitments there are still challenges to be faced, particularly in the extent of under-reporting and the comparably low satisfaction levels of victims who report hate crimes to authorities.

WHAT HAS CHANGED SINCE 1993?

As suggested earlier, most countries will not fit exclusively into any one of the categories we set out above but we would argue that in 1993, England and Wales was predominantly in the third category (legal equality but practical inequality), which, to the extent that provisions existed, included theoretical equality under law, but in practice this was not effectively delivered, particularly to minority citizens. The initial UK Government response to the Inquiry came in the Home Secretary's Action Plan published in April 1999, and updated in an Annual Report published in February 2000 (Home Office 1999). The then Home Secretary Jack Straw MP accepted the vast majority of the seventy recommendations and committed to significant policy and legislative change. The Inquiry findings still inform policy today and have introduced a number of key underlying principles that similarly inform the legal and policy response, including:

PERCEPTION-BASED RECORDING

The Inquiry believed professionals were making decisions influenced by their own prejudices and that if the victim, or any other person, perceived a crime to be racist then the police should record it as such.

RESPONDING TO INCIDENTS AS WELL AS CRIMES

The Inquiry recognized the importance of early responses to hostility and presumed that offenders motivated by racism that go on to commit serious crime would have demonstrated that hostility at an earlier stage.

THERE IS A NEED TO IMPROVE THE RECORDING, AND ADDRESS THE UNDER-REPORTING, OF HATE CRIME

This challenge has been a major thrust of policy since 1999, with successive Governments recognizing that most crimes are unrecorded and wishing to see increased levels of recorded hate crime, so long as the actual incidence of hate crime does not increase.

THAT THE RACIST ELEMENT SHOULD NOT BE SUBJECT TO 'PLEA BARGAINING' DURING PROSECUTIONS

In addition to the initial Government response, the police and Crown Prosecution Service issued guidance to professionals. The police produced their first national guidance in the 2000 Hate Crime Manual, issued by the Association of Chief Police Officers (ACPO 2000), and the Director of Public Prosecutions issued guidance to prosecutors, including an instruction that prosecutors should never use the racist element of the crime as a bargaining tool to secure guilty pleas from defendants.

It is perhaps understandable, given the significance of the Stephen Lawrence Inquiry and the fact that the majority of hate crimes recorded are racist in nature (True Vision 2015), that this would be the focus of early attention. However, since then other types of hate crime have been added to the policy response. Since 2007, criminal justice agencies have shared a common definition which recognizes five 'monitored strands' of hate crime, these being disability, race, religion, sexual orientation, and transgender. The same five categories are the basis of the English and Welsh hate-based legislation, discussed below.

In reality there is no single strategic document that encompasses all of the changes to hate crime responses that we have seen in the last two decades. Whilst most provisions can be traced back to the Stephen Lawrence legacy, the legislation and policies that have brought around change have developed in a piecemeal way.

POLITICAL LEADERSHIP

One consistent factor of the state response has been the political commitment to reduce the harm that hate crime causes and to encourage those who are victimized to seek the services of the police and other agencies (HM Government 2012; True Vision 2015). Since 1999 all three major parties (Conservative, Labour, and Liberal Democrat) have been in power in national government, either alone or as part of a coalition, and all have demonstrated their commitment to combating hate crime. As well as the Home Secretary's Action Plan, mentioned above, the Labour administration published an action plan in 2009 (Home Office 2009) and the Coalition Government (comprising the Conservatives and Liberal Democrats) replaced this with its own plan in 2012 (HM Government 2012). As we write, the now-majority Conservative government has begun the process of creating a new action plan, to be published in 2016.

Political leadership is an essential part of any effective response, and the fact that all three main parties have included manifesto commitments on the subject has prevented it becoming a 'political football' and has allowed progress to continue even when there has been a change of government. There are some on the extremes of politics who would argue against the policy, often claiming that it creates a two-tier criminal justice system with preferential treatment of some over others (in line with academic arguments proffered by, e.g., Jacobs and Potter 1998; Sullivan 1999), but their views are isolated and they have not achieved broad electoral support.

In addition to the strategic oversight and provision of legislation and resources, ministers have had to show an element of political courage, particularly around increased reporting. It is perhaps counterintuitive for politicians to put in place measures to increase levels of recorded crime, but that is effectively what happens with hate crime in England and Wales. Whilst all politicians in power would wish to see fewer victims of any crime, the knowledge that so many hate crimes are never reported to the police has led to the principal measurement of success being a reduction in the under-reporting of hate crime (College of Policing 2014; HM Government 2012). Increases in recorded hate crime are welcomed so long as they are the result of better reporting, rather than there being a real increase in the total number of victims experiencing hate crimes.

GOVERNANCE

The initial response to the Stephen Lawrence Inquiry was led by central government. The Home Secretary's response included commitments from the police and others and was overseen by the Stephen Lawrence Steering Group, chaired by the Home Secretary personally until it was dissolved in October 2005. This decision received some criticism, including from Stephen's mother Doreen, now Baroness Lawrence of Clarendon.

In 2006, the then Attorney General, Baroness Scotland of Asthal, commissioned a task force to consider progress in relation to hate crime. As a result of the review she established the Race for Justice Programme to address the challenges that were faced. The programme, which is now called the Cross-Government Hate Crime Programme, is still in operation. It recognizes that effective responses require coordination across all relevant Whitehall departments and with each of the criminal justice agencies. The Programme is overseen by a Strategy Board, which includes representatives from ministers and criminal justice executives (from government departments including the Home Office, the Ministry of Justice, the Department for Communities and Local Government, amongst others, and representatives from the various agencies of the criminal justice system).

Most importantly, it has a standing Independent Advisory Group (IAG). A key principle of successive governments has been that hate crime policy should be informed by the views of those with varying experience and expertise in the subject. Since 2007 this has been delivered by the IAG. The group brings together victims, advocates, activists, and academic experts. Members of the group have expertise and involvement in all five strands of 'Monitored Hate Crime', these being disability, race, religion, sexual orientation, and transgender, as well as other related areas. The group is self-selecting and is led by an independent chair of their choosing, who also sits on the Strategy Board. This helps to ensure that their views are understood by Ministers and executives as they develop both their policy and practice responses.

We believe that the coordination of policy and operational responses, highlighted above, has been an essential and transferable factor in the progress achieved within England and Wales. It has led to a more cohesive response and, in essence, it has allowed the voices of victims to be at the heart of government and criminal justice agency decision-making.

WHAT CHANGES HAVE TAKEN PLACE?

When we look back over the past two decades, we can see significant changes in the response to hate crime in England and Wales (see Hall, Grieve, and Savage 2009, for a more detailed discussion of the 'legacies of Lawrence' in relation to policing in the UK). Rather than providing a chronological list we have selected some of the most significant milestones along the journey and concentrated on those that could be transferable to other states who are considering their own response. We have listed them in three sections below, categorized as legislation, policy and culture. We see these three strands as integral to an effective strategy for improving responses to hate crime, and consider them to be of equal importance. To use an analogy, they are like the three legs of a milking-stool that is rendered useless if only two of the legs are strong.

LEGISLATION

Although England and Wales does not have generic hate crime legislation per se, it nevertheless has a relatively robust legal framework for penalizing hate crime perpetrators. It also provides a positive legal duty on all agencies to help counter hate crimes. This framework has provided three specific options to assist in combating hate crime, these being:

    racially or religiously aggravated offences;
    specific offences that will always be classified as a 'hate' crime;
    enhanced sentencing legislation for any offence.

RACIALLY OR RELIGIOUSLY AGGRAVATED OFFENCES

The Crime and Disorder Act 1998 introduced racially aggravated offences and these were extended to include religious hostility in the Anti-terrorism, Crime and Security Act 2001. Sections 29–32 of the 1998 Act identify a number of offences which, if motivated by hostility or where the offender demonstrates hostility, can be treated as racially or religiously aggravated. These offences cover assaults, criminal damage, public order offences, and harassment. Whilst these offences are often not the most serious of offences they are amongst the most commonly recorded hate crimes (True Vision 2015), and they provide a transparency that has been welcomed by some victim groups.

In 2013 the UK Government asked the independent Law Commission to examine these offences to advise whether they should be extended to cover hate crime that targets sexual orientation, transgender status, and disability. As we write this, we are waiting on the Government response to their report, which was published in 2014 (Law Commission 2014).

SPECIFIC OFFENCES THAT WILL ALWAYS
BE CLASSIFIED AS A HATE CRIME

From an English and Welsh legal perspective, there are a small number of specific offences that would always be considered a 'hate' crime. These include racist chanting at a designated football match (Football Offences and Disorder Act 1999), but the most notable offences outlaw the incitement of hatred. The Public Order Act 1986 (Part 3) makes it an offence for a person to use threatening, abusive, or insulting words or behaviour, or to display any written material which is threatening, abusive, or insulting, intending to stir up racial hatred, or where, having regard to all the circumstances, racial hatred is likely to be stirred up. The Act provides similar provisions on the grounds of religion and sexual orientation, although the threshold for these latter offences is higher (see Part 3A). In these latter offences the behaviour must be threatening, and has to be intended to stir up hatred rather than it being likely to do so.

ENHANCED SENTENCING LEGISLATION FOR ANY OFFENCE

The 'cornerstone' of the legislative framework is the enhanced sentencing provision, which is provided by sections 145 and 146 of the Criminal Justice Act 2003. This provision instructs the courts to enhance a sentence for an offender and to declare in court that they are doing so, when it is found that an offender demonstrated, or was motivated by, hostility based on disability, race, religion, sexual orientation, or transgender status.

POSITIVE DUTY ON AGENCIES

The Equality Act 2010 creates a positive duty on public bodies, including on the police and other criminal justice agencies. Essentially this compels agencies to consider issues such as hate crime. Section 149 of the Act requires:

A public authority must, in the exercise of its functions, have due regard to the need to (amongst other duties):
a. eliminate discrimination, harassment, victimisation and any other conduct that is prohibited by or under this Act; and
b. foster good relations between persons who share a relevant protected characteristic and persons who do not share it.

POLICY

A key characteristic of the response to the Stephen Lawrence Inquiry has been the production and publication of policy documents that set out both the strategic goals and the operational guidance for government departments and criminal justice professionals.

A particular feature of the Stephen Lawrence Steering Group and the Cross-Government Hate Crime Programme has been the recognition of the need for joint working across agencies and departments. This has led to some key decisions being made holistically which has enabled progress to be made in key areas. One example of this is the development of hate crime data. In 2007 the programme was asked to agree a common definition of hate crime, which had not been in place beforehand. Indeed, the police and prosecution service had different definitions and recognized different strands within their respective policies.

Moreover, there was little consistency between police forces. Given the importance of the Stephen Lawrence Inquiry, all agencies had a policy response to racism, but the other victim groups included within the policy varied significantly. The Cross-Government Hate Crime Programme carried out a consultation, both with its own Independent Advisory Group and also with broader community groups and agencies. All forces agreed the resulting definition(s) (below) in November 2007, as did the Crown Prosecution Service shortly afterwards (True Vision 2015). This definition was important because it provided the ability to produce national hate crime data for the first time, with an unprecedented degree of consistency. As such, national recorded hate crime data has been provided since April 2008, initially by the police, and since April 2011 as part of the National Crime Statistics. Prosecution data has also been provided by the Crown Prosecution Service.

Table 12.1 Agreed criminal justice definitions in England and Wales

Title	Definition	Included subjects
Hate Motivation	'Hate crimes and incidents are taken to mean any crime or incident where the perpetrator's hostility or prejudice against an identifiable group of people is a factor in determining who is victimized'.	This is a broad and inclusive definition. A victim does not have to be a member of the group. In fact, anyone could be a victim of a hate crime.
Hate Incident	'Any non-crime incident which is perceived by the victim or any other person, to be motivated by a hostility or prejudice based on a person's race or perceived race' Or; 'Any non-crime incident which is perceived, by the victim or any other person, to be motivated by a hostility or prejudice based on a person's religion or perceived religion' Or; 'Any non-crime incident which is perceived, by the victim or any other person, to be motivated by a hostility or prejudice based on a person's sexual orientation or perceived sexual orientation'	Any racial group or ethnic background including countries within the United Kingdom and 'Gypsy & Traveller groups'. Any religious group including those who have no faith. Any person's sexual orientation. Any disability including physical disability, learning disability, and mental health. Including people who are transsexual, transgender, transvestite, and those who hold a Gender Recognition Certificate under the Gender Recognition Act 2004.

(continued)

Table 12.1 Continued

Title	Definition	Included subjects
	Or;	
	'Any non-crime incident which is perceived, by the victim or any other person, to be motivated by a hostility or prejudice based on a person's disability or perceived disability'	
	Or;	
	'Any non-crime incident which is perceived by the victim or any other person, to be motivated by a hostility or prejudice against a person who is transgender or perceived to be transgender'	
Hate Crimes	'A hate crime is any criminal offence which is perceived, by the victim or any other person, to be motivated by a hostility or prejudice based on a person's race or perceived race'.	Any racial group or ethnic background including countries within the United Kingdom and 'Gypsy & Traveller groups'.
		Any religious group including those who have no faith.
	'A hate crime is any criminal offence which is perceived, by the victim or any other person, to be motivated by a hostility or prejudice based on a person's race or perceived race'	Any racial group or ethnic background including countries within the United Kingdom and 'Gypsy & Traveller groups'.
	Or;	Any religious group including those who have no faith.
	'Any criminal offence which is perceived, by the victim or any other person, to be motivated by a hostility or prejudice based on a person's religion or perceived religion'	Any person's sexual orientation.
		Any disability including physical disability, learning disability, and mental health.
	Or;	Including people who are transsexual, transgender, transvestite, and those who hold a
	'Any criminal offence which is perceived, by the victim or any other person, to be motivated by a hostility or prejudice based on a person's sexual orientation or perceived sexual orientation'	Gender Recognition Certificate under the Gender Recognition Act 2004.
	Or;	
	'Any criminal offence which is perceived, by the victim or any other person, to be motivated by a hostility or prejudice based on a person's disability or perceived disability'	

(continued)

Table 12.1 Continued

Title	Definition	Included subjects
	Or;	
	'Any criminal offence which is perceived, by the victim or any other person, to be motivated by a hostility or prejudice against a person who is transgender or perceived to be transgender'	
Hate Crime Prosecution	'A hate crime prosecution is any hate crime which has been charged in the aggravated form or where the prosecutor has assessed that there is sufficient evidence of the hostility element to be put before the court when the offender is sentenced'.	

In addition to the recorded crime data, in 2008 questions were added to the national Crime Survey of England and Wales, which is an extensive household survey that measures people's experience of crime and the quality of service they received. This provides a rich source of information that can indicate the quality and extent of the service that is provided to victims.

Despite this progress, there are still some data yet to be provided from England and Wales. One is in the application of the sentencing provisions by the courts, as prescribed by the Criminal Justice Act 2003, and another is the effect of efforts to rehabilitate perpetrators.

CULTURE

The third leg of the effective response is addressing the issue of culture within society, politics, and criminal justice agencies (the former two will be discussed further, below). We would argue this is the most important but perhaps the most difficult issue to quantify or to identify evidence of change. We have outlined above the positive intentions of leaders from the mainstream political parties, but assessing degrees of hostility in society generally, and of the openness of criminal justice professionals specifically, is a much more difficult task.

The Stephen Lawrence Inquiry had assessed that, in 1993, the Metropolitan Police Service was 'institutionally racist' and that this unwitting bias affected the way the organization investigated Lawrence's murder, so there needed to be a robust response from police leaders. There is of course a vast body of literature that illustrates the ways in which organizational and individual cultures within policing can affect the implementation of policy into effective practice; and the adverse effect of culture on service provision to minority communities both generally, and more specifically in hate crime cases, is similarly well documented (see Hall 2013: ch 7 for an overview of this literature). It has been argued (Hall, Grieve, and Savage 2009) that one of the legacies of Lawrence has been to bring about a considerable degree of positive cultural change within policing, but this undoubtedly remains an ongoing challenge both here and in the police services of other states.

In England and Wales, Hall et al. (2009) have described post-Lawrence policing reform as a 'paradigm shift', resulting in a number of far-reaching and complex legacy areas (categorized variously as cultural, governance, political, legal, intelligence, and international). For our purposes here, the cultural impact on policing is defined as the impact of the 'Lawrence agenda' on the police 'mind-set'—ways of thinking about policing and the police role that have direct or indirect consequences for policing practices. Although there isn't the space here for a full discussion, for Hall et al. (2009), cultural change is evidenced through issues such as changes to police training; the adoption of a victim-centred definition of hate crime; third-party reporting systems; a shift towards recognizing the needs of victims in relation to service provision; 'colour-blind' and 'appropriate' approaches to policing that recognize the different needs of diverse communities; specific policing policies and instructions in relation to hate crime; and changes to investigative strategies.

HOW TRANSFERABLE IS THE ENGLISH AND WELSH EXPERIENCE?

Whilst the circumstances will vary from country to country and at different times, we believe there are many lessons we can take from the English and Welsh response to the racist murder of Stephen Lawrence, and the improvements that have occurred as a result, that would be likely to assist in other states, whether they are responding to a similar tragedy or proactively seeking to provide protection for citizens from targeted abuse. We would argue that effective strategies and operational improvements will be identified if the following key factors are adopted and effectively implemented:

Political leadership is an essential driver for change. It is needed to provide the legal framework, the resources needed to implement change, and to ensure that suitable performance targets are established.

Whilst the police will play a major part in any response to hate crime, *inclusive and coordinated governance* is needed to ensure that all state actors play their role in reducing hostility including in areas of indirect influence such as educators and victim services. We believe the England and Wales model of inclusive governance is transferable and could benefit most states, whether it is implemented at a local or national level.

Victim involvement in policy is another significant characteristic of the England and Wales model. The inclusion of a standing IAG gives credibility to the response and is likely to build confidence and provide more effective solutions.

Hate crime activity attracts greater scrutiny than most law enforcement practices, variously from victims, academics, and those opposed to policies. By providing *transparent policy*, particularly for police and prosecutors, we can begin to allay some of these fears and perceptions.

Accurate and published *hate crime data* provides the ability to measure progress and to highlight areas where intervention is necessary. This can seek to reassure affected communities but also to inform effective policing responses. Surveys to help indicate the extent of under-reporting and quality of service are also invaluable to help understand the problem.

- We have to accept that many victims of hate crime will not have confidence in the police and some would face accessibility challenges through language or other factors. It is important then that the police seek to encourage reporting by *providing accessible routes for reporting*, including through the provision of online resources such as the True Vision web facility (www.report-it.org.uk) or through third-party reporting facilities within communities.

However, meaningful engagement and strategies of the types discussed above can, inevitably, only take place if governments, and therefore policy makers, together with the agencies of the criminal justice system, have an interest in furthering the hate crime agenda, and regard it as a priority. The role and political inclinations of the state and its institutions can therefore have serious implications for shaping an environment in which hate can potentially flourish. The extent to which a country's political stance serves either to protect or infringe human rights therefore represents an important issue for consideration. One might reasonably assume that the numbers of recorded hate crimes in any given country are, at least in part, an indication of the importance (or otherwise) with which it is held politically.

Of course there are different ways in which the politics of a country can shape its policy responses to these issues. This is illustrated by Bleich (2007), for example, who notes that different countries of the European Union have pursued distinctive paths in their responses to hate crimes. To illustrate this Bleich highlights the primacy of a criminal justice approach in the UK, whilst Germany has devoted resources to civil society groups with the intention of countering right-wing extremism, and France has taken symbolic and educational approaches to the problem. As Bleich (2007: 160–2, emphasis added) suggests:

broadly speaking, states have choices to make about how much they use repressive policies aimed at preserving public order versus instructive policies aimed at promoting tolerance and liberal democratic values . . . Most commentators agree that much has changed during the past few years, yet most also agree that each state's commitment to eradicating racist violence is not as strong as it could be. *Developing nationally effective policies thus depends on learning from other states about the pragmatic steps a country can take.* It also depends on responding to domestic actors who articulate concerns about specific problems and suggest possible solutions. Obeying this rule of thumb will go a long way toward limiting the impact of racist violence and toward promoting national cohesion.

Of course, 'commitment', the 'international learning process', and listening and responding to 'articulated concerns' are by no means guaranteed. In comparative terms, then, in our view England and Wales is the 'world leader' in terms of responding to hate crimes. This position, as one of us has argued elsewhere (Hall, Grieve, and Savage 2009), is largely a product of the 'legacies of Lawrence', which have been instrumental in generating or accelerating far-reaching and multi-tiered changes to political and policy responses to hate crime.

The outcomes of this 'paradigm shift' in terms of radically changing the goals of policy and practice, which in many ways is still in progress, can be seen in the range of outcomes that appear to set the England and Wales example apart from its international counterparts. As we have variously considered elsewhere in this chapter, these include, but are not limited to, the broad and inclusive definitions of hate crime employed; the focus on appropriate service provision to victims and communities; the True Vision online (and other) third-party reporting system: the volume of incidents reported to the police; the number of diversity strands for which data is collected and published; the scope and strength of legal recognition for diversity issues; the number of cases prosecuted; the level of financial support thus far provided by government, most noticeably through the Victim's Fund, to support the valuable work of NGOs in this area; the previous and current government's Hate Crime Action Plan; the engagement with Independent Advisory Groups and other community representatives; the various Hate Crime Policing Manuals; and the demand from other countries for knowledge transfer (Hall 2013).

But, whilst the comparative position of England and Wales should be a source of some satisfaction, it should not become a source of complacency, and nor would we wish to convey a message of 'Britain knows best'; far from it. Indeed, in recent times, the political commitment of government has attracted some criticism. In 2009, the tenth anniversary of the publication of the Public Inquiry into Stephen Lawrence's murder provided an opportunity to reflect on the extent of progress made in relation to the areas covered by the Inquiry's original recommendations. The general consensus of opinion was that 'much had been achieved, but that much still remained to be done' (EHRC 2009; Hall, Grieve, and Savage 2009; Rollock 2009; Stone 2009). Nevertheless, the period since the tenth anniversary has seen two changes of government, and the 'hate crime' agenda is no longer under the guardianship of the Labour administration that instigated it. This situation has been the source of some anxiety for many who hold concerns relating to the subsequent governments' desire and commitment to further pursuing the agenda set in motion by its predecessor (Muir 2012), not least in times of considerable financial austerity.

In what are increasingly difficult times globally, sustaining political interest and creating and maintaining an environment in which hate cannot flourish therefore seem to us to be critical issues for the furtherance of the hate crime agenda, not least because, as we have alluded to throughout this chapter, much still remains to be done in terms of addressing hate and hate crime internationally. Notwithstanding recent domestic concerns, we would still contend that those of us in England and Wales are in a *comparatively* privileged position in this regard, although much still remains to be done here too.

However, the question as to how to secure the protection of human rights of others elsewhere in the world where combating hate crime has been, and remains, somewhat less of a political priority (perhaps shaped by deep-rooted cultural differences) remains both problematic and unanswered. As Perry (2001: 179) suggests:

hate-motivated violence can flourish only in an enabling environment...such an environment historically has been conditioned by the activity—or inactivity–of the state...State practices, policy, and rhetoric often have provided the formal framework within which hate crime—as an informal mechanism of control—emerges.

The monumental challenge in this regard, it would seem, is to secure the complicity of states in terms of rhetoric, policy, and practice, in the creation of *dis-enabling* environments where the human rights of all are both respected and protected. On the available evidence, then, international organizations seeking to improve national responses to hate crime, including England and Wales, undoubtedly have some way to go in this unenviable undertaking.

This undertaking is further complicated by the fact that, as complex events, hate crimes pose significant challenges to law makers, the police, and prosecutors. There are many issues both internal and external to those individuals and agencies responsible for law enforcement, and over which they have varying degrees of control, that inevitably impact upon their ability to enforce the law, regardless of jurisdiction, and to respond effectively and to provide a service appropriate to the needs of victims and wider communities.

The potential for practical difficulties in law enforcement in hate crime cases are reflected in the problems experienced in the prosecution of such cases, as illustrated by the relatively low rates of conviction for these offences in most countries where such laws exist (OSCE 2014). At one level the potential for difficulty arises because, arguably, the law in this field reflects a number of the elements that Pound (1917) argued would limit legal effectiveness, not least because of the problems associated with proving the motivation behind an offence, or that the offence was aggravated by some prejudice-based hostility, and the extent to which the law is able to achieve its intended purposes.

In addition, Pound (ibid) rightly notes the importance of the role of law enforcement agencies, most notably the police, in the process of law enforcement. The role of the police is crucial, as noted by Cotterrell (1992: 56):

How the law is put into effect is clearly as important as its content. The nature of the enforcement agencies used, the degree of commitment of enforcement agents to implementation of the law, their morale and—a closely related factor—the amount of resources available to ensure compliance, are all shown to be extremely significant factors. In addition, the particular strategy of coercion or persuasion employed in regulation is clearly of great importance.

The theoretical issues concerning 'street-level bureaucrats' (Grimshaw and Jefferson 1987; Lipsky 1980) demonstrate the powerful position held by those often in lower ranks of law enforcement agencies, and the potential for these employees to determine the outcomes of both law and organizational policy through their use of discretion and the related influence of individual and organizational culture.

With these issues in mind, it is important to note that in some countries, notably in England and Wales, law enforcement is only one aspect of the policing response to hate crimes. It is therefore important to consider measuring 'success' in policing in other ways. For example, the 'success' of policing in relation to hate crimes might be better measured against the numbers of hate crimes reported by victims, where, depending on the circumstances, an increase may signify an increase in trust and confidence in the police, or by victim satisfaction with the police response, as indicated by qualitative and quantitative surveys. The latter is of significant importance in assessing the 'success' of the police and is of far greater informational value than clear-up rates.

It may also be possible to further measure 'success' against the educative role achieved by policing activities in the community, or the strength of the message conveyed to the public that hate crimes will not be tolerated and the suffering of victims will be treated seriously. One might also consider the ability of the police to respond proactively to a perceived threat or tension in a community; the collecting and dissemination of hate-related intelligence; the training of other police officers to respond appropriately to hate crimes; or the ability of the police to liaise with advocacy groups and 'build bridges' between minority communities and the police. All of these represent significant functions undertaken by some police services which are not measurable simply by considering clear-up rates, or whether numerically hate crime goes up or down. That said, their importance should not be underestimated, particularly given the difficulties in law enforcement in this field. In other words, enacting and attempting to enforce hate crime legislation is not a panacea to the problem of hate crime.

CONCLUSION

In this chapter we have drawn upon the learning acquired from England and Wales' experience of responding to hate crimes and attempted, as far as is possible, to extract the elements that may, depending on domestic circumstances, prove to be transferable to other states who may be seeking a transition from their current position towards what we have termed the 'utopian option'. We are not naïve enough to think that the situation here in England and Wales is perfect. Indeed, it is far from it. But undoubtedly much progress has been made in the past twenty years or so, much of which is derived from the painful lessons learned from all too tragic events and subsequent criminal justice failures. Therefore, if these lessons, where appropriate, can be learned elsewhere and responses to hate crime improved without the need for similar events to have necessarily taken place first, then that is clearly preferable. At this point in time the 'utopian option' may simply be an impossible dream, but as we stated at the outset of this chapter, that should not stop us from doing all that we can to try to improve the situation of those whose lives are blighted by hate and hate crime. The sharing of experiences, policies, and practices is just one step on the road to achieving that.

REFERENCES

ACPO 2000. *ACPO Guide to Identifying and Combating Hate Crime*. London: ACPO.

Bleich, E. 2007. 'Hate Crime Policy in Western Europe: Responding To Racist Violence in Britain, Germany and France'. *American Behavioral Scientist*, 51(2): 149–65.

College of Policing 2014. *Tackling Hate Crime—A National Hate Crime Strategy and Operational Guidance*. London: The College of Policing.

Cotterrell, R. 1992. *The Sociology of Law* (2nd edition). London: Butterworths.

EHRC 2009. 'Police and Racism: What Has Been Achieved 10 Years after the Stephen Lawrence Inquiry Report?' http://www.equalityhumanrights.com/uploaded_files/raceinbritain/policeandracism.pdf

Grimshaw, R. and Jefferson, T. 1987. *Interpreting Policework*. London: Allen and Unwin.

Hall, N. 2005. *Hate Crime*. Cullompton: Willan Publishing.

Hall, N. 2013. *Hate Crime* (2nd edn.). London: Routledge.

Hall, N., Grieve, J., and Savage, S. (eds.) 2009. *Policing and the Legacy of Lawrence*. London: Willan Publishing.

Hall, N., Corb, A., Giannasi, P., and Grieve, J. (eds.) 2014. *The Routledge International Handbook on Hate Crime*. London: Routledge.

HM Government 2012. *Challenge It, Report It, Stop It: The Government's Plan to Tackle Hate Crime*. London: HM Government.

Home Office 1999. *The Home Secretary's Action Plan*. London: Home Office.

Home Office 2009. *Hate Crime—A Cross-Government Action Plan*. London: Home Office.

Jacobs, J. B. and Potter, K. 1998. *Hate Crimes: Criminal Law and Identity Politics*. New York: Oxford University Press.

Law Commission 2014. *Hate Crime: Should the Current Offences be Extended?* London: The Law Commission.

Lipsky, M. 1980. *Street-level Bureaucracy*. New York: Russell Sage Foundation.

Macpherson, W. 1999. *The Stephen Lawrence Inquiry Report*. London: Home Office.

Muir, H. 2012. 'Coalition responds to Doreen Lawrence over race equality'. *The Guardian*, 23 December. http://www.guardian.co.uk/uk/2012/dec/23/coalition-respond-doreen-lawrence-equality

OSCE 2013. *Hate Crimes in the OSCE Region: Incidents and Responses. Annual Report for 2012*. Warsaw: OSCE.

OSCE 2014. *Hate Crimes in the OSCE Region: Incidents and Responses. Annual Report for 2013*. Warsaw: OSCE.

Perry, B. 2001. *In the Name of Hate: Understanding Hate Crimes*. New York: Routledge.

Pound, R. 1917. 'The Limits of Effective Legal Action'. *International Journal of Legal Ethics*, 27: 150–67.

Rollock, N. 2009. 'The Stephen Lawrence Inquiry 10 Years On: An Analysis of the Literature'. http://www.runnymedetrust.org/uploads/publications/pdfs/StephenLawrenceInquiryReport-2009.pdf

Scarman, L. 1981. *The Brixton Disorders: 10–12 April 1981: Report of an Inquiry: Presented to Parliament by the Secretary of State for the Home Department, November*. London: HMSO.

Smith, K., Lader, D., Hoare, J., and Lau, I. 2012. *Hate Crime, Cyber Security and the Experience of Crime among Children: Findings from the 2010/11 British Crime Survey*. London: Home Office.

Stone, R. 2009. 'Stephen Lawrence Review – An Independent Commentary to Mark the 10th Anniversary of the Stephen Lawrence Inquiry'. http://www.stoneashdown. org/images/stories/slr_report.pdf

Sullivan, A. 1999. 'What's so Bad About Hate? The Illogic and Illiberalism Behind Hate Crime Laws'. *New York Times Magazine*, 26 September.

True Vision 2015. *True Vision*. http://www.report-it.org.uk/reporting_internet_hate_crime

United Nations 1948. The Universal Declaration of Human Rights. Paris: The General Assembly of the United Nations.

PART III

INTERNATIONAL RESPONSES TO HATE CRIME

13

NATIONAL MONITORING OF HATE CRIME IN EUROPE: THE CASE FOR A EUROPEAN LEVEL POLICY

Michael Whine

INTRODUCTION

European states have been under a duty to combat hate crime for a number of years; both as a consequence of their general duty to protect human rights and because of the development of case law on discrimination based on Article 14 of the European Convention on Human Rights. Three agreements in particular established these duties: the European Convention on Human Rights established judicial mechanisms for dealing with breaches of the human rights contained therein; with regard to the EU and its Member States, the Treaty on the Functioning of the European Union required the Union to ensure a high level of security through measures to prevent and combat crime, racism, and xenophobia, while the Charter of Fundamental Rights of the European Union, legally binding since December 2009, guarantees, among others, the rights to human dignity on grounds such as religion, ethnic origin, and sexual orientation.

However, it is only since 2003 that states have also been required to collect and publish data on hate crime, in order to ensure consistency in formulating counterstrategies and to combat such crime more effectively. The term 'hate crime' itself is relatively recent, only coming into general use by policy makers in Europe in 2003 when participating states of the Organization for Security and Co-operation in Europe (OSCE) made a commitment to 'collect and keep records on reliable information and statistics on hate crimes, including on forms of violent manifestations of racism, xenophobia, discrimination, and anti-Semitism' (OSCE 2003: 2). Their decision came in the wake of previously expressed concerns over the increase in hate crimes, and when they pledged to 'take effective measures, including the adoption, in conformity with their constitutional systems and their international obligations, of such laws as may be necessary, to provide protection against any acts that constitute incitement to violence against persons or groups based on national, racial, ethnic or religious discrimination, hostility of hatred, including anti-Semitism' (OSCE 1990: 21).

Despite such pledges, European policy makers have noted that states are failing to implement the agreements they have entered into in the full spirit in which they were intended. They have recognized that the rise in hate crime, fuelled by economic distress, large-scale migration, and other concerns, has the capacity to de-stabilize the Union. There is also growing recognition that the internet facilitates and enhances these developments and enables the spread of hate against minorities, as well as the growth of extremist politics (Council of the European Union 2013; OSCE 2009).

Inter-regional agencies have also voiced their concern. Citing obligations under the International Convention on the Elimination of All Forms of Racial Discrimination and the International Covenant on Civil and Political Rights, the United Nations Commissioner for Refugees noted in 2009 that incidents of hate crimes that came to the attention of UNHCR and its network of partners needed to be recorded and reported to the authorities to promote comprehensive, timely, and impartial investigations of bias-motivated crimes (UNHCR 2009). In 2012, the UN Secretary-General presented the report of the Special Rapporteur on contemporary forms of racism to the UN General Assembly in which he lamented the 'lack of sufficient data collection mechanisms and the absence of statistics on hate crimes' (UNGA 2012: 22).

In this chapter I employ a policy perspective to examine the obligations undertaken by European states to monitor hate crime. The chapter outlines the reasons why many states are failing to effectively monitor hate crime, and highlights the measures they are expected to take to improve their performance. In doing so, I shall also be updating the information I have previously published elsewhere (Whine 2015).

DEALING WITH THE THREAT OF HATE CRIME

A recent OSCE report notes that there is a 'chronic lack of reliable and comprehensive data on hate crimes across the region' (OSCE 2014: 1). This matters because hate crime is a human rights issue with wide social and political ramifications. Hate-motivated crime undermines the victim's sense of worth, self-confidence, and right to a place in society. The message that the hate crime perpetrator sends is that the victim has no right to be what he is, to live where he does, and at its most extreme, no right to life, with the effect being magnified as it extends to the victim's community. This may have a mobilizing or retaliatory effect on the victim's community, and for these reasons the European agencies rightly see hate crime as a threat to the security of Member States, and to Europe itself. Moreover, the harm caused is greater when the victim belongs to a group that suffers from long-term victimization or deprivation, who may suffer from secondary victimization when the police or other criminal justice agencies fail to respond in a sensitive manner or disregard the bias motive behind the crime. Hate crime therefore undermines European commitments to democracy and the fundamental rights of equality and non-discrimination.

The failure of European states to collect and maintain statistics therefore frustrates any effective policy formulation and appropriate resource allocation to counter hate crime. But for such data to be usable it must be comparable, that is, like-for-like. It must be disaggregated by type of crime (e.g., assaults, incitement, etc.) and by targets to establish which groups are suffering. Data on prosecutions and convictions are likewise required to assess the seriousness with which states treat the problem, and details of punishments are required to determine if states are unmasking the motive behind hate crime, and uplifting sentences on conviction. This results from decisions by the European Court of Human Rights (ECtHR), which has ruled in a number of cases that states are obliged to 'unmask' the motivation behind racist crimes or crimes committed because of the victim's religious belief (FRA 2012). If the criminal justice system overlooks the bias motivation behind a crime then this can amount to a violation of Article 14 of the European Convention on Human Rights.

Recognizing that states fail to monitor hate crime has led the European agencies to encourage civil society groups to provide data in addition to states parties. Non-governmental organizations (NGOs) may have an interest in publicizing the crimes committed against those on whose behalf they work, and they can access those victims who are unable or unwilling to report directly to the police. Civil society groups can add context to their reporting in a way that criminal justice agencies cannot. They can report the build-up of non-crime incidents in an area or against a community which the police might ignore; and they can more effectively describe the harm suffered by communities and how communities respond, that officials may dismiss.

Nevertheless, civil society reporting is too often based on anecdotal or media reporting and may not be evidenced. Consequently the agencies encourage and fund civil society initiatives such as Facing Facts, a partnership between the Brussels-based CEJI—a Jewish response to an inclusive Europe; the UK-based Community Security Trust; the Dutch Jewish monitoring group CIDI; and the international lesbian, gay, bisexual, transgender, and intersex group ILGA, which trains civil society groups to monitor and record hate crime to criminal justice standards (Facing Facts Forward 2015). Another is the annual Shadow Reports of the European Network Against Racism, which represents anti-racist monitoring groups across Europe, and which are designed to fill the gaps in official and academic data (ENAR 2013–14).

Aside from the legal and convention considerations, it is apparent that hate crime easily crosses borders in a post-Schengen Europe, facilitated by universal access to the internet, electronic media, and the persistence of populism, racism, and anti-immigrant movements which link internationally with each other, overtly and covertly (Whine 2012). Police and criminal justice systems, particularly in the new Member States of central and eastern Europe, also now have to understand their human rights' duties and responsibilities in a democratic society, and reorganize to recognize and investigate crimes motivated by hate (COREPOL 2014).

EUROPEAN POLICIES ON MONITORING
HATE CRIME

The legal obligation to combat hate crime in Europe is contained within the Council Framework Decision on combating certain forms of racism and xenophobia by means of criminal law, which EU Member States agreed in 2008.That they took seven years to negotiate the agreement gives some idea of the complexities they encountered in defining a common criminal approach and establishing legislative and judicial cooperation (Council Framework Decision 2008).

The Framework Decision requires states, amongst other things, to criminalize public incitement to violence or hatred against religious, racial, ethnic, and other groups; to criminalize the public condoning, denying, or grossly trivializing genocide, crimes against humanity, and war crimes; and to ensure that racist and xenophobic motivation is considered an aggravating circumstance during sentencing. Its purpose is to approximate domestic laws, and to promote full and effective judicial cooperation. Member States were given two years to comply, in recognition that each would be approaching the agreement from different legal and political positions. In 2013 and 2014, respectively, two reviews on states' compliance were published.

The first review, in the form of an Opinion by the European Union Agency for Fundamental Rights (FRA), was compiled in response to a two-part request by the Council of the European Union, the European Commission, and the European Parliament. The authors of the Opinion noted that theirs was an assessment of the impact of the Framework Decision on Member States, and in so doing, asked what more should be done to better protect and acknowledge the rights of hate crime victims (FRA 2013). They added that the Framework Decision itself contains two sections: the first and main part aims at harmonizing states' penal laws against hate crime and 'negationism' (i.e. denial of genocide and the Holocaust); the second requires states' courts to 'unmask' the discriminatory motives of offenders, that is, the hate element of the crime (FRA 2013). The first part of the Opinion briefly assessed the impact of the Framework Decision on the rights of victims, and contrasted this with an assessment of certain aspects of victims' rights recognized in other instruments of secondary legislation. The second explored options and requirements to improve the victim's rights.

The Framework Decision obliges EU Member States to ensure that racist motives behind offences are not overlooked, that criminal justice systems give them appropriate attention and reflect the crucial rights of hate crime victims, as required by established European case law (*Nachova and Others v Bulgaria*, 2005). In that sense it also supports the 2012 EU Victims Directive, due to be transposed at Member State level by November 2015. This provides for the rights of crime victims to recognition, effective access to justice, participation in proceedings, and protection against repeat victimization, and is more fully explained below.

The second part of the request was to examine areas of concern where FRA is of the opinion that EU action could and should improve the situation of the rights of victims of hate crime, and bring the Framework Decision into line with the Victims' Directive. Here the Opinion authors noted that FRA has compiled the most extensive set of EU-wide data on different groups' experiences of hate crime, based on an EU-wide survey of a randomly selected sample of 23,500 migrants and minorities (EU-MIDIS), and cited by way of illustration some of its published research reports: Data in Focus report—Minorities as Victims of Crime; Making Hate Crimes Visible in the European Union: acknowledging victim's rights; Discrimination and Hate Crimes against Jews in EU Member States, etc. (FRA 2013).

The FRA Opinion recommended that Member States take a number of actions to ensure full compliance with the Framework Decision. These included taking appropriate measures to facilitate the reporting of hate crime; encouraging victims and witnesses to report such crime; raising awareness among those at particular risk; and in doing so, working closely with civil society and human rights organizations. It further recommended providing appropriate training for officials who come into contact with victims of hate crime; establishing special hate crime units in police services; paying particular attention to victims' needs; ratifying the Additional Protocol on Cyberhate to the Council of Europe Convention on Cybercrime; and assessing whether police and public prosecutors are sufficiently staffed and equipped to respond to hate crimes. An important recommendation within the Opinion was that Member States should collect and publish data on hate crimes, on the basis of clear and comprehensive guidelines, and on an annual basis. These are, at a minimum: the number of incidents which are crimes; the number of convictions of offenders; the grounds on which the offences are found to be discriminatory; and the punishment handed down to offenders (FRA 2013: Action 23).

It is instructive to note that Member States were urged within the twenty-five recommendations to acknowledge and pay proper attention to the discriminatory motive behind, and the nature of, hate crime and not to simply label it as the consequence of 'right-wing extremism' or 'left-wing extremism'. This practice, by Germany, Austria, and some Nordic states, tends to obscure the element of discrimination present in hate crime, and conceals the particular victimization suffered by hate crime victims. For instance, FRA has noted in this context that 'research also shows that right-wing extremism is a relatively rare phenomenon' (FRA 2013: 3). In this respect it is also noteworthy that research in the UK and Europe generally has shown that hate crimes may not be mission-oriented by extremists, but are often the consequence of abrasive encounters on the streets, or occur as an overspill of events elsewhere (EU-Midis 2012; Iganski et al. 2005).

Expanding on the need to collect data, the Opinion noted that the lack of a consistent approach between Member States results in gaps in data collection across the EU. Differing legal approaches and interpretations of what constitutes hate crime influence the depth and breadth of official data collection mechanisms. These disparities mean that Member States may measure different realities, complicating any analysis of the prevalence of hate crimes across the EU. Data collected by FRA, and published in its reports, consistently show that persistent gaps exist in data collection on crimes motivated by racism, xenophobia, antisemitism, and especially crimes motivated by another person's sexual orientation, gender identity, or disability, or because of their presumed identification with these grounds (FRA 2013).

To pre-empt governments using the excuse that data protection laws prevent the compilation and publication of statistics, Member States are advised to collect and publish hate crime data at an aggregate level and on an anonymous basis so that no individual case can be identified. This would serve to acknowledge victims' rights flowing from ECtHR case law decisions to 'unmask' bias motives underlying criminal offences (EU 2008; FRA 2013).

The Framework Decision contains other weaknesses which it notes, as does the Opinion. These are that states experience difficulties regarding judicial cooperation; that there is a need for further approximation of criminal laws; that full harmonization may not be possible because of long-standing traditions; and that Member States may choose to punish only conduct which is either carried out in a manner likely to disturb public order or which is threatening, abusive, or insulting, ignoring other forms of hate crime (FRA 2013).

The second report on the Framework Decision was compiled by the European Commission on behalf of the European Parliament and the Council, and was delivered in January 2014. Its primary focus is on its transposition into domestic law by Member States. The report examines how states have adopted the main elements, and their reasons for not doing so, if applicable. It concludes that 'at present it appears that a number of Member States have not transposed fully and/or correctly all the provisions of the Framework Decision and notes that the Commission will engage in bilateral dialogues with them during 2014 with a view to ensuring full and correct transposition' (European Commission 2014: 9).

The report added that the existence of reliable, comparable, and systematically collected data can contribute to more effective implementation of the Framework Decision, and noted that hate speech and hate crime incidents should always be registered, as well as their case history, in order to assess the level of prosecutions and sentences. It further added that the collection of hate speech and hate crime data was not uniform across the EU and consequently did not allow for reliable cross-country comparisons. The Commission therefore asked all Member States to provide it with data on the incidence of, and the criminal response to, hate speech and hate crime (European Commission 2014).

THE EU VICTIMS' DIRECTIVE

The 2012 EU Victims' Directive established minimum standards on the rights, support, and protection of victims of crime, and replaced the 2001 Council Framework Decision, which required Member States, inter alia to approximate their laws and regulations to afford victims of crime a high level of protection, to develop cooperation between them, and to improve and train victim support services.

Referencing the Treaty on the Functioning of the European Union, and in particular Article 82(2) thereof which calls for judicial cooperation on criminal matters, the mutual admissibility of evidence between Member States, and the rights of individuals and crime victims, the 2012 Directive noted that the Union has set itself the objective of maintaining and developing freedom, security, and justice, and that a cornerstone of this is the mutual recognition of 'judicial decisions in civil and criminal matters', and 'the establishment of minimum standards in regard to victims of crime' (Directive 2012/29/EU 2012: 1).

The preamble to the Victims' Directive notes inter alia that victims must be encouraged to report crimes in order to break the cycle of repeat victimization, and that the response by authorities in a respectful, sensitive, professional, and non-discriminatory manner will increase victims' confidence in criminal justice systems, and reduce the number of unreported crimes (Directive 2012/29/EU 2012). A second introductory note states that the collection of systematic and adequate statistical data is recognized as an essential component of effective policy making, and that states are therefore required to communicate relevant statistical data on crime victims, including at least the number and type of the reported crime, and, as far as is known, the number, age, and gender of the victims. Relevant data can also include that recorded by judicial and law enforcement agencies, and as far as possible, administrative data compiled by healthcare and social welfare services by public and non-governmental victim support or restorative justice services, and other organizations working with victims of crime (Directive 2012/29/EU 2012).

None of these provisions specifically apply to hate crime, but an introductory note in the Directive lists protected characteristics, which include race, colour, ethnic or social origin, genetic features, language, religion or belief, political or any other opinion, membership of a national minority, property, birth, disability, age, gender, gender expression, gender identity, sexual orientation, residence, status, or health, which are to be recognized and taken into account. This is clearly too long and no state will have the resources, or the political will, to include all of them, but race, religion, ethnic or social origin, gender and gender expression or identity, as well as national minority, are generally regarded as necessary to monitor. Another notes that systematic and adequate statistical data collection is an essential component of effective policymaking, that reliable support services should be made available to victims, and that competent authorities should encourage and facilitate reporting of crimes and allow them to break the cycle of repeat victimization. The Victims' Directive therefore is an important step forward which strengthens European guidelines: all crime is a wrong against society and a violation of individual rights; victims should be recognized and treated in a respectful, sensitive, and professional manner without discrimination of any kind; the competent authorities should address victims' needs, their personal situation, ensure that they are protected from secondary and repeat victimization, and receive appropriate support to facilitate their recovery (Directive 2012/29/EU 2012).

However, like the Framework Decision, the Victims' Directive contains inherent weaknesses. Not the least of these is the overlong list of protected characteristics which no government is willing to monitor, although the minimum relevant statistical data should be achievable by all, in time.

THE EUROPEAN UNION AGENCY
FOR FUNDAMENTAL RIGHTS (FRA)

The first Europe-wide report on hate crime was undertaken in April 2005 by the European Union Monitoring Centre on Racism and Xenophobia (EUMC), the predecessor to FRA. Their report presented the information gathered from 2001 up to part of 2004 by the EUMC RAXEN network of national focal points.

The first part of the report presented an overview of legal obligations of 'race', 'ethnicity', and 'racism', and offered critical commentary on attempts to measure the extent and nature of racist violence, particularly as a comparative cross-national undertaking. It also sought information on the effectiveness of official and alternative data collection mechanisms. In the second part, the EUMC explored the available data from each of the (then) fifteen Member States. The third part presented a comparative review, noting the limitations of trying to compare the sparse and different data sets, an examination of the cultural and criminological context in which racist violence occurs, and finally an assessment of states' responses (EUMC 2005).

In summary, the EUMC found that no two states had data that was strictly comparable; three states had no public official data at all; one state released only limited figures; three states concentrated their data collection on 'discriminatory offences' alone; two states focused their attention on the activities of (right wing) extremists only; and only four had comprehensive data collection mechanisms (EUMC 2005).

The discrepancies in collected hate crime data were therefore apparent and it was obvious that official data under-recorded hate crime to a substantial degree, either because official recording systems did not exist, or because they were not thorough or comprehensive enough. Since then data collection systems have improved and the 2011 FRA Annual Report acknowledged that some states had improved data collection on racist crime but that they still have a long way to go, and many still did not have systematic data collection mechanisms in place. FRA therefore concluded that it remained difficult to quantify the prevalence of racist crime in the EU, or to compare trends over time (EUMC 2011). Some improvements were noted in the 2012 report as more states had changed and improved their data collection systems. But in yet another 2012 report it observed that no further progress had been made despite states' commitments to counter discrimination, intolerance, and hate crime (EUMC 2012).

FRA accordingly recommended the introduction of legislation at the EU and national level that would oblige Member States to collect and publish data, recognizing that this would encourage confidence among victims to report hate crime. Law enforcement agencies were urged to be attentive to bias motivation when investigating and prosecuting crime. FRA further recommended enhanced penalties for hate crime in order to underline their seriousness, and that courts should address these bias motivations publicly (FRA 2012).

In order to circumvent under-recording by states, and to fill in the gaps, FRA instituted a series of Europe-wide surveys on experiences of criminal victimization.

The first, the *European Union Minorities and Discrimination Survey* (EU-MIDIS), reported its findings in 2009. Among the questions asked were a series about respondents' experiences of being a victim of crime in five areas (theft of or from a vehicle, burglary or attempted burglary, theft of personal property not involving force or threat, assault, and threat and harassment of a serious nature). The focus of the survey was on the largest migrant or indigenous minority ethnic groups in each Member State, such as Roma and North African migrants, whose direct experience of discrimination and hate crime was under-recorded. The survey found that the overwhelming majority of correspondents actually never reported incidents of hate crime or discrimination to law enforcement or other public authorities because they did not know this was unlawful, in the case of discrimination, or it would not change anything, in the case of hate crime (EU-MIDIS 2012).

In 2012, FRA published a detailed analysis of the EU-MIDIS survey data examining in more detail information, including on whether racially or religiously offensive language was used, whether the matter was reported to the police, and the reasons why no report was made to the police in cases of negative responses. Among the key findings in the Report were that every fourth person from a minority group had been the victim of crime at least once in the twelve months preceding the survey; Sub-Saharan Africans, closely followed by Roma, experienced the highest overall victimization; minorities are victims of personal theft and assault or threat of assault more than the majority population; more than one in four respondents from some minorities considered they were the victim of racially motivated crime in the previous twelve months; and most incidents of assault or threat of assault were not committed by members of right-wing extremist groups (EU MIDIS 2012).

Since then three other FRA surveys have covered issues of hate crime: the survey on experiences and perceptions of antisemitism among Jewish communities (FRA 2012); the survey on discrimination against, and victimization of, lesbian, gay, bisexual, and transgender persons (EU LGBT 2013); and the survey on violence against women (FRA 2014). Taken together, these surveys provide a more complete picture of hate crime and criminal victimization among some of the most populous minority groups, as well as among the general population (women), demonstrating the serious extent of under-reporting by states parties. They further show that despite legislation and improved practices, the reality, and the fear, of hate crime is growing.

The latest FRA report based on official data for 2013 notes that only five states provided comprehensive data as required (Finland, Netherlands, Spain, Sweden, and United Kingdom). It notes that the twenty-eight Member States of the EU differ on the data they record and publish, and that the data are not comparable between them. The report adds that official data collection systems often fail to capture the situation on the ground, and that the states which record the highest number of crimes are not necessarily those where most crimes are committed. FRA therefore suggest looking at trends in collected data to provide an indication of the increase or decrease in hate crime, but also changes in recording procedures. They urge states to intensify their efforts to collect data and to implement awareness-raising activities in order to encourage reporting, and to provide law enforcement and judicial authorities with specialist training to enable them to effectively identify, investigate, and prosecute hate crimes, and to respond sensitively to the rights and needs of victims (FRA 2015).

THE ORGANIZATION FOR SECURITY AND CO-OPERATION IN EUROPE (OSCE)

OSCE commitments to combating hate crime were laid down by the 2006 Ministerial Council meeting, which tasked the Office for Democratic Institutions and Human Rights (ODIHR) to serve as a collection point for information and statistics on hate crimes and relevant legislation; make this information publicly available through its Tolerance and Non Discrimination Information System (TANDIS 2015a); strengthen its early warning function to identify, report, and raise awareness of hate-motivated incidents and trends; provide recommendations and assistance to participating states; and report annually on challenges and responses to hate-motivated incidents in the OSCE region (Decision No. 13/06 2006).

This mandate was subsequently developed and strengthened by the Ministerial Council in 2009, where participating states committed to enact specific tailored legislation to combat hate crimes; encourage victims to report hate crime (recognizing that under-reporting prevents states from devising effective policies); facilitate the cooperation of civil society; improve hate crime victims' access to counselling and legal assistance; introduce or further develop professional training and capacity-building activities for law enforcement, prosecution, and judicial officials dealing with hate crimes; and use ODIHR education and training resources to ensure a comprehensive approach to the tackling of hate crimes (Decision No.9/09 2009).

Additionally, ODIHR recognized specific types of hate crime, including those against Jews, Muslims, Roma, and Sinti, and lesbian, gay, bisexual, and transgender (LGBT) communities. These categories have also been recognized in Ministerial Council decisions, and latterly by the appointment of Special Representatives of the Chairman in Office, whose tasks are to focus participating states' attention on the threats encountered by these communities (TANDIS 2015b).

However, ODIHR also complains about the paucity of data. In its Annual Report for 2012 it records that fifty-one states reported that they collect hate crime data, and that forty-one states had completed questionnaires or otherwise provided updated information on data collection for 2012, but only twenty-seven states had actually submitted official statistics or information on incidents of hate crimes. The Report adds that where hate crime statistics are collected, it may be by the police, prosecutors, or other agencies, but that some states do not collect any data or do not make their data public. Information provided by a number of police officers and officials to this author, though not empirically collected data, suggests that the reasons for this are either lack of money for instituting the required system changes, or that the governments concerned have other priorities.

ODIHR gathers data for its annual hate crime report through a questionnaire sent to states' National Point of Contact on hate crime (NPC), which contains questions about data-collection methods, legislation, reported hate crime, and policies and initiatives. NPCs in turn respond by completing a questionnaire on a restricted access section on the TANDIS website, where information provided in previous submissions can also be accessed (TANDIS 2015c). Non-governmental organizations are also invited to submit reports on hate crime to fill the gaps left by NPC reports, and to add context. Intergovernmental organizations, including the United Nations, EU agencies, and others are also consulted.

ODIHR hate crime reports therefore differ from those of FRA as they include larger quantities of data submitted by partner organizations, international governmental organizations (IGOs), and NGOs. In its recommendations to states, ODIHR has noted that the lack of accurate and comprehensive data undermines the ability of states to understand fully and to deal effectively with the problem of hate crime. It adds that they need to collect, maintain, and make public reliable data and statistics in sufficient detail, and that such data should include the number of cases reported to police as well as the number of cases prosecuted and the sentences imposed. They should also separate hate crimes from other crimes, disaggregate bias motivations, and encourage victims to report the crimes against them (OSCE ODIHR 2013).

EUROPEAN COMMISSION AGAINST RACISM AND INTOLERANCE (ECRI)

ECRI is a monitoring body of the Council of Europe with the mandate to review Member States' legislation, policies, and other measures to combat racism, racial discrimination, xenophobia, antisemitism , and intolerance, and their effectiveness; to propose further action at local, national, and European level; to formulate general policy recommendations (GPRs) to Member States; and to study international legal instruments applicable in the matter with a view to their enforcement where appropriate. Its investigative reports on Member States are published in a five-yearly cycle, and are used as a primary source of information by FRA and ODIHR. Indeed, the three agencies increasingly cooperate, share information, and attend each other's meetings in order to improve their coordination (ECRI 2008).

ECRI too is concerned with monitoring hate crime, and in its first GPR it noted that:

Since it is difficult to develop and effectively implement policies in the areas in question (ie combating racism, xenophobia, antisemitism and intolerance) without good data, to collect, in accordance with European laws, regulations and recommendations on data-protection and protection of privacy, where and when appropriate, data which will assist in assessing and evaluating the situation and experiences of groups which are particularly vulnerable to racism, xenophobia, antisemitism and intolerance. (ECRI 1966)

In its 2013 Annual Report, ECRI noted the increasing support for aggressive nationalist and populist xenophobic parties, and its concern that these will have an overall negative effect on the political climate in Europe. It applauded the dismantling and banning of some neo-Nazi political parties, but noted the worrying consequence of the rise of nationalist populist parties rooted in profound hostility to ethnic, religious, and cultural diversity. In its 2014 Annual Report, it drew attention to the need to tackle the problem of under-reporting of discrimination, and that a comparison between official and civil society statistics suggests substantial discrepancies. In its country reporting work, ECRI now encourages states to take a more vigorous approach to prosecuting discrimination, harassment, and cyberhate. In its current fifth round of country monitoring it will focus on racist and homophobic/transphobic violence and the response of the authorities to these phenomena.

In order to enhance these efforts, ECRI held a seminar in May 2014 for national 'Specialised Bodies' to discuss cooperation mechanisms between themselves and local and regional authorities in countering hate speech and racist and homophobic/transphobic violence, and what more could be done in practical terms to prevent and combat hate speech and hate crime at a local level (ECRI 2014).

Arising from the conclusions reached by the participants at that seminar, ECRI held a second seminar in May 2015 on 'The role of national Specialised Bodies in addressing underreporting of discrimination and hate crime'. Agenda items included 'Underreporting and its causes', and 'Good practices in addressing underreporting'. No conclusions from the seminar have been made public, but it was agreed that cooperation between local authorities and national Specialised Bodies offers benefits, although many are under-resourced and political effort is required to enhance their capacities (ECRI 2015).

TACKLING THE LACK OF PROGRESS

In 2013, the EU Justice and Home Affairs Council adopted a resolution that declared that 'measures to tackle discrimination, racism, antisemitism, xenophobia and homophobia must be vigorously pursued'. The Council invited Member States to ensure that the 2008 Framework Decision has been fully transposed into national legislation and implemented in practice. They asked states to ensure that they collect and publish comprehensive and comparable data on hate crimes, including the number of such incidents reported by the public and recorded by law enforcement authorities, the number of convictions, the bias motives behind these crimes, and the punishments handed down to offenders. The Council further invited states to facilitate the exchange of good practice and invited FRA to continue to assess the extent of racism, xenophobia, antisemitism, and other forms of hate crime through EU-wide surveys (Council of the European Union 2013).

Building on this new initiative, ODIHR published a guide to collecting data provided by governments, civil society, and intergovernmental organizations. *Hate Crime Data-Collection and Monitoring Mechanisms: A Practical Guide* is intended as a step towards overcoming national and organizational differences between jurisdictions and criminal justice agencies. In recognition of the complexities created by different approaches in multiple jurisdictions, governments are urged to adopt a clear approach that allows for flexibility (OSCE 2014). ODIHR reorganized its training programmes to support police officers who deal with hate crimes, as they are the first responders. The Training against Hate Crimes for Law Enforcement (TAHCLE) programme is designed to enable them to effectively recognize such crimes and therefore record them more accurately. Likewise criminal prosecutors, who deal with the next step in the criminal justice process, are to be trained under a new programme, Prosecutors and Hate Crimes Training Programme (PAHCT).

However, under-reporting of hate crimes remains a major concern, and authorities are urged to work around the difficulties thrown up by cultural barriers, language difficulties, mistrust, and fear of reprisals. Among the most worrying of these barriers is the widespread belief that authorities simply do not act on hate crime reports. For example, the FRA survey on perceptions of antisemitism indicated that 76 per cent of victims of antisemitic crime do not report either to the police or Jewish community monitoring groups as they believe that nothing will happen (FRA 2012).

The following year, FRA noted in two publications that hate crime data should be freely available and in the public domain to increase the visibility of hate crime in the EU, and that few states have mechanisms in place to record hate crime comprehensively. In its latest published report, *Fundamental Rights: Challenges and Achievements in 2013*, FRA noted that few changes had taken place in the status of official data collection mechanisms. It noted therefore that 'the collection of reliable, comparable and comprehensive data on racist and related crime would contribute to the Framework Decision's effective implementation. Public authorities in Member States will be increasingly called on to collect and publish data on such crime, including details of such prosecutions and sentences handed down' (FRA 2014: 159).

While applauding some improvement in the submission of data, ODIHR has pointed out that 'it remains difficult to identify trends and obtain a complete picture of the true extent of the problem due to remaining significant gaps in data collection and the use of different definitions across the region' (OSCE 2011). Frustrated by the slow progress in monitoring and publishing hate crime data, FRA, in cooperation with the Lithuanian Presidency of the Council of the EU, held a two-day conference on *Combating hate crime in the EU*, in Vilnius in December 2013. Thematic working groups discussed a range of relevant issues including: evidence on the extent of hate crime; under-reporting of hate crime; victim support services; effective investigatory practices and prosecutions; discriminatory aspects of hate crime; capacity building for law enforcement; and criminal justice systems, among other themes. The conference was attended by over 400 participants, representing the international organizations, national law enforcement agencies, judiciary, two Member States' government ministers with justice or interior department portfolios, as well as the European Home Affairs Commissioner, who lamented the lack of political will to deal effectively with hate crime. There was overwhelming consensus that measures to address hate crime should be extended to cover all forms of bias, that legal frameworks need to reflect the new comprehensive approach, and that a directive should replace the

Framework Decision. This would provide the EU with enforcement power (FRA 2013; Malstrom 2013).

All EU Member States are now required to comply with all the provisions of the Framework Decision and the Victims' Directive as well as to ratify the Additional Protocol to the Council of Europe Convention on Cybercrime, which requires signatory states to criminalize online incitement to hate crime, denial of genocide, and denial of the Holocaust. Increased inter-institutional coordination between EU agencies and intergovernmental agencies is to be further encouraged to give practical effect to the recommendations, and FRA was asked to work together with them all to facilitate the exchange of good practice and to assist Member States (Council conclusions on combating hate crime in the European Union 2013: 5). The police and prosecution services were urged to establish specialized units or focal points for dealing with hate crime, to review their practices regularly, and to build trust with victim communities (Council conclusions on combating hate crime in the European Union 2013: 4).

With regard to data collection, the conference recommended that a group of experts be assembled to exchange expertise and review data collection systems to increase comparability, that they cover all grounds protected under Article 21 of the Charter of the EU (sex, race, colour, ethnic or social origin, genetic features, language, religion or belief, political or any other opinion, membership of a national minority, property, birth, disability, age, or sexual orientation), that police, prosecutors, and judiciary publish their separate data, that more victimization surveys be conducted, and that FRA continuously assess the situation (FRA 2013).

In December 2013, the EU Justice and Home Affairs Council published the *Council Conclusions on Combating Hate Crime*. This agreement quoted relevant EU agreements, notably Article 2 of the Treaty of the European Union, which refers to the rule of law and respect for human rights, the Stockholm Programme 2010–2014, which required Member States to provide a safe environment and the need to tackle discrimination vigorously, and the Framework Decision (Council of the European Union 2013). The Council invited Member States to ensure that the Framework Decision has been fully transposed, provide prompt and effective investigation and prosecution of hate crimes, facilitate the reporting of hate crimes by victims and as far as possible support mechanisms, and collect and publish comprehensive and comparable hate crime data. The EU itself was invited to contribute to improving the collection of reliable and comparable data and its analysis, and improve strategic cooperation with external stakeholders such as the international organizations and civil society.

Thus began the process of improving the reporting of hate crime in Europe. The first initiative was a seminar on how to combat hate crime effectively and sustainably, held in Thessaloniki in April 2014. Representatives of twenty-five Member States, and the EU, together with human rights bodies, civil society, and intergovernmental bodies discussed practical and policy measures in order to implement the Council conclusion. Discussion focused on improving hate crime data collection by states, with additional comments from expert civil society groups (FRA 2014). The end result was the appointment of a Working Party with a mandate to develop an understanding of hate crime in the national context, enhance multi-agency partnerships, encourage reporting, and identify gaps in training, which has met twice thus far; in November 2014 and March 2015. Its focus has been on improving victims' confidence to report hate crimes, transferability of existing practices, improving coordination between national criminal justice agencies, improving supervision of cases going through criminal justice systems, and sharing understanding of hate crimes between criminal justice agencies. The UK Ministry of Justice thereafter hosted a seminar on behalf of FRA for European police officers and other criminal justice agency representatives in March 2015, with the aim of assisting their work by showcasing British methods, including presentations by Muslim and Jewish hate crime recording bodies which work closely with the police.

CONCLUSIONS

Despite policy makers' best intentions, European states have yet to fully transpose agreements, are slow in their approximation of legal systems, and are failing to provide statistical data on hate crime. These failures apply to new Member States as well as early members of the EU and Council of Europe, and may reflect their long-standing political traditions and practices which they are unwilling to change, but also in some cases different priorities, and/or money to institute the changes required.

The requirement to monitor hate crime began with the 2003 OSCE Ministerial Council Decision, and was given a legal basis with the 2008 Council Framework Decision, but doubts were expressed even at that time that some states would fail to fulfil their obligations. The then Commissioner for Human Rights at the Council of Europe noted, 'Steps should be taken to ensure that bias-motivated crimes are monitored and that data is collected on them and their circumstances. Unfortunately, there is an information gap in several countries due to lack of official determination' (Hammerberg 2008).

In many ways he minimized the problems, as the complexities of persuading states to monitor and publish their hate crime data in a comparable fashion were always going to lead to a politically difficult and time-consuming task. European states have different legal systems which have evolved over time, and accordingly they have different approaches and priorities in collecting data on all forms of crime. It is even more problematic when some states still fail to recognize the very existence of hate crime, despite the fact that OSCE-participating states agreed a common definition with which to work, that is, 'hate crimes are criminal offences committed with a bias motive' (OSCE 2009: 1). That said, the Commissioner did reflect, even then in 2008, a mounting concern among many European leaders that unchecked hate crime threatens stability. The recession of the last few years, disillusionment with the European experiment, and populist anti-migrant politics which dominates national and European discourse adds to this concern, as does the realization that movement within the Schengen area and malign use of the internet allow extremist ideas to cross borders more easily. European-level policy to monitor hate crime therefore exists, and it is clear that it is accorded a high priority by the European agencies, but it lacks proper or continent-wide application by the states who lack the political will at the national level to institute the changes, or lack money for system improvements and training for the criminal justice services.

Although European police and prosecutors now have the legal tools and the incentive to record hate crime as racist, the issue remains for many that everyday violent racism is usually dealt with as violent crime only, if it is reported at all. Further, it occurs widely and frequently, and not just as a consequence of political extremism. However, the proposed 'victim-centred' approach mandated by the Victims' Directive should overcome any dependency on reports or accusations by victims who are particularly vulnerable and reluctant to initiate legal proceedings. The Directive places the victim at the heart and the focus of states' criminal justice systems.

It might be added that when governments publicly recognize the problem of hate crime, and invest efforts into identifying and effectively responding to it, they create a climate that supports additional research. Data collection, including on hate crimes, therefore appears more routine on a range of social phenomena. Moreover, the growing political representation of minority and immigrant groups becomes the focus of media attention which in turn can put pressure on governments to react more effectively.

Despite the oversight and enforcement powers given to the Framework Decision and the Victims' Directive, the monitoring of hate crime across all states and in the detail agreed is still a distant policy goal. States may properly transpose the agreements into domestic law, but they still lack sufficient trained police officers, prosecutors, and judges to use the laws, and without substantial overhaul of criminal justice systems, they lack the capacity and infrastructure to use them. Further progress will continue to be dependent on funding, and the determination of governments and political leaders.

REFERENCES

Article 67, Consolidated Version of the Treaty on the Functioning of the European Union, Official Journal of the European Union, C 326/73, 26 October 2012, http://eur-lex.europa.eu/legal-content/EN/TXT/PDF/?uri=CELEX:12012E/TXT&from=EN, downloaded 9 March 2015.

Charter of Fundamental Rights of the European Union, http://www.europarl.europa.eu/charter/pdf/text_en.pdf, downloaded 5 March 2015.

Community Security Trust, Antisemitic Incidents Report 2014, Community Security Trust, London, https://cst.org.uk/data/file/5/5/Incidents-Report-2014.1425053165.pdf, downloaded 29 April 2015.

COREPOL, Police profession as a human rights service, 2014, COREPOL, German Police University (DHPol) et al, Germany.

Council Framework Decision 2008/913/JHA of 28 November 2008 on combating certain forms and expressions of racism and xenophobia by means of criminal law, Official Journal of the European Union (EU), http://eur-lex.europa.eu/LexUriServ/LexUriServ.do?uri=OJ:L:2008:328:0055:0058:en:PDF, downloaded 9 March 2015.

Council of Europe, Additional Protocol to the Convention on Cybercrime, concerning the criminalisation of acts of a racist and xenophobic nature committed through computer systems, 28 January 2003, Council of Europe, Strasbourg, http://conventions.coe.int/treaty/en/Treaties/Html/189.htm, downloaded 19 May 2015.

Council of Europe–European Commission against Racism and Intolerance, ECRI's mandate, 2008, Council of Europe–European Commission against Racism and Intolerance, Strasbourg, http://www.coe.int/t/dghl/monitoring/ecri/activities/mandate_en.asp, downloaded 18 May 2015.

Council of the European Union, Council conclusions on combating hate crime in the European Union, 5 and 6 December 2013, The Council of the European Union, Brussels, http://www.consilium.europa.eu/uedocs/cms_data/docs/pressdata/en/jha/139949.pdf, downloaded 15 May 2015.

Decision No.4/03, Tolerance and Non-Discrimination, 1–2 December 2003 (OSCE 2003), Eleventh Meeting of the Ministerial Council, Maastricht, http://www.osce.org/mc/19382?download=true, downloaded 9 March 2015.

Decision No. 9/09, Combating Hate Crimes, 2 December 2009, Ministerial Council, OSCE, Athens, http://www.osce.org/cio/40695?download=true, downloaded 30 April 2015.

Decision No. 13/06, Combating Intolerance and Discrimination and Promoting Mutual Respect and Understanding, MC.DEC/13/06, OSCE, 5 December 2006, Ministerial Council, http://www.osce.org/mc/23114?download=true, downloaded 30 April 2015.

Directive 2012/29/EU of the European Parliament and of the Council establishing minimum standards on the rights, support and protection of victims of crime, and replacing Council Framework Decision 2001/220/JHA, 25 October 2012, pt. 11, Official Journal of the European Union, Brussels.

European Commission, Report from the Commission to the European Parliament and the Council on the implementation of the Council Framework Decision 2008/913/JHA on combating certain forms and expressions of racism and xenophobia by means of criminal law, 27 January 2014, European Commission, pp. 9–10, Brussels, http://ec.europa.eu/justice/fundamental-rights/files/com_2014_27_en.pdf, downloaded 9 March 2015.

European Commission against Racism and Intolerance, ECRI General Policy Recommendation No.1 on combating racism, xenophobia, antisemitism and intolerance, adopted 4 October 1996, European Commission against Racism and Intolerance, Strasbourg, http://www.coe.int/t/dghl/monitoring/ecri/activities/GPR/EN/Recommendation_N1/ Reco1en.pdf, downloaded 18 May 2015.

European Commission against Racism and Intolerance, Annual Report on ECRI's Activities covering the period from 1 January to 31 December 2013, European Commission against Racism and Intolerance, Strasbourg, http://www.coe.int/t/dghl/monitoring/ecri/activities/Annual_Reports/Annual%20report%202013.pdf, downloaded 15 May 2015.

European Commission against Racism and Intolerance, The role of national Specialised Bodies in supporting local authorities in the fight against racism and intolerance, ECRI's seminar with national Specialised Bodies, 22–23 May 2014, European Commission against Racism and Intolerance, Strasbourg, http://www.coe.int/t/dghl/monitoring/ecri/activities/48-Seminar_national_specialised_bodies_2014/Draft%20programme%20NSBR%202014-en.pdf, downloaded 29 July 2015.

European Commission against Racism and Intolerance, Annual Report on ECRI's Activities covering the period from 1 January to 31 December 2014, European Commission against Racism and Intolerance, Strasbourg.

European Commission against Racism and Intolerance, The role of national Specialised Bodies in addressing underreporting of discrimination and hate crime, ECRI's seminar with national Specialised Bodies, 28–29 May 2015, European Commission against Racism and Intolerance, Strasbourg, http://www.coe.int/t/dghl/monitoring/ecri/Library/PressReleases/1882015_05_26_NSBR2015_en.asp, downloaded 29 July 2015.

European Convention on Human Rights, Council of Europe, Strasbourg, 4 November 1950, amended text at: http://www.echr.coe.int/Documents/Convention_ENG.pdf, downloaded 5 March 2015.

European Monitoring Centre on Racism and Xenophobia, Racist violence in 15 EU Member States: a comparative overview from the RAXEN national focal point reports 2001–2004, Summary Report, April 2005, EUMC, Vienna, http://fra.europa.eu/en/publication/2005/racist-violence-15-eu-member-states, downloaded 31 April 2015.

European Network Against Racism, Shadow Reports on racism in Europe, European Network Against Racism, Brussels, http://www.enar-eu.org/Shadow-Reports-on-racism-in-Europe-203, downloaded 7 August 2015.

European Union Agency for Fundamental Rights, Fundamental rights: challenges and achievements in 2011, 2012, European Union Monitoring Centre (EUMC), FRA, Vienna.

European Union Agency for Fundamental Rights, Data in focus report—minorities as victims of crime, 2012, European Union Minorities and Discrimination Survey, FRA, Vienna.

European Union Agency for Fundamental Rights, EU-MIDIS at a glance, Introduction to the FRA's EU-wide discrimination survey, 2012, FRA, Vienna.

European Union Agency for Fundamental Rights, European Union lesbian, gay, bisexual and transgender survey, FRA, Vienna, 2012, http://fra.europa.eu/sites/default/files/eu-lgbt-survey-results-at-a-glance_en.pdf,downloaded 30 April 2015.

European Union Agency for Fundamental Rights, FRA survey of Jewish people's experiences and perceptions of antisemitism in European Union Member States, 2012, FRA, Vienna, http://fra.europa.eu/sites/default/files/fra-2013-factsheet-jewish-people-experiences-discrimination-and-hate-crime-eu_en.pdf, downloaded 30 April 2015.

European Union Agency for Fundamental rights, Making hate crime visible in the European Union: acknowledging victims' rights, 2012, lists cases where the ECtHR ruled that courts have a duty to consider and publicize the motivation for crimes, FRA, Vienna, http://report-it.org.uk/files/fra-2012_hate-crime[1].pdf, accessed 7 August 2015.

European Union Agency for Fundamental Rights, Fundamental rights: challenges and achievements in 2012, 2013, FRA, Vienna, http://fra.europa.eu/sites/default/files/annual-report-2012_en.pdf, downloaded 15 May 2015.

European Union Agency for Fundamental Rights, Discrimination and hate crime against Jews in EU Member States: experiences and perceptions of antisemitism, 2013, FRA, Vienna, http://fra.europa.eu/sites/default/files/fra-2013-discrimination-hate-crime-against-jews-eu-member-states_en.pdf, downloaded 15 May 2015.

European Union Agency for Fundamental Rights, EU LGBT survey–European Union lesbian, gay, bisexual and transgender survey, 2013, FRA, Vienna, http://fra.europa.eu/sites/default/files/eu-lgbt-survey-results-at-a-glance_en.pdf, downloaded 7 August 2015.

European Union Agency for Fundamental Rights, FRA brief: crimes motivated by hatred and prejudice in the EU, 2013, FRA, Vienna, http://fra.europa.eu/sites/default/files/fra-brief_hatecrime_en.pdf, downloaded 18 May 2015.

European Union Agency for Fundamental Rights, Fundamental Rights Conference 2013, Combating hate crime in the EU—giving victims a face and a voice, Conference conclusions, 1 –13 November 2013, Vilnius, Lithuania, FRA, Vienna, http://fra.europa.eu/sites/default/files/frc2013-conclusions_en.pdf, downloaded 19 May 2015.

European Union Agency for Fundamental Rights, Fundamental rights: challenges and achievements in 2013, 2014, FRA, Vienna, http://fra.europa.eu/sites/default/files/fra-2014-annual-report-2013-0_en.pdf, downloaded 15 May 2015.

European Union Agency for Fundamental Rights, Fundamental rights: key legal and policy developments in 2013, 2014, FRA, Vienna, http://fra.europa.eu/sites/default/files/fra-2014-annual-report-2013-0_en.pdf, downloaded 7 August 2015.

European Union Agency for Fundamental Rights, FRA survey on gender-based violence against women, 2014, FRA, Vienna, http://fra.europa.eu/sites/default/files/fra-2014-vaw-survey-main-results-apr14_en.pdf, downloaded 30 April 2015.

European Union Agency for Fundamental Rights, Seminar report—How can EU Member States combat hate crime effectively? Encouraging reporting and improving recording, 28–29 April 2014, FRA, Thessaloniki, http://fra.europa.eu/sites/default/files/hate-crime-seminar-report-2014_en.pdf, downloaded 19 May 2015.

European Union Agency for Fundamental Rights, Violence against women, an EU-wide survey, 2014, FRA, Vienna, http://fra.europa.eu/sites/default/files/fra_images/fra-2014-vaw-survey-main-results-cover_en.jpg, downloaded 7 August 2015.

European Union Agency for Fundamental Rights, Fundamental rights: challenges and achievements in 2014, 2015, FRA, Vienna, http://fra.europa.eu/sites/default/files/fra-annual-report-2014_en.pdf, downloaded 7 August 2015.

European Union Agency for Fundamental Rights, FRA holds second meeting of Working Party on combating hate crime, 30 March 2015, FRA, Vienna, http://fra.europa.eu/en/news/2015/fra-holds-second-meeting-working-party-combating-hate-crime, downloaded 19 March 2015.

Facing Facts, 2015, Brussels, http://www.facingfacts.eu/, downloaded 7 August 2015.

Hammerberg, T., Hate crimes—the ugly face of racism, anti-Semitism, anti-Gypsyism, Islamophobia and homophobia, 12 July 2008, Commissioner for Human Rights, The Council of Europe, http://www.coe.int/t/commissioner/viewpoints/default_en.asp?toPrint=yes&downloaded, downloaded 19 May 2015.

Iganski, P., Keilinger, V., and Paterson, S., 2005, *Hate Crimes against London's Jews–An Analysis of Incidents Recorded by the Metropolitan Police Service 2001–2004*, Metropolitan Police Service and Institute for Jewish Policy Research, London.

Malstrom, C., Combating Hate Crime in the EU Conference, Press release, European Union Agency for Fundamental Rights, 13 November 2013, http://fra.europa.eu/en/news/2013/combating-hate-crime-eu-conference, downloaded 19 May 2015.

Nachova and Others v Bulgaria, 6 July 2005, European Court of Human Rights, Strasbourg, http://hudoc.echr.coe.int/eng?i=001-69630#{"itemid":["001-69630"]}, downloaded 30 July 2015.

ODIHR, Hate Crimes Remain Serious Problem across OSCE Region–ODIHR Report, Press release, 16 November 2011, OSCE ODIHR, Warsaw, http://www.osce.org/odihr/85099, downloaded 19 May 2015.

ODIHR, Hate Crime Data-Collection and Monitoring Mechanisms—A Practical Guide, 2014, OSCE ODIHR, Warsaw, http://www.osce.org/odihr/datacollectionguide, downloaded 15 May 2015.

ODIHR, Hate Crimes in the OSCE Region: Incidents and Responses–Annual Report for 2012, 2013, OSCE ODIHR, Warsaw, http://tandis.odihr.pl/hcr2012/pdf/Hate_Crime_Report_full_version.pdf, downloaded 30 April 2015.

ODIHR, Personal Representatives' Appointments and Reports to OSCE Chairman in Office, Tolerance and Non Discrimination Information System (TANDIS), http://tandis.odihr.pl/?p=qu-pr,pr-all, downloaded 30 April 2015.

ODIHR, Prosecutors and Hate Crimes Training (PAHCT), OSCE ODIHR, Warsaw, 2014, http://www.osce.org/odihr/pahct?download=true, downloaded 15 May 2015.

ODIHR, Tolerance and Non-Discrimination Information System (TANDIS), OSCE, Vienna, http://www.osce.org/odihr/44066, downloaded 7 August 2015.

ODIHR, Tolerance and Non-Discrimination Information System (TANDIS), Personal Representatives, 2015, OSCE ODIHR, Warsaw. http://tandis.odihr.pl/?p=qu-pr, downloaded 11 August 2015.

ODIHR, Tolerance and Non-Discrimination Information System (TANDIS), National Points of Contact, 2015, OSCE ODIHR, Warsaw, http://tandis.odihr.pl/?p=ki-hc,downloaded, downloaded 11 August 2015.

ODIHR, Training against Hate Crimes for Law Enforcement, Programme Description, OSCE ODIHR, Warsaw, http://www.osce.org/odihr/tahcle?download=true, downloaded 15 May 2015.

Opinion of the European Union Agency for Fundamental Rights on the Framework Decision on Racism and Xenophobia—With Special Attention to the Rights of Victims of Crime, FRA Opinion 02/2013, 15 October 2013, Vienna, http://fra.europa.eu/sites/default/files/fra-opinion-2-2013-framework-decision-racism-xenophobia_en.pdf, downloaded 9 March 2015.

OSCE, Document of the Copenhagen Meeting of the Conference on the Human Dimension of the OSCE, 5–29 June 1990, OSCE, Copenhagen, http://www.osce.org/odihr/elections/14304?download=true, downloaded 7 August 2015.

Secretary General, United Nations General Assembly, Contemporary Forms of Racism, Racial Discrimination, Xenophobia and Related Intolerance, 22 August 2012, p. 22, Note by the Secretary General, United Nations General Assembly (UNGA), New York.

United Nations High Commissioner for Refugees, Combating Racism, Racial Discrimination, Xenophobia and Related Intolerance through a Strategic Approach, December 2009, United Nations High Commissioner for Refugees (UNHCR), Geneva.

Whine, M., 2012, 'Trans-European Trends in Right-wing Extremism'. In Mapping the Extreme Right in Contemporary Europe, edited by Godin, E., Jenkins, B., and Mammone, A., London, pp. 317–333. Routledge Studies in Extremism and Democracy.

Whine, M., 2015, 'Hate Crime in Europe'. In The Routledge International Handbook on Hate Crime, edited by Hall, N., Corb, A., Giannasi, P., and Grieve, J., London, pp. 95–104. Routledge International Handbooks.

14

THE EUROPEAN COURT OF HUMAN RIGHTS AND DISCRIMINATORY VIOLENCE COMPLAINTS

Jasmina Mačkić

INTRODUCTION

29 January 1996, Razgrad, Bulgaria. It is around midnight when a seventeen-year-old Bulgarian national of Roma origin, Anguel Zabchekov, is meandering near parked vehicles at the front of a block of flats. Neighbours spot Anguel and start shouting at him, thinking that he is trying to steal a car. At this very moment, an off-duty police officer is passing by and is stopped by the neighbours. He starts chasing Anguel in order to arrest him. After approximately twenty minutes, Anguel is arrested by the policeman and is taken to the police station where he dies later that day. 'An abnormally thin skull' (*Anguelova v Bulgaria*, 2002, para. 61) is put forward as the main explanation for his death. According to one of the investigators, the skull was severely damaged by Anguel's frequent falls during the chase; a conclusion that is accepted by the Bulgarian domestic courts, but not by the mother of the victim. She believes that her son's death and the lack of a meaningful investigation into the incident have been the result of racial hatred. Anguel is not the first Roma in Bulgaria who was stopped by the police while in good health, but who did not return from custody alive. The mother's belief is further strengthened by the conduct of the police officers during the investigation: they referred to Anguel as 'the Gypsy' (*Anguelova v Bulgaria*, 2002, para. 66) even in their official statements.

This case eventually appeared before the European Court of Human Rights ('ECtHR' or 'Court') in which the mother of the victim, Ms Anguelova, claimed that Bulgaria had violated Article 14 (prohibition of discrimination) read in conjunction with Article 2 (right to life) of the European Convention for the Protection of Human Rights and Fundamental Freedoms ('ECHR' or 'Convention'). The Court rejected her complaint, stating that it was unable 'to reach the conclusion that proof beyond reasonable doubt has been established' (*Anguelova v Bulgaria*, 2002, para. 168) that the violence was motivated by racial prejudice.

The *Anguelova* case is just one example of an allegation of a hate crime that has appeared before the ECtHR, an institution that ensures the observance of the undertakings made by the forty-seven Member States of the Council of Europe ('CoE') in the Convention and the Protocols thereto. Hate crime is here taken to mean 'violence directed towards groups of people who generally are not valued by the majority society, who suffer discrimination in other arenas, and who do not have full access to institutions meant to remedy social, political and economic injustice' (Wolfe and Copeland 1994: 201). In this chapter, it is used interchangeably with the term 'discriminatory violence'.

In approximately the past twenty years, minority groups such as Roma, Kurds, and Chechens frequently alleged before the Court that they were ill-treated by state officials or that their family members were killed by state agents due to discriminatory motives. In this context, they complained that Article 14 ECHR read in conjunction with Article 2 or 3 (prohibition of torture) was violated. In most of these cases it was alleged that the authorities of the respondent states failed to conduct an effective investigation into the circumstances surrounding the events. Consequently, for these applicants the ECtHR was the only institution they could turn to. Although the Court has sometimes discussed complaints regarding discriminatory violence and, occasionally, even established a violation of the Convention in this context (e.g., *Nachova and Others v Bulgaria* [GC], 2005; *Identoba and Others v Georgia*, 2015), there are still cases in which the Court appears to be reluctant in addressing this issue.

This chapter demonstrates why the ECtHR ought to play more of a role in emphasizing the problem of hate crime in Europe. The Convention mechanism, allowing individuals and CoE Member States to complain about human rights violations committed by other Member States, is generally regarded as 'the most successful and influential international human rights regime' (Neumayer 2005: 938). The Court has delivered prominent and effective judgments on various matters which have had a considerable impact on Member States of the CoE in practice. For instance, several European governments have revised their legislation on Lesbian, Gay, Bisexual, and Transgender (LGBT) rights (see, e.g., *Dudgeon v United Kingdom* [GC], 1981). Additionally, regarding the effect of the Convention mechanism, it has been observed that the 'direct impact of international human rights law in Europe is not only comparable to that of domestic constitutional law in developed democracies, but greater than that of domestic law in nations where the rule of law has yet to take hold or is crippled by corruption' (Cassel 2001: 132). Thus, it is assumed here that the ECtHR may also play a valuable role as an international body in the process of condemning hate crime in Europe, particularly in those CoE countries where there is a lack of adequate hate crime legislation, or where the domestic authorities fail to apply existing hate crime laws in practice.

This chapter first briefly illustrates the Court's reluctance in addressing discriminatory violence complaints. Thereafter, it lists a number of arguments which underline why the Court is a valuable actor in addressing discriminatory violence complaints in Europe. As shall be indicated hereunder, through a more elaborate reasoning of the discriminatory violence claims and, if possible, a greater condemnation of this type of wrongful conduct, the Court would not merely recognize the individual complaints of applicants and observe whether domestic authorities ful-filled their obligations under the Convention in this field, but also reassert certain fundamental norms in European human rights law through its judgments.[1]

ECtHR'S RELUCTANCE IN ADDRESSING DISCRIMINATORY VIOLENCE COMPLAINTS

Applications concerning discriminatory violence before the ECtHR have taken dif-ferent forms. First, applicants have alleged that state agents ill-treated or took vic-tims' lives due to prejudice-based motives ('the negative, substantive obligation to refrain from inflicting violence'; e.g., *Stoica v Romania*, 2008). Second, applicants have argued that state authorities failed in conducting an effective investigation into cases involving discriminatory violence, or that they showed discriminatory attitudes while investigating violent crimes committed against minority groups ('the procedural obligation to investigate'; e.g., *Nachova and Others v Bulgaria* [GC], 2005). Finally, they have complained that the domestic authorities refused to protect the victims from discriminatory violence ('the procedural obligation to take pre-ventive measures'; e.g., *Identoba and Others v Georgia*, 2015).

Notwithstanding the different ways in which complaints about discriminatory violence can be made, there has remained reluctance on the part of the Court to rec-ognize, or to even discuss, the nature of such violence. This is illustrated through the following examples. The first example is derived from the case law on anti-Roma vio-lence. In 2012, Möschel assessed more than forty ECtHR cases which involved vio-lence committed against individuals with a Romani ethnic background (Möschel 2012: 479). However, in only one case did the Court actually establish a violation of Article 14 read in conjunction with Article 3 under the substantive limb. This occurred in *Stoica*, which concerned the alleged ill-treatment of a Roma individual by Romanian police officers. The Court was able to establish that the beatings were racially motivated because witnesses reported that the police officers asked another Roma individual, who was beaten together with Mr Stoica, whether he was 'Gypsy or Romanian' before assaulting him, at the deputy mayor's request, to teach the Roma 'a lesson'. The Court also took into consideration the remarks from a police report which described the Romani villagers' alleged aggressive behaviour as 'pure Gypsy'. According to the Court, these remarks are clearly stereotypical and indicate that the police officers were motivated by bias during the incidents and during the domestic investigation into the events (*Stoica v Romania*, 2008, paras 128–32).

[1] This chapter was delivered as a paper at the International Network for Hate Studies (INHS), University of Sussex, in May 2015. The research presented here is derived from PhD study conducted at Leiden Law School under the supervision of Prof. Larissa van den Herik and Dr. Pınar Ölçer. The author wishes to thank her supervisors and Prof. Janneke Gerards (Radboud University Nijmegen) who read and commented upon an earlier draft of this text. Also, she wishes to thank the participants of the INHS symposium 'Globalising Hate Crime' for their helpful comments on earlier versions of this chapter.

Similarly, in *Carabulea v Romania*, the applicant claimed that his brother's death in custody, the ill-treatment that he had suffered, and the refusal of the military prosecution to investigate the conduct of the state agents who were involved in his brother's death were partially because of his Roma ethnicity. Therefore, he was of the opinion that the Romanian government had violated Article 14 read in conjunction with Articles 2, 3, and 13 (right to an effective remedy) of the Convention. Nevertheless, as a response to the applicant's complaint, the Court stated that it 'considers that it is not necessary to examine this complaint separately' (*Carabulea v Romania*, 2010, para. 168). The Court did not address the question as to whether state agents displayed any discriminatory behaviour during the incidents or the investigation. Moreover, it did not even elaborate on the question as to why it was unnecessary to examine the discrimination issue in this case.

Another, more recent, example of the Court's reluctance to recognize discriminatory violence occurred in *Karaahmed v Bulgaria*. The issue at stake was a demonstration organized by the Bulgarian nationalist party Ataka. Demonstrators gathered outside the Banya Bashi Mosque in Sofia in order to protest against what they called the 'howling' coming from the mosque's loudspeakers. Between 100 and 150 Ataka supporters attacked approximately thirty or forty Muslim worshippers who had gathered in and around the mosque for their regular Friday prayer. Video recordings of the event made by the media displayed the demonstrators wearing black t-shirts with inscriptions such as 'Erdogan, you owe us 10 billion' (*Karaahmed v Bulgaria*, 2015, para. 16). The footage also showed the demonstrators shouting insulting remarks at the worshippers, such as 'Turkish stooges' and 'filthy terrorists'. The recordings even showed one participant slowly cutting a Turkish fez with a pocket knife, saying 'Can you hear me? We shall now show you what will happen to each one of you!' (*Karaahmed v Bulgaria*, 2015, para. 17). The recordings also captured some of the demonstrators climbing onto the roof of the mosque trying to disrupt the sound of the loudspeakers, and several more entering the mosque and hitting the worshippers with wooden flagpoles and metal pipes. Some of the worshippers are seen hitting back in response. The police were present and attempted to intervene. The two investigations that were opened after the demonstration were suspended without anyone being charged. A third investigation resulted in charges being brought against seven people, although there was no information available on whether they were eventually prosecuted (*Karaahmed v Bulgaria*, 2015, paras 19–41).

The applicant first complained that Bulgaria had breached its duty to protect the worshippers from the ill-treatment inflicted by the demonstrators and that it failed to properly investigate the events. The Court rejected this complaint, which concerned an alleged violation of Article 3 alone and also when considered in conjunction with Article 14, as manifestly ill-founded. It did not find that the inflicted violence was sufficiently severe 'as to cause the kind of fear, anguish or feelings of inferiority that are necessary for Article 3' (*Karaahmed v Bulgaria*, 2015, para. 75). The applicant also claimed that the Member State's failure to take preventive measures in this case violated Article 9 ECHR (freedom of thought, conscience, and religion). The Court found a violation in this regard, stressing that the domestic authorities failed to strike a proper balance in ensuring the effective and peaceful exercise of the rights of the demonstrators, and the rights of the applicant and the other worshippers to pray to-gether. It also established that the domestic authorities failed to properly respond to the relevant events (*Karaahmed v Bulgaria*, 2015, para. 111). Although the conclusion under the Article 9 complaint is reasonable, the reasoning of the Court seems to be inappropriate here, since the facts of this case indicate that the Ataka demonstrators did not have the intention to peacefully assemble, but rather to provoke and to hurt individuals who only gathered in front of and around the mosque for their Friday prayers. The Court also found it unnecessary to separately assess the applicant's complaint concerning Article 14 read in conjunction with Article 9, by emphasizing that it had already examined the circumstances of this case under Article 9 alone and found a violation of the right to freedom of thought, conscience, and religion (*Karaahmed v Bulgaria*, 2015, para. 112). The Court's choice not to evaluate the com-plaint under Article 14 is incomprehensible, taking into account the clear indica-tions of the discriminatory nature of violence in this case, which was even recorded by the media (see also Spiliopoulou Åkermark 2002, who noted the uncertainty as to when and why the ECtHR chooses to examine Article 14).

To sum up, the Court's reluctance to recognize discriminatory violence becomes particularly visible in cases which concern the negative, substantive duty (anti-Roma violence cases) and from the Court's (sometimes incomprehensible) unwillingness to address discriminatory aspects in violence matters, despite clear signs that the events were caused by prejudice (*Karaahmed*). Such cases are missed opportunities for the Court which could play a valuable role in actively addressing the problem of hate crime in Europe.

Before turning to the arguments which justify a Court that is more engaged in hate crime matters, it is necessary to highlight that ECtHR judgments are 'essentially declaratory in nature' (*Assanidze v Georgia* [GC], 2004, para. 202). This means that the finding that a Member State has violated the Convention results in a declaration from the Court that such a violation occurred. The Court may, additionally, reward compensation and costs to the applicants. However, the Court does not have the power to quash decisions of the national authorities or courts, strike down domestic legislation, require a state to alter its legislation, or otherwise require a state to take particular measures within the domestic legal system (Leach 2011: 83–4). The ECtHR is, for instance, not in a position to order the punishment of a state agent who has committed a hate crime in the territory of that Member State. Nevertheless, there are sev-eral reasons why the ECtHR is a suitable actor in emphasizing the issue of dis-criminatory violence. Where Member States fail to take adequate preventive measures, conduct an effective investigation into this type of wrongful con-duct, or punish the perpetrators, the ECtHR is the final organ to which the victims may turn. Despite its limited powers in this regard, the judgments of the Court have an important symbolic effect in shaming the conduct of certain Member States. Furthermore, ECtHR judgments help to create awareness that particular Member States ought to alter their stance towards discriminatory violence. It is in these two regards that the ECtHR can help to address hate crime internationally.

JUSTIFICATIONS FOR ADDRESSING DISCRIMINATORY VIOLENCE FOUND WITHIN THE *TELOS* OF THE COURT ITSELF

There are different reasons why the Court in particular ought to dedicate special attention to discriminatory violence complaints and, where appropriate, find violations of the Convention in this regard. The first reason for this may partly be reduced to the original purposes and functions of the ECtHR. The Court's initial role, originating from the 1950s, was to act like an 'alarm bell' warning other nations of democratic Europe that one of their members was going 'totalitarian' (Bates 2011: 21) through its judgments. One example of a case where the Court responded to such an event occurred in *Moldovan*, concerning the Hădăreni pogrom. This case involved the killing of three Romani men, the subsequent destruction of fourteen Roma houses in the village of Hădăreni, and, finally, the degrading circumstances under which the Roma victims were forced to live after the pogrom. Faced with complaints about these events, the Court established a violation of, amongst others, Article 3 of the Convention (*Moldovan and Others v Romania (No 2)*, 2005). Cahn argues that in this case 'the Court was confronted with an event echoing the reasons for which the Court was founded. With the past as mirror, the Court recognised the harms at issue' (Cahn 2006: 19). The 'past' then most probably refers to the atrocities inflicted upon Roma during the Second World War and 'the reasons for which the Court was founded' emphasizes the Court's alarm bell function. Therefore, the initial roles of the Convention and the Court to serve as guardians of peace in Europe may gain particular prominence in times where there is a threat that isolated, violent acts committed against individuals who are members of certain minorities in the Member States might escalate into large-scale, systemic violent events directed towards vulnerable groups.

Second, growing concerns for discrimination generally in the CoE nourish the argument for more attention for discriminatory violence claims by the ECtHR. In approximately the past twenty years, there were two developments which created a shift in the CoE's approach to discrimination. The first concerns a number of violent conflicts within the European territory throughout the 1990s. According to Weller, 'the shock of the interethnic violence that afflicted Eastern Europe with the unfreezing of the Cold War' (Weller 2005: vii) sparked an interest in the field of minority issues. Consequently, the realization developed that minority-related tensions are capable of destabilizing the whole region (Ringelheim 2010: 106). The second development concerns the expansion of the CoE: most Central and Eastern European states became Contracting Parties to the Convention after the fall of the Iron Curtain. What is even more pertinent here is that their accession brought with it an increase in the number of indigenous groups falling under the Convention's protection (Thornberry 2002: 290–1). It is claimed that these two developments created a shift in political and legal thinking: this shift moved from a 'politics of ideology', dominating the 1950s, to a 'politics of identity', prevailing since the 1990s. This means that rather than debating the relationship between the individual, society, the state, and the market ('politics of ideology'), parties now rather conflict over the cultural, ethnic, linguistic, and religious identity of the state ('politics of identity') (Greer 2006: 30–1). These developments imply more attention for minority rights and—more specifically—attention for minorities' protection from discriminatory violence. The Court, monitoring whether Member States adhere to Convention's provisions, must not ignore such developments.

Separately from these developments, it may be observed that twenty-eight of the CoE's Member States, which are also members of the European Union, have adopted the 'EU Directive establishing minimum standards on the rights, support and protection of victims of crime', which entered into force on 15 November 2012. Article 22§3 calls on EU Member States to pay particular attention, amongst others, to 'victims who have suffered a crime committed with a bias or discriminatory motive which could, in particular, be related to their personal characteristics'. This provision continues by underlining that 'victims of terrorism, organised crime, human trafficking, gender-based violence, violence in a close relationship, sexual violence, exploitation or hate crime, and victims with disabilities shall be duly considered'. So, more than half of the CoE's Member States realize that there is a need to address hate crime issues at domestic levels. This signals to the ECtHR that there is a growing consensus in Europe to tackle hate crime; it may inspire the Court to emphasize hate crime concerns even more through its judgments.

A study conducted by Pentassuglia into the jurisprudence of the ECtHR reveals that the Court has already become more sensitive towards the rights of minority groups, by underpinning themes such as pluralism, identity, and non-discrimination in its case law from the late 1990s and onwards (Pentassuglia 2012: 2). The Court, for instance, made the general observation that 'the existence of minorities and different cultures in a country was a historical fact that a "democratic society" had to tolerate and even protect and support according to the principles of international law' (*Sidiropoulos and Others v Greece*, 1998, para. 41). In a case where the Court had to determine whether a Gypsy woman's right to private life (Article 8 ECHR) was violated after she was refused planning permission to station caravans on her land, it observed:

an emerging international consensus amongst the Contracting States of the Council of Europe recognising the special needs of minorities and an obligation to protect their security, identity and lifestyle (. . .), not only for the purpose of safeguarding the interests of the minorities themselves but to preserve a cultural diversity of value to the whole community (*Chapman v United Kingdom* [GC], 2001, para. 93).

In the specific context of discriminatory violence, in *Nachova*, the Grand Chamber noted that '[r]acial violence is a particular affront to human dignity and, in view of its perilous consequences, requires from the authorities special vigilance and a vigorous reaction' (*Nachova and Others v Bulgaria* [GC], 2005, para. 145). Pentassuglia argues that these developments are 'at the core of a wider legal reasoning which is rendering the ECHR an increasingly functional instrument in the field of minority protection' (Pentassuglia 2012: 7). In *Antayev*, the ECtHR underlined that difference in treatment based exclusively on a person's ethnic origin can never be objectively justified in 'a contemporary democratic society built on the principles of pluralism and respect for different cultures' (*Antayev and Others v Russia*, 2014, para. 124).

A third reason for the ECtHR to specifically address discriminatory violence may be sought in the so-called agenda-setting function of the Court. Gerards emphasizes in that light the ECtHR's ability to place—through declaration of judgments in individual cases—certain topics on the regulative or policy agendas of national legislatures and executive bodies; for instance, the criminalization of homosexual contacts or state refusals to grant residence permits to HIV-positive immigrants (Gerards 2012: 185). She explains how it may occur that a state criminalizes homosexual contacts without considering its own stance on this matter as problematic. This may especially be the case if the state's attitude results from deeply rooted cultural, traditional, or legal phenomena. It is equally imaginable that the national authorities have not realized that their attitude is problematic or that they *do* indeed see the problem, yet omit to solve it. The ECtHR, acting as an external Court that is far-removed from daily domestic concerns, can respond to such domestic issues in an assertive manner. It can visualize these problems for the Member States and possibly effectuate domestic legal change and alterations in the perception of rights through its rulings (Gerards 2012: 186).

Gerards' views align with claims that Çali (2008) has made. Çali noted the tendency amongst majorities in societies to marginalize, victimize, and exclude minority groups and identified a new function for the contemporary Court from this: the protection of minority views against the majority. In that sense, ECtHR judges can conduct a prominent role, since they are 'removed from the political climate or practices that may have popular support in a country' (Çali 2008: 302).

Following from this, it may be argued that the Court's agenda-setting function can become highly valuable if the Court would, for instance, condemn discriminatory violence committed towards members of minorities in each case before it, regardless of whether such actions of violence may have been inflicted by state agents and/or are tolerated by the domestic authorities in a Member State. Additionally, it may serve the goal in combating discriminatory violence committed by private persons. In that regard the following two examples may be relevant. First, in the United Kingdom, there is anxiety over hatred towards asylum seekers. O'Nions observes that their constant problematization in the British media and in political rhetoric contributes to 'anti-immigrant' prejudice becoming mainstreamed as a common-sense response. She notes in this context particular problems with racist violence in Scotland (O'Nions 2010: 235). The second example concerns prejudice that may be observed towards certain groups in Russia. This country was recently criticized for introducing anti-homopropaganda laws, which essentially prohibit acts that aim at propagating homosexuality. The emergence of this Russian-led campaign, specifically enacted to gain recognition for 'traditional values', has been accompanied by a rise in homophobic violence in the Russian territory. It is even said that the Kremlin's current homophobia shows resemblance to Third Reich activities (Wilkinson 2014: 372). Notwithstanding, regardless of whether such governmental policies may be considered as popular (in the United Kingdom) or as being justified through tradition (Russia), the fact is that they condition violent behaviour and, consequently, encroach upon the most fundamental human rights. It is exactly in these types of cases that the relevance of the Court's agenda-setting function appears. The Court has the ability to condemn policies that condition discriminatory violence by pronouncing judgments on incidents of discriminatory physical abuse. Through its judgments the Court can then protect core rights in times when the policies and sentiments in certain Member States threaten to throw them overboard. This places the ECtHR in a more advantageous position in contrast to the national judiciary, especially in those countries where certain minority groups are not properly protected. In countries where there may be heated debates over whether and how to provide sufficient protection to individuals of certain groups who are frequent victims of discriminatory violence, and where, because of the heated situation, the national judges are unable to respond adequately, the ECtHR may prove valuable in observing whether the situation is in accordance with the norms of the Convention. More specifically, it is stressed that under these circumstances, '[t]he ECtHR should then operate as a barometer, pointing to dangerous levels of populism, deep prejudices and the reactionary or hostile treatment of individuals who hold minority views or belong to minority groups' (Çali 2008: 302).

A fourth argument for the Court's valuable role in condemning hate crimes lies in the fact that a more elaborate reasoning in discriminatory violence cases would be particularly appropriate given the Court's constitutional nature. In recent years, a fierce debate has been held regarding the categorization of the ECtHR: more precisely it is being asked whether the Court possesses a constitutional nature or whether it aims at serving individual justice. Greer frames how these two doctrines are opposed to one another. The individual justice model 'exists primarily to provide redress for Convention violations for the benefit of the particular individual making the complaint, with whatever constitutional or systemic improvements at the national level might thereby result' (Greer 2008: 684). This stands in contrast with the constitutional model which implies that the Court's primary responsibility is to select and to adjudicate the most serious alleged violations and to highlight specific systemic compliance problems in Member States which are related to human rights matters (Greer 2008: 684–5).

It may be argued, especially in the light of the constitutional approach, that discriminatory violence claims deserve more attention in the Court's case law due to their particularly grave nature. As indicated earlier, discriminatory violence complaints encroach upon Article 14 read in conjunction with Articles 2 and 3. Together, these provisions represent the most fundamental principles in Europe. The last two provisions enshrine 'the basic values of the democratic societies making up the Council of Europe' (*McCann and Others v United Kingdom* [GC], 1995, para. 147; *Soering v United Kingdom* [GC] 1989, para. 88). Article 2 is one of the few provisions in the Convention that cannot be derogated from in time of war or other public emergency. Breaches under Article 3 are *never* permitted, since this provision is an absolute right prohibiting torture (Harris, O'Boyle, Bates, and Buckley 2014: 203, 235–6).

The Court is generally known for allowing Member States a certain margin of appreciation when fulfilling their obligations under the Convention (Spielmann

2012: 2). This doctrine is closely connected to the principle of subsidiarity, since it follows from the perception that domestic courts are often better placed than the ECtHR to give an opinion on the necessity of a state measure. However, the Court is barely willing to provide a margin where non-derogable rights, namely those enshrined within Articles 2 and 3 are at stake. It is argued that in scenarios where applicants rely on these two articles the phrase margin of appreciation is virtually nonexistent (Spielmann 2012: 7, 11). This also goes for discriminatory violence cases. Besides, in discrimination complaints in general the margin may be narrowed down, particularly in those cases in which members from minority groups complain about wrongful state acts. In the context of Article 14 matters, the Court stressed that Contracting states enjoy a certain margin of appreciation in the assessment whether and to what extent differences in otherwise similar situations justify a different treatment. However, if the treatment were based exclusively on the ground of ethnic origin, very weighty reasons would have to be put forward to justify such treatment (*Oršuš and Others v Croatia* [GC], 2010, para. 149). Little space for manoeuvre has equally been provided in cases where distinctions were based, for instance, on the ground of religion alone (*Hoffmann v Austria*, 1993, para. 36) or sex (*Abdulaziz, Cabales and Balkandali v United Kingdom*, 1985, para. 78).

Apart from the fundamental importance of the rights embedded in Articles 2, 3, and 14, there is another reason that renders discriminatory violence complaints significantly more serious than other acts. This argument may be derived from Lawrence, who asserts that bias crimes affect larger circles within society and impact individuals in three different ways: first, they affect the victim in a particular emotional and psychological manner, by encroaching not merely upon a person's physical being, yet also on the very core of his identity; second, the crimes have an impact on the so-called 'target-community', meaning the community that belongs to the same 'targeted' group as the victim; third, bias crimes affect an even wider circle, notably the general society (Lawrence 2002: 39–44).

The outmost circle, impacting the general society, deserves a bit more elaboration. In the common law legal systems of the United States and the United Kingdom it is generally stressed that bias crime laws or penalty enhancements for this type of crime in essence reflect a social aversion to racism, religious intolerance, and other forms of bigotry. They represent those values that matter in a society and those that are particularly affected by discriminatory violence, such as harmony between different groups and the equality principle. Since bias crimes often affect victims belonging to groups that had to endure suffering and loss in the past, measures condemning such crimes may particularly be justified (Lawrence 2002: 161–75).

It must be observed, though, that all the arguments in favour of bias crime laws have been refuted by those who find harsher penalties or distinct provisions prohibiting this type of crime unjust. This also applies in the context of the argument which underlines the beneficence of bias crime laws or enhanced penalties for the community as a whole. Sullivan, for instance, claims that the existence of bias crime legislation would rather highlight social divisions amongst different societal groups (Sullivan 1999). Additionally, it is sometimes claimed that prioritization of minority groups may even cause aversion from the majority towards minority groups rather than combat social divisions due to the perception that minority groups receive preferential treatment (Hall 2013: 176).

It is to be questioned how far this criticism can be transposed to the European human rights level. Those who are opposed to the measures that essentially reflect harsher condemnation of bias crimes raise their claims in domestic criminal spheres. Hate debates dominating common law countries address the question of why hate crime ought to be recognized as a distinct category of *criminal* offence. Hate crime laws in common law legal systems are usually created in the field of criminal and sentencing law, which enhance the punishments for convicted offenders. Occasionally, there is a possibility for civil litigation paving the way for damage awards to the victims. Critics within these systems do not question the wrongfulness of discriminatory violence, but rather they question their position in the hierarchy vis-à-vis parallel crimes and, subsequently, express that tougher punishments ought not to be attached to such crimes (Jacobs and Potter 1998: 90–1). The ECtHR, not being a civil or criminal court, is unable to punish the respondent state or to rule on civil liability. In addition, neither the Convention nor the Protocols to it contain provisions similar to those formulated in common law hate crime legislation. Whereas a country such as the United Kingdom might ask whether imposing tougher punishments for discriminatory violence is warranted, the same question cannot be posed in an ECHR context since the European human rights mechanism does not possess the power to punish agents who act on behalf of the respondent states.

This may be where the Court's strength lies. Where domestic debates may block the development of hate crime laws, the ECtHR can serve its function of 'merely' declaring on state responsibility in this field. The Court was established in the 1950s to serve a more symbolic function in preserving peace. At present, the Court may equally serve such a function by condemning the issue of discriminatory violence and, through this path, underline the importance of minority rights. Viewed from this perspective, the Court may, through a greater elaboration on discriminatory violence complaints, not just show attentiveness towards the potential individual victims, but may even emphasize the generality of this problem and in that way serve the purpose of constitutionalism.

One final note here relates specifically to the question as to what the positive impact may be for victimized groups if the Court dedicated more attention to discriminatory violence. This next argument is most valuable in cases concerning Contracting Parties where there are repeated, isolated incidents of discriminatory violence or where there are violent acts that are committed against a minority group at large on the grounds of prejudice-based motives, such as pogroms in Romani-populated areas. Judgments that discuss the hate crime concerns write down the historical memory of the events. If the Court additionally condemns such events it may even contribute to the prevention of their repetition (Burgorgue-Larsen and Úbeda de Torres 2011: 318–20). Court decisions on human rights are capable of setting examples and may be instructive. Where an ordinary court decision may do its job without critical reflections on the facts or the social contexts in which breaches of the law have taken place, a human rights tribunal aiming to create awareness of human rights concerns and prevent new breaches from taking place, ought to consider the context in which the atrocities took place.

CONCLUSION

This chapter has highlighted one way in which the phenomenon of discriminatory violence may be addressed at an international (European) level, namely through the ECtHR. In the last couple of decades, this Court has faced numerous complaints concerning discriminatory violence. Although the ECtHR is not in a position to penalize CoE's Member States or the agents employed by them for this type of wrongful conduct, the ECtHR may nonetheless play a more normative role in addressing hate crimes in Europe. This function of the Court is particularly necessary in those Contracting Parties of the CoE in which domestic authorities fail to conduct an effective investigation into hate crimes or fail to take preventive measures against such crimes.

Problems related to hate crimes are widespread within the territory of the CoE. This chapter mentioned only a few examples of pogroms and violent incidents in certain European states. There are reports about hate crimes towards asylum seekers in the United Kingdom and reports about anti-homopropaganda laws in Russia. The Court can signal these issues, create more awareness of their existence, and condemn these types of conduct by engaging in discussions about such complaints that are presented to it under the heading of Article 14 of the Convention read in conjunction with Article 2 or Article 3, and by establishing violations where appropriate.

The Court's extraordinary position in Europe allows it to contribute to the condemnation of hate crimes in different ways. The Court may, for instance, evaluate in each case concerning Article 14 read in conjunction with Article 2 or Article 3 whether a complaint concerns violent conduct which occurs at a more pervasive, systemic basis. In such a case, the Court can pronounce that there is an alarming situation in a Contracting Party which requires immediate attention and effective measures to be undertaken. In addition, the ECtHR may through its judgments place the issue of discriminatory violence high on the regulative or policy agendas of national legislatures and executive bodies. There may be different reasons why discriminatory violence is not properly combated at a domestic level. Yet, regardless what these reasons may be, the Court, serving as a supervisory human rights organ for the whole of Europe, can possibly trigger alterations in the domestic hate crime legislation or policy. Now that the Court is in great part constitutional in nature, it ought to prioritize issues related to discriminatory violence as a matter of special concern.

REFERENCES

Bates, E. 2011. 'The Birth of the European Convention on Human Rights–and the European Court of Human Rights' in Christoffersen, J. and Rask Madsen, M. (eds) *The European Court of Human Rights between Law and Politics*, New York: Oxford University Press, pp. 17–42.

Burgorgue-Larsen, L. and Úbeda de Torres, A. 2011. *The Inter-American Court of Human Rights: Case Law and Commentary*, New York: Oxford University Press.

Cahn, C. 2006. 'The Elephant in the Room: On Not Tackling Systemic Racial Discrimination at the European Court of Human Rights' *European Anti-Discrimination Law Review*, (4), 13–20.

Çali, B. 2008. 'The Purposes of the European Human Rights System: One or Many?' *European Human Rights Law Review*, (3), 299–306.

Cassel, D. 2001. 'Does International Human Rights Law Make a Difference?' *Chicago Journal of International Law*, 2(1), 121–35.

Gerards, J. 2012. 'The Prism of Fundamental Rights' *European Constitutional Law Review*, 8(2), 173–202.

Greer, S. 2006. *The European Convention on Human Rights. Achievements, Problems and Prospects*, New York: Cambridge University Press.

Greer, S. 2008. 'What's Wrong with the European Convention on Human Rights?' *Human Rights Quarterly*, 30, 680–702.

Hall, N. 2013. *Hate Crime*, Abingdon: Routledge.

Harris, D.J., O'Boyle, M., Bates, E.P., and Buckley, C.M. 2014. *Harris, O'Boyle & Warbrick: Law of the European Convention on Human Rights*, New York: Oxford University Press.

Jacobs, J.B. and Potter, K. 1998. *Hate Crimes: Criminal Law & Identity Politics*, New York: Oxford University Press.

Lawrence, F.M. 2002. *Punishing Hate. Bias Crimes under American Law*, Cambridge/London: Harvard University Press.

Leach, P. 2011. *Taking a Case to the European Court of Human Rights*, New York: Oxford University Press.

Möschel, M. 2012. 'Is the European Court of Human Rights' Case Law on Anti-Roma Violence "Beyond Reasonable Doubt"?' *Human Rights Law Review*, 12(3), 479–507.

Neumayer, E. 2005. 'Do International Human Rights Treaties Improve Respect for Human Rights?' *The Journal of Conflict Resolution*, 49(6), 925–53.

O'Nions, H. 2010. 'What Lies Beneath: Exploring Links between Asylum Policy and Hate Crime in the UK' *Liverpool Law Review*, 31(3), 233–57.

Pentassuglia, G. 2012. 'The Strasbourg Court and Minority Groups: Shooting in the Dark or a New Interpretative Ethos?' *International Journal on Minority and Group Rights*, 19(1), 1–23.

Ringelheim, J. 2010. 'Minority Rights in a Time of Multiculturalism–The Evolving Scope of the Framework Convention on the Protection of National Minorities' *Human Rights Law Review*, 10(1), 99–128.

Spielmann, D. 2012. *Allowing the Right Margin, the European Court of Human Rights and the National Margin of Appreciation Doctrine: Waiver or Subsidiarity of European Review?*, University of Cambridge: CELS Working Paper Series.

Spiliopoulou Åkermark, S. 2002. 'The Limits of Pluralism-Recent Jurisprudence of the European Court of Human Rights with Regard to Minorities: Does the Prohibition of Discrimination Add Anything?' *Journal on Ethnopolitics and Minority Issues in Europe*, (3), 1–24.

Sullivan, A. 1999. 'What's so Bad about Hate? The Illogic and Illiberalism behind Hate Crime Laws' *New York Times Magazine*, 26 September.

Thornberry, P. 2002. *Indigenous Peoples and Human Rights*, Manchester: Manchester University Press.

Weller, M. 2005. 'Preface' in Weller, M. (ed.), *The Rights of Minorities in Europe: A Commentary on the European Framework Convention for the Protection of National Minorities*, New York: Oxford University Press, pp. vii–x.

Wilkinson, C. 2014. 'Putting "Traditional Values" Into Practice: The Rise and Contestation of Anti-Homopropaganda Laws in Russia' *Journal of Human Rights*, 13(3), 363–79.

Wolfe, L. and Copeland, L. 1994. 'Violence against Women as a Bias-Motivated Hate Crime: Defining the Issues in the USA' in Davies, M. (ed.), *Women and Violence*, London: Zed Books Ltd, pp. 200–13.

CASE LAW

Abdulaziz, Cabales, and Balkandali v United Kingdom, (Apps. 9214/80, 9473/81, and 9474/81), 28 May 1985 [GC], Series A, No 94, (1985) 7 EHRR 471.

Anguelova v Bulgaria, (App. 38361/97), 13 June 2002, (2004) 38 EHRR 659, ECHR 2002-IV.

Antayev and Others v Russia, (App. 37966/07), 3 July 2014.

Assanidze v Georgia, (App. 71503/01), 8 April 2004 [GC], (2004) 39 EHRR 653, ECHR 2004-II.

Carabulea v Romania, (App. 45661/99), 13 July 2010.

Chapman v United Kingdom, (App. 27238/95), 18 January 2001 [GC], (2001) 33 EHRR 399, ECHR 2001-I.

Dudgeon v United Kingdom, (App. 7525/76), 22 October 1981 [GC], Series A, No 45, (1982) 4 EHRR 149.

Hoffmann v Austria, (App. 12875/87), 23 June 1993, Series A, No 255-C, (1994) 17 EHRR 293.

Identoba and Others v Georgia, (App. 73235/12), 12 May 2015.

Karaahmed v Bulgaria, (App. 30587/13), 24 February 2015.

McCann and Others v United Kingdom, (App. 18984/91), 27 September 1995 [GC], Series A, No 324, (1996) 21 EHRR 97.

Moldovan and Others v Romania (No 2), (Apps. 41138/98 and 64320/01), 12 July 2005, (2007) 44 EHRR 302, ECHR 2005-VII.

Nachova and Others v Bulgaria, (Apps. 43577/98 and 43579/98), 6 July 2005 [GC], (2006) 42 EHRR 933, ECHR 2005-VII.

Oršuš and Others v Croatia, (App. 15766/03), 16 March 2010 [GC], (2009) 49 EHRR 572.

Sidiropoulos and Others v Greece, (App. 26695/95), 10 July 1998, (1999) 27 EHRR 633, ECHR 1998-VI.

Soering v United Kingdom, (App. 14038/88), 7 July 1989 [GC], Series A, No 161, (1989) 11 EHRR 439.

Stoica v Romania, (App. 42722/02), 4 March 2008.

15

HOW SHOULD WE LEGISLATE AGAINST HATE SPEECH? FINDING AN INTERNATIONAL MODEL IN A GLOBALIZED WORLD

Viera Pejchal and Kimberley Brayson

INTRODUCTION

Hate speech constitutes a growing phenomenon around the globe (Pillay 2013). In order to better address problems linked to hate speech, such as discrimination and the commission of physical hate crimes, policy- and law-makers have tried, un-successfully, to define it. To date, no satisfactory definition or legal approach has been presented that would curtail hate incidents (Weber 2009). This chapter questions whether a uniform definition is possible and/or even desirable. Therefore the chapter does not propose a rigid definition of what hate speech is or how it should be addressed in legislation. Instead, the chapter focuses on the development of inter-national treaties that seek to tackle the problem of hate speech in order to establish how this phenomenon should be responded to in a globalized world. The prohib-ition of hate speech is a positive obligation for states in order to protect citizens from verbal and physical harm. However, the paradox arises that this obligation often leads to protecting the rights of one group while curtailing the rights of others. Such a situation presents a conundrum for states and raises the question of how to justify preferring the rights of one group over another.

At the core of this problem has been finding a balance between protecting freedom of expression on the one hand and protecting vulnerable groups from verbal (and in turn potentially physical) persecution on the other. Any attempt to limit free speech has been perceived as an attack on the foundations of Western society, where freedom of expression has been considered a developmental cornerstone (Hare and Weinstein 2009). Nevertheless, freedom of expression is not an absolute right, it is a qualified right, meaning that in some cases a violation of the right to freedom of speech can be justified. This reflects the fact that legally established limitations on speech are crucial to ensuring that all people receive equal treatment and that their rights are not infringed upon (Egendorf 2003). Just as governments have the duty to protect from racial discrimination as forming part of their *jus cogens*[1] obligations,[2] protection from hate speech that incites racial discrimination is herein understood as the obligation to ensure equal enjoyment of all rights to all people and should similarly enjoy the status of *jus cogens*. Such limitations on hate speech should be established by law. Simultaneously, governments must ensure that free speech is protected as vital for social democratic development. These competing obligations have resulted in high levels of legal and judicial protection of freedom of expression as a general rule, and permissible limits of freedom of expression as an exception.

The task of defending the right to freedom of expression, whilst at the same time defending the right to not be discriminated against, is not an easy one. The philosophical foundations for numerous international conventions that promote respect for the rights of others concentrate on the start and end of one's liberty. These conventions oblige Member States to adopt domestic legislation and policies that prohibit discrimination, hostility, and violence. Limits to free speech have evolved over time and correspondingly so have the obligations for states that ratify them. One theory that has arisen as a result of these evolving obligations for states in relation to limits on free speech is that hate speech has emerged as a limitation on free speech. This thesis is explored herein by outlining the stages of evolution of hate speech after the Second World War through to the present day. For the purposes of analysis we will use the notion of 'generations' of hate speech to chart the genesis of hate speech. Such a schema draws upon Vasak's (1977) notion of the three generations of human rights: civil-political, socio-economic, and collective-developmental. Accordingly, the chapter sets out three different generations of what constitutes hate speech. Understanding hate speech in terms of generations shall be read in accordance with limits on freedom of expression. Thinking in terms of generations of hate speech thus enables the analysis to track the evolution of a global understanding as to what legal and public goods are protected by international human rights treaties. In accordance with Vasak's three generations of human rights, there should be no hierarchy established in understanding the generations of hate speech. This observation can help us to better apprehend past, present, and future interpretations of the norms limiting the exercise of freedom of expression in cases of hate speech. It must be noted that while the concept of hate speech 'generations' is inherently linked to chronological development, treaties on the international level legitimize state intervention in free speech on numerous grounds. For the purpose of this chapter, the chronology of hate speech generations will be considered as secondary to the content of different treaties which draw on elements from all three generations of hate speech, without strictly following the time frame in which these treaties were adopted. This reflects the fact that hate speech has evolved over time in line with constantly shifting societal attitudes towards different social groups. All relevant international and regional treaties, both binding and non-binding, will be examined in order to establish the

---

[1] *Jus cogens* obligations are fundamental principles of international law. Derogations from *jus cogens* principles are never permitted.

[2] See Barcelona Traction, Light and Power Company, Limited, Second Phase, Judgment of 5 February 1970, ICJ Reports (1970), p. 3, at p. 32.

three generations of hate speech. This threefold analysis is presented as a promising way to understand and tackle hate speech in a globalized world.

THE FIRST GENERATION OF HATE SPEECH: GENOCIDE AND WAR CRIMES

The Convention on the Prevention and Punishment of the Crime of Genocide (here-after Convention on Genocide, CoG) established express limits on freedom of expression, by banning direct and public incitement to commit the crime of genocide.[3] While the prevention of racial or religious hate propaganda is not mandated by this Convention, enacting anti-vilification or hate speech laws may nonetheless be a legitimate measure for the systemic prevention of genocide (Saul 2009). Article 3 of the CoG aimed to limit free speech and was largely criticized on this basis. For example, American diplomats objected that the prohibition of propaganda inciting group hatred or provoking genocide could be used as a pretext for governmental control of the press (Lippman 1984).

The Convention on Genocide was the first international treaty to ban genocide and incitement to genocide as an imperfect offence. Notwithstanding, the Convention was first applied only after such crimes of genocide had already been committed, and it was not until 2003 that the meaning of direct and public incitement to commit genocide was elaborated upon by the International Criminal Tribunal for Rwanda (ICTR). The ICTR identified the existence of hate and violence as a cause of the conflict in Rwanda. This hate was present between two ethnic groups: the Hutus and the Tutsis, and despite widespread hatred among members of those two groups, the Court established individual responsibility for the crimes committed by prosecuting high-ranking media figures in Rwanda (Bemba 2008). The ICTR recognized the role of the mass media—specifically of the *Radio-Télévision Libre de Milles de Collines*—as contributing to a hateful campaign against the Tutsis (Thompson 2007). During the trial process, the ICTR clarified the way in which incitement should be considered: '... the direct element of incitement should be viewed in the light of its *cultural and linguistic content*. Indeed, a particular speech may be perceived as "direct" in one country, and not so in another, depending on the audience.'[4]

For the ICTR, incitement to genocide was directly linked to hate speech. However, the ICTR made a distinction between 'mere' hate speech as part of the context surrounding incitement to genocide and the offence of direct incitement to commit genocide.[5] Hate speech that does not instigate violence cannot constitute the factual

---

[3] *Convention on the Prevention and Punishment of the Crime of Genocide*, adopted on 9 December 1948. Article 3 states: The following acts shall be punishable: (a) Genocide; (b) Conspiracy to commit genocide; (c) *Direct and public incitement to commit genocide*; (d) Attempt to commit genocide; (e) Complicity in genocide; emphasis added.

[4] Case No. ICTR-99-52-A (ICTR Appeal Chambers 2007), para. 698; emphasis added.

[5] Case No. ICTR-99-52-A (ICTR Appeal Chambers 2007), paras 715, 955, 988.

basis for prosecution for incitement to genocide[6] and accordingly the ICTR did not offer any further definition of it.

There have been other contemporary examples of hate speech acting as a catalyst for genocide. For instance, ethnic hate speech was present before and during the Bosnian genocide (Southwick 2005). The International Criminal Tribunal for the Former Yugoslavia (ICTY) considered the relevance of hate speech in 2001 in *Prosecutor v Kordi & Čerkez*. The trial chamber of the ICTY considered that calls for 'cleansing the area of Muslim inhabitants' as part of a campaign of propaganda constituted hate speech and incitement to genocide. Nevertheless, similarly to the ICTR, the ICTY went on to state that these allegations, hate speech and incitement to genocide, did not constitute 'persecution' as defined under its competencies.

It has been highlighted several times that this kind of speech was present during war propaganda across the globe and thus should be outlawed. International consensus on this issue was confirmed by adopting Article 20[7] of the International Covenant on Civil and Political Rights which prohibits propaganda for war. Partsch (1981) has referred to Article 20 as being practically a fourth paragraph of Article 19, the right to freedom of expression[8]; indeed, the two should be read in close connection. Article 20, unlike Article 19, does not guarantee a right; rather, it restricts the right to freedom of expression enshrined in Article 19 ICCPR. Article 20 contains mandatory limitations to freedom of expression by requiring states parties to outlaw war propaganda (McGoldrick 1994). The Human Rights Committee (HRC) has not yet had the opportunity to consider the application of Article 20.1 of the ICCPR.

Taking the above into consideration, the first generation of hate speech should be understood as the strict prohibition of any speech that incites war, the commission of genocide, and crimes against humanity. This prohibition should be enshrined in domestic legal frameworks and the exercise of freedom of expression in these cases should not be permitted. Accordingly, when applying international norms or domestic laws, it should not be open to courts to engage in the balancing of the competing rights and associated interests of free speech and the protection of the nation. The prohibition on hate speech in these instances and the limitation on the right to free speech should be understood as absolute with no room for derogation or justification.

---

[6]   Case No. ICTR-99-52-T (ICTR Trial Chamber 2003), paras 13–14, 21.

[7]   ICCPR, International Covenant on Civil and Political Rights Adopted on 16 December 1966: Article 20:

1.   Any propaganda for war shall be prohibited by law.
2.   Any advocacy of national, racial or religious hatred that constitutes incitement to discrimination, hostility or violence shall be prohibited by law.

[8]   ICCPR Article 19:

1.   Everyone shall have the right to hold opinions without interference.
2.   Everyone shall have the right to freedom of expression; this right shall include freedom to seek, receive and impart information and ideas of all kinds, regardless of frontiers, either orally, in writing or in print, in the form of art, or through any other media of his choice.
3.   The exercise of the rights provided for in paragraph 2 of this article carries with it special duties and responsibilities. It may therefore be subject to certain restrictions, but these shall only be such as are provided by law and are necessary:
    (a) For respect of the rights or reputations of others;
    (b) For the protection of national security or of public order (ordre public), or of public health or morals.

THE SECOND GENERATION OF HATE SPEECH: FREEDOM OF EXPRESSION VS. PUBLIC ORDER

The first generation of hate speech identified above does not encounter major academic or legal disagreement as to when a particular speech act should be prohibited if its effect is to incite war crimes. However, the second generation of hate speech is more problematic. The second generation of hate speech requires states to balance the protection of freedom of expression with the protection of public order and therefore runs to the heart of the democratic state and its institutions. In analysing the second generation, Article 19 of the ICCPR (as set out above) is of paramount importance.

Article 19 has been regarded as an important pillar for democratic societies. When the HRC debated what restrictions to include in Article 19, it highlighted that the basic purpose was to protect the rights of the individual to freedom of opinion and expression and that the Article should therefore contain as few restrictions as possible (Bossuyt 1987). Thus the first two paragraphs affirm a commitment to a 'right to hold opinions without interference' and to 'freedom to seek, receive, and impart information and ideas of all kinds'. Nevertheless, Article 19 does disclose some restrictions on freedom of speech. The third paragraph of Article 19 allows states to restrict this freedom, inter alia, 'for the protection of national security or of public order'. The idea of violence and hostility within a society is a justifiable limit on free speech. In order to limit free speech, cumulative conditions must be observed. The restriction must be 1) prescribed by law; 2) addressed towards the aims set out in paragraphs 3(a) and (b) of Article 19; and 3) necessary to achieve a legitimate purpose (Bossuyt 1987).

On this basis many states have sought to restrict the freedom of expression of certain individuals. For example, Canada restricted the right to freedom of expression of a teacher who was publishing antisemitic opinions.[9] The Government justified the restriction through its obligation to protect the community from hostility and from a 'poisoned environment'. In addition, it presented arguments based on its obligation enshrined in Article 20.2 of the ICCPR. This Article can be read in the way that 'any advocacy of hatred that constitutes incitement to hostility or violence shall be prohibited by law'. The HRC considered in this case that Canada had complied with its positive duties under the ICCPR.

In spite of the lack of cases regarding hate speech before the HRC, its main concern has been to protect society as a whole, that is, public order, from hostility and violence based on harmful ideas that emerged in the last century in the period of National Socialism in Germany. *J.R.T. and the W.G. Party v Canada*,[10] *Zundel v Canada*,[11] and *Faurisson v France*[12] are all significant cases which dealt with the dissemination

---

[9] CCPR/C/70D/736/1997, Communication No. 736/1997, *Malcolm Ross v Canada*.
[10] CCPR/C/18D/104/1981, Communication No. 104/1981, *J.R.T. and the W.G. party v Canada*.
[11] CCPR/C/89/D/1341/2005, Communication No. 1341/2005, *Zundel v Canada*.
[12] CCPR/C/58/D/550/1993, Communication No. 550/1993, *Faurisson v France*.

of hateful opinions towards the Jewish community. In all of the above cases, hate speech authors claimed in vain to have had their right to freedom of expression violated. In this way, the HRC has determined that punishment of holocaust denial is a legitimate restriction on free speech. Otherwise, by not banning antisemitic speech, society allows diffusion of discriminatory and offensive statements that attack not only the Jewish community but undermine principles of peaceful coexistence within a society.

The second generation of understanding what kind of speech constitutes hate speech can thus be linked to incitement to violence and hostility which undermines public order in a variety of ways including genocide denial. The obligation for states to prevent violence and hostility is also outlined in the International Convention on the Elimination of Racial Discrimination (ICERD).[13] One of the main catalysts for the adoption of the ICERD was the acknowledgement that the dissemination of ideas of racial superiority was linked to activities that incited violence in the Second World War. The ICERD embodied the first international consensus opposing the superiority of one race of people over another, and prohibited both colonialism and apartheid as forms of racial discrimination. Although discrimination will be linked to hate speech in the third generation, it is important to highlight here that failure to punish hate speech may in fact provoke feelings of hostility in a society, thereby exacerbating inter-group tensions. Such an outcome was evident in the Committee on Elimination of Racial Discrimination's (CERD) decision in the case of *L.K. v the Netherlands*. This case, decided in 1991, involved a Moroccan citizen residing in the Netherlands.[14] The applicant had been offered social housing on a street in Utrecht and when he turned up to view the house, a group of twenty people had gathered outside. The group could be heard shouting 'no more foreigners', 'we've got enough foreigners in this street', and 'they wave knives about and you don't even feel safe in your own street'. In addition the group threatened the applicant. The applicant lodged a complaint which the police initially refused to register. In its decision, the CERD condemned the Netherlands for its failure to fulfil its obligations under the ICERD. The CERD considered that the statements aimed at the applicant passed the threshold between permissible speech and speech that incites hostility. Under the obligations established in the ICERD, speech inciting hostility must be punished by a penal law. The Dutch authorities failed to comply with this obligation through their uncompleted police investigation into the matter and inadequate judicial proceedings which did not demonstrate the requisite due diligence. Had the Dutch authorities undertaken their duties under the ICERD diligently and punished those responsible for remarks constituting incitement to racial discrimination, hostility between the parties could have been mitigated and mediated; potentially minimizing inter-group tensions.

It seems clear that states have a duty to protect citizens from violence and hostility. Indeed, international frameworks demand fulfilment of this obligation. However,

---

[13] ICERD, International Convention on the Elimination of All Forms of Racial Discrimination, Adopted on 21 December 1965.

[14] CERD/C/42/D/4/1991, Communication No. 4/1991, *L.K. v the Netherlands*.

a lack of case law suggests how difficult it is to directly link speech with the commission of violence. Criminologists have linked hate speech to the commission of hate crimes, which are more easily identified as hatred or bias-motivated violence (Perry 2001; Walters 2014). If hate speech is defined within the second generation of understanding hate speech, it can be considered as a type of 'hate crime' and thus penal provisions and sanctions must be established. Any verbal incitement to violence and hostility must be penalized as it targets one of the most precious public goods: human life. Nevertheless, it is not just public order and protection from violence that is important to a discussion about the regulation of hate speech. We need also understand that the commission of verbal hate abuse has its roots in discrimination and denial of equal dignity towards *all* human beings. We turn now to the third generation of hate speech in order to examine how this element of bias-motivated violence can be better addressed.

THE THIRD GENERATION OF HATE SPEECH: DISCRIMINATION

Although deciding *what* constitutes incitement to violence, war, or genocide is not simple, the first two generations share similarities with regards to the definition of those terms. Mendel (2006) has highlighted the problematic nature of hate speech, which is vague and contextual, standing in stark contrast to the clear definition of genocide. If hate speech is linked to the commission of hate crimes, it becomes easier to define. In addition, hate-motivated crimes have arguably been well-defined within national legal frameworks throughout the Western world (Walters 2014: ch 1). The third generation of hate speech, though, is harder to define. This third generation tends to address the origin of hate speech and the consequences that this speech has on its victims. Delgado (1982) has observed that speech that incites hatred has far-reaching effects, including the internalization of insults, negative psychological responses to stigmatization, and the reinforcement of social stratification. Such effects have led to efforts internationally to address hate speech that incites discrimination or the full enjoyment of the rights of victims on the basis that attacks on dignity should be properly addressed. In addressing hate speech and its effects, states send an important signal to vulnerable groups that their protection is paramount, and simultaneously to perpetrators that their freedom of expression is not absolute. Prohibition of discrimination and the promotion of equality are crucial for social cohesion. It is for this reason that several international treaties oblige states to punish acts linked to incitement to discrimination, including hate speech.

ICERD has been regarded as central to the struggle against racial discrimination (Lerner 1980). Article 4 of it states:

States Parties condemn all propaganda and all organizations which are based on ideas or theories of superiority of one race or group of persons of one colour or ethnic origin, or which attempt to justify or promote *racial hatred and discrimination* in any form, and undertake to adopt immediate and positive measures designed to eradicate all incitement to, or acts of, such discrimination and, to this end, with due regard to the principles embodied in the Universal Declaration of Human Rights and the rights expressly set forth in Article 5 of this Convention, inter alia:

(a) Shall declare an offence punishable by law all dissemination of ideas based on racial superiority or hatred, *incitement to racial discrimination*, as well as all acts of violence or incitement to such acts against any race or group of persons of another colour or ethnic origin, and also the provision of any assistance to racist activities, including the financing thereof;

(b) Shall declare illegal and prohibit organizations, and also organized and all other propaganda activities, which promote and *incite racial discrimination*, and shall recognize participation in such organizations or activities as an offence punishable by law;

(c) Shall not permit public authorities or public institutions, national or local, to promote or *incite racial discrimination*.[15]

However, despite its importance in eliminating racial discrimination, Article 4 has been considered by some to jeopardize both the right to freedom of opinion and expression and the right to freedom of peaceful assembly and association (Korengold 1993).

The obligations enshrined in Article 4(a) have been subject to various analyses with differing results.[16] According to the CERD, Article 4(a) requires states parties to *penalize* four categories of misconduct: 1) dissemination of ideas based upon racial superiority or hatred; 2) incitement to racial hatred; 3) acts of violence against any race or group of persons of another colour or ethnic group; and 4) incitement to such acts. As mentioned in the previous section, the second generation of hate speech evolved from legally punishing incitement to violence and the commission of violent acts. This is a historical consequence of apartheid, segregation, and other hate crimes motivated by the belief of racial superiority. Nevertheless, Article 4(a) offers a new legal basis for the Committee's latest interpretation of what constitutes hate speech. This interpretation provides the foundations for what is termed herein the 'third generation' of hate speech.

In their Concluding Observations and General Recommendations,[17] the CERD observed that racial discrimination can take different forms such as xenophobia, Islamophobia, or antisemitism. In addition, the CERD recognized that racial hate speech and a lack of punishment and/or proper investigation of incitement to racial discrimination had arisen in several cases. On two occasions, in 2006[18] and 2010,[19] during political discussions about Female Genital Mutilation in Denmark, the

---

[15] Emphasis added.

[16] For example, Nicolas Lerner (1980) identifies five categories; and D. Mahalic and J.G. Mahalic, in 'The Limitation Provisions of the International Convention on the Elimination of All Forms of Racial Discrimination', *Human Rights Quarterly* 9(1) (1987), established six different categories.

[17] Regarding the interpretation of Article 4, the Committee elaborated four General Recommendations: No. 1 about *States parties' obligations (Art. 4)*, U.N. Doc. A/8718 at 37 (1972); General Recommendation No. 7 about *Legislation to eradicate racial discrimination (Art. 4)*, U.N. Doc. A/40/18 at 120 (1985); General Recommendation No. 15 *Organized violence based on ethnic origin (Art. 4)*, U.N. Doc. A/48/18 at 114 (1994); General Recommendation No. 35 about *Combating racist hate speech*, CERD/C/GC/35 (23 September 2013).

[18] CERD/C/68/D/34/2004, Communication No. 34/2004, *Mohamemed Hassan Gelle v Denmark*.

[19] CERD/C/77/D/43/2008, Communication No. 43/2008, *Saada Mohamada Adan v Denmark*.

Somali minority was compared to rapists and paedophiles. Members of the CERD concluded that the fight against xenophobia and Islamophobia includes striking an effective balance between freedom of expression and gratuitous insults that do not construct a basis for public debate. Furthermore, that political debate on harmful practices on girls and women within African culture should have been supported by objective facts without racist content; such content, they stated, hinders the integration of Muslim immigrants.

Racial hate speech in the form of antisemitism was also recognized in a case against Norway[20] for failing to investigate properly favourable promotion of the ideologies of Adolf Hitler and Rudolf Hess. The CERD found that promotion of Nazi ideas constituted propaganda based on theories of superiority and, therefore, should have been condemned by Norway. The most recent case concerning a violation of Article 4 for incitement to racial discrimination and hatred was against Germany in 2010.[21] The former German Finance Minister blamed Turkish and Arab immigrants for poor levels of integration attributable to their economic conditions, culture, and intelligence. The CERD was not unanimous in its decision in this case. Defenders of freedom of expression argued that questioning immigration plays an important role in political debate and that it was essential for a democratic society. On the other hand, for the majority of the CERD, the rise of Islamophobia in Germany and the promulgation of the superiority of Germans over Turkish immigrants constituted propaganda of racial superiority and thus should be sanctioned—a step which Germany failed to take. Sensitivity towards the limits of what is permissible in political debate and when the protection of a vulnerable group should prevail is very contextual. Due to the relatively recent German history of racial propaganda, the CERD opted to silence any speech that might incite discrimination and held Germany in violation of Article 4.

These case law examples of decisions made by the CERD confirm that the third generation of understanding hate speech is intrinsically linked to discrimination. It is not merely a case of semantics in ensuring that speech acts and statements should be politically correct. More fundamentally the third generation of hate speech seeks to capture an understanding that the verbal promotion of stereotypes can have far-reaching effects leading to discrimination in access to education, employment, healthcare, and other services. Discrimination is also prohibited under the ICCPR. Article 20.2 of ICCPR, set out above, requires states to outlaw 'any advocacy of national, racial or religious hatred that constitutes incitement to discrimination'.[22] Discrimination can be understood as an obstacle to the full enjoyment of the rights to which a person is entitled. Accordingly, the third generation of hate speech should be understood as encompassing any speech that hampers the full enjoyment of these rights. This is in line with Article 19.3a of the ICCPR which recognizes as a limit

---

[20] CERD/C/67/D/30/2003, Communication No. 30/2003, *The Jewish Community of Oslo et al. v Norway.*

[21] CERD/C/82/D/48/2010, Communication No. 48/2010, *TBB-Turkish Union in Berlin/Brandenburg v Germany.*

[22] Art. 20.2 ICCPR, emphasis added.

to free speech the respect for the rights or reputations of others. In this context, it is important to recall the general limit to the exercise of rights under the ICCPR Article 5.1.[23] This provision discloses a general limit to freedom of expression and is recognized in the Human Rights Committee's General Comment No.34. In this comment, the HRC affirms that Article 20 may be considered as *lex specialis* in relation to Article 19. A major concern in qualifying speech as hate speech is determining whether Article 19.3 or Article 20.2 should be applied. Certainly, Article 20.2 offers a wider scope of offences as legally punishable. The obligation under Article 20.2 requires states to prohibit specific conduct and verbal expressions. The state's duty to prevent the advocacy of hatred that incites unlawful actions requires a clear and narrow interpretation of what elements constitute advocacy and incitement. In this respect Nowak (2005) has noted the lack of uniformity in interpretation of 'incitement' and the extraordinary vagueness which characterizes the term 'advocacy', leading to a risk of abuse of the term. In addition to the notion of public order as justifying limitations on free speech, the Human Rights Committee in all of the above analysed cases also used the argument of the rights of others and the protection of morals to justify limits on free speech. The HRC are thus drawing on justifications from both the second and third generations of hate speech to support their conclusions.

The third generation of hate speech can also be understood as speech attacking human dignity without a direct link to violence. Waldron (2012) equates human dignity with citizenship. Any assault on a person's dignity means an assault on the basic rights and status of a person integral to the proper functioning of any democratic society in which all its members are respected as equals. Punishment of expressions that undermine human dignity represents a moral statement of what society values and is an expression of solidarity with the objects of hate speech (Mendel 2012). Today, with profound changes within society, increasing migration, and the impact of social media, the cohesion of society is even more necessary and requires a clear intolerance of hate speech towards minority communities. For a long time, free speech has been protected and regarded as an important public good and a *sine qua non* for the development of a democracy. However, as demonstrated above in the three generations of hate speech that have been outlined, freedom of expression is not absolute and limitations on what is tolerable have evolved. Today, the protection of other public goods enters into conflict with free speech. Social peace and human dignity are important values, which any democratic society should defend. Indeed, these values are fundamental for a democratic society. As Lord Acton (2005) has noted, the most certain test by which we judge whether a country is really free is the amount of security enjoyed by minorities. Thus, democratic societies should not only guarantee freedom of expression but freedom from fear as well. Such fear is captured by the different generations of hate speech. The first generation of hate speech relates to concerns that bring into question the existence of a nation or a people and

---

[23] Art. 5.1 ICCPR: Nothing in the present Covenant may be interpreted as implying for any state, group, or person any right to engage in any activity or perform any act aimed at the *destruction of any of the rights and freedoms* recognized herein or at their limitation to a greater extent than is provided for in the present Covenant. Emphasis added.

is characterized by genocide and war crimes. The second generation of hate speech relates to the debate around free speech and public order whereby competing concerns come to the fore. On the one hand, concerns relate to permitting hate speech as free speech, which will disrupt public order and potentially lead to the physical integrity of citizens being violated. On the other hand, concerns are raised that in prohibiting hate speech, free speech is limited and infringed. The third generation of hate speech relates to concerns which manifest in discrimination, the hindrance of enjoyments of rights, and a threat to moral integrity of members of society. Hence, when states opt to address hate speech they are making a statement about what kind of society we want to live in. No concern is more or less important than another. Similarly, no generational understanding of hate speech is more important than other generations. They are complementary and not mutually exclusive. In tackling hate speech, states have at their disposal a wide range of options, from legal obligations under their ratification of international treaties to non-legal measures such as educational and informative campaigns proposed by governmental and non-governmental organizations.

According to Sadurski (1994), the existence of hate speech can make the public sensitive to prevailing racist trends in their community, thus prompting a doubling of efforts to eradicate such speech through educational and other initiatives. The international governmental and non-governmental community provides us with different approaches to finding a balance between protecting free speech and regulating hate speech. Frank La Rue (2011), former Special Rapporteur on the promotion and protection of the right to freedom of opinion and expression, has emphasized the need to distinguish between three types of expression:

(1) expression that constitutes an offence under international law and can be prosecuted criminally;
(2) expression that is not criminally punishable but may justify a restriction and a civil suit; and
(3) expression that does not give rise to criminal or civil sanctions, but still raises concerns in terms of tolerance, civility, and respect for others.[24]

According to him, laws prohibiting incitement to hatred in accordance with international human rights law are necessary and required to ensure that perpetrators are punished, victims receive effective remedies, and to prevent the recurrence of such acts. Nevertheless, penal codes alone will rarely provide the solution to the challenges of incitement to hatred. Education, consciousness-raising campaigns, and integration programmes for minorities are essential in order to deconstruct historical stereotypes.

The most recent global initiative to compile all regional and national mechanisms combating hate speech is the Rabat Plan of Action (RPA).[25] The purpose of this Plan

---

[24] UNGA, *Report of the Special Rapporteur on the Promotion and Protection of the Right to Freedom of Opinion and Expression*. A/66/290, 10 August 2011, para. 18.

[25] OHCHR, *Rabat Plan of Action on the Prohibition of Advocacy of National, Racial or Religious Hatred That Constitutes Incitement to Discrimination, Hostility or Violence*. 2012, available at http://www.ohchr. org/EN/Issues/FreedomReligion/Pages/RabatPlanOfAction.aspx (accessed on 11 March 2015).

is to identify elements to determine the threshold of 'advocacy of national, racial or religious hatred that constitute incitement to discrimination, hostility or violence'. Palmar (2014) argues that the RPA draws legitimacy and credibility from both the process that led to its drafting (input), as well as its substantive content (output). The RPA, as a soft law instrument, offers a series of conclusions, and recommendations in the area of legislation, jurisprudence, and policy. Amongst other things, it affirms that the three part test (legality, proportionality, and necessity) for restrictions on freedom of expression should be respected in examining cases of incitement to hatred. It recommends that restrictions should be: i) clearly and narrowly defined and respond to a pressing social need; ii) the least intrusive possible; iii) not overly broad, so they do not restrict speech in a wide or untargeted way; and iv) proportionate (the benefit of protected interest outweighs the harm to free speech), including in respect to the sanctions they authorize.

In addition, the RPA also encourages states to adopt comprehensive anti-discrimination legislation that includes preventive and punitive action to effectively combat incitement to hatred. It recommends that policies aim towards the creation and strengthening of a culture of peace, tolerance, and mutual respect among individuals, public officials, and members of the judiciary as well as rendering media organizations and religious/community leaders more ethically aware and socially responsible. Indeed, a multi-stakeholder approach is required to realize these aims.[26]

The most relevant outcome of the RPA is the suggestion of a case-by case analysis provided by judicial systems in applying the six-part test to determine whether the threshold of incitement to discrimination, hostility, or violence has been reached. This test includes an in-depth analysis of context, speaker, intent, content, extent of the speech, and likelihood-imminence.[27] This examination allows for clarification of what kind of generational understanding of hate speech a particular state has. In clarifying what hate speech is, the dilemma of justification might be presented. The key elements to take into account when understanding whether speech passes the threshold and becomes hate speech are the context of speech and its likelihood of commission of a hate crime, discrimination or attack on human dignity, and the curtailment of enjoyment of rights. However, recognizing hate speech is not always easy or automatic in a democratic society.

Across the globe two broad democratic responses to the issue of free speech are discernible. The first response opts for the sacrosanct nature of free speech in line with the classical democratic model. This approach can be closely associated with the United States where freedom of speech is protected under the Constitution. The second response is to choose the egalitarian democratic model by providing protection and equal values to all members of society, both majority and minority

---

[26] At the regional level, important suggestions have been made by the European Union's Agency for Fundamental Rights. OSCE's Office for Democratic Institutions and Human Rights offers an important range of tools on combating, analyzing, and responding to all hate crimes, including hate speech. To see more: http://fra.europa.eu/en/theme/hate-crime (accessed on 19 May 2015).

[27] This test is identical to the test proposed by a non-governmental organization, called ARTICLE 19, in December 2012.

communities. This second model is the one more closely aligned with Western European countries where rights to free speech are balanced with rights to be protected from verbal persecution. In Europe, Article 10 of the European Convention on Human Rights allows for balancing the exercise of freedom of expression with 'public security, commission of crimes, rights of others or morals'.[28] Indeed, incitement, glorification of violence, and dissemination of violent propaganda[29] are all examples of unprotected speech. A former judge to the Court, Tulkens (2012), has explained that from 2008 onwards the cases to do with freedom of expression related more to racial/ethnic hate speech. Some of the cases reflect anti-immigration[30] and anti-Islamic[31] discourse found in many European countries and mainly concern hate propaganda. A move from the second generation of hate speech to the third can be observed by this evaluative interpretation from judges in Strasbourg. In addition, cases dealing with negationism, revisions, and discourse inspired by a totalitarian doctrine or expressing ideas that represent a threat to the democratic order are not all scrutinized by the European Court of Human Rights. Instead the guillotine effect of Article 17 ECHR, the prohibition of abuse of rights, is applied in these instances (Flauss 1992).

Provisions similar to Article 10 ECHR can be found in other regional human rights instruments. Article 13 of the Inter-American Convention on Human Rights enshrines freedom of expression and also establishes its limits: (a) War Propaganda and advocacy of hatred that constitutes violence; (b) Direct and public incitement to Genocide; and (c) Infantile pornography. Seemingly, in a case of conflict of rights, this treaty offers an understanding in line with the first and second generations of hate speech. The third generation of hate speech can also be recognized when applying the most recent Inter-American regional treaties that deal with Discrimination and Tolerance.[32]

Africa has known some of the worst crimes against humanity fuelled by hatred—such as the genocide in Rwanda or apartheid in South Africa—but, paradoxically, the regional treaty does not offer a first generation understanding of hate speech: that is, incitement to genocide. Heyns (2002) correctly observes that freedom of expression,

---

[28] Art.10.2 Freedom of expression, the European Convention on Human Rights: The exercise of these freedoms, since it carries with it duties and responsibilities, may be subject to such formalities, conditions, restrictions or penalties as are prescribed by law and are necessary in a democratic society, in the interests of *national security, territorial integrity or public safety, for the prevention of disorder or crime, for the protection of health or morals, for the protection of the reputation or rights of others*, for preventing the disclosure of information received in confidence, or for maintaining the authority and impartiality of the judiciary. Emphasis added.

[29] See, for example, *Gündüz v Turkey* (2003), *Sener v Turkey* (2000), *Gerger v Turkey* (1999), *Sürek (no.1) v Turkey* (1999), etc.

[30] See, for example, *Soulas and Others v France* (2008), *Féret v Belgium* (2009), *Jersild v Denmark* (1994).

[31] See, for example, *Leroy v France* (2008).

[32] The *Inter-American Convention against Racism, Racial Discrimination, and Related Forms of Intolerance* and the *Inter-American Convention against All Forms of Discrimination and Tolerance*. Both treaties stipulate that 'states undertake to prevent, eliminate, prohibit, and punish' acts that 'advocate, promote, or incite hatred, discrimination, and intolerance'. 'Promotion' is a newly added word emphasizing that repeating old stereotypes is punishable and all members of society should act responsibly in order to avoid discrimination of others.

as defined in Article 9.2 of the African Charter on Human and Peoples' Rights is not subject to special duties as was the case in the international treaties scrutinized above. Notwithstanding, it provides for non-discrimination in the enjoyment of rights and general limitations, in particular, in Articles 2, 19, 27.2,[33] and 28. Such provisions promote compassion, solidarity, morality, mutual respect, and tolerance (Winks 2011) and thus would correspond well with the third generation of hate speech characterized by attacks on human dignity.

CONCLUSION

On the one hand, international awareness of the existence of hate speech has not yet been translated into a uniform international legal response. On the other hand, the international legal and non-legal framework allows states to tackle the phenomenon of hate speech according to its national, historical, and social contexts. Perception, tolerance, and understanding of hate speech are thus contextual and may be different in every society. As such, a single universal definition of hate speech is not necessarily desirable.

The evolution of the genesis of understanding of hate speech can be summarized as follows. The first generation of hate speech is characterized as direct incitement to the severe crimes of genocide and war crimes. The second generation is linked to direct incitement to violence and endangering public order. The third generation of hate speech is linked to instances of incitement to discrimination and attacks on human dignity. All three generations of hate speech are relevant today. No one definition is more valuable than the other but they all provide insights into the development of public goods and values which members of a society seek to protect. National and international judges are best placed to develop new understandings of what hate speech is.

The third generation of hate speech as an attack on human dignity begins to reveal greater consensus about the kind of globalized society we want to live in. Freedom of expression, a cornerstone for democracies, is highly protected to avoid such democracies from becoming dictatorships. Classical democracies have long been concerned with censorship and lack of free speech as the pathway to dictatorship. However, once democratic regimes are stable, there is little evidence to show that restricting free speech in order to protect social peace and guaranteeing the full enjoyment of all members' rights will result in the longer-term dismantling of social democratic freedom. These democracies are protected from such an existence by placing emphasis on egalitarianism. Respect for the rule of law is maintained while simultaneously adopting anti-hate speech laws. In international law this is

---

[33] Communications 140/94, 141/94, 145/95–Constitutional Rights Project, Civil Liberties Organization, and Media Rights Agenda/Nigeria, para. 41 affirmed that the only legitimate reasons for limitations of the rights and freedoms of the African Charter rights exercised with due regard to the rights of others, collective security, morality, and common interest.

best achieved by states respecting the tripartite standard: limits on free speech are prescribed by law; those limits pursue a legitimate aim; and such limits are necessary in a democratic society. If a democratic society wishes to be tolerant, respectful, and egalitarian, it is its duty to prevent all forms of expression that spread, incite, promote, or justify hatred. Judges play a crucial role in ensuring equal enjoyment of all rights by all members of society. This can be most effectively achieved by drawing on insights from all three generations of hate speech coupled with an appreciation that hate speech is context-dependent.

REFERENCES

Acton, John E.E. Dalberg. 2005. *The History of Freedom and Other Essays*. New York: Cassimo Classics.

Bemba, Joseph. 2008. *Justice International et Liberté d'expression: Les Médias Face aux Crimes Internationaux*. Paris: L'Harmattan.

Bossuyt, Marc J. 1987. *Guide to the "Travaux Préparatoires" of the International Covenant on Civil and Political Rights*. Dordrecht: Martinus Nijhoff.

Delgado, Richard. 1982. 'Words That Wound: a Tort Action for Racial Insults, Epithets and Name-Calling'. *Harvard Civil Rights-Civil Liberties Law Review* 17: pp. 133–81.

Egendorf, Laura K. 2003. *Should there be Limits to Free Speech*. Detroit: Greenhaven Press.

Flauss, Jean-François, 1992. 'L'abus de droit dans le cadre de la C.E.D.H', *Revue Universelle des droits de l'homme* 4(12): pp. 461–8.

Hare, Ivan and James Weinstein. 2009. *Extreme Speech and Democracy*. New York: Oxford University Press.

Heyns, Christof. 2002. 'Civil and Political Rights in the African Charter'. In *The African Charter on Human Rights and Peoples' Rights: The System in Practice, 1986–2000*, edited by Malcolm David Evans and Rachel Murray, pp. 137–77. Cambridge: Cambridge University Press.

Korengold, Michael A.G. 1993. 'Lessons in Confronting Racist Speech: Good Intentions, Bad Results, and Article 4(a) of the Convention on the Elimination of All Forms of Racial Discrimination'. *Minnesota Law Review* 77: p. 719.

Lerner, Natan. 1980. *The U.N. Convention on the Elimination of All Forms of Racial Discrimination*. Alphen aan den Rijn: Sijthoff & Noordhoff.

Lippman, Matthew. 1984. 'The Drafting of The 1948 Convention on the Prevention and Punishment of the Crime of Genocide', *Boston University International Law Journal* 3: 1–65.

McGoldrick, Dominic. 1994. *The Human Rights Committee: its Role in the Development of the International Covenant on Civil and Political Rights*. Oxford: Clarendon Press.

Mendel, Toby. 2006. *Study on International Standards Relating to Incitement to Genocide or Racial Hatred for the UN Special Advisor on the Prevention of Genocide*. Geneva: UN Publications.

Mendel, Toby. 2012. 'Does International Law Provide for Consistent Rules on Hate Speech?'. In *The Content and Context of Hate Speech: Rethinking Regulation and Responses*, edited by Michael E. Herz and Péter Molnár, pp. 417–29. New York: Cambridge University Press.

Nowak, Manfred. 2005. *U.N. Covenant on Civil and Political Rights, CCPR Commentary*. Kehl: NP Engel Publisher.

Palmar, Sejal. 2014. 'The Rabat Plan of Action: A Global Blueprint for Combating "Hate Speech"'. *European Human Rights Law Review* 1: pp. 21–31.

Partsch, Karl Joseph. 1981. 'Freedom of Conscience and Expression, and Political Freedoms'. In *The International Bill of Rights: the Covenant on Civil and Political Rights*, edited by Louis Henkin, pp. 209–45. New York: Columbia University Press.

Perry, Barbara. 2001. *In the Name of Hate: Understanding Hate Crimes*, New York: Routledge.

Pillay, Navi. 2013. 'Freedom of Expression and Incitement to Hatred in the Context of International Human Rights Law' (Speech, London, 15 February 2013).

Sadurski, Wojciech. 1994. 'Racial Vilification, Psychic Harm and Affirmative Action'. In *Freedom of Communication*, edited by T. Campbell and W. Sadurski, pp. 77–94. Aldershot: Dartmouth Publishing Company.

Saul, Ben. 2009. 'The Implementation of the Genocide Convention at the National Level'. In *The UN Genocide Convention: a Commentary*, edited by Gaeta Paola, pp. 58–83. New York: Oxford University Press.

Southwick, Katherine G. 2005. 'Srebrenica as Genocide—The Krstic Decision and the Language of the Unspeakable', *Yale Human Rights & Development Law Journal* 8: 188.

Thompson, Allan. 2007. *The Media and the Rwanda Genocide*. New Delhi: International Development Research Centre.

Tulkens, Françoise. 2012. 'Freedom of Expression and Hate Speech in the Case-Law of the Court'. In *Freedom of Expression, Essays in Honour of Nicolas Bratza*, edited by Josep Casadevall et al., pp. 349–62. Oisterwijk: Wolf Legal Publisher.

Vasak, Karel. 1977. *Human Rights: a Thirty-Year Struggle: the Sustained Efforts to Give Force of Law to the Universal Declaration of Human Rights*, UNESCO Courier 30:11, Paris: United Nations Educational, Scientific, and Cultural Organization.

Waldron, Jeremy. 2012. *The Harm in Hate Speech*. Cambridge, MA: Harvard University Press.

Walters, Mark Austin. 2014. *Hate Crime and Restorative Justice*. Oxford: Oxford University Press.

Weber, Anne. 2009. *Manual on Hate Speech*. Strasbourg: Council of Europe Publishing.

Winks, Benjamin E. 2011. 'A Covenant of Compassion: African Humanism and the Rights of Solidarity in the African Charter on Human and Peoples' Rights', *African Human Rights Law Journal* 11(2): pp. 447–64.

16

REGULATING HATE CRIME IN THE DIGITAL AGE

Chara Bakalis

INTRODUCTION

The questions surrounding the regulation of online hatred have become progressively more significant over the past twenty years because of the growing presence of the internet in our professional, social, and private lives. The extensive use of social networking sites such as Twitter and Facebook, as well as our mounting utilization of online discussion forums and comments sections in newspapers, have led to a vast increase in the amount of ways in which cyberhate can now be perpetrated.

It is important at the outset to start with some important definitions. Cyberhate will be taken to mean the use of electronic communications to express in written form hateful comments, insults, or discriminatory remarks about a person or group of persons based on, for example, their race, religion, ethnicity, sexual orientation, disability, or transgender identity. This will incorporate all written content, including images such as memes, but will not include any forms of Voice over IP or instant messaging. It is important to state that 'cyberhate' is distinct from broader conceptions of 'hate crime', although it should be noted that certain forms of cyberhate might also be classified as a type of hate crime.

This chapter will consider the issue of cyberhate from the point of view of legal regulation. It will explore the particular challenges that globalization poses to the combating of online hatred effectively, and it will determine what the global response to cyberhate should be. First it will discuss the ways in which the legal regulation of hate speech online differs from the regulation of 'offline' hate speech. Then it will reflect on how globalization poses additional challenges to legal responses to online hatred. The third section will evaluate the current international response to cyberhate and will conclude with some suggestions for ways forward. The chapter argues that the issues surrounding freedom of speech and the harm caused by cyberhate need to be reconsidered in light of the way in which online hatred is committed. It will also suggest that a united global response is the most effective way to progress, while acknowledging that differing cultural and legal norms make this a slow and difficult process.

ISSUES OF PRINCIPLE

The first issue of vital importance is the need to justify, from a principled point of view, the criminalization of online hate speech. This is because if a state or international body proposes the creation of a new piece of legislation or legal framework, it needs to be demonstrated that there is a strong case in favour of using the law to prohibit such behaviour. Traditionally, J.S. Mill's (1991) notion of 'harm' has been used as a guiding principle, which stipulates that the criminal law should only be used to prohibit behaviour if it can be shown to cause 'harm' to others. Mill's 'harm' principle has been subjected to a number of criticisms and modifications over the years, but has had enduring appeal for many contemporary legal philosophers (e.g., Raz 1986). By contrast, legal moralists believe that a necessary (although not sufficient) condition for criminalization is that the underlying behaviour which the law aims to prohibit is morally 'wrong' (e.g., Finnis 1980). Within both schools of thought, views differ as to the essential qualities of 'harm' or 'wrongfulness'. For the purposes of a discussion on cyberhate, what this debate demonstrates is the need to articulate clearly the underlying 'harm' or 'wrong' which a particular piece of legislation seeks to outlaw.[1]

Identifying the harm caused by hate speech is also important in that it will enable states to ensure that any legal response constitutes a legitimate incursion into free speech. The issue of free speech is central to the debate on cyberhate. Free speech lies at the core of our democratic society for a number of reasons and is regarded as protection against abuse of power. J.S. Mill (1991: 20) in *On Liberty* wrote about the need for democratic states to ensure 'the fullest liberty of professing and discussing ... any doctrine'. Such a right exists in most modern democratic states albeit in different forms such as for example the First Amendment under the US Constitution or Article 10 of the European Convention on Human Rights (ECHR). However, the right to freedom of expression is not absolute. J.S. Mill himself acknowledged that '... even opinions lose their immunity, when the circumstances in which they are expressed are such as to constitute ... a positive instigation to some mischievous act' (1991: 56). As such, the right to freedom of expression can be restricted under certain conditions. Regulating hate speech is a prima facie violation of freedom of expression, and there has been a wide-ranging debate amongst hate crime scholars about the extent to which hate crimes are compatible with free speech (e.g., Blazak 2011) and a similar discussion has been undertaken by scholars on the relationship between hate speech and freedom of speech (e.g., Waldron 2012). The most commonly used argument is that the regulation of hate speech can be justified if to do so is warranted by the level of harm caused by the speech. Thus, this is an additional reason as to why it is imperative at the outset of a discussion of the regulation of cyberhate to have a clear understanding of the harm caused by online hate speech.

---

[1] In order to simplify the discussion, the term 'harm' will be used from now on whilst acknowledging that legal moralists would prefer the word 'wrong'.

To some extent, the discussion about the harm in online hate speech will mirror the ongoing debate that hate crime scholars engage in when attempting to identify why hate crime or hate speech should be prohibited. Two particular explanations stand out as they have been very influential in the development of hate crime legislation. The first is that the harm lies in the fact that victims of hate crime hurt more (Iganski 2001) and/or hate crime offenders are more blameworthy because of their bias motivation (Lawrence 1999). The second is that the harm in hate speech lies in the damage to public order or in the fact that it pollutes the sense of security in the public space we all inhabit (Waldron 2012). Conceptualizing the harm of hate crime and hate speech along these lines results in two sets of distinctions being made: the first is between the *personal* and the *impersonal*, and the second is between the *public* and the *private*. If the harm in hate crime lies in the greater harm caused to the individual because of the offender's motivation, then hate crime legislation needs to reflect this. This results in legislation that treats hate crime as a problem that is *personal* to the victim, rather than an impersonal harm which is directed in a more abstract sense at a group of people. Meanwhile, if the harm in hate speech lies in the pollution of the public space or in the threat to *public* security and peace, legislation will focus primarily on protecting the public arena and will not be concerned with the exclusively private domain.

In some jurisdictions, these distinctions are intrinsic to the legal framework on hate speech. For example, in England and Wales the existing legislation which can be used in cases involving cyberhate can be divided broadly along the personal/impersonal divide and the public/private divide. On the one hand there are the offences under the Malicious Communications Act 1988, the Communications Act 2003, and the Protection from Harassment Act 1997 which are aimed at protecting the individual from behaviour that has caused the recipient or was meant to cause them harassment, alarm, distress, annoyance, inconvenience, or anxiety, such as an email sent to the victim threatening to assault them because they are Muslim. These offences are designed to deal with targeted attacks on individuals and are not aimed at impersonal attacks. On the other hand, the offences under the Public Order Act 1986 make it an offence to stir up hatred on the grounds of race, religion, or sexual orientation. An example that would fall under these provisions would be displaying in a public place a poster encouraging the killing of gay people. These provisions are aimed at regulating speech which is deemed to be a threat to public disorder as s 18(2) stipulates that these measures do not apply to speech that is expressed in a dwelling, or to speech that is only seen or heard by someone in a dwelling. Thus, the Act makes a distinction between words expressed in a home, and those expressed outside a home. The speech does not have to be aimed at anyone personally, and can be an impersonal attack on a group of people. This pattern can be seen in legislation in other countries as well. For instance, in the US there is a raft of state legislation which can give protection to individual victims of hate such as where threats have been made to the victim *personally*, or the behaviour is covered by stalking and harassment charges (Citron 2014: 123–5). Meanwhile the Supreme Court allows for the existence of hate speech laws as long as they only cover 'fighting words'

(*Chaplinsky v New Hampshire*) which threaten *public* security by inciting imminent lawlessness (*Brandenburg v Ohio*).

Undoubtedly some online hate speech will fall into the category of either personal attacks or public incitement, and so would potentially be covered by the relevant legislation. However, not all hate speech appearing on the internet will fall neatly into this divide. This is because the nature of the internet and the way it is used challenges the traditional divisions between personal/impersonal and public/private. Thus, there is a need for the law to reconceptualize the notion of the harm caused by cyberhate in order to inform legal reform in this area, both at an international level and at a local level.

The distinction made between public and private discourse by the law is fundamentally challenged by the way in which the internet functions. Whilst some operations are clearly private—such as emails—what constitutes a 'public' space on the internet is harder to identify clearly. As already noted, under English and Welsh law, activities which take place in the 'home' are not covered by the public order offences (Public Order Act, s 18(2)). In other countries such as Canada a 'private conversation' is exempt from the provisions (s 319(2) of the Canadian Criminal Code). Nevertheless, at a very basic level, these distinctions between a private/public space will not work for the internet given that online hate speech can be written by someone in their home, and read by someone else in their home on the other side of the globe. Similarly, identifying what constitutes a 'private conversation' on the internet is not straightforward as different levels of privacy are expected depending on which internet service is being used. For example, whether a conversation over Twitter or Facebook or in private chatrooms is public or private may depend on the number of people involved, as well as the privacy settings adopted by different users. We may find it easy to argue that an online newspaper available to all without subscription is public, but there may be much disagreement about whether or not this is also true of all freely available websites, including blogs. In an era when there are serious concerns over government surveillance of the internet, it is problematic to suggest that all content available on the internet should fall into the public domain.

From a legal point of view, this requires some thought. Jeremy Waldron in his book *The Harm in Hate Speech* (2012) sets out some persuasive arguments in favour of prohibiting hate speech. He likens the harm in hate speech to pollution that contaminates the environment and poisons the atmosphere. Hate speech, he argues, undermines the dignity of those who are targeted, and weakens their ability to be treated as equals. For this reason, he argues, prohibiting hate speech is a legitimate incursion on freedom of expression. To illustrate this, he gives the example of a Muslim father who walks his children to school, and on the way is confronted by posters with Islamophobic slogans, such as 'Muslims and 9/11! Don't serve them, don't speak to them, and don't let them in' (Waldron 2012: 1). These posters make him and his children feel unwelcome and threatened. This is a powerful image and demonstrates well how hate speech can deeply affect the daily lives of citizens. However, in order to employ these arguments to justify infringing free speech by regulating cyberhate, a further explanation is required because of some crucial differences between the online and offline world.

To begin with, as already argued, the 'public' space as defined in the physical world is more limited in scope and so, therefore, it is easier to defend placing restrictions on free speech. It is much harder to rationalize such curbs on our freedom when it involves our online behaviour which is now integral to our everyday lives. In fact, research suggests that young people see little difference in their online and offline identities, often making no distinction between the two (Miller 2013). Another difference lies in the way in which we come across material on the internet and the fact that we have varying degrees of control over what we encounter online. Whilst it might be possible to avoid looking at racist websites by not searching for them, or by not clicking on the relevant link if you accidentally come across them whilst searching for something else, there will be some situations where a user comes across hateful content whilst using a website that they have a reasonable expectation will not publish this sort of material, such as for example on the comments sections of an online newspaper. Interestingly, researchers have found that contrary to expectations, even on social media websites such as Facebook, users come across a substantial amount of ideologically diverse material (Bakshy et al. 2015). This suggests that we have less control over the content we encounter on social media than we would expect. Consequently, it might be necessary to consider a more nuanced approach to online hatred whereby differing levels of responsibility exist depending on the context. For instance, we might wish to impose an obligation on certain websites to police their online content, but might not want to necessarily extend this responsibility to *all* websites for fear that this would infringe free speech.

These fundamental differences between the online and offline world have profound implications for the debate surrounding the regulation of the internet. It means that we cannot simply rely on the same arguments used by scholars in favour of banning hate speech, such as those employed by Waldron. It also means that we have to go much further in giving particular thought to how we use the internet, how hate speech online is viewed and by whom, and consequently where its harm lies. A salutary illustration of the importance of constructing clear arguments in relation to free speech is the recent repeal of s 13 of the Canadian Human Rights Act. This made it an offence to communicate via the internet any 'undertaking... that is likely to expose a person or persons to hatred or contempt'. In its original form, s 13 applied only to telecommunications, and the infringement on free speech had been deemed legitimate and constitutional by the Supreme Court of Canada in *Canada (Human Rights Commission) v Taylor*. However, after s 13 was extended to undertakings over the internet in 2001, this initiated a very public debate about the constitutionality of s 13. Concerns were expressed, particularly over the freedom of the press (Walker 2013), and ultimately the pro-free speech arguments were deemed to be stronger and s 13 was finally repealed in 2013 (c. 37, s 2).

The impersonal/personal distinction that is usual in hate crime legislation might also not work as well when applied to hateful content on the internet. Whilst attacks on an individual by email or targeted attacks on Twitter could fall foul of offences which deal with injury caused to the victim, there may well be other ways in which hate perpetrated over the internet has far-reaching consequences that extend beyond harm to a particular individual. For example, Perry and Olsson (2009) have argued that the internet provides those who belong to groups we might broadly define as ones peddling 'hate' with the opportunity to 'retrench and reinvent...as a viable collective' (Perry and Olsson 2009: 185). It allows them to establish a collective identity and, Perry and Olsson argue, could potentially lead to a 'global racist subculture' (ibid). The permanency of the material that appears on the internet also contributes to this. As these hateful messages can be read by anyone at any time, this means that hate on the internet transcends the victim/perpetrator model, and instead can help create a wider global hate environment. It could, therefore, be said that the harm in hate speech over the internet is not limited to the injury it causes to an individual but also lies in the damage it causes to the social fabric of our global society by bolstering and intensifying certain hate movements. This aspect of cyberhate is not currently given enough attention by the law.

Another characteristic of internet use that has important implications for cyberhate legislation is the dichotomy between on the one hand the ease with which comments can be published on the internet, and on the other the permanent nature of internet publication along with its global reach. This presents a difficult dilemma for legislators. The casual nature of much internet 'chatter' presents a challenge to legal regulation as these types of comments may lack the intention usually necessary for hate speech. This has led commentators such as Rowbottom (2012) to caution against the over-criminalization of low-level online speech. Notwithstanding, even if an intention to cause injury may be lacking in many such cases, the harm caused can nevertheless be considerable (Fearn 2014). It is also a paradox of internet use that even though the reach of the internet is much more extensive than traditional forms of print media, the regulation, whether legal or non-legal, is minimal in comparison. Newspaper editors, for example, will take carefully considered decisions about what material to include in their newspaper. Meanwhile, the internet makes it possible for anyone to easily disseminate to the public their views and ideas through a number of means such as the creation of blogs, by posting comments at the end of newspaper articles, or via social media. This means that those thoughts and ideas are not necessarily well-thought out, and can be intemperate and uncontrolled. This lack of restraint or self-regulation means that speech that in the past would not have been published by traditional print media is now available to all. The internet can also embolden those who would never threaten or attack another person in the physical world to do so online. This has led to a worrying increase in the number of people, particularly women, who have been subjected to online abuse, harassment, or threats. The European Agency for Fundamental Rights (FRA) found in a gender-based violence against women survey that one in ten women in the European Union (EU) said they had been the victim of cyber harassment since the age of 15, and it was found that 'cyber harassment' was the most common form of harassment that women had experienced in the twelve-month period running up to the survey (FRA 2013). It also found that young women were most at risk of being targeted in this way (ibid). FRA's survey of discrimination and hate crime against Jews also found that 10 per cent of Jews said they had experienced offensive or threatening antisemitic comments made about them online (ibid). Meanwhile, the American Association of University Women surveyed almost 2,000 students in 2010–11 and found that

30 per cent of them said they had experienced some form of online harassment (Citron 2014: 16).

This discussion highlights the fact that relying on traditional measures used to combat hate crime is not sufficient, and there is a need for specific legislation aimed at targeting digital hate crime (see also Guichard 2009). A large part of the legislative exercise will require a reconsideration of free speech in light of the points made above about the challenges of cyberhate. In the context of 'offline' hate crime and hate speech, this debate has been characterized by interplay between two important values: on the one hand there is the important democratic value of freedom of speech, and on the other there is the equally important concept of equality. Hate crime legislation is seen as an important tool in the push towards equality, but this necessarily entails an incursion on our freedom of expression. Citron (2014) and Brennan (2009) have both argued that when considering the extent to which an infringement on freedom of speech is justified by legal regulation of cyberhate, more emphasis should be placed on the concept of equality. Citron (2014) has explored cyberhate in depth and has focused particularly on the way in which women are exposed to hate online, and how this affects their ability to participate fully in society and thereby threatens the principle of equality. She outlines a number of examples of cyberhate attacks where women have abandoned their online presence as a consequence. Citron views this as an affront to civil liberties as these attacks hinder women from enjoying their right to access to education and employment. This illustrates how in the context of the discussion of online regulation, it is wrong to assume that the relationship between free speech and equality is mutually exclusive whereby any step towards greater equality necessarily involves an incursion into free speech. This is because in many instances, online regulation of hateful messages may in fact help preserve free speech rather than diminish it. If the internet is meant to be a platform for free speech, then this has to apply equally to all groups in society. If cyberhate is impeding this, then legal regulation must be employed to even the scales.

TECHNICAL AND PRACTICAL ISSUES

Having looked at some of the issues of principle pertaining to online hate crime, it is necessary next to consider some of the technical and practical concerns regarding the legislative response to cyberhate. These relate in particular to the international nature of the internet, given that globalization poses a number of difficulties to the legal regulation of cyberhate. These challenges are of particular importance as they indicate that ordinary criminal offences such as those relating to harassment or stalking are not sufficient to deal with online hatred, and that what is needed instead is a legal response which is more tailored to the specific requirements of cyberhate.

The first challenge relates to the global nature of cyberhate. Unlike most 'ordinary' hate crime which is perpetrated by offenders who live in the same jurisdiction as the victims, online hatred can be carried out by offenders who live in a different country or even a different continent to their victim. This transnational nature of online hate crime generates a number of problems from a legal perspective. First, it would be necessary to decide which jurisdiction has authority to punish the perpetrator's actions. From the victim's point of view, there are disadvantages whatever the outcome. If jurisdiction lies with the perpetrator's legal system, the victim will encounter a number of potential hurdles when attempting to access justice in a foreign country. There may be no existing legislation in the perpetrator's legal system that covers the offending behaviour, and even if there is, there may be obvious cultural, linguistic, logistical, and financial difficulties which would confront the victim who is attempting to persuade the police in another country to take their case forward. If jurisdiction lies with the victim's legal system, justice can only be achieved if the perpetrator is extradited to the victim's country. Inevitably, this will not be straightforward as extradition treaties are neither universal nor comprehensive, and so there is no guarantee that a victim will find it easy to bring a perpetrator to court. This illustrates how cooperation between states is required. The international harmonization of laws relating to cyberhate, as well as effective extradition treaties, would go some way to solving these difficulties.

In practice, though, this is likely to be very difficult to achieve as different cultural and legal traditions across the world act as an enormous stumbling block to harmonization. For example, the US approach to free speech is very different to that of the ECHR. The US First Amendment right to free speech is framed in absolutist terms. This means that although in practice exceptions to the First Amendment do exist (Citron 2014), the rhetoric surrounding free speech is that of assertive guardianship. By contrast, freedom of expression under Article 10 of the ECHR is given protection subject to certain limitations. This has meant that the US has traditionally been less open to persuasion when drafting laws that may infringe freedom of speech. The divergence in approach to free speech extends beyond the US and Europe. Countries at different stages of political development will also have distinct needs in relation to the balance that needs to be struck between free speech and cyberhate. Whilst it could be argued that that the political development of Western liberal democracies allows for greater restrictions on free speech (Waldron 2012), other emerging nations might still require the scales to be balanced more in favour of free speech (Gagliardone et al. 2014). Given the importance of international cooperation and the crucial role the US would play in this, international agreement on cyberhate legislation appears a long way off (Banks 2011).

One particular practical difficulty associated with the regulation of cyberhate relates to the anonymity of the internet. Even if we were able to achieve international harmonization of laws and broker far-reaching extradition treaties, these will only be effective if it is possible to identify and track down the perpetrators. This is not necessarily straightforward given the ease with which it is possible to conceal one's identity online. Email accounts can be obtained using false information, and software is available that allows a user to hide the origin of an email or their physical location. Once a false email has been obtained, a perpetrator is able to join discussion groups, chat forums, and social media without their true identity becoming known to the victim. In countries where Internet Service Providers (ISPs) do not provide anonymous accounts it is possible, in principle, to obtain the Internet Protocol (IP) addresses of a perpetrator's computer, and thus track down the physical location of the computer which was used to carry out the attack. However, ISPs do not give out IP addresses easily and will often only do so under a court order. In the US, the courts have allowed 'John Doe subpoenas'[2] to be issued to a website or an ISP in order to compel the handing over of details of a particular poster in cases involving civil claims (Citron 2014: 223). Currently there is no similar provision in relation to criminal claims, and so these subpoenas are of limited use in most cyberhate cases which are better tackled through the criminal law.

A further problem is the issue of policing. It is imperative that any regulatory regime can be policed effectively if we are to justify the use of the criminal law and criminal punishment. Packer (1968) argues that one of the pre-conditions for the legitimate use of the criminal law is if doing so will not expose that process to severe qualitative and quantitative strains. This is a particular challenge for the policing of cyberhate given the scale and complexity of the internet. It is important to note, though, that the predominant role of the police with regard to cyberhate is to respond to complaints by individual victims, and not to police the entire World Wide Web. Thus, the police need to be given the appropriate tools and resources to deal effectively with individual incidences of cyberhate that are brought to their attention, but they do not need to be given the power or responsibility to regulate all online content. Coliandris (2012) suggests that a Problem-Oriented Policing (POP) approach would be necessary so as to identify the root cause of the behaviour before finding effective measures to deal with it. Clearly, there is still much work to be done to identify and develop best practice in this area and this will require a deep dialogue between governments, the security services, the police, and academics.

A combination of the global reach of the internet, the problems regarding policing, the difficulties surrounding international agreement over free speech, and the complications posed by anonymity forces us to consider whether the responsibility for online hatred needs to be shifted to, or at least shared by ISPs. The current situation means that many victims of online hatred face considerable difficulties in locating their assailant, and even greater problems with bringing them to justice. In such cases, where tracing an offender is too complicated either because of geographical impediments or because of technical difficulties in identifying them, an alternative solution for the victim would be to force ISPs to take responsibility for policing their websites. This already happens in cases involving defamation in English law. Under s 5 of the Defamation Act 2013, website operators are given a defence to defamation claims if they comply with certain procedures. Thus, if they are able to show that they provided the complainant with sufficient details of the poster's identity which would enable them to bring proceedings against them, or they took down the offending material when asked to by the complainant, they will have a defence in law under s 5(3) of the Defamation Act 2013. Although there is no direct legal obligation on websites to provide identification information, or to take down offending

---

[2] These subpoenas enable a plaintiff to file suit even if they do not yet know the identity of the defendant.

speech, there is a very strong incentive for them to do so in cases involving defamation. It is too soon to evaluate the effectiveness of s 5, and its success depends on how clear the accompanying regulations prove to be. Arguably it is not an excessively onerous responsibility on ISPs, but the issue does raise broader questions about the importance of privacy on the internet. At a time when tensions are running high over state surveillance of internet communications both in the United States and elsewhere, any obligation on ISPs to hand over personal information to the authorities will have to be carefully worded in order to ensure this does not breach privacy rights. The main concern has been with unlimited and indiscriminate surveillance (e.g., UN 2013) and so it would be possible for similar criminal provisions to be drafted narrowly enough to strike a balance between freedom of speech and privacy rights on the one hand, and the right of victims of cyberhate to achieve justice by resolving some of the difficulties surrounding anonymity on the other.

Another important part of the solution to cyberhate will be a continuation and intensification of the informal techniques that already take place. Currently, there is a proliferation of different approaches that attempt to help solve the problem of online hatred in an informal non-legal way. For instance, the Anti-Defamation League (ADL) has produced a set of best practices which guide providers and the internet community on how best to tackle online hatred (ADL 2014). The emphasis is on cooperation by industry providers such as through the voluntary enforcement of terms of service and the provision of effective mechanisms for reporting and removing offensive comments (ADL 2015). There is a concern that over-reliance on private contractors to deal with cyberhate essentially gives those companies the power to make decisions on free speech, but equally, as a recent report by UNESCO on online hatred points out, 'focusing exclusively on repressive measures can miss the complexity of a phenomenon that is still poorly understood and which calls out for tailored and coordinated responses from a range of different actors in society' (Gagliardone et al. 2015: 53). Other initiatives, such as Belgium's 'Stop Hate' website, aim to give parents, teenagers, and teachers information and support on how to recognize and combat online hatred. The Council of Europe's 'Young People Combating Hate Speech Online' campaign has also sought to mobilize young people from around Europe to take a proactive stance against hate speech they confront online.

The globalization of online hatred means that in order to achieve the most effective response, international cooperation is required. However, this is not an easy solution, as attempting to reach a consistent approach across different countries with vastly different legal systems and cultural approaches to issues such as free speech has proven to be very difficult. This will become clear in the following section which evaluates the attempts made so far at international collaboration. Nevertheless, the globalization of cyberhate also requires us to consider refocusing attention on those who enable it, rather than adopting a traditional response which concentrates on the perpetrators of hate. This corroborates the argument put forward in the first section above that we need to design a specific response to online hatred that requires us to think beyond the traditional measures usually adopted to combat physical hate crimes.

CURRENT INTERNATIONAL RESPONSE

At the global level, there has been a concerted effort over a number of years to establish a cohesive international response to hate crime. Article 20 of the International Covenant on Civil and Political Rights (ICCPR) and Article 4 of the International Convention on the Elimination of All Forms of Racial Discrimination both call on states to outlaw any dissemination or advocacy which incites discrimination or violence. The provisions in both articles are couched widely enough that legislation outlawing hate speech online (subject to freedom of expression) could be included. However, online hatred is not specifically mentioned, and so no guidance is provided on how these prohibitions would operate in relation to cyberhate. At the EU level, the EU Framework Decision on combating certain forms and expressions of racism and xenophobia by means of the criminal law requires states to harmonize their laws on racism and xenophobia. Whilst all of these initiatives constitute a constructive approach to hate crime, they do not provide a solution to any of the particular problems relating to online hatred outlined in the previous two sections. By the same token, the Organization for Security and Co-operation in Europe (OSCE) has produced under its Office for Democratic Institutions and Human Rights (ODIHR) a Practical Guide (2009) which provides a very useful framework for hate crime legislation, but it is less concerned with hate speech. Its recommendations will only apply to online hatred which falls into the category of an already existing criminal offence and, as such, they are of limited use to a wider discussion on cyberhate which seeks to establish both a reconceptualization of traditional notions of harm and a practical solution to some of the particular problems associated with digital hate speech. Thus, the current approach which subsumes cyberhate within the broader problem of hate crime is ultimately insufficient.

The only international agreement targeted expressly at online hate is the Council of Europe's Additional Protocol to the Convention on Cybercrime concerning the criminalization of acts of a racist and xenophobic nature committed through computer systems. To date, the Protocol has had limited success due to the reluctance by a number of states, such as the US, Russia, Turkey, Sweden, and the UK, to ratify it. Brennan (2009) has written in detail about the shortcomings of the Protocol and has argued that, even if ratified by a state, it is too narrow a document to provide an effective response to online hatred. She identifies a number of defects with the Protocol, such as the reference to 'intention' which potentially limits the extent to which ISPs can be held liable for publishing hate material online, and the free speech exception under Article 3(3) which allows states to not implement cyberhate measures even if they ratify the Protocol. Furthermore, she contends that the emphasis on free speech undermines the underlying objectives of the Protocol, and she argues that more weight should instead be placed on the concept of equality and non-discrimination which states are under a duty to promote.

The legislative response to hate crime at the international level does, therefore, appear to be insufficient. Nevertheless, there is a growing recognition that cyberhate should be treated as a distinct category of hate crime which requires special attention. For example, the report by the EU into the implementation of its Framework Decision points out that: '[d]ue to its special character, including the difficulty of identifying the authors of illegal online content and removing such content, hate speech on the internet creates special demands on law enforcement and judicial authorities in terms of expertise, resources and the need for cross-border cooperation' (European Commission 2014: para. 4).

Meanwhile, the working group on cyberhate at the EU Agency FRA conference on Hate Crime in 2013 considered the need for a targeted legislative approach to cyberhate (FRA 2013). In parallel to this, civil society groups have already taken steps to combat cyberhate as a discrete problem. The ADL treats cyberhate as a specific policy area, and has implemented a number of initiatives to combat online hatred, such as the Cyber-Safety Action Guide which aims to provide internet users with a simple way of registering any hatred they find online. The International Network against Cyberhate (INACH) aims to bring the internet in line with human rights by uniting organizations to tackle online hate and to raise awareness of discrimination which takes place online.

CONCLUSION

Taken together, several themes emerge from the current international and national approach to hate crime. The first is that we need a targeted approach to cyberhate. There are a number of ways in which the nature and impact of cyberhate differs from offline hate speech, and which therefore require us to go beyond traditional definitions of harm to capture the complex and subtle distinctiveness of the damage caused by online hatred. Particular attention needs to be paid to the fact that online interactions between individuals can bolster hate movements, whilst the prevalence of online hatred on heavily used websites, such as online newspapers, may impact certain groups and affect their ability to enjoy the internet. In addition to this, more thought needs to be given to adopting a more nuanced approach to the concept of what constitutes a 'public' space on the internet. Finally, there will need to be a recognition that freedom of speech arguments need to be reconsidered in light of the harm caused by online hatred. In particular, the principle of equality as a competing value must be given greater attention in order to determine the correct limits of legal regulation.

The second point to make is that we need a globalized approach to cyberhate. The very nature of internet use means that the perpetrator and the victim will not necessarily be in the same country, and so without an international response, victims will often find they have no legal solution to their problem. In addition to this, we need to hold ISPs at least partially responsible for enabling cyberhate that comes to their attention, and this cannot easily be achieved without an international response. This international response also needs to take into account the unique nature of cyberhate. It is not sufficient to rely on efforts that are already being made at the international level in relation to hate crime more generally. Cyberhate needs to become a priority policy in its own right. Currently, the Council of Europe's Additional Protocol is the only international framework on cyberhate. Other international bodies such as the UN and the EU should reflect on the special requirements of online hatred as outlined in the previous paragraph, and establish agreements which are tailored towards the broader harm caused by cyberhate, and the need for social equality.

Third, although an international response is the ideal, it seems unlikely that a coherent approach will be achieved in the short-term. In the meantime, though, there is still much that can be done at the national level. National governments can still achieve results by adopting effective legislation aimed at online hatred. It is also imperative that European states which have not already ratified the Council of Europe's Additional Protocol do so because, in spite of its deficiencies, it signals a first step in the right direction.

The regulation of online hate speech is still in its infancy, and a number of challenges lie ahead. The difficulties are undoubtedly substantial, but the problems caused by cyberhate are equally significant and should not be underestimated. The regulation of cyberhate needs to become a top priority for those with responsibility in this field as the situation is pressing and action can no longer be deferred.

REFERENCES

ADL. 2014. 'Cyberhate Responses. Best Practices for Responding to Cyberhate'. ADL website at: http://www.adl.org/combating-hate/cyber-safety/best-practices/#.VX_9vflViko

ADL. 2015. 'Report of the Anti-Defamation League on Confronting Cyberhate'. ADL website at: http://www.adl.org/assets/pdf/combating-hate/ICCA-report-2015-With-hyperlinks-May-8-2015_final.pdf

Bakshy, Eytan, Solomon Messing, and Adamic Lada. 2015. 'Exposure to Diverse Information on Facebook'. Facebook blogpost at: https://research.facebook.com/blog/1393382804322065/exposure-to-diverse-information-on-facebook

Banks, James. 2011. 'European Regulation of Cross-Border Hate Speech in Cyberspace: the Limits of Legislation'. *European Journal of Crime, Criminal Law and Criminal Justice* 19(1), 1.

Blazak, Randy. 2011. 'Isn't Every Crime a Hate Crime? The Case for Hate Crime Laws'. *Sociology Compass* 5(4), 244.

Brandenburg v. Ohio, 395 U.S. 444 (1969).

Brennan, Fernne. 2009. 'Legislating Against Internet Race Hate'. *Information & Communications Technology Law* 18, 123.

Canada (Human Rights Commission) v. Taylor [1990] 3 S.C.R. 892.

Chaplinsky v. New Hampshire 315 U.S. 568 (1942).

Citron, Danielle Keats. 2014. *Hate Crimes in Cyberspace*, Harvard University Press.

Coliandris, Geoff. 2012. 'Hate in a Cyber Age'. In *Policing Cyber Hate, Cyber Threats and Cyber Terrorism*, edited by Imran Awan and Brian Blakemore, Ashgate, pp. 173–92.

European Commission. 2014. 'Report from the Commission to the European Parliament and the Council on the implementation of Council Framework Decision 2008/913/JHA on combating certain forms and expressions of racism and xenophobia by means of criminal law'. At: http://eur-lex.europa.eu/legal-content/EN/TXT/?uri=celex:52014DC0027

Fearn, Harriet. 2014. 'Experiences of Online Hate Crime'. Conference of the International Network for Hate Studies: Understanding Hate Crime: Research, Policy and Practice. Sussex University, 8–9 May.

Finnis, John. 1980. *Natural Law and Natural Rights*, OUP.

FRA. 2013. 'Working Group II. Challenges of Cyberhate'. At: http://fra.europa.eu/sites/default/files/frc2013-12-11-wg02-challenges_of_cyberhate.pdf

Gagliardone, Iginio, Alisha Patel, and Matti Pohjonen. 2014. 'Mapping and Analysing Hate Speech Online: Opportunities and Challenges for Ethiopia'. Working paper at: http://pcmlp.socleg.ox.ac.uk/wp-content/uploads/2014/12/Ethiopia-hate-speech.pdf

Gagliardone, Iginio, Danit Gal, Thiago Alves, and Gabriela Martinez. 2015. 'Countering Online Hate Speech'. Unesco Publishing at: http://unesdoc.unesco.org/images/0023/002332/233231e.pdf

Guichard, Audrey. 2009. 'Hate Crime in Cyberspace: The Challenges of Substantive Criminal Law'. *Information and Communications Technology Law* 18(2), 201.

Iganski, Paul. 2001. 'Hate Crimes Hurt More'. *American Behavioural Scientist* 45(4), 626.

Irish Examiner. 2011. 'Man cleared of online hatred against Travellers'. At: http://www.irishexaminer.com/ireland/man-cleared-of-online-hatred-against-travellers-169325.html

Lawrence, Frederick. 1999. *Punishing Hate: Bias Crimes under American Law*, Harvard University Press.

Mill, J.S. (1991). *On Liberty and Other Essays*, OUP.

Miller, Danny. 2013. 'Future Identities: Changing identities in the UK—the next 10 years DR 2: What is the relationship between identities that people construct, express and consume online and those offline?' *Government Office for Science*. At: https://www.gov.uk/government/uploads/system/uploads/attachment_data/file/275750/13-504-relationship-between-identities-online-and-offline.pdf

OSCE/ODIHR. 2009. 'Hate Crime Laws: A Practical Guide'.

Packer, Herbert. 1968. *The Limits of the Criminal Sanction*, Stanford University Press.

Perry, Barbara and Patrik Olsson. 2009. 'Cyberhate: the Globalization of Hate'. *Information and Communications Technology Law* 18(2), 185.

Raz, Joseph. 1986. *The Morality of Freedom*, OUP.

Rowbottom, Jacob. 2012. 'To Rant, Vent and Converse: Protecting Low Level Digital Speech'. *Cambridge Law Journal* 71(2), 355.

UN. 2013. 'UN resolution to the right to privacy, a first step—UN expert on freedom of expression'. UN website at: http://www.ohchr.org/EN/NewsEvents/Pages/DisplayNews.aspx?NewsID=14033&

Waldron, Jeremy. 2012. *The Harm in Hate Speech*, Harvard University Press.

Walker, Julian. 2013. 'Canadian Anti-Hate Laws and Freedom of Expression'. Parliament of Canada Research Publications at: http://www.parl.gc.ca/content/lop/researchpublications/2010-31-e.htm#a8

17

STATE-SPONSORED HATRED AND PERSECUTION ON THE GROUNDS OF SEXUAL ORIENTATION: THE ROLE OF INTERNATIONAL CRIMINAL LAW

Ruby Axelson

INTRODUCTION

The criminalization of 'massacres and other violent conduct against targeted groups' (Pocur 2008: 356) under Article 7(1)(h) of the Rome Statute offers an important opportunity to provide accountability for crimes committed against marginalized peoples. It is under this framework that instances of state-sponsored hate occurring in Africa against sexual minorities will be addressed in this chapter. Whilst it is stressed that such acts are neither limited to nor representative of African society, situating the debate within the African context highlights both theoretical concerns that attempt to stifle the recognition of sexual orientation as a protected group and the severity of abuse.[1]

This chapter begins by examining instances of state-sponsored hate and hate speech as crimes against humanity of persecution. State-sponsored hate against sexual minorities can be expressed in a variety of forms and typically manifests as physical acts of violence against individuals and hate speech that is characterized by propaganda, as well as calls to inflict such violence. However, despite an abundance of evidence of persecution against sexual minorities, the Rome Statute does not specifically include such groups due to the historic heteronormativity of international law. Instead, the Statute offers protection to 'any identifiable group or collectivity on political, racial, national, ethnic, cultural, religious, gender... or other grounds that are universally recognized as impermissible under international law' (Rome Statute, 1998, Article 7(1)(h)). This chapter attempts to marry the principles espoused in both universalism and postcolonialism, in order to consider how universal protection of sexual

---

[1] For instance, Mauritania, Sudan, northern Nigeria, and southern Sudan all retain the death penalty for 'homosexuals' (Amnesty International 2015).

minorities may be legitimized in the face of varying cultural contexts. An attempt is then made to situate protection of sexual minorities within the existing framework of persecution, under either 'gender' or 'other grounds universally recognized'.

STATE-SPONSORED HATE CRIME AND THE *ACTUS REUS* OF PERSECUTION

The Rome Statute provides that persecution is 'the intentional and severe deprivation of fundamental rights contrary to international law by reason of the identity of the group or collectivity' (Article 7(2)(f)), committed in connection with other enumerated acts under the jurisdiction of the Court (Article 7(1)(h)). Additionally, the persecution must satisfy the chapeau of crimes against humanity, namely that it must be 'committed as a part of a widespread or systematic attack directed against any civilian population, with knowledge of the attack' (Article 7(1)). The criminalization of homosexuality, occurring in thirty-six African countries (Amnesty International 2015) and recognized as unlawful by international human rights tribunals (*Toonen v Australia*, 4 April 1994, para. 86), offers the clearest example of a persecutory act, in connection with 'imprisonment or other severe deprivation of physical liberty in violation of fundamental rules of international law' (Rome Statute, Article 7(1)(e)). Moreover, since the criminalization of homosexuality has led to the 'arrest, blackmail, mob justice and "Othering" of homosexuals' (Jjuuko 2013: 382), it can be directly connected to state-sponsored hate and to the individual hate crimes that are committed against those with perceived dissident sexualities.

In addition to satisfying the chapeau of crimes against humanity by being part of a widespread or systematic attack against the civilian population, state-sponsored violence, as a form of hate against sexual minorities, must also be committed in connection with another crime under the jurisdiction of the Court (Article 7(1)). For example, instances of unlawful and intentional killing due to perceived homosexual status, such as that of prominent activist David Kato,[2] may amount to persecution in connection with Article 7(1)(a). Moreover, in Mauritania, Sudan, northern Nigeria, and southern Somalia, individuals found guilty of 'homosexuality' may face the death penalty (Amnesty International 2013: 7). In Cameroon, evidence that those convicted of 'homosexuality' suffer malnutrition and regular beatings whilst detained (Amnesty International 2013: 60) suggests the occurrence of torture under Article 7(1)(f). Furthermore, alleged incidences of corrective rape, as well as other forms of sexual violence, not limited to 'physical invasion of the human body' in the form of penetration (*Prosecutor v Akayesu*, 1998, para. 888), may also amount to persecution in connection to Article 7(1)(g).

---

[2] BBC (2011) "Uganda gay rights activist David Kato killed" downloaded at: http://www.bbc.co.uk/news/world-africa-12295718

Additionally, hate speech that gives 'permission to a culture of extreme and violent homophobia, whereby the state and non-state actors are free to persecute' sexual minorities with impunity (Sexual Minorities Uganda (SMUG) 2014b: 1), may amount to persecution rising to the level of 'other inhumane acts of a similar character' (Article 7(1)(k)). For example, in Uganda, assertions that sexual minorities have a 'compulsion to sexually abuse children' (*Sexual Minorities Uganda v Scott Lively* 2013: 10) link same-sex activity with violent sexual perversion and antagonize a climate of hatred. The criminalization of hate speech has been recognized in international criminal jurisprudence since the International Military Tribunal (IMT) case of *Streicher*, which held that as the editor of *Der Stürmer*, a 'virulently anti-Semitic weekly-newspaper' that regularly called for the extermination of the Jews, the accused had 'incited the German people to active persecution' (*IMT Judgment* 1947: 294). The Appeals Chamber of the International Criminal Tribunal for Rwanda (ICTR) has offered that while hate speech does amount to 'actual discrimination', other people must intervene before a finding of persecution may occur since 'a speech cannot, in itself, directly kill members of a group, imprison or physically injure them' (*Prosecutor v Nahimana*, 2007, para. 986). Although the Court declined to rule on whether hate speech not accompanied by calls to violence could reach a level of gravity equivalent to other crimes against humanity, this question appears to be 'purely academic given the realities of mass atrocity', since 'hate speech will necessarily be accompanied by other widespread or systematic inhumane treatment in the [crime against humanity] context' (Gordon 2013: 307). It is contended here that homophobic hate speech initiated against sexual minorities by the religious and political elite in certain African countries amounts to persecution considering the context of 'widespread and systematic' persecution under which it operates.

Despite cogent evidence that state-sponsored violence may amount to the *actus reus* of persecution, historically sexual minorities have been omitted from the groups protected. The Nuremberg Charter recognized only 'persecution on political, racial and religious grounds' (Charter of the IMT, 1945, Article 6(c)), and the Tokyo Charter recognized only 'political or racial grounds' (Charter of the IMT for the Far East, 1946, Article 5(c)). These Statutes fail to mention other groups facing group-based attacks by the Nazis, including homosexuals, the aged or the infirm, and the mentally ill (Luban 2004: 100). This limited applicability of persecution continued in the ad hoc Tribunals. Though reflecting a modernization of the legal framework, the Rome Statute's more recent expansion to protect 'political, racial, national, ethnic, cultural, religious, gender as defined by paragraph 3, or other grounds that are universally recognized as impermissible under international law' arguably maintains the heteronormativity of the law by failing to explicitly include sexual minorities. The presumed heteronormativity of the law is challenged later in this Chapter via the suggestion that sexual minorities can (and should) be included within the scope of either 'gender' or 'other grounds universally recognised as impermissible under international law' in the absence of its explicit inclusion.

First it is important to ascertain why sexual minorities continue to be excluded whilst other group identities have found protection under the Statute. Part of the answer is found within debates surrounding cultural relativism, and in particular the assertion that respect must be maintained for cultures that are yet to accept homosexuality as part of 'normal' society. Yet deference to cultural relativism does not necessarily mean that the persecution of sexual minorities must be accepted in absolute terms. As we will see, the universalizing project of international criminal law may well be reconciled with the varying cultural contexts under which sexual identities exist.

UNIVERSALISM, CULTURAL RELATIVISM, AND POSTCOLONIALISM

This chapter recognizes the importance of universalism in the fight against hate crime by promoting the idea of universally recognized human rights being 'protected by a universal, interculturally recognised criminal law' (Ambros 2013: 308). Through the conceptualization that 'all human beings are born free and equal in dignity and rights' (Universal Declaration of Human Rights (UDHR), 1948, Article 1), the protection of sexual diversity may be advanced in international criminal law; understanding that the aims of the International Criminal Court (ICC) to 'protect fundamental human rights by prosecuting and punishing international crimes' (Ambros 2013: 294) are essentially connected to the guiding notions of universality and non-discrimination. A failure to incorporate protection for sexual diversity under these conceptions would therefore render the sexual subject dehumanized (United Nations General Assembly (UNGA) 2011b, para. 19). Nevertheless, the postcolonial context under which sexuality is situated stipulates an imagining of how international law can be legitimized by succumbing to neither 'homogenising universalism' nor the 'paralysis of relativism' (Cook 1994: 7). Indeed, espousals of cultural relativism that maintain sexuality as a 'site where ideological independence from Western influence is expressed' (Oliver 2013: 98) have pronounced homosexuality as 'unAfrican'. Yet historical analyses reveal a long history of diverse sexualities across Africa. In Uganda, for example, same-sex activity has been documented among the Bahima, the Bantoro, and the Buganda people (Tamale 2007: 18). Contrary to contemporary rhetoric, the criminalization of homosexuality was first introduced during the colonial era. By creating the myth that the African man was the 'essence of nature', his sexuality being devoted purely to heterosexuality and procreation, the colonial powers were able to position him as uncivilized and thus justify their rule (Oliver 2013: 92).

In addition to being historically inaccurate, cultural relativism, the idea that cultures must profess their own moral understandings, is also theoretically unsound since it results in the 'political silencing' of 'improperly decolonised subjects' (Smith 2010: 56). Indeed, it is the political, cultural, and religious fundamentalisms that often drive the backlash against sexual diversity, justifying persecution on unsound understandings of homogenous heterosexuality in Africa and the denial of pluralities within African sexualities (Nyanzi 2013: 952). Alternatively, by locating the debate in concepts such as *ubuntu*, understood as the 'idea that people are truly human only when they affirm the humanity of others', protection for all people, regardless of sexual orientation, can be based in African traditions (Kaomo 2009: 8).

Despite this defence, the Western predication of universalism and international law must continue to be acknowledged in order to profess a more nuanced vision of universalism not implicated in imperialism. It is not only relativism, but the 'gay rights' movement also, that views sexuality through the lens of 'colonial myth-making' (Lewis 2011: 210). Rendering Africa as essentialized and uniformly homophobic, Western discourse regenerates 'racialised and paternalistic' (Oliver 2011: 84) assumptions instigated during colonialism. By creating a victimized homosexual 'Other', who is in need of liberation, the continued influence of the West is justified. Moreover, the globalization of gay identities has occurred due to the 'gay rights' movement situating the 'Western subject as universal, while the racialised subject is particular, but aspires to be universal' (Smith 2010: 42). Indeed, Western binary notions of homo/heterosexuality and gender identity fail to appreciate the variety of sexual relationships evident in African history. For example, among the Iteso communities in northwest Kenya, same-sex relationships existed between men who behaved as and were socially accepted as women (SMUG 2014a: 10). For the incorporation of a truly universal understanding of sexual orientation, the ICC must understand that indigenous sexualities may not be reduced to Western understandings. Considering the history of sexuality in Africa, while it is true no one can claim a monopoly on same-sex sexual activity (Hoad 1999: 564), the Western 'gay identity' fails to recognize the variety of ways sexual orientation and sexuality is experienced. Indeed, certain Western terminology, reflecting a view of sex and sexual roles constructed far from the realities of African society, may be problematic; for example, in Uganda the identification of *kuchu*, similar to the identification of 'queer' and including diverse sexual and gender identities, is utilized to describe a variety of behaviours and identities not subsumed within the lesbian/gay dichotomy (Gay Uganda 2007), as well as existing to construct an 'alternative positive and empowering self-identification' (Tamale 2007: 20).

Additionally, any formulation of protection for sexual minorities under the Rome Statute must recognize that homophobic discourses also have their own unique trajectories that occur across disparate social milieus (Boyd 2013: 699). As such, were it to be included as a category for protection the ICC must reject a 'monolithic concept of homophobia in sub-Saharan Africa', and instead comprehend that there are multiple homophobias (Thoreson 2014: 24). Through a rejection of collective guilt, international criminal law focuses on holding individuals accountable for state-sponsored violence contrary to myths of cultural or 'tribal' hatred (Akhavan 2001: 7). This renders international criminal law unique in enabling justice to prevail over imperialist and myopic conceptions of a homogenous homophobic Africa by focusing on the individual trajectories of hate.

Despite both universalism and cultural relativism being 'guilty of essentialising' that which they aim to protect (Reitman 1997: 106), a more holistic approach, open to the multifaceted identities inhabited by sexual minorities, informed by sexuality, gender, and culture, is possible. Marrying the maxim that 'human rights are the rights one has simply by being human' (Donnelly 1999: 93) with this more nuanced view of the relationship between culture and sexuality fosters a space for theoretical grounding of this debate within universalism. It is the 'tendency of universal claims to intellectually obscure and politically repress difference' that is condemned, rather than universal rights per se (Donnelly 2007: 298). The attempt of this Chapter to promote universal protection for sexual minorities against state-sponsored hate, through the employment of international criminal law, may thereby be legitimized under a more nuanced understanding of universalism and engagement with postcolonial critique.

The existing nature of international law necessitates the adoption of identifiable points of reference. Therefore utilization of terms such as 'sexual minorities', 'sexual orientation', 'sexual identities', and 'sexual diversity' is advocated, understanding that these terms are 'more inclusive, being open to any group (previously, presently, or in the future) stigmatised or despised as a result of sexual orientation, identity or behaviour' (Donnelly 1999: 97). Such analysis, it is hoped, will promote understandings of sexuality beyond Western binary models of gender and sexual identity, to incorporate the diverse array of sexual practices and identities present worldwide. As such, the utilization of postcolonialism, which renders visible a plurality of sexual identities, ensures universality through the appreciation of a greater variety of sex and gender arrangements (Altman 1996: 81). Demonstrating the need for an understanding of groups lacking clearly defined boundaries, such as ethnic groups, international criminal law has utilized a subjective approach to overcome problems inherent with group identification (*Prosecutor v Rutaganda*, 1999, para. 56). As such, a reliance on the perpetrator's perception of the groups as ethnically distinct has enabled the ICTR to bypass the ambiguous question of whether the Tutsi are in fact objectively distinct from the Hutu (Schabas 2006: 1713). It is suggested that the utilization of a subjective approach to group identification may comprehend the variety of ways people identify and express themselves within the category of sexual minority, so as to avoid 'applying western preconceptions of behaviour, mannerisms and appearance to individuals' (Arnold 2013: 27). Returning to a primary focus on the perpetrator's subjective stigmatization of the group (Nersessian 2003: 311) enables a more nuanced approach, focusing on the actual discrimination faced by victims to acknowledge that it is not logically necessary to delineate objective 'distinctions among groups of people to prove that a particular group was stigmatised and targeted' (Sanga 1997: 112).

THE IMPORTANCE OF 'GENDER'

Without the specific inclusion of sexual minorities within the Rome Statute we are forced to examine other ways in which protection may be maintained in law. One such avenue is through an interpretation of 'gender' that is broad enough to include sexual orientation. Described as an 'inelegant working', though one necessary due to 'very delicate negotiations' (von Hebel and Robinson 1999: 101), the definition designates 'gender' as the 'two sexes, male and female, within the context of society' and 'does not indicate any meaning different from above' (Rome Statute, Article 7(3)). At Rome a divergence of opinion occurred in the construction of the term; while many believed the inclusion of sexual orientation was 'not only desirable, but also necessary to prosecute the kind of homophobic persecution that had occurred in World War II' (Oosterveld 2011: 96), other more conservative states regarded gender as 'potentially subversive' due to the implied consideration of sexuality, preferring a definition that reduced gender to biological differences (Oosterveld 2005: 76). As such, despite signifying a sociological dimension in the term 'gender', the qualifier 'two sexes, male and female', continues to ensure the 'binary Western' notion that there remains only two genders (O'Flaherty and Fisher 2008: 208).

Scholars also disagree regarding the inclusion of sexual minorities within 'gender', and ultimately, since no consensus was reached during negotiations, the ambiguity leaves the term open for interpretation by the Court (Steins 1999: 374). A consideration of 'gender' as a 'construct built upon social understandings of what is expected of those of the male and female sex' would render imperative a discussion of sexuality by the ICC, on account of the fundamental links between gender identity and oppression of sexual minorities (Oosterveld 2006: 77, 81). Understanding while the definition affirms biological aspects of gender, it situates this within the 'context of the societal roles men and women are expected to play' (von Hebel and Robinson 1999: 101). This understanding enables sexual orientation to be included within the ground of 'gender' on account of the culturally ascribed roles associated with heterosexuality. Such an understanding ensures that a prohibition of sex or gender discrimination inevitably leads to a conclusion that it is also unlawful to discriminate on the basis that a person's choice of partner is not in conformity with dominant stereotypes (Kukuru 2005: 184). Following this analysis Oosterveld contends that a consideration of gender by the ICC would be incomplete without a proper 'evaluation of whether the collective norm in society understands "femaleness" and "maleness" only to include heteronormativity, or to include different sexual identities' (Oosterveld 2005: 79). Indeed, attitudes throughout Uganda have been 'deeply shaped by notions of kinship and lineage which tightly bind experiences of sexuality and reproduction', which in turn influence ideas about archetype gendered behaviours and situate homosexuality as a threat to conceptions of the traditional family unit (Boyd 2013: 704). Narratives of 'traditional sexuality' involving a 'hearty yet wholesome heterosexual appetite', standing in 'proud opposition to the dominant emasculating colonial discourse' (Epprecht 2009: 1262), when deployed to justify persecution of sexual minorities, should lead to such persecution as covered by 'gender' under the Rome Statute.

International legal understandings of gender may therefore support such reasoning by indicating that gender connotes the 'socially constructed roles played by women and men that are ascribed to them on the basis of their sex' (UNGA 1996: para. 9). This is in line with other international instruments such as the International Convention on the Elimination of all Forms of Discrimination against Women (ICEDAW), which requires the eradication of practices that are based on the 'idea of the inferiority of either of the sexes or on stereotype roles for men and women'

(Article 5). It is understood that stereotypical views of women may cause them to be discriminated 'on grounds such as sexual orientation' (Committee on the Elimination of All Forms of Discrimination against Women (CEDAW) 2010: para. 10). Similarly, the Special Rapporteur on Torture notes that 'members of sexual minorities are disproportionately subjected to torture and other forms of ill-treatment because they fail to conform to socially constructed gender expectations' (UNGA 2011b: para. 19). The Human Rights Committee (HRC) in *Toonen v Australia* has also explicitly connected gender and sexual identity, signifying that 'the reference to "sex" in Article 2(1), and Article 26 International Covenant on Civil and Political Rights (ICCPR) is to be taken as including sexual orientation' (1994: para. 87). Finally, the UN High Commissioner for Refugees (UNHCR) has recognized the relevance of the 'refusal to adhere to socially or culturally defined roles or expectations' of the biological sexes to the discrimination of sexual minorities (2002: para. 16).

It is clear that certain branches of international law now promote a broader definition of 'gender'. Yet certain practical and theoretical limitations exist on the extent to which these may be utilized by the ICC. Reflecting upon the debates in Rome, it is not improbable that the definition of 'gender' will be construed to ensure the continued heteronomativity of international law, considering the static nature of the definition that restricts conceptions of gender to biological sex. Being required to 'strictly' construe terms and unable to extend them by analogy (Article 7(3)), the ICC will be faced with a situation whereby the meaning of 'two sexes, male and female... elides the notions of gender and sex', preventing an approach reliant on the social construction of gender (Charlesworth 1999: 394). This regression away from common international legal understandings of gender, by representing gender as an issue of biology rather than social construction, limits the progressive nature of the definition. The qualification that gender 'does not indicate any meaning different from above' offers another substantial blow to a broad interpretation, being a seeming attempt to exclude sexual orientation. Forestalling suggestions that sexual orientation is covered by Article 7(3), the additional qualifier that gender persecution be 'within the context of society' renders legitimate persecution on the ground of sexual orientation when approved by a 'vicious religion or culture' (Robertson 2006: 343). In consideration of the explicit rejection by certain states of a broad definition at Rome, many consider Article 7(3) as operating as a 'distasteful but realistic reminder that a majority of states in 1998 still favoured the withdrawal of human rights from homosexuals' (Robertson 2006: 343).

Moreover, an interpretation of gender broad enough to encompass sexual orientation neglects to appreciate that the underlying forces of patriarchy and heterosexual dominance are two separable systems. Although clearly interlinked, even whilst the two concepts work in tandem, it remains possible to differentiate between the patriarchal aspects of male–female relationships and their heterosexual dimensions (Calhoun 1994: 562). Advocating for persecution towards sexual orientation to be identified separately from gender, acknowledging the 'invidious distinctions' made on account of sexuality (Stein 2002: 1028) would provide unambiguous protection. Despite perhaps proving a useful tool in the struggle for recognition of sexual diversity, a broad interpretation of 'gender' to include sexual minorities ultimately mitigates an understanding that 'same-sex desire should be of the same legal status and ethical status as opposite-sex sexual acts' (ibid: 1038), rendering an analysis beyond 'gender' necessary.

'UNIVERSALLY RECOGNIZED AS IMPERMISSIBLE UNDER INTERNATIONAL LAW'

Allowing for non-exhaustive expansion, the ground of 'universally recognized as impermissible under international law' (Article 7(1)(h)) may provide an alternative strategy for incorporation of sexual minorities within the framework of persecution. Despite this phrase maintaining a 'higher threshold than requiring that certain distinctions are impermissible under international law in general' (Boot 2002: 521), it is understood to entail wide recognition rather than complete state agreement, thereby negating concerns that the absence of protection in international human rights treaties may exclude sexual minorities. While some states proposed the requirement that grounds be 'universally recognised under customary international law', such wording was 'vigorously opposed' since no ground would meet this threshold (ibid). In addition, concern that the application of this drafting technique may risk 'watering down the meaning of already established rights' (Kukuru 2005: 185) fails to comprehend the continuously changing and developing nature of international law which necessitates dynamic interpretation. By allowing room for the progressive articulation of new grounds, this phrase anticipates evolution of human rights jurisprudence. The International Law Commission has understood this fluidity in international law, and has provided that where a treaty provision is 'not static but evolutionary', it may be reasonably inferred that states parties intended its meaning to evolve over time (UNGA 2006: para. 478).

To aid interpretation of 'universally recognized', the ICC may look to international human rights law, as anticipated by Article 21(3), recognizing the importance of international human rights treaties, court decisions, and statements. Previously utilizing this approach, the Court applied Article 21(3) to explicitly state that reparations should be given to victims without adverse distinction on the grounds of, inter alia, sexual orientation; referring simply to the idea that reparations should be 'consistent with international human rights law', and be 'without distinction of any kind or any ground, without exception' (*Prosecutor v Lubanga* 2012: para. 191).

Although absent from protection under international human rights treaties, a conclusion affirming the absence of sexual orientation as a form of discrimination from international law would be mistaken, having regard for a body of law that has developed protecting sexual diversity. A comprehension that the distinctions set out in human rights treaties will inevitably be considered as 'universally recognized' enables us to draw on human rights jurisprudence that widely recognizes sexual orientation within the scope of 'other status' to advocate for the inclusion of sexual minorities under the crime of persecution. With judicial and political human rights monitoring bodies utilizing such an interpretation, it is widely understood that international anti-discrimination provisions protect sexual minorities. UN bodies have demonstrated a deepening acknowledgement that violence and persecution against sexual minorities is impermissible, by recognizing that states have a 'legal obligation...to ensure to everyone the rights recognized...without discrimination on the basis of sexual orientation' (UNHRC 2006: para. 25). Having been much criticized for reducing sexual orientation to 'sex' rather than utilizing 'other status' and neglecting to rule on the right to equality in *Toonen v Australia* (Kukuru 2005: 183), the HRC has since progressed its reasoning to recognize that discrimination against same-sex couples amounts to unjustifiable discrimination on the basis of the complainant's sex or sexual orientation (*Young v Australia*, 2003: para. 6.1). The ICC has regularly acknowledged that 'guidance should be sought from human rights', relying on 'internationally recognised human rights jurisprudence' in previous cases (*Prosecutor v Lubanga*, 2007: paras 38, 73), and may therefore follow the progressive reasoning deployed by the HRC.

The jurisprudence of the HRC, in becoming more open to deciphering sexual orientation as incorporated under 'other status', explicitly places protection for sexual minorities under the framework of the ICCPR. Such reasoning has become extensively endorsed by the wider UN system, exemplified by the understanding that 'the obligations of states to prevent violence and discrimination based on sexual orientation and gender identity are derived from various international human rights instruments' (UNGA 2011a: para. 8). Ensuring that a 'person's sexual orientation is not a barrier to realizing Covenant rights', the Committee on Economic, Social, and Cultural Rights (CESCR) has explicitly placed sexual orientation within the corpus of 'other status' (CESCR 2009: para. 32). The Committee against Torture has also signified 'the protection of certain minority or marginalised individuals or populations especially at risk of torture is a part of the obligation to prevent torture or ill-treatment' including on account of, inter alia, 'gender, sexual orientation, transgender identity' (2007: para. 21).

This emergent consensus in international law is also evident within regional human rights systems, particularly in the European Court of Human Rights (ECtHR) where sexual orientation has been acknowledged as a prohibited ground of discrimination. Adding credence to the suggestion that protection for sexual minorities is universal, the ICC may utilize the reasoning exhibited by regional human rights bodies. In fact, the Court has previously looked to Article 5(1)(c) of the European Convention on Human Rights (ECHR) and the interpretations of the Inter-American Court of Human Rights for guidance in its understanding of Article 58(1) and (7) regarding the issuance of a warrant of arrest or summons to appear (*Prosecutor v Al Bashir*, 2009: para. 32). Reiterating that the list of discriminated grounds under the ECHR is 'illustrative and not exhaustive', the ECtHR has affirmed 'a difference of treatment [. . .] based on the applicant's sexual orientation' is a 'concept which is undoubtedly covered by Article 14 of the Convention' (*Salgueiro da Silva Mouta v Portugal*, 1999: para. 28). This trend is also illustrated by the Inter-American Commission on Human Rights, signifying that the criminalization of homosexuality and deprivation of liberty, simply because of sexual preference, are practices 'contrary to the provision of various articles of the American Convention' (International Commission of Jurists 2009: para. 38). Despite rhetoric in international human rights advocacy of the homogenized nature of homophobia in Africa, a more appropriate reading of the African Charter on Human and People's Rights enlightens an understanding for the incorporation of sexual minorities, through the affirmation of the equality of all people and anti-discriminatory principles, with the provisions on 'people's rights' adding additional scope. Accepting that 'the exact content of the Charter will not be frozen in time', Commissioner Taklula has observed that discrimination on the basis of sexual orientation is incompatible with Article 2 of the African Charter (Murray and Viljoen 2007: 91, 103), a position outlined by the Commission stating the purpose of the anti-discrimination principle was to 'ensure equality of treatment for individuals irrespective of nationality, sex... or sexual orientation' (African Commission on Human and Peoples' Rights 2006: para. 169). Finally, the recent Resolution on Protection against Violence and Violations against Persons on the Basis of their Real or Imputed Sexual Orientation or Gender Identity offers the strongest confirmation that the 'increasing incidence of violence and other human rights violations, including murder, rape, assault, arbitrary imprisonment and other forms of persecution of persons on the basis of their imputed or real sexual orientation or gender identity' (African Commission on Human and Peoples' Rights 2014: para. 1) are condemned in Africa, exemplifying the emerging universal consensus on sexual orientation rights in international law.

Additionally, international refugee law jurisprudence adds credence to the understanding of sexual orientation as universally recognized under international law. While a direct transfer of persecution law from international refugee law has been cautioned against (*Prosecutor v Kuspreškić*, 2000: para. 589), a link between the developments of gender-related persecution under the two regimes clearly exists. Having been recognized as incorporated under 'membership of a particular social group' by the key receiving nations, sexual orientation has gradually been accepted as incorporated under this ground in international refugee law. First identified in the *Matter of Toboso-Alfonso* (1990), it is now firmly understood that sexual orientation is protected in the same way as those persecuted because of more traditional grounds. The UNHCR has explicitly conveyed the understanding that, similarly to other grounds of persecution, 'sexual orientation is a fundamental part of human identity' (UNHCR 2008: para. 8). Particularly illuminating for the ICC is the reliance on human rights law in formulating protection for sexual minorities, recognizing that the guarantees of the UDHR are 'fundamental to a proper understanding of the Convention' (*HJ (Iran) and HT (Cameroon) v Secretary of State for the Home Department*, 2011: para. 15). By recognizing that the principles of equality and human dignity are at the heart of the Convention, international refugee law explicitly bases its protection of sexual minorities within universally recognized international human rights law. Through this recognition, that having due regard to fundamental rights and the principle of non-discrimination requires protection of sexual orientation (UNHCR 2012: para. 6), international refugee law establishes progressive reasoning that highlights the human rights of sexual minorities, thereby adding authority to claims that protection is 'universally recognized'.

Through a thorough examination of the sources of international law, despite a lack of consolidated customary law (Reeves 2009: 281), a strong argument may be formed in support of the protection of sexual minorities from state-sponsored forms of hate and the combating of hate-motivated violence. Even as an opponent of the Court, Wilkins has suggested it is 'hardly far-fetched' to imagine incorporation of sexual minorities through the use of international guidelines that call for penalties for those who vilify homosexual behaviour, based on developments that are mandated by international human rights law (Wilkins 2002: 8). Universal consensus on the protection of sexual minorities from hate-motivated violence and persecution is continuingly developing, exemplified by the rapidly increasing number of states decriminalizing same-sex activity. A collection of countries have decriminalized same-sex activity since the Rome Statute was introduced (UNGA 2011a: para. 43). Sable contends that this 'rapid' trend towards decriminalization at state level and the recognition of sexual minorities at the international level 'reflects a change in state behaviour and collective sense of obligation' (Sable 2010: 115), with some regions exhibiting the creation of customary international law on the matter (ibid: 127).

CONCLUSION

By locating the assessment of individual criminal responsibility for persecution on account of sexual orientation within the context of the African continent, both the severity of abuse and theoretical concerns can be brought into focus. It is suggested that universality, implicit in a proper understanding of crimes against humanity as both 'offences against humankind' and 'injuries to humanness' (Luban 2004: 90), provides the theoretical basis upon which to situate protection for sexual minorities against state-sponsored hate. However, in order to profess a truly universal conception of sexual minorities protected under the crime against humanity of persecution, this chapter has utilized postcolonial critiques to acknowledge the nuances in how sexual orientation is understood and experienced across the continent. By presuming 'sexual orientation' to encompass diverse sexualities, beyond Western understandings of the 'homosexual', this chapter advocates for a culturally sensitive means of universally protecting sexual minorities. This critique can be operationalized in international criminal law by taking account of the diversity of sexual orientation and by focusing on the different trajectories of sexual orientation persecution.

Furthermore, a broad interpretation of gender, as a concept based on socially constructed roles males and females are expected to play, also provides an *initial* opportunity for sexual orientation to be recognized under Article 7(1)(h). Nevertheless, considering both practical and theoretical problems regarding such interpretation, an examination of sexual orientation under the ground of 'universally recognized as impermissible under international law', appreciating the growing trend for recognition in international human rights, may be preferable since it recognizes that patriarchy and heterosexual dominance are two separable systems.

Nevertheless, the current maintenance of heteronormativity in international law, combined with the lack of specific enumeration for sexual orientation under international human rights treaties, means that protection for sexual diversity under the Rome Statute is far from guaranteed. As such, it is essential that further attempts be initiated to advocate for the expansion of Article 7(1)(h) to explicitly recognize sexual minorities.

REFERENCES

African Commission on Human and Peoples' Rights 2006. *Zimbabwe Human Rights NGO Forum v Zimbabwe*, AHRLR 128.

African Commission on Human and Peoples' Rights 2014. *Resolution on the Protection against Violence and Violations against Persons on the Basis of their Sexual Orientation or Gender Identity*, 55th Ordinary Session, Res.275.

Akhavan, P. 2001. 'Beyond Impunity: Can International Criminal Justice Prevent Future Atrocities', 95 *American Journal of International Law* 7.

Altman, D. 1996. 'Rapture or Continuity? The Internationalisation of Gay Identities', 48 *Social Text* 77.

Ambros, K. 2013. 'Punishment without a Sovereign? The *Ius Puniendi* Issue of International Criminal Law: a First Contribution towards a Consistent Theory of International Criminal Law', 33 *Oxford Journal of Legal Studies* 293.

Amnesty International 2013. *Making Love a Crime: Criminalisation of Same-Sex Conduct in Sub-Saharan Africa*, Amnesty International Publications, London.

Amnesty International 2015. *Mapping Anti-Gay Laws in Africa*, available at: http://www.amnesty.org.uk/lgbti-lgbt-gay-human-rights-law-africa-uganda-kenya-nigeria-cameroon#.VcsaL51Viko (Accessed 12 August 2015).

Arnold, S.K. 2013. 'Identity and the Sexual Minority Refugee: Discussion of Conceptions and Preconceptions in the UK and Ireland', 20 *Human Rights Brief* 26.

Boot, M. 2002. *Nullem Crimen Sine Lege and the Subject Matter Jurisdiction of the International Criminal Court: Genocide, Crimes against Humanity and War Crimes*, Intersentia, Antwerp.

Boyd, L. 2013. 'The Problem with Freedom: Homosexuality and Human Rights in Uganda', 88 *Anthropological Quarterly* 697.

Calhoun, C. 1994. 'Separating Lesbian Theory from Feminist Theory', 104 *Ethics* 558.

CEDAW 2010. *Concluding Observations of the Committee on the Elimination of Discrimination against Women: Panama*, CEDAW/C/PAN/CO/7.

Charlesworth, H. 1999. 'Feminist Methods in International Law', 93 *American Journal of International Law* 379.

Cook, R.J. 1994. *Human Rights of Women: National and International Perspectives*, Pennsylvania University Press, Pennsylvania.

Council of Europe, European Court of Human Rights 1999. *Salgueiro da Silva Mouta v Portugal*, Application No. 33290/96.

Donnelly, J. 1999. 'Non-Discrimination and Sexual Orientation: Making a Place for Sexual Minorities in the Global Human Rights Regime', in Baehr, P., Flintermann, C., and Senders, M. (eds.), *Innovation and Inspiration: Fifty Years of the Universal Declaration of Human Rights*, Royal Netherlands Academy of Arts and Sciences, Amsterdam, pp. 93–110.

Donnelly, J. 2007. 'The Relative Universality of Human Rights', 29 *Human Rights Quarterly* 281.

Epprecht, M. 2009. 'Sexuality, Africa, History', 114 *The American Historical Review* 1258.

Gay Uganda 2007. *Kuchu Identities*, available at http://gayuganda.blogspot.co.uk/2007/10/kuchu-identities.html (Accessed 19 June 2005).

Gordon, G.S. 2013. 'Hate Speech and Persecution: A Contextual Approach', 46 *Vanderbilt Journal of Transnational Law* 303.

HJ (Iran) and HT (Cameroon) v Secretary of State for the Home Department [2011] 1 AC 596.

Hoad, N. 1999. 'Between the White Man's Burden and the White Man's Disease: Tracking Lesbian and Gay Human Rights in Southern Africa', 5 *GLQ: A Journal of Lesbian and Gay Studies* 559.

ICC 29 January 2007. *Situation in the Democratic Republic of Congo in the Case of The Prosecutor v Thomas Lubanga Dyilo, (Decision on the Confirmation of Charges)*, (Pre-Trial Chamber I), ICC-01/04-04/06.

ICC 4 March 2009. *Situation in Darfur, Sudan in the Case of The Prosecutor v Omar Hassan Ahmed Al Bashir, (Decision on the Prosecutor's Application for a Warrant of Arrest against Hassan Ahmed Al Bashir)*, (Pre-Trial Chamber I), ICC-02/05-01/09.

ICC 7 August 2012. *Situation in the Democratic Republic of the Congo in the Case of the Prosecutor v Thomas Lubanga Dyilo, (Decision Establishing the Principles and Procedures to be Applied to Reparations)*, (Trial Chamber I), ICC-01/04-01/06.

ICTR 2 September 1998. *Prosecutor v Jean-Paul Akayesu (Judgment)*, (Chamber I), ICTR-96-4-T.

ICTR 6 December 1999. *Prosecutor v Georges Anderson Underubumwe Rutaganda (Judgment and Sentence)*, (Trial Chamber 1), ICTR-96-3-T

ICTR 28 November 2007. *Ferdinand Nahimana, Jean-Bosco Barayagwiza, Hassan Ngeze v The Prosecutor (Judgment)*, (Appeals Chamber), ICTR-99-52-A.

ICTY 14 January 2000. *Prosecutor v Kupreškić et al. (Trial Judgment)*, (Trial Chamber), IT-95-16-T.

International Commission of Jurists 2009. *Sexual Orientation, Gender Identity and International Human Rights Law: Practitioners Guide No.4*, International Commission of Jurists, Geneva.

Jjuuko, A. 2013. 'The Incremental Approach: Uganda's Struggle for the Decriminalisation of Homosexuality', in Lennox, C. and Waites, M. (eds.), *Human Rights, Sexual Orientation and Gender Identity in the Commonwealth: Struggles for Decriminalisation and Change*, Human Rights Consortium, London, pp. 381–408.

Judgment of the Nuremburg International Military Tribunal 1946, 1947, 41 *American Journal of International Law* 172.

Kaomo, K. 2009. *Globalising the Cultural Wars: US Conservatives, African Churches and Homophobia*, Political Research Associates, Somerville.

Kukuru, E. 2005. 'Sexual Orientation and Non-Discrimination', 17 *Peace Review: A Journal of Social Justice* 181.

Lewis, D. 2011. 'Representing African Sexualities', in Tamale, S. (ed.), *African Sexualities: A Reader*, Pambazuka Press, Cape Town, pp. 199–216.

Luban, D. 2004. 'A Theory of Crimes against Humanity', 29 *Yale Journal of International Law* 85.

Murray, R. and Viljoen, F. 2007. 'Towards Non-Discrimination on the Basis of Sexual Orientation: The Normative and Procedural Possibilities before the African Commission on Human and Peoples' Rights and the African Union', 29 *Human Rights Quarterly* 86.

Nersessian, D.L. 2003. 'The Razor Edge: Defining and Protecting Human Groups Under the Genocide Convention', 36 *Cornell International Law Journal* 293.

Nyanzi, S. 2013. 'Dismantling Reified African Culture through Localised Homosexualities in Uganda', 15 *Culture, Health And Sexuality* 952.

O'Flaherty, M. and Fisher, J. 2008. 'Sexual Orientation, Gender Identity and International Human Rights Law: Contextualising the Yogyakarta Principles', 8 *Human Rights Law Review* 207.

Oliver, M. 2013. 'Transnational Sex Politics, Conservative Christianity, and Antigay Activism in Uganda', 7 *Studies in Social Justice* 83.

Oosterveld, V. 2005. 'The Definition of "Gender" in the Rome Statute of the International Criminal Court: A Step Forward or Back for International Criminal Justice?' 18 *Harvard Human Rights Journal* 55.

Oosterveld, V. 2006. 'Gender, Persecution, and the International Criminal Court: Refugee Law's Relevance to the Crime against Humanity of Gender-Based Persecution', 17 *Duke Journal of Comparative and International Law* 49.

Oosterveld, V. 2011. 'Gender-Based Crimes against Humanity', in Sadat, L.N. (ed.), *Forging a Convention for Crime Against Humanity*, Cambridge University Press, Cambridge, pp. 78–101.

Pocur, F. 2008. 'Persecution as Crime under International Criminal Law', 2 *Journal of National Security and Policy* 355.

Reeves, A.R. 2009. 'Sexual Identity as a Fundamental Human Right', 15 *Buffalo Human Rights Law Review* 215.

Reitman, O. 1997. 'Cultural Relativist and Feminist Critiques of International Human Rights—Friends or Foes?', 1 *Statsvetenskaplig Tidskrift* 100.

Robertson, G. 2006. *Crimes against Humanity: The Struggle for Global Justice*, Penguin, London.

Sable, S.M. 2010. 'A Prohibition on Antisodomy Laws Through Regional Customary International Law', 19 *Law and Sexuality: Review of Lesbian, Gay and Bisexual and Transgender Legal Issues* 95.

Sanga, L.S. 1997. *The Emerging System of International Criminal Law: Developments in Codification and Implementation*, Kluwer Law International, The Hague.

Schabas, W.A. 2006. 'Genocide, Crimes against Humanity and Darfur: The Commission of Inquiry's Findings on Genocide', 27 *Cardozo Law Review* 1703.

SMUG 2014a. *Expanded Criminalisation of Homosexuality in Uganda: A Flawed Narrative: Empirical Evidence and Strategic Alternatives from an African Perspective*, Sexual Minorities Uganda, Kampala.

SMUG 2014b. *From Torment to Tyranny: Enhanced Persecution in Uganda Following the Passage of the Anti-Homosexuality Act 2014*, Sexual Minorities Uganda, Kampala.

Smith, A. 2010. 'Queer Theory and Native Studies: The Heteronormativity of Settler Colonialism', 16 *GLQ: A Journal of Lesbian and Gay Studies* 42.

Stein, E. 2002. 'Law, Sexual Orientation, and Gender', in Coleman, J. and Shapiro, S. (eds.), *The Oxford Handbook of Jurisprudence & Philosophy of Law*, Oxford University Press, Oxford, pp. 990–1039.

Steins, C. 1999. 'Gender Issues', in Lee, S.K. (ed.), *International Criminal Court: The Making of the Rome Statute*, Kluwer Law International, The Hague, pp. 357–90.

Tamale, S. 2007. 'Out of the Closet: Unveiling Sexuality Discourses in Uganda', in Cole, C.M., Manuh, T., and Miescher, S. (eds.), *Africa After Gender?*, Indiana University Press, Bloomington, pp. 17–29.

Thoreson, R.R. 2014. 'Troubling the Waters of a "Wave of Homophobia": Political Economies of Anti-Queer Animus in Sub-Saharan Africa', 17 *Sexualities* 23.

UN CESCR 2009. *General Comment No.20: Non-Discrimination in Economic, Social and Cultural Rights (art.2, para.2, of the International Covenant on Economic, Social and Cultural Rights)*, E/C.12/GC/20.

UN Committee against Torture 2007. *General Comment 2, Implementation of Article 2 by States Parties*, CAT/C/GC/2/CPR.1/Rev.4.

UNGA 1948. *Universal Declaration of Human Rights*, Resolution 217 A (III).

UNGA 1979. *Convention on the Elimination of All Forms of Discrimination against Women (ICEDAW)*, A/RES/34/180.

UNGA 1996. *The Implementation of the Outcome of the Fourth World Conference on Women: Report of the Secretary-General*, A/51/322.

UNGA 1998. *Rome Statute of the International Criminal Court*, A/CONF.183/9.

UNGA 2006. International Law Commission, *Fragmentation of International Law: Difficulties Arising from the Diversification and Expansion of International Law, Report of the Study Group of the International Law Commission, Finalised by Martti Koskenniemi*, A/CN.4/L.682.

UNGA 2011a. Human Rights Council, *Discriminatory Laws and Practices and Acts of Violence against Individuals Based on their Sexual Orientation and Gender Identity: Report of the United Nations Commissioner for Human Rights*, A/HRC/19/41.

UNGA 2011b. *Questions of Torture and other Cruel, Inhumane or Degrading Treatment or Punishment: Note by the Secretary General*, A/56/156.

UNHCR 2002. *Guidelines on International Protection No. 1: Gender-Related Persecution with the Context of Article 1(a)(2) of the 1951 Convention and/or its 1967 Protocol Relating to the Status of Refugees*, HCR/GIP/02/01.

UNHCR 2008. *Guidance Note of Refugee Claims Relating to Sexual Orientation and Gender Identity*, Geneva.

UNHCR 2012. *Guidelines on International Protection No 9: Claims to Refugee Status based on Sexual Orientation and/or Gender Identity within the context of Article 1A(2) of the 1951 Convention and/or its 1967 Protocol relating to the Status of Refugees*, HCR/GIP/12/09.

UNHRC 4 April 1994. *Toonen v Australia*, Communication No. 488/1992, CCPR/C/50/D/488/1992.

UNHRC 18 August 2003. *Young v Australia*, Communication No. 941/2000, CCPR/C/78/D/941/2000.

UNHRC 2006. *Consideration of Reports Submitted by States Parties Under Article 40 of the Covenant: Concluding Observations of the Human Rights Committee—United States of America*, CCPR/C/USA/CO/3/Rev.1.

UN Security Council 1994a. *Statute of the International Criminal Tribunal for the former Yugoslavia*, UN Doc SC/Res/827/94, Article 5(h).

UN Security Council 1994b. *Statute of the International Criminal Tribunal for the former Yugoslavia*, UN Doc SC/Res/955/94, Article 3(h).

UN 8 August 1945. *Charter of the International Military Tribunal—Annex to the Agreement for the Prosecution and Punishment of the Major War Criminals of the European Axis*, United Nations Treaty Series 82, p. 279.

UN 1946. *Charter of the International Military Tribunal for the Far East*, 2 Bevans 20.

United States Board of Immigration Appeals 1990. *Matter of Toboso-Alfonso*, Interim Decision 3222.

United States District Court for the District of Massachusetts, *Sexual Minorities Uganda v Scott Lively*, [2013], C.A No. 12-cv-30051-MAP.

von Hebel, H. and Robinson, D. 1999. 'Crimes within the Jurisdiction of the Court', in Lee, S.K. (ed.), *International Criminal Court: The Making of the Rome Statute*, Kluwer Law International, The Hague, pp. 79–126, p. 101.

Wilkins, R.G. 2002. 'Ramifications of the International Criminal Court for War, Peace and Social Change', *The Federalist Society for Law and Public Policy Studies*. Available at: http://www.fed-soc.org/publications/detail/ramifications-of-the-international-criminal-court-for-war-peace-and-social-change (Accessed 4 February 2016).

18

CHALLENGING ORTHODOXY: TOWARDS A RESTORATIVE APPROACH TO COMBATING THE GLOBALIZATION OF HATE

Mark Austin Walters

INTRODUCTION

The final part of this book illustrates how important international and domestic legislation has become in challenging, and perhaps in time eradicating, the globalization of hate. Yet, to rely solely on the blunt instrument of the law and its established enforcers to counter such a phenomenon would be to underestimate the complex nature of hate-based conflicts.[1] Indeed, legislatures and policy makers must seek to employ a combination of criminal, social, and educational measures if the international community is to provide a truly comprehensive response to the global spread of hate-motivated violence. In this regard, this chapter explores whether domestic and international justice agencies should move towards a restorative justice (henceforth RJ) approach to addressing such conflicts.

This chapter asserts that the globalization of crime control has, in the main, reproduced neo-liberal conservative justice policies that have resulted in carceral expansion. There are few other examples that so neatly exemplify such an approach than the proliferation of hate crime punishment enhancers. Laws have been enacted across the globe aimed primarily at combating hate crime by punishing offenders more harshly (OSCE 2009). Though there are a number of strengths to legislating against hate (and cogent arguments for the retention of such laws), I argue that equal emphasis should be given to a restorative approach to tackling globalized forms of hatred. Such an approach should be underlined by processes that utilize inclusive dialogue and which are focused on the values of mutuality, equality, and respect.

---

[1] 'Hate-based conflict' is used throughout this chapter as an umbrella term that encompasses: interpersonal hate-motivated crimes and non-criminal incidents; community-based conflicts that involve identity-based hostilities; and cases involving state-promoted policies and practices that have been used to persecute groups of people based on their identity characteristics.

In exploring the global dimensions of hate-based violence, this chapter examines three *intersecting* levels of conflict (macro, meso, and micro) and the restorative practices that have been used to address them. It is argued that a restorative approach to addressing different forms of hate, though itself limited, will construct a new lens through which we are better able to understand, and in turn, combat the varying levels of hate-based conflict that continue to blight communities globally.

THE INTERNATIONALIZATION
OF CRIME CONTROL

The formation of our globalized society during the post-modern period has had a number of significant implications on the ways in which individual states now respond to crime. In particular, the proliferation of international human rights law combined with the creation of international governing bodies such as the United Nations has created the foreground for a growing and strengthening policy basis for the internationalization of crime control. For many, the growth in international justice mechanisms is conceived as a marker of the neo-liberal project that began in Anglo-American states, most prominently in the twentieth century (Christie 2000; Findlay 2008; Garland 2001). The decline in social welfarism, partly a result of the 'nothing works' mentality that pervaded much of the latter part of the century, gave way to both conservative and neo-liberal thinking on crime control, including amongst other things the growth of punitive penal policies (Garland 2001). Most prominent amongst these policies has been the expansion of the prison estate (Christie 2000). This has been aligned to the emergence of retributive justice during the 1980s and 1990s in the United States (US) and United Kingdom (UK) as the 'cornerstone' of criminal justice policy (Ashworth 2010). Such a system of justice has placed emphasis on imposing *deserved* punishments while maintaining defendant rights within a framework of proportionate sentencing. This approach was fostered in order to maintain consistency and equity in sentencing by ending the judicial discretion that was central to previous welfarist approaches to justice. However, the renewed focus on retributivism at the turn of the twentieth century was not only about protecting the rights of offenders through due process, but was also used a means of getting 'tough on crime'—at least rhetorically (Garland 2001). The language of needs, care, and protection therefore gave way to that of individual responsibility and obligations (often referred to as 'responsibilization') and to the need to protect society against the *risk* of crime and disorder (Garland 1996; Muncie 2005). Punitive policies established in the US and, in turn, the UK, have been 'exported' globally, both into domestic and international frameworks of justice (Baker and Roberts 2005). These have included amongst other policies: zero tolerance policing, mandatory minimum sentences, electronic tagging, private prisons, naming and shaming of offenders, anti-social behaviour orders, and, of particular importance to this chapter, penalty enhancers for hate crimes.

Notwithstanding the vast expansion of punitive interventions, the Anglo-American approach to criminal justice cannot be described as an all-encompassing monolith which has pervaded global justice systems in absolute terms. The transfer of justice models is often a two-way process and different countries across the world will employ varying and intersecting ideologies and practices in the administration of justice (Baker and Roberts 2005; Vogler 2005). As we will see below, the rise of restorative justice practices, which many believe have drawn from indigenous models of justice, has made significant inroads into justice systems across the world.[2] This has ultimately given rise to a tension between two paradigms of justice that draw from competing ideological backgrounds.

THE INTERNATIONALIZATION OF HATE CRIME: THE RISE OF PUNISHMENT ENHANCERS

During the 1980s and 1990s dozens of hate crime laws were enacted throughout the US. Common amongst almost all of these laws were the enhanced penalties that were imposed on offenders convicted of hate-motivated offences (see Lawrence 1999). The increased use in penalty enhancers for hate crimes has quickly spread further afield. The Organization for Security and Co-operation in Europe (OSCE) has been particularly influential in internationalizing both the concept of hate crime and its legal proscription (Goodall 2013). At their Ministerial Council meeting in Maastricht in 2003, participating members of the OSCE made an official commitment to combat 'crimes motivated by intolerance towards certain groups in society' (ODIHR 2009). Participating states proceeded by making a commitment to 'consider enacting or strengthening, where appropriate, legislation that prohibits discrimination based on, or incitement to hate crimes' (ibid: 7). A guide was subsequently developed as a tool to assist states in implementing that commitment, published in 2009 by the Office for Democratic Institutions and Human Rights (ODIHR)—the human rights organization that operates within the OSCE. The aim of the guidance is to support participating states when legislating against hate crime. The practical guide is drafted so as to be inclusive of the varied histories of participating members. Hate crimes are specifically defined as offences where the 'perpetrator intentionally chose the target of the crime because of some protected characteristic' (ibid: 16). This follows the discriminatory model of legislation first developed in the US, that is, it does not require an offender to be motivated by identity-based hostility (Lawrence 1999). Rather, the selection of the victim *because of* a characteristic becomes central to determining whether an offence is a hate crime. The language used by ODIHR reflects closely that

---

[2] Though it should be noted that for some critics these new approaches have been maintained within a neo-liberal approach to 'doing justice' (Cunneen 2012).

which has developed within neo-liberal discourse on hate crime in the US (including their use of the term 'bias crime' within guidance documents).

ODIHR's influence on hate crime policy, including their extensive consultations with member governments, has certainly been impactful on a number of participating states' approach to proscribing hate crime. Goodall identifies Moldova, Bosnia and Herzegovina, and Macedonia as three recent instances where ODIHR has directly helped to shape domestic hate crime legislation. In each of these cases she asserts that 'ODIHR's amendments were decisive' (Goodall 2013: 216). ODIHR's online resource shows that amongst the fifty-seven OSCE participants, fifty-four states now have specific hate crime laws. It is outside of the scope of this chapter to critique the details of any of these state provisions here.[3] I note simply that ODIHR's work has been instrumental in proliferating hate crime laws internationally; laws that focus on criminalizing bias motivation and enhancing punishment. It has meant that the international policy domain for hate crime, as originating in the US, has been focused predominantly on neo-liberal and punitive approaches to addressing the problem.

INTERNATIONAL LAW AND HATE CRIME

Few international instruments specifically call on signatories to criminalize hate-motivated offences. However, for those that have, the emphasis has again been on increasing penalties for offenders. For example, Article 4 of the European Union Framework Decision on Racist and Xenophobic Crime (2008) states that Member States 'shall take the necessary measures to ensure that racist and xenophobic motivation is considered an aggravating circumstance, or, alternatively that such motivation may be taken into consideration by the courts in the determination of the penalties'. This means that all members of the EU must have provisions in law that consider hate-motivation as an aggravating factor for any offence; or, put more simply, Member States must punish hate-motivated offenders more severely.

More recently the Council of the EU's conclusions on combating hate crime (December 2013) 'invited' members to 'ensure' that they have transposed the provisions of the Framework Decisions 2008 (i.e. to introduce punishment enhancers) and to 'consider the experience of other Member States in extending within their criminal legislation, the scope of punishable hate crime offences'. A single point in the document mentions the need for preventive measures, including 'taking steps to educate the public on the values of cultural diversity and inclusion'. No part of the document mentions the use of alternative justice mechanisms such as RJ as a response to hate crime.

---

[3] http://www.legislationline.org/topics/subtopic/79/topic/4. It should be noted, though, that this total is based on members of the OSCE region only.

Supporting the Council's approach to combating hate crime is the Fundamental Rights Agency (FRA) which operates as the research and policy arm on human rights within the EU. FRA has published widely on the need to combat hate crime, providing both research reports on the pervasiveness of different types of hate crime (FRA 2012a, 2012b) as well as a number of reports examining the effectiveness of responses to tackling it (FRA 2013a). FRA's work has been pivotal in highlighting the destructive nature of different forms of hate-motivated conduct throughout Europe, giving the social problem direct policy relevance. Notwithstanding, it too is yet to recognize the potential of community-based solutions when combating hate-based conflict within the EU.[4] With current policy focus remaining on criminalization and punitive penalties, it looks unlikely that it will embrace alternative measures for dealing with hate crime any time soon.

TOWARDS A RESTORATIVE APPROACH TO COMBATING GLOBALIZED HATE?

There are a number of criticisms that can be made about the use of penalty enhancers for hate crime offenders (see, generally, Jacobs and Potter 1998)—not least the fact that penalty enhancement rarely decreases offending levels (see, generally, Doob and Webster 2003). Still, there is much to be said for legislating against hate. It is outside the scope of this chapter to analyse these reasons in detail; indeed, a number of scholars, including this author, have examined the benefits that specific legislation can bring in combating hate crime (Lawrence 1999; Walters 2014a). In brief, these can be summarized as: providing symbolic messages of support to historically marginalized groups in society; providing specific censure and moral denunciation of prejudice and hate-motivated conduct; supporting longer-term educative deterrence by publically denouncing hate-motivated behaviour; and ensuring the effective operationalization of hate crime by law enforcement agencies via recording and prosecution policies that are attendant to specific legislation (Schweppe and Walters 2015).

Nevertheless, legislating to combat hate crime cannot, by itself, immobilize the globalization of hate. Recent statistics have shown significant increases in the number of hate-motivated offences across Europe (e.g., FRA 2015; Home Office et al. 2013). Though statistics do not always reveal a completely accurate picture of the number of hate-motivated offences committed, they remain a reliable indicator of the growing problem of hate crime. Such data is an important reminder that the law, and more specifically punishment enhancers, has a limited impact in reducing overall hate crime. As such, we need to consider carefully other measures that can be used to prevent hate incidents from occurring, or escalating.

---

[4] Though the conclusions document from the FRA conference on hate crime held in Lithuania in 2013 states at 5.4: 'Redress mechanisms, including the provision of compensation and restitution, must be strengthened' (FRA 2013b). No mention of how RJ might be used for hate crime is made.

The failure of punitive sanctions to reduce general crime rates has led many crimi-nologists to advocate for alternative justice frameworks and practices that aim to repair harm and reintegrate offenders back into communities where they are less likely to reoffend (Christie 1977; Zehr 1990). During the late 1970s, scholars began to theorize about new restorative approaches for crime that focused on communi-tarian concepts of crime control (see, e.g., Christie 1977). This gave birth to a modern RJ movement whose advocates argued for a new lens through which we should con-sider both the causes and consequences of crime (Zehr 1990).

Central to the theory and practice of RJ is the notion of 'community' (McCold 2004). Community is a complex concept that is not easily defined. As such it has not always been easy to comprehend how community works within RJ (Pavlich 2004). Braithwaite (1989: 85) has described community as a set of 'dense networks of in-dividual interdependencies with strong cultural commitments to mutuality and obligations'. Others have referred to community as collections of individuals who share an essence that bonds them together, whether that is based on morals, aes-thetics, or group identities (see further Walters 2014b: 167–74). At its most simple we might refer to community as a 'perception of togetherness' (McCold and Wachtel 1997 cited in Walgrave 2002: 74). Needless to say, the concept of community can be very broad, fluid, and subject to metamorphosis. How then can it be applied to RJ practice? I offer here several interconnecting forms of community that apply to RJ practice, and which in turn can be aligned to the varying levels of hate conflict, as expounded below.

The most common type of community within RJ practice is that of the 'micro-community'. Micro-communities comprise individuals who are directly affected by inter-personal (micro-level) crimes/conflict (McCold 2004). This will typically include family members and other individuals who have a meaningful relationship with either the direct victim or the offender of a crime. Collectively, these individu-als are often referred to as the 'community of care' and participate in restorative dialogue in a supportive role to either of the main stakeholders of an offence/con-flict. Micro-communities play an important role in providing emotional and social support to those directly impacted by the conflict, especially during the preparation stage of RJ and within direct meetings. However, beyond the role of 'care', these indi-viduals can also be conceptualized as a community 'tool' by forming a constellation through which dialogue can be facilitated. In other words, micro-communities are groups of people who act both as a support mechanism while additionally forming a collective space within which restorative goals can be achieved (see further below).

Linked to, and often intersecting with, micro-communities are individuals who make up what I refer to as 'meso-communities". These communities can be defined by localized geographical space (such as neighbourhoods) or through identity membership (for example the 'gay community' or 'Muslim community').[5] Meso-communities typically have little direct personal connection with the direct victim but may still be concerned with the indirect harms caused by crime, or as is the

[5] Others have referred to these communities as 'macro-communities', see McCold (2004). I differen-tiate between meso and macro for the reasons outlined below.

case in hate crimes may fear that they too will be targeted. In some cases (as we will see below) meso-communities may retaliate against a perceived threat, leading to an escalation in hostilities that results in entire groups of people (communities) coming into conflict. If RJ is to grapple with inter-group hostilities that proliferate across and within geographical/identity-based communities it must seek to include many of these individuals in dialogical processes that aim to resolve conflict. For instance, members of the 'Muslim community' may attend restorative meetings in order to support directly targeted individuals but also so that they too can articulate the *indirect* impacts that Islamophobic hate incidents have on Muslim people in the local area. As with micro-communities, the role of meso-communities can also extend beyond their role as participants in restorative dialogue to that of assisting individuals to move beyond conflict. By this I mean that meso-communities can also become a tool through which restorative goals are achieved, such as where a perpetrator makes reparations to the wider community (e.g., voluntary work for a local charity), and where he or she is then reintegrated into the local neighbourhood, whereby community members offer ongoing social support (such as that offered by youth groups, schools, etc.).

Finally, it is important for the purposes of this chapter to understand the role of the state in relation to community. The delineation of state and citizen often precludes state entities from being understood as forming a component part of any community. Indeed there are fundamental constitutional and political reasons for separating state from community (not least that the state has direct powers over members of micro and meso communities and has the role of serving and protecting citizens). Nevertheless, in terms of restorative practice, there are several legitimate reasons for viewing certain local agency employees as potentially forming part of 'community' during the restorative process.

First and foremost, state representatives (such as housing officers, police officers, school teachers, social care workers), though *politically* separated from the community, in *reality* form an important constituent component of any local social milieu. For example, in relation to hate crime, local state agencies frequently play a pivotal role in supporting victims' needs and addressing criminal behaviour. Community police officers, for instance, often become important parties to inter-personal and community-based conflicts as they attempt to address and resolve these. In a practical sense at least, state agency employees become party to the 'cultural commitments to mutuality and obligations' by becoming 'community supporters' to those who seek out their help. Such individuals often participate in restorative justice meetings by supporting the parties and engaging in dialogue about what has happened (see in more detail Walters 2014b: ch 6). Though many do so in the capacity of service provider, they are also there to uphold normative community values and to reassure that there is a community infrastructure that protects against victimization.

Conversely, these same institutions can also be responsible for the commission of individual and social harms. Poor service delivery (secondary victimization), or worse still, direct victimization by agency employees can mean that local agencies move from 'community supporter' to become community harmers (see ibid: 169–74). In fact, I have observed several restorative conferences facilitated by independent

mediators that involved state agency employees that have been accused of inflicting harm. Many of these representatives have been asked to explain their actions
and later repair the traumas that they (and their institution) have caused (see case
studies, ibid: ch 6). In doing so, they in effect traverse the roles of micro and meso
community participation. As we will see below, where state activities become pervasive and systemic, state agencies not only become implicated in micro-meso level
incidents of hate, but can also be directly responsible for macro-level human rights
violations.

If RJ theory and practice pivots on the concept of community (Christie 1977) and
state actors were to fall outside of its scope, restorative practices would be impo-
tent in addressing some of the broader structural harms perpetrated by state agents
during micro and meso level conflicts. The involvement of the state during community dialogue therefore becomes fundamental to the realization of restorative justice
goals. While the state, as an institution, must be treated with caution in relation to
RJ practice (especially with regards to state control over RJ processes; Christie 1977),
in a practical sense state representatives will often have to be integrated as part of
the 'stakeholders' of a conflict, if communities are to find resolution to the different
types of harms they have suffered (see more detailed analysis Walters 2014b: chs 6
and 7).

Collectively then, victims, offenders, along with micro, meso, and occasionally
state representatives can be included in a variety of different types of RJ through
practices that aim to repair harm—whether it be material, emotional, relational,
and even institutional. The aim of restorative practices is to utilize these diverging
levels of communities as the basis for structured dialogue, where all parties are able
to discuss what has happened, why it occurred, and how it has impacted upon each
individual. Unlike other forms of interpersonal communication, any pre-existing
dynamic of power between the stakeholders is shifted to that of non-domination
and mutuality.[6] This is best achieved where an independent mediator ensures that
no individual is silenced during the process and by framing communication so that
it is focused on how the conflict, and its injured parties, can be restored (Braithwaite
2003). The restorative process is typically completed with one or more parties
offering a written or verbal apology, and often a promise that the incident/s will
not be repeated. Other forms of reparation include: financial restitution; repairing
of damaged property; participation in community work; and engagement/volun-
tary work with local community organizations. For many stakeholders, the dialogical process is itself a constructive form of reparation, enabling participants to
feel empowered and less fearful of the other parties (Walters 2014b; see below). In
cases involving intergroup conflict such processes may be particularly promising as
they create opportunities for empathy by allowing participants to share emotions
such as guilt, shame, and sympathy for one another (Harris et al. 2004). Such emotional connections can help to break down identity-based stereotypes, thereby revealing the humanity of each of the stakeholders. If this is possible, communities

[6] This is most effectively achieved where the process is facilitated by an independent mediator.

can resolve conflicts by sharing perspectives, comprehending each other's suffering, and experiencing greater levels of respect for those perceived as 'different' (Walters 2014b: ch 8).

GLOBALIZATION AND RESTORATIVE JUSTICE: MACRO-LEVEL RESPONSES TO STATE-SPONSORED HATE

Restorative theorists often assert that RJ is rooted in ancient or indigenous methods of conflict resolution that focused on communitarian and welfarist approaches to resolving inter-personal conflicts (such as Maori and Pacific nation philosophies; Consedine 1995). Braithwaite (1999) has argued that in many ancient societies, crime was seen not as individual violations, but as harms to community wellbeing, which in turn gave rise to community responsibility and community-based solutions. In the modern context, such approaches to justice have been heralded as the antidote to the socially marginalizing effects of neo-liberal justice interventions (Christie 1977; Zehr 1990). This rethinking of criminal justice has seen the rebirth of RJ as a twenty-first century solution to the problem of crime, both at a domestic and international level. Such has been its popularity that RJ is now being incorporated into justice systems across the world in an attempt to resolve both micro-level inter-personal incidents (McCold 2006) as well as much larger-scale human rights abuses (Cunneen 2008).

The international proliferation of RJ practices has, as with their punitive predecessors, been the product of a globalized criminal justice knowledge exchange (Cunneen 2012: 147). By the early 2000s the use of RJ as a means of crime control had been embraced by the UN, who in 2002 introduced the *Basic Principles on the Use of Restorative Justice Programs in Criminal Matters* (Basic Principles). Part IV, para 20 states: 'Member States should consider the formulation of national strategies and policies aimed at the development of restorative justice and at the promotion of a culture favourable to the use of restorative justice among law enforcement, judicial and social authorities, as well as local communities.'

In the same year, the Council of Europe recommended to Member States that RJ should be made available at all stages of the criminal process (see more recently Directive 2012/29/EU 2012 'The Victims' Directive'). The promotion of RJ at these and other international levels has certainly supported the growth of restorative practices across jurisdictions. In fact, most countries in Europe now use some form of RJ within their justice/legal frameworks; though there is by no means uniformity in the approaches taken (Varfi et al. 2014). This means that RJ practices are now being used for a number of different crimes at various different stages of the criminal process (as well as outside the criminal process altogether) in countries across the world.

Yet despite the rapid expansion of RJ globally, there are few practices being used *specifically* to address hate-based conflicts (Walters 2014b). The lack of RJ practices for hate crime is likely to be the result of both the current focus on punitive measures to tackle the problem and the perceived risk that RJ will exacerbate tensions within communities by exposing participants to further hostilities. This is reflected in the 2012 EU Victims' Directive, which states at paragraph 46:

Factors such as the nature and severity of the crime, the ensuing degree of trauma, the repeat violation of a victim's physical, sexual, or psychological integrity, power imbalances, and the age, maturity or intellectual capacity of the victim, which could limit or reduce the victim's ability to make an informed choice or could prejudice a positive outcome for the victim, should be taken into consideration in referring a case to the restorative justice services and in conducting a restorative justice process.

Conversely, there has been a much greater willingness to utilize restorative processes in cases involving the most extreme forms of hatred, including those committed by the state itself. Such conflicts have typically involved systemic faith-based or ethnic persecution that has resulted in the infliction of mass personal and social violence. For instance, the creation of the Truth and Reconciliation Commissions (TRC) in South Africa (SA) in 1995 was one of the first macro-level processes guided by restorative principles to help repair the harms inflicted during Apartheid (Daly 2002). Apartheid had instituted a regime of oppression and domination by white people over all other (though mainly Black African) ethnic and racial groups. After the abolition of Apartheid in 1994, the TRC was created as a platform from which individuals could be identified as victims of gross human rights violations.[7] The TRC had six main purposes, including: to record the extent and nature of the incidents; to name those responsible; to provide a public forum for victims to express themselves; to make recommendation to prevent future violations; to make reparations to victims; and to grant amnesty to those who made full disclosure (Cunneen 2008: 362). During its seven years in operation, both victims and witnesses were invited to give statements about their experiences with many taking part in public hearings. In total, the TRC heard testimony from approximately 21,000 victims, with 2,000 appearing at public hearings.[8] Those responsible for the violations were provided with the opportunity to give testimony and in turn they could request amnesty from both civil and criminal prosecution.[9]

The TRC distinguished between four different levels of reconciliation including: individual—coming to terms with painful truths; interpersonal—between victims and offenders; community—the role of local populations; and national—the role of the state and non-state institutions (Cunneen 2008). The significance of these forms of reconciliation is magnified in societies where extreme forms of prejudice have been embedded within social and cultural structures over many years. It is not always possible, or even desirable, to implement punitive forms of 'justice' during times of political and social unrest, especially where the system itself has been at the

---

[7] This was in stark contrast to the approach taken by the Nuremberg Trials after the Second World War that focused on 'victor's justice' as a way of addressing the horrific genocides committed during this period.

[8] See Truth and Reconciliation Commission Website, 'AMNESTY HEARINGS & DECISIONS' at: http://www.justice.gov.za/trc/amntrans/index.htm

[9] Amnesty was granted in 849 cases and refused in 5,392 cases. Ibid.

heart of identity-based persecution. Few perpetrators are ever caught or punished for the violence inflicted on fellow citizens where those responsible remain in positions of power during periods of transition.

The TRC offered an alternative approach to criminal prosecution which encouraged the process of 'truth-telling' (Weitekamp et al. 2006). Such a process can be especially significant to relatives who want to know what has happened to their loved ones, while society more broadly needs to be aware of patterns of gross violations (ibid). The offer of amnesty, though highly controversial, is sometimes the only opportunity for the *truth* to emerge. The SA Constitutional Court reflected upon the symbolic significance of the TRC:

> The families of those unlawfully tortured, maimed or traumatized become more empowered to discover the truth, the perpetrators become exposed to opportunities to obtain relief from the burden of a guilt or an anxiety they might be living with for many long years, the country begins the long and necessary process of healing the wounds of the past, transforming anger and grief into a mature understanding and creating the emotional and structural climate essential for the 'reconciliation and reconstruction' which informs the very difficult and sometimes painful objectives of the amnesty...[10]

Many believe that the TRC has enabled SA to move beyond the historical traumas caused by Apartheid towards a more peaceful, free, and democratic society (see, e.g., Daly 2002). Notwithstanding the Commission's many criticisms (see further below), the perceived success of the TRC resulted in significant international pressure for state-based reparation in post-conflict societies. This resulted in the establishment by the UN General Assembly of the *Basic Principles and Guidelines on the Right to a Remedy and Reparation for Victims of Gross Violations of International Human Rights Law and Serious Violations of International Humanitarian Law* in 2005. Principles 16–25 outline the right to adequate, effective, and prompt reparation. Principle 18 states:

> ...victims of gross violations of international human rights law and serious violations of international humanitarian law should, as appropriate and proportional to the gravity of the violation and the circumstances of each case, be provided with full and effective reparation...which include the following forms: restitution, compensation, rehabilitation, satisfaction and guarantees of non-repetition.

This means that at an international level at least, reparation, restoration, and restitution are now fundamental principles that *should* be utilized in cases involving the most extreme forms of hate. As a result, a number of other restorative processes have been used to respond to human rights violations in a number of post-conflict societies (see Sullivan and Tifft 2008: Section V).[11]

Despite its popularity, a number of criticisms have been levelled at restorative approaches to addressing macro-level hate violence (Cunneen 2008; Waldorf 2008).

---

[10] *Azanian Peoples Organisation (AZAPO) and Others v President of the Republic of South Africa and Others*, 1996 (8) BCLR 1015 (CC at 17), 1996 SACLR LEXIS 20 at 37–8.

[11] See, e.g., Truth and Reconciliation in Serbia (Nikolic-Ristanovic 2008); and the use of gacaca courts in Rwanda (Waldorf 2008).

Waldorf (2008) notes that although macro-level restorative programmes have provided some 'reparations', the outcomes have not always been *fully* restorative in that not all stakeholders of the original abuses are present; some participants receive no reparation at all; clear examples of inclusive and two-way dialogue are rare; while the structural harms caused by ongoing incidents are not always properly acknowledged (see also Weitekamp et al. 2006). This has led some critics to suggest that practices such as TRCs are little more than instruments of political settlement (see, e.g., Cunneen 2012; Lin 2005). Lin (2005), for instance, has claimed that the SA TRC was a reflection of the political interests of achieving less legal pluralism and more centralization and not about RJ at all (see also, Cunneen 2012). She goes on to argue that the international community, however, has perpetuated a 'restorative justice mythology' based largely on the ideological reformulation of the TRC, as expressed by Bishop Desmond Tutu and Dr Alex Boraine who were at the helm of the Commission (see Lin 2005: 56–63).

Cunneen (2012) has gone on to criticize the TRC and similar macro-level restorative processes by arguing that in many countries localized and non-state practices used for resolving inter-personal conflicts have been replaced by Western interpretations of conflict resolution that impose hegemonic ideals of RJ, thereby displacing indigenous and customary forms of justice. Conceived in such terms, RJ may be seen as little more than an appropriation of ancient practices, which are reformulated into Western principles and translated into processes that actually fulfil the cultural values that underpin neo-liberal approaches to criminal justice. Cunneen argues that RJ theory and practice does little to challenge the orthodoxy of criminology that maintains a dichotomous division between 'offenders' and 'victims'. Although RJ attempts to re-orientate crime control from state to community, in reality it may simply create an 'individualized sense of civic obligation' (Cunneen 2012: 148), while simultaneously reproducing the role of law and conventional processes of criminalization as maintained by Western neo-liberal states (Cunneen and Hoyle 2010). Moreover, RJ—at least in its current form—fails to adequately address the structural inequalities that give rise to various social harms and to an environment where hate crime flourishes (Cunneen 2012: see also Walters 2014b: chs 3 and 9). The challenge for RJ is that it currently operates within a system that is set up to reproduce outcomes that partly sustain an unequal society. As such, some critics argue that we should remain sceptical about RJ's ability to truly challenge the neo-liberal formulations of criminalization and state control mechanisms (including policing) that disproportionately impact upon already marginalized communities (Christie 2000; Cunneen 2012).

AT THE INTERSECTIONS
OF GLOBALIZATION: FROM MACRO TO MESO

In the introduction to this book we summarized some of the contemporary macro-level geo-political events that have led to the proliferation of hate incidents across the world. In particular, the human rights violations that have occurred in Gaza and Israel during recent years have affected not just those who inhabit this region (though they are certainly most affected), but millions of others across the globe. The effects of globalization, as promulgated by social media and traditional media coverage, as well as the diaspora of peoples from this region, mean that religious, political, and historical hostilities have rippled out across the world. Directly connected to these geo-political tensions has been a polarizing discourse that pits religious identity against freedom of expression. An acrimonious debate has erupted, fuelled by fear of the Islamisation of American and European cultures, which has in turn given rise to a 'defence' of Western democratic freedoms.[12] This has resulted in tensions across communities leading to entire groups of people coming into conflict. Political responses to this perceived threat, such as the depictions of the prophet Mohammed by cartoonists in Denmark and France, have inevitably triggered other extreme incidents of hate-motivated violence that affect entire groups of people (CST 2015). These tensions move beyond isolated incidents of hatred to the promulgation of ongoing and retaliatory violence between communities.

So what is to be done to quell the proliferation of this community-level violence? As with other forms of hate, extremist violence (including terrorist attacks) has been met with forceful political rhetoric that is aimed at conveying a punitive response to the problem. In the fight to combat extremism, governments have declared a 'war on terrorism' by increasing surveillance measures in order to help capture perpetrators, while additionally extending military campaigns in certain 'problem zones'. Yet these deterrent measures have undoubtedly failed to prevent terrorist activities abroad or what are considered 'extremist' acts at home (Tschudi 2008). Indeed, it would not be implausible of me to suggest that government policy has led to greater geo-political destabilization, further entrenching the division between Western and Eastern civilizations, and in turn exacerbating the problem of hate crime.

Whether RJ could be used more successfully to resolve such cases remains unclear. There are few RJ programmes being used in such complex contexts and therefore much is yet to be learnt about the use of inclusive structured dialogue to resolve meso-level hate conflicts. One salient example of good practice is that of the Victim-Combatant Dialogue of the LIVE programme established by the Glencree Centre in Ireland, whose objective is peace-making within and between communities in Ireland and Britain. The primary aim of the LIVE programme was to rebuild the relationships between victims who had suffered as a result of the political, religious, and sectarian conflict in Northern Ireland during the twentieth century (White 2003). The secondary aim was to facilitate dialogue between former IRA combatants and the victims of the conflict (ibid: 91). In total, the programme involved sixty victims from Northern Ireland, and twenty each from Britain and Ireland (ibid: 92). There were three stages to the programme, including: victims from each of the three regions meeting separately in workshops; dialogue between the victim groups across locations; and finally direct meetings between former paramilitary combatants and all the victim-survivors.

---

[12] See websites such as SIOE: https://sioeeu.wordpress.com/

White (2003: 93) notes that victim-survivors had many questions they had been waiting to ask for a number of years. The retelling of participants' stories also brought much grief. In response, the former combatant was able to explain some of the historical causes of the conflict. He went on to offer the group a sincere apology for the casualties of his actions, though he did not apologize for the broader conflict itself, which he still believed was 'a just war' (White 2003: 93). He then told his own story, speaking of the injustice he had experienced as a young man, which provided his main motivation to actively participate in the conflict. Following the direct dialogue a follow-up reflection session was organized allowing for the participating victim-survivors to fully process the encounter.[13] An ongoing telephone support service for the participants was also extensively used to provide further support.[14]

The LIVE-programme illustrates how meso-level RJ processes *may* help those involved in extreme forms of violence to understand loss and to ask questions to those responsible for hurting loved ones. Yet this example alone does not provide unequivocal proof of the effectiveness of RJ for meso-level hate conflicts. There will remain several barriers to the successful implementation of such initiatives. First, RJ is likely to be of limited use for community-level violence where macro-level (i.e. state) responses to addressing such conflicts are focused solely on punitive interventions. Governments' focus on punishment and imprisonment, combined with their often rhetorical responses to extremism—which often portrays certain community members as dangerous 'Others'—means that community dialogue for intergroup conflict is likely to remain restricted by political barriers to resolution. After all, RJ is a voluntary process that seeks to repair harms through inclusive participation in dialogue aimed at reintegrating stakeholders back into the community. This will be problematic where certain individuals feel that they do not have a stake in the broader community, or at least in the 'right' community (Pavlich 2004). For instance, the alienation of Muslim (and various other) people in Western societies via political, legal, cultural, and other structural processes means that many will not feel that they are 'equals' within any given meso-level community (Fekete 2009). As such, they are unlikely to embrace any justice mechanism that involves them participating in a community-based solution to their experiences of (perceived) victimization.

Such a situation is exacerbated further where participants hold diametrically opposing political and ideological (religious) views. Indeed it is the divergence in such perspectives that is causal to incidents of extreme violence between the parties in the first place. Religious or sectarian conflicts, for instance, expose complex histories involving myriad cultural variables that are linked to long-term animosities. The desire to kill and maim during such conflicts is often an expression in absolutist terms of one group's righteousness over another (Marshall 2006). Perpetrators of extremist violence are unlikely to feel respect for victims, be open to treating them

---

[13] Some participants engaged with further non-structured dialogue with the former combatants and others with therapy sessions.

[14] For another example of meso-level RJ in such conflicts see Parents Circle Families Forum (PCFF), who state that they are 'a grassroots organization of bereaved Palestinians and Israelis [that] promotes reconciliation as an alternative to hatred and revenge' (http://www.theparentscircle.com).

as 'equals', or accept any culpability for the harms they have inflicted (Staiger 2010: 313–14). Such acts of hate must therefore be understood within the broader socio-cultural contexts in which they occur if we are to truly address them in any mean-ingful way (ibid: 315). The complexity of these extreme expressions of hate may mean that processes that emphasize the values of mutuality and respect for *all* parties may be easier stated than they are realized. This is not to say that such meso-level dia-logue is not possible (see examples above and those below); however, engaging these stakeholders in such a process is likely to be complicated by the entrenched social attitudes that divide groups of people.

FROM MACRO-MESO TO MICRO

Extreme forms of community-based violence that are linked to macro-level events demonstrate how hate incidents are perpetuated via continuous cycles of hate-based conflict. Such a cycle not only leads to large-scale violence, such as that in France and elsewhere, but also frequently serves as the catalyst for lower-level inter-personal hate incidents across the globe. These more sporadic incidents result in micro-level interpersonal hate crimes. This has been observed during the aftermath of terrorist attacks such as 9/11 and 7/7 where large spikes in hate-motivated assaults against individuals in various parts of the US and the UK have been recorded (see studies detailed in Benier, this collection). These individual, though pervasive, incidents make up the very end of the spectrum of hate; that which is propelled by the various dynamics of globalization.

As noted above, despite the rapid growth in RJ globally, only a few practices have been used specifically to address micro-level hate crime. In the US context, Coates et al. (2006) provide a useful case study illustrating the potential benefits of using a restorative approach to resolving isolated hate incidents in the aftermath of large-scale incidents of extreme hatred. In their case study in Oregon an offender had made death threats to an Islamic cultural centre directly after the terrorist attacks of September 11 in New York. The offender was thereafter apprehended and in response, two restorative conferences were facilitated between the offender, the victim, and his family. During these meetings the victim spoke of how the phone call had impacted him and his family, noting that it had instantly changed their lives for fear that they would be hurt or, worse, killed. The meetings additionally included more general discussion about the current political cli-mate towards Muslims as well as the role that the media and films had played in depicting Muslim people negatively. The offender also opened up to the group, telling them of his experience of losing his child and being angry at the world. He apologized for his actions and as part of the reparation agreement was asked to attend lectures on Islam, which he did. He also agreed to attend counselling for his anger issues and later became involved in helping at a juvenile detention centre. The pursuit of a dialogical process between the stakeholders of this offence had the effect of humanizing both parties. Ultimately, it was the bridging of empathic divides that allowed both sides to move on with their lives in a more positive and peaceful way.

A number of other case studies have been documented by Gavrielides (2012) and Walters (2014b), each highlighting the potential benefits of RJ for micro-level hate crimes. Such examples illustrate how RJ might diffuse conflict and expose ignorance and bigotry to critical scrutiny. For example, Walters' (2014b: ch 4) empirical study into the use of RJ for hate crime in England found that of greatest importance to the victims of hate-motivated incidents was that they were offered an opportunity to participate in the resolution of their case. This was best achieved by giving them a voice. It was this voice that enabled participants to develop their stories of personal suffering, which they now felt was finally being listed to. It was also important that individuals had the opportunity to talk more indirectly about their experiences of being 'different' within the community, thereby allowing them to articulate their broader experiences of identity-based prejudice (as was the case in Coates et al.'s case study). This aspect of RJ was particularly significant to hate crime victims who often felt that they were without a voice in their local community, and moreover that their plights had been ignored by the local state agencies to whom they had turned for help (Walters 2014b: ch 6). In addition, most victims wanted the perpetrator(s) to promise that they would not repeat their actions: such promises were frequently included in mediation agreements signed at the end of the process (see further, Walters 2014b: ch 4).

CONCLUSION: RESTORATIVE JUSTICE FOR GLOBALIZED HATE— LIMITATION OR EXPECTATION?

The case examples presented throughout this chapter demonstrate the *potential* of RJ to address the various intersecting hate-based conflicts that occur globally. It has been outside the scope of this chapter to explore all the criticisms that can be made about RJ for hate crime (see these detailed in Walters 2014b). It suffices to say that both ideological and practical tensions remain between conventional processes of justice and the restorative practices proliferating within criminal justice systems throughout the world. Perhaps then, RJ is best situated somewhere between the neo-liberal approach to hate crime (that which promotes individual responsibility through criminalization and punishment) and an approach that aims to repair both individual *and* structural harm (emphasizing welfarist and communitarian considerations). It cannot be denied that hate crimes are real life expressions of violent prejudice, involving both individual and social responsibility, and which invariably cause immense individual and social harms (Iganski and Lagou 2015). Without a legal framework for hate crime it would be difficult to pinpoint when harmful hate-motivated conduct has been committed (how would it be reported? Who would respond and offer support to those affected?). The law is required not only as a formal proscription of these acts of hate, but its rules play an important symbolic function by conveying to the public social disapproval of hate crimes; acts that have led in the past to the most serious escalation of violence. This does not, though, automatically mean that the law must be supported by *more* punishment (Walters 2016). Nor does it necessarily follow that the law, in and of itself, serves a hegemonic or marginalizing function as Cunneen (2012) has suggested (see above). Rather, it is the disproportionate enforcement of the law and the ensuing implementation of punishments by certain criminal justice agencies that has led to the racialized and gendered aspects of criminalization.

Thus while we must be attuned to the *risk* of RJ becoming another means through which the 'Other' is oppressed, we need not yet conclude that this is an inevitability. The risk is greatest where centralized state agencies take control of restorative practices and align them to the more punitive elements of the justice system. However, the philosophy and practice of RJ, as advocated by its practitioners and theorists, actively resists social marginalization via the practical application of its key values, including mutuality, equality, and respect (Braithwaite 2003). Those who administer RJ must serve only as facilitators of community-based dialogue that is inclusive, structured, and focused on harm reparation. Practices can create opportunities for broader discussion about community *and* structural harm where micro (victims, offenders, and their supporters), meso (other affected community members), and even state representatives are engaged as equal participants in the dialogical process (Walters 2014b: ch 6). In this regard, RJ may help to open 'a space to consider a series of replacement discourses of "social harm", "social conflict" and "redress" to challenge conservative neo-liberal conceptions of punitive populism and retributive justice' (Muncie 2005: 44).

Whether the international community is ready to embrace a restorative approach to hate-based conflict depends largely on what our expectations are for RJ to address the global threats of hate. Those who seek a completely new system of social governance that reformulates our understanding of crime will inevitably remain sceptical about the ability of RJ to challenge the inequalities that currently exist in society. For others, including this author, RJ can be envisaged as multiple dialogical practices that help to deconstruct our current understanding of crime, including hate crime, by allowing affected community members to participate in various forms of communication that seek to explore harm, the meaning of identity difference, and to repair damaged inter-personal relationships. By understanding hate-based violence as a continuum of micro, meso, and macro level conflict, all of which at various times intersect, we may *begin* to help reformulate social structures, institutional processes, and social systems by creating localized platforms from which both individual and structural harm can be explored and (partly) resolved (Walters 2014b: chs 4 and 6).

No social paradigm is static. Political, legal, cultural, and economic change becomes possible where those who were once silenced are brought to the fore via practices that give voice to those affected by crime, conflict, and persecution. The internationalization of RJ may be just one way that people affected by hate-based conflicts can challenge its global effects. This is not to suggest that RJ is a panacea. It may, nevertheless, be one way in which we can move towards a more peaceful future.

REFERENCES

Ashworth, Andrew. 2010. *Sentencing and Criminal Justice*, 5th edn. Cambridge: Cambridge University Press.

Baker, Estella and Roberts, Julian B. 2005. 'Globalization and the New Punitiveness'. In *The New Punitiveness: Current Trends, Theories and Perspectives*, edited by John Pratt, David Brown, Mark Brown, Simon Hallsworth, and Wayne Morrison, pp. 121–38, Cullompton: Willan Publishing.

Braithwaite, John. 1989. *Crime, Shame, and Reintegration*, Cambridge: Cambridge University Press.

Braithwaite, John. 1999. 'Restorative Justice: Assessing Optimistic and Pessimistic Accounts'. *Crime and Justice: A Review of Research*, 25: pp. 1–127.

Braithwaite, John. 2003. 'Restorative Justice and Social Justice'. In *Restorative Justice: Critical Issues*, edited by Eugene McLaughlin, Ross Fergusson, Gordon Hughes, and Louise Westmorland, pp. 157–63, London: Sage.

Christie, Nils. 1977. 'Conflicts as Property'. *British Journal of Criminology*, 17(1): pp. 1–15.

Christie, Nils. 2000. *Crime Control as Industry*, 3rd edn. London: Routledge.

Coates, Robert B., Umbreit, Mark S., and Vos, Betty. 2006. 'Responding to Hate Crimes through Restorative Justice Dialogue'. In *Contemporary Justice Review: Issues in Criminal, Social, and Restorative Justice*, 9(1): pp. 7–21.

Community Security Trust. 2015. *Antisemitic Incidents Report 2014*, Community Security Trust: London.

Consedine, Jim. 1995. *Restorative Justice: Healing the Effects of Crime*, New Zealand: Ploughshares Books.

Cunneen, Chris. 2008. 'Exploring the Relationship between Reparations, the Gross Violation of Human Rights, and Restorative Justice'. In *Handbook of Restorative Justice: a Global Perspective*, edited by Dennis Sullivan and Larry Tifft, pp. 355–68, London: Routledge.

Cunneen, Chris. 2012. 'Restorative Justice, Globalization and the Logic of Empire'. In *Borders and Crime: Pre-Crime, Mobility and Serious Harm in an Age of Globalization*, edited by Sharon Pickering and Jude McCulloch, pp. 99–113, New York: Palgrave Macmillan.

Cunneen, Chris and Hoyle, Carolyn. 2010. *Debating Restorative Justice*, Oxford: Hart Publishing.

Daly, Erin. 2002. 'Transformative Justice: Charting a Path to Reconciliation'. *International Legal Perspectives*, 12(1&2): pp. 73–183.

Directive 2012/29/EU of the European Parliament and of the Council of 25 October 2012– establishing minimum standards on the rights, support and protection of victims of crime, and replacing Council Framework Decision 2001/220/JHA.

Doob, Anthony N. and Webster, Cheryl M. 2003. 'Sentence Severity and Crime: Accepting the Null Hypothesis'. *Crime and Justice*, 30: pp. 143–95.

Fekete, Liz. 2009. *A Suitable Enemy: Racism, Migration and Islamophobia in Europe*, London: Pluto Press.

Findlay, Mark J. 2008. *Governing through Globalized Crime: Futures for International Criminal Justice*, Cullompton: Willan Publishing.

FRA (European Union Agency for Fundamental Rights). 2012a. *Discrimination and hate crime against Jews in EU Member States: Experiences and perceptions of anti-Semitism*, FRA.

FRA (European Union Agency for Fundamental Rights). 2012b. *Making hate crime visible in the European Union: Acknowledging victims' rights*, FRA.

FRA (European Union Agency for Fundamental Rights). 2013a. *Racism, discrimination, intolerance and extremism: Learning from experiences in Greece and Hungary*, FRA.

FRA (European Union Agency for Fundamental Rights). 2013b. *Fundamental Rights Conference 2013 'Combating hate crime in the EU': Conference conclusions*, FRA.

FRA (European Union Agency for Fundamental Rights). 2015. *Antisemitism: Overview of data available in the European Union 2004–2014*, FRA.

Garland, David. 1996. 'The Limits of the Sovereign State: Strategies of Crime Control in Contemporary Society'. *British Journal of Criminology*, 36(4): pp. 445–71.

Garland, David. 2001, *The Culture of Control*, Oxford: Oxford University Press.

Gavrielides, Theo. 2012. 'Contextualising Restorative Justice for Hate Crime'. *Journal of Interpersonal Violence*, 27(18): pp. 3624–3643.

Goodall, Kay. 2013. 'Conceptualising "Racism" in Criminal Law'. *Legal Studies*, 33(2): pp. 215–38.

Harris, Nathan, Walgrave, Lode, and Braithwaite, John. 2004. 'Emotional Dynamics of Restorative Conferences'. *Theoretical Criminology*, 8(2): pp. 191–210.

Home Office, Office for National Statistics, and Ministry of Justice 2013. *An Overview of Hate Crime in England and Wales*, London: Home Office, Office for National Statistics, and Ministry of Justice.

Iganski, Paul and Lagou, Spiridoula. 2015. 'Hate Crimes Hurt Some More Than Others: Implications for the Just Sentencing of Offenders'. *Journal of Interpersonal Violence*, 30(10): pp. 1696–718.

Jacobs, James B. and Potter, Kimberly. 1998. *Hate Crimes: Criminal Law & Identity Politics*, New York: Oxford University Press.

Lawrence, Frederick M. 1999. *Punishing Hate: Bias Crimes under American Law*, Cambridge, MA: Harvard University Press.

Lin, Olivia. 2005. 'Demythologizing Restorative Justice: South Africa's Truth and Reconciliation Commission and Rwanda's Gacaca Courts in Context'. *ILSA Journal of International & Comparative Law*, 12: pp. 41–85.

Marshall, Christopher D. 2006. 'Terrorism, Religious Violence and Restorative Justice'. In *Handbook of Restorative Justice*, edited by Gerry Johnstone and Daniel W. Van Ness, pp. 372–94. Cullompton: Willan Publishing.

McCold, Paul. 2004. 'What is the Role of Community in Restorative Justice Theory and Practice?'. In *Critical Issues in Restorative Justice*, edited by Howard Zehr and Barb Toews, pp. 155–71, Cullompton: Willan Publishing.

McCold, Paul. 2006. 'The Recent History of Restorative Justice: Mediation, Circles, and Conferencing'. In *The Handbook of Restorative Justice: a Global Perspective*, edited by Dennis Sullivan and Larry Tifft, pp. 23–51, London: Routledge.

Muncie, John. 2005. 'The Globalization of Crime Control—the Case of Youth and Juvenile Justice: Neo-liberalism, Policy Convergence and International Conventions'. *Theoretical Criminology*, 9(1): pp. 35–64.

Nikolic-Ristanovic, Vesna. 2008. 'Truth and Reconciliation in Serbia'. In *The Handbook of Restorative Justice: a Global Perspective*, edited by Dennis Sullivan and Larry Tifft, pp. 369–86. London: Routledge.

Office for Democratic Institutions and Human Rights (ODIHR) (2009), *Hate Crime Laws: A Practical Guide*, Warsaw: ODIHR, OSCE.

Pavlich, George. 2004. 'What are the Dangers as well as the Promises of Community Involvement?'. In *Critical Issues in Restorative Justice*, edited by Howard Zehr and Barb Toews, pp. 173–84, Cullompton: Willan Publishing.

Schweppe, Jennifer and Walters, Mark A. 2015. *Hate Crimes: Legislating to Enhance Punishment.* In: Oxford handbooks online. Criminology and criminal justice. Oxford: Oxford University Press.

Staiger, Ines. 2010. 'Restorative Justice Responses to Terrorism'. In *Assisting Victims of Terrorism: towards a European Standard of Justice*, edited by Rianne Letschert, Ines Staiger, and Antony Pemberton, pp. 267–337, London: Springer Science.

Sullivan, Dennis and Tifft, Larry (eds.). 2008. *The Handbook of Restorative Justice: A Global Perspective*, London: Routledge.

Tschudi, Finn. 2008. 'Dealing with Violent Conflicts and Mass Victimisation: a Human Dignity Approach'. In *Restoring Justice after Large-scale Violent Conflicts*, edited by Ivo Aertsen, Jana Arsovska, Holger-C. Rohne, Marta Valinas, and Kris Vanspauwen, pp. 46–69. Cullompton: Willan Publishing.

Varfi, Tzeni, Parmentier, Stephan, and Aertsen, Ivo. (eds.). 2014. *Developing Judicial Training for Restorative Justice: Towards a European Approach*, Final Research Report, (JUST/2011/JPEN/AG/2977), Leuven: European Forum for Restorative Justice.

Vogler, Richard. 2005. *A World View of Criminal Justice*, Aldershot: Ashgate.

Waldorf, Lars. 2008. 'Rwanda's Failing Experiment in Restorative Justice'. In *The Handbook of Restorative Justice: a Global Perspective*, edited by Dennis Sullivan and Larry Tifft, pp. 422–32. London: Routledge.

Walgrave, L. (2002), 'From Community to Dominion: In Search of Social Values for Restorative Justice'. In *Restorative Justice: Theoretical Foundations*, edited by E. Weitekamp and H. Kerner, pp. 71–109. Collumpton: Willan Publishing.

Walters, Mark A. 2014a. 'Conceptualizing "Hostility" for Hate Crime Law: Minding "the Minutiae" when Interpreting Section 28(1)(a) of the Crime and Disorder Act 1998'. *Oxford Journal of Legal Studies*, 34(1): pp. 47–74.

Walters, Mark A. 2014b. *Hate Crime and Restorative Justice: Exploring Causes, Repairing Harms.* Oxford: Oxford University Press.

Walters, Mark A. 2016. 'Readdressing Hate Crime: Synthesizing Law, Punishment and Restorative Justice'. In Thomas Brudholm and Birgitte Johansen (eds.), *Hate, Politics, Law*, Oxford: Oxford University Press, *forthcoming*.

Weitekamp, Elgar G.M., Parmentier, Stephan, Vanspauwen, Kris, Valiñas, Marta, and Gerits, Roel. 2006. 'How to Deal with Mass Victimization and Gross Human Rights Violations: A Restorative Justice Approach'. In *Large-Scale Victimisation as a Potential Source of Terrorist Activities–Importance of Regaining Security in Post-Conflict Societies*, edited by Uwe Ewald and Ksenija Turkovic, pp. 217–41. Amsterdam: IOS Press.

White, Ian. 2003, 'Victim–Combatant Dialogue in Northern Ireland' from *Reconciliation after Violent Conflict*, IDEA, pp. 89–96.

Zehr, Howard. 1990. *Changing Lenses: A New Focus for Crime and Justice*, Scottdale, PA: Herald Press.

CONCLUSION: TOWARDS AN INTERNATIONAL RESPONSE TO HATE CRIME

Jennifer Schweppe and Mark Austin Walters

There remains a lack of consensus internationally as to what hate crime encompasses. Despite this there is a *general* agreement that, as a concept, hate crime refers to criminal incidents that are at least partly motivated by prejudice, bias, bigotry, or identity-based hostility (OSCE 2009). Barbara Perry (2015) recently observed that what is not clear is the extent to which such definitions reflect the global reality of hate. In beginning to investigate Perry's observation, this book has explored first, how globalization has led to the proliferation of different forms of hate crime; and second, whether an international approach to combating hate crime both domestically and globally can be realized.

As we noted in the introduction, there have been a number of recent global events that have had consequences reaching across oceans and between continents. These events have a ripple effect that is fuelled by media coverage, social media platforms, physical travel, and a virtual world that knows few borders. Barbara Perry and Ryan Scrivens illustrated the extent to which the internet has impacted the spread of hate, showing how the World Wide Web is proving a powerful means of constructing hate-based identities, as well as a recruitment tool to radical hate groups. Similarly, Kathryn Benier tracked the manner in which terrorism events can have a global impact in the context of retaliatory incidents. Irene Zempi continued this theme using her empirical research in the United Kingdom to highlight the international reach of Islamophobia, including the manner in which hate crime attacks affect not only the direct geographical community from which a victim comes, but also the worldwide, transnational Muslim community, called the 'ummah'. Paul Iganski and Abe Sweiry's presentation of research on the spatial and psychosocial harms of hate violence also showed that what we know about hate crime in a national context translates on a global scale, giving rise to what they call a major international public health problem.

If we accept that hate crime is an issue that is of global concern, the next question is the extent to which an international response to the phenomenon is possible. In this context, we were repeatedly reminded of Perry's statement that hate crime is 'historically and culturally contingent' (2003: 7). Thus, in searching for an international response to hate crime, and means by which it can be combated globally, a persistent theme throughout the book has been the extent to which we must accept national and regional cultural, legal, and historical differences that, arguably, have a diluting effect on any collective response. This balancing act is simultaneously set against an American-Western European policy domain for hate crime that has dominated international responses to hate crime. This has meant that our current understandings and responses to hate crime have been framed broadly within the dominant neo-liberal philosophy of the West.

In some respects our book perpetuates this approach, as indeed some of our chapters advocate the expansion of a policy domain, originating in the US, where new laws enhancing penalties for hate crime offenders were first established (e.g., Giannasi and Hall). As many of you will no doubt agree, there is much to be said for this approach to hate crime—which has also been adopted by the key international body working to combat hate crime: the Office for Democratic Institutions and Human Rights (ODIHR) situated in Warsaw, Poland (part of the Organization for Security and Co-operation in Europe (OSCE)). One certainly cannot deny the popularity of new laws aimed at preventing hate crime by punishing hate offenders more severely. More debatable, though, is whether this approach is the most *suitable* way of responding to hate crime in jurisdictions within and beyond US/Western Europe.

In response to this, efforts were made by some of our contributors to question the recent developments in international responses to hate crime. The inclusion of work by scholars from outside of the US/Western Europe helped to bring different perspectives to tackling the problem. Both Bengi Bezirgan's and Piotr Godzisz and Dorota Pudzianowska's chapters reminded us of the importance of understanding historical, cultural, religious, and political variations in conceptualizing hate, which bears heavily on the ways in which these societies are willing to tackle the problem. Duncan Breen, Ingrid Lynch, Juan Nel, and Iole Matthews further elaborate on the peculiar and sometimes devastating historical contexts in particular countries, such as the situation in post-Apartheid South Africa, which they examine as a means of explaining specific concerns of transitional communities in the context of hate crime. Garland and Funnell also outline some of the key issues and conundrums that could potentially cause international initiatives to fail. Even in a relatively small group of nation states that are reasonably homogenous, the European Union, they note that there are considerable differences in terms of 'conceptualization, measurement, victim group recognition, types of legal intervention, and forms of crime included within it'. In fact while many commonalities in approaches across jurisdictions can be found (most commonly legislation aimed at tackling racism and racist violence) there remains a lack of agreement as to what other groups should be protected by law, which may (partly) be influenced by a political resistance to being told 'what to do' by the West.

Some of our contributors offered ways in which some of these concerns might be surmounted. For instance, Ruby Axelson provided a sophisticated analysis of how cultural relativism and universalism might be reconciled in the application of international criminal law. Most importantly, Western notions of hate and human rights must be re-understood within (in this case) African notions of identity and justice, if we are to avoid the imposition of colonial understandings of identity-difference and the ways in which prejudice should be addressed by the courts. Similarly, Mark Walters offered an alternative approach to responding to hate that focused on restorative (indigenous) approaches to conflict resolution. Such an approach does not outright reject the criminalization of hate as an international response to hate crime, but replaces neo-liberal punitive narratives with dialogical processes that focus on inclusive communication about identity-difference and harm reparation.

Irrespective of what the international approach to hate crime should be, by far the biggest barrier to developing an effective international legal/policy framework is the attitude of international and supranational organizations to the issue. A number of our contributors highlighted a range of issues in this context. The most prevalent theme was the lack of enforcement mechanisms at an international level. Thus, while policies exist which are in some cases progressive and engaged, the bodies from which they emit have no capacity to enforce the policy, or ensure that states parties adequately transpose the policy at a domestic level (Haynes and Schweppe, Godzisz and Pudzianowska, Mačkić, Axelson, Whine). Brudholm provides an important contribution in this regard. He argues that while hate crimes can be viewed as a human rights *issue*, most inter-personal hate crimes cannot be conceptualized as human rights violations. The vast majority of hate crimes are committed by private citizens (as against by state agents). As such, most international human rights instruments become utterly redundant as they operate to protect citizens' rights in relation to the actions of the state (and in Brudholm's opinion rightly so). This means that those who seek an international framework for hate crime based on human rights may in fact be undermining the development of effective international responses to *most* hate crimes.

A second issue which was highlighted throughout the book related to the lack of engagement amongst international bodies with the issue of hate crime. While some international organizations such as the EU Agency for Fundamental Rights (FRA), the European Commission against Racism and Intolerance (ECRI), the United Nations Committee on the Elimination of Discrimination (UNCERD), and the United Nations Convention on the Rights of Persons with Disabilities (UNCRPD) are conversant in the language of hate crime, at least in the context of their own remit, as discussed by Mike Whine, others have not yet addressed it in any meaningful way. Jasmina Mačkić, for example, notes that while the European Court of Human Rights has addressed the question of violent discrimination in a number of contexts through the mechanism of Article 14, it has not yet fully embraced hate crime as an issue to concern itself with—perhaps for the very reasons put forward by Brudholm.

Further, the silo-driven nature of international discourses on the issue means that whilst there are clear policies on the issue of racist and religious hate crime, there is little or no engagement at an international level with, for example, homophobic or transphobic hate crime (Axelson). This, of course, reflects national concerns regarding the politicization of the issue in the context of characteristics named and protected by such bodies (as noted above). Bezirgan as well as Godzisz and Pudzianowska, for example, speak to engrained attitudes in Turkey and Poland, respectively, which have dictated the exclusionary manner in which hate crime legislation has been drafted, thus further marginalizing certain groups of people.

Finally, the book asks, given the ways the World Wide Web has impacted on the global spread of hate, can a digital response to it be more fully utilized? Indeed, we might ask ourselves whether an almost unregulated internet (Perry and Scrivens) makes it possible to adequately address online hate crime internationally? Chara Bakalis offers suggestions as to how we might tackle hate crime that occurs in the borderless space of the World Wide Web; though she too admits that different cultural and legal norms make achieving this aim a slow and difficult process. Perhaps of greatest challenge to combating cyberhate is the issue of freedom of expression. A number of problems present themselves here. Perhaps the most pertinent two issues are that different countries take starkly divergent approaches to regulating speech (see Pejchal and Brayson), and that the borderless character of the internet means that it is not always possible to trace where an offender expressed his hateful speech. Bakalis notes that the virtual nature of cyberhate means that legislatures (and researchers) need to re-understand hate crimes that occur online in order to reflect the fact that their commission and impacts may be very different to those which occur offline. This means that online regulation will need to take a new approach to hate crime that responds to the differing ways in which it is committed, while also acknowledging that it may have tangibly different emotional, behavioural, community, and global impacts. We see here how globalization (through the internet) may directly change the way we think about and, in turn, respond to vast amounts of hate crime that occur globally.

Given these difficulties, it could be argued that a major barrier to addressing hate crime internationally is the lack of a dedicated organization which, rather than addressing racist or xenophobic crimes as part of its broader body of work, is tasked with addressing hate crime (more broadly conceived) as its sole preoccupation. Such an organization would allow for the multi-faceted approach required to combating hate crime, which would address issues such as recording, reporting, legislative, and non-legislative responses to addressing the phenomenon. Without this the silo-driven approach at an international level will persist, allowing entrenched positions of discrimination against, and marginalization of, minority communities to persist, seen in this book in the cases of Poland (Godzisz and Pudzianowska) and Turkey (Bezirgan). Whilst ODIHR in particular does perform some of these functions, the fact that it can only act in an advisory capacity means that recalcitrant nation states (such as those identified by Haynes and Schweppe) can simply ignore any such advice and recommendations without fear of penalty or international opprobrium. Thus, this proposed international organization would also need clear enforcement powers.

Naturally, the first obstacle to such an initiative would be that states would simply not sign and ratify such an agreement. However, even if they did—in this 'best case scenario'—they would need a common definition of hate crime that can be applied across jurisdictions. How 'global' any agreement on hate crime could be remains to be seen. Many members within the OSCE region are already using ODIHR's definition of hate crime as 'a criminal act motivated by bias towards a certain group'. Yet even this basic definition is fraught with complexities when attempts are made to operationalize hate crime across jurisdictions. In response to these problems, David Brax argues that for a universal model of hate crime to work it must encompass a number of intersecting concepts, some or all of which may apply in any given context. Only when such a model is agreed can we develop a truly international framework of legislation and policy for hate crime.

Whether the application of a universal definition (model) of hate crime is possible depends largely on whether scholars, policy makers, and practitioners can agree on the concepts that underlie the phenomenon. We argue that such a framework is possible, so long as it remains open to a certain degree of flexibility. As to the question of *how* a global society should address the causes and consequences of hate crime, much remains open to debate. Many question marks remain, not least the question of whether the punitive measures advocated by ODIHR and other international bodies are the most effective way of addressing the globalization of hate.

The debates and discourses highlighted in this book are intrinsic to the future development of an international hate studies that moves beyond the parochial analyses currently found within the field. This is not to suggest that the extant literature is without validity: far from it, we have learnt much about the causes and consequences of hate over the past thirty years. Rather, the aim of this book has been to add to the discipline by expanding our lens beyond the conventional US/European approach to theorizing hate. The eighteen chapters that make up this collection are by no means a comprehensive review of the ways in which hate crime is affected by globalization. Much more needs to be done if we are to create a truly inclusive dialogue that reflects the diversity of thinking on this topic. We hope simply that the contributions you have read here help to advance the field of hate studies in a direction that encourages future dialogue and research on the differing ways that hate manifests globally.

REFERENCES

Organization for Security and Co-operation in Europe (OSCE) 2009, *Hate Crime Laws: a Practical Guide*, Warsaw: ODIHR, OSCE.

Perry, B. 2003. 'Where do we go From Here? Researching Hate Crime', *Internet Journal of Criminology* 1–60.

Perry, J. 2015. 'A Shared Global Perspective on Hate Crime?' *Criminal Justice Policy Review* (advance access doi: 10.1177/0887403415601473)

INDEX

abortion 104
Ackland, R. 67
actus reus 278–80
Additional Protocol to the Council of Europe Convention on Cybercrime 217, 226
advocacy groups 177, 184, 207
Africa 5, 259, 315
  see also sexual orientation in Africa: state-sponsored hatred and persecution
African Charter on Human and Peoples' Rights 260, 287
African Commission on Human and People's Rights: Resolution on Protection against Violence and Violations against Persons on the Basis of their Real or Imputed Sexual Orientation or Gender Identity 287
age 23, 25, 123, 149, 180–2
Alevi people 149
Allen, C. 84
alternative subcultures 23, 25, 175
Alvi, S. 121
Amnesty International 136–7
Amsterdam, Treaty of 19
ancestry *see* national origin/ancestry
anonymity 270–2
anti-Arab crimes 81, 85
Anti-Defamation League (ADL) 272
  Cyber-Safety Action Guide 274
antisemitism 2, 22, 27, 98–9, 254–5
  cyberhate 268
  Europe 15, 213, 217, 221, 223, 224, 225, 227
  global 5
  Ireland 162, 165, 167
  Poland 177
  South Africa 131
  Turkey 145
Apartheid 127, 252, 254, 259, 303–4
Arab Anti-Discrimination Committee 81
Arendt, H. 33
argumentum ad necessarium 37
Asquith, N. 25
assimilation 170
asylum seekers 240, 244
Australia 1, 2, 5, 16, 23, 70, 85–9
  Arabic Council 82
  Cronulla race riots (2005) 87
  global terrorism database 86
  international variations in legislation 25–6
  Islamophobia Register Australia 88–9, 90
  Law Enforcement Assistant Program (LEAP) database 86
  relationship between terrorism and hate crime 87–8
  right-wing extremism 69
  Sydney terrorist attack (2014) 15, 88–9, 90
  terrorism events and retaliatory hate crime 79, 82, 91
  Victoria Police incident data 85–6
  Victoria Police Prejudice Motivated Crime Strategy 86
  see also terrorism events globally and retaliatory hate crime
Austria 217
Axelson, R. 10, 315

Bahrain 120
Bakalis, C. 10, 317
Bali bombings (2002) 84–5
Balicki, S.S. 147
behaviour impacts 102
Belgium 21, 99, 100, 215
  banning of niqab 116
  Brussels attack (2014) 96
  Stop Hate website 272
Benier, K. 7, 314
Bezirgan, B. 8, 315, 316
bias-motivated crimes 22, 34, 41, 45, 54, 58–60, 265
  Poland 175, 182
  see also hate crime
Biedron, R. 177n
bisexuals 175n, 177, 221
  see also Lesbian, Gay, Bisexual, Transgender (LGBT)
Bjørgo, T. 5
Black, D. 67
Bleich, E. 204
Boomgaarden, H.G. 90
Boraine, Dr. A. 305
Bosnia & Herzegovina 21, 22, 100, 104, 297
Bowling, B. 118
Braithwaite, J. 299, 302
Brax, D. 6, 317
Brayson, K. 10
Brazil 15

Breen, D. 8, 315
Brennan, F. 269
Brudholm, T. 6, 316
Byrd, J. Jr. 184n

Cahn, C. 238
Çali, B. 240
Cameroon 278
Campaign Against Antisemitism 99
Canada 1, 5, 21, 161
    cyberhate 266–7
    freedom of expression v public order 251
    international variations in legislation 25
    politics of justice 27
    right-wing extremism 69
    Unit 14 67
Card, C. 36n
Carr, J. 114
Central and Eastern Europe (CEE) 5, 174, 177,
    215, 238
Centre for Information and Documentation
    (CIDI) (Netherlands) 215
Chakraborti, N. 18, 25, 51n, 112, 113
Charter of Fundamental Rights of the
    European Union 19, 213, 226
citizenship 143, 256
Citron, D.K. 269
civil society organizations (CSOs) 105,
    135, 274
    Europe 215, 217, 222, 226
    Ireland 158, 159–61, 163, 165, 166
    Poland 175, 176, 186
    South Africa 126, 129, 131, 132, 134,
        135–6, 137
    Turkey 142, 147
    United Kingdom 204
classical democratic model 258
Coates, R.B. 308
Coliandris, G. 271
collective action 105
collective identity 66–7, 68–9, 70, 72–4,
    122, 268
collective impacts 121–3
collective self/collective other 70
collective solidarity enhancement 80
Colombia 5
colonialism 127, 252, 281
colour-blindness 203
Combat 18 73–4
community, concept of 299–302
community resilience-building 105
Community Security Trust (CST) 99
consciousness-raising campaigns 257

constitutional model (European Court of
    Human Rights) 241
Copsey, N. 111
Cotterrell, R. 206
Council of Europe (CoE) 123, 162, 191, 216,
    218, 223, 227, 234, 238–9, 241, 244,
    297–8, 302
    Committee of Ministers 19
    Convention on Cybercrime (Additional
        Protocol) 217, 226, 273, 275
    defining hate crime 32
    Young People Combating Hate Speech
        Online campaign 272
crimes against humanity 19, 35–6, 104, 147,
    181, 216, 277, 288
    see also genocide
criminal damage 198
criminality 133
criminalization 152, 264, 273, 279
Crisafi, A. 66
Croatia 21, 22, 104
culpability 58, 62
cultural difference 70
cultural identity 17
cultural and legal traditions,
        differing 270, 272
cultural racism 113–14, 120
cultural relativism 279–82
cultural rights 146–7
cumulative impact 17
Cunneen, C. 305, 310
cyberhate: online hate speech 1, 2, 66,
    263–75, 317
    anonymity 270–2
    bias motivation 265
    criminalization 264, 273
    cultural and legal traditions,
        differing 270, 272
    current international response 273–4
    cyber harassment 268–9
    dignity, undermining 266
    equality concept 269, 273, 274
    Europe 224
    freedom of expression 264, 266, 270, 273
    freedom of the press 267
    free speech 264, 267, 269–70, 271, 272, 273, 274
    gender issues 269
    globalization/global nature of 269–70,
        274, 572
    harm 264–6, 268
    incitement to hate crime 226
    informal techniques, continuation and
        intensification of 272

Internet Protocol (IP) 270-1
Internet Service Providers (ISPs) 270-1,
    272, 273-4
issues of principle 264-9
jurisdiction 270
monitoring systems 160
non-discrimination 273
online discussion forums and comments
    sections 263
personal/impersonal distinction 265-8
policing 271
privacy rights 272
Problem-Oriented Policing (POP) 271
public order, damage to 265
public and private discourse
    distinction 265-7
public security, threat to 266
social networking sites 263
surveillance, unlimited and
    indiscriminate 272
technical and practical issues 269-72
wrongfulness 264
cybermedia see cyberhate: online hate speech
Czech Republic 24n

Dack, J. 111
Dalberg, J.E.E. (Lord Acton) 256
Data in Focus report 217
Delgado, T. 253
Deloughery, K. 83-4
democracy 146, 258-9
Denmark 2, 15, 24n, 306
    Copenhagen murders (2015) 84, 96-7
    Female Genital Mutilation 254-5
    terrorism events and retaliatory hate
        crime 82, 84, 90
de Vreese, C.H. 90
difference 18, 27, 149, 152
    cultural 70
    gender 70, 82
    see also Other; Othering; Otherness
differing understandings and protected
    characteristics 232
dignitarian conception 39-41, 42-4, 45
disability 24-6, 55n, 97n, 131, 175, 180,
    182-3, 198
    discrimination 15, 23, 24, 27, 86, 111, 149, 151,
        191, 199, 218, 263
    monitoring and reporting 185, 196-7
    prevention of discrimination 19
    protected category 23, 150, 219, 226
    protection from victimization 19, 181
    sentence enhancement 25-6

discrimination 26, 34, 55-6, 60-1, 85, 213, 273
    Europe 213, 217, 224, 234
    institutionalized 130
    South Africa 126, 127, 131
    Turkey 146-7, 151
discriminatory selection model 54n, 55, 60
Drink, H. 147

Echebarria-Echabe, A. 85
education to combat hate crime 105, 257
egalitarian democratic model 258-9
Egypt 120
electronic media 215
    see also cyberhate: online hate speech
emotional and psychological
    consequences 102-4, 136, 242
emotional terrorism 121
enforcement mechanisms, lack of 316
equality, principle of 60, 126, 253, 269, 273,
    274, 287
ethnic cleansing 104
    see also crimes against humanity; genocide
        Holocaust
ethnic groups 60, 61
ethnic identity 17, 100
    Turkey 143, 149, 151-2
ethnicity/ethnic origin 19, 55, 97n, 263, 279
    differing understandings and protected
        characteristics 22, 23
    Europe 216, 219, 220
    international variations in
        legislation 24, 25, 26
    Ireland 159
    Poland 178-9, 184, 185
    politics of justice 27
    South Africa 127
    Turkey 145-6, 151
    United Kingdom 115, 123, 191
ethnic minorities 55
    Poland 175, 184
    South Africa 128
    Turkey 146, 148, 150, 153
ethnocentrism 152
Europe 1-5, 15, 16, 17, 71, 116, 213-28, 298, 315
    conditionality 177
    cyberhate 275
    expression - 'symbolic' crimes 56
    intergovernmental agencies 223
    international variations in legislation 26
    inter-regional agencies 214
    monitoring policies 20-2, 216-18
    nationalism 68
    police services 217, 225

Europe (*cont.*)
    spatial impact of hate violence 98, 99
    terrorism events and retaliatory hate
        crime 79, 82, 84, 86, 91, 96–7
    white supremacy 76
    see also Central and Eastern Europe;
        European Union
European Commission 147, 162, 216, 218
European Commission against Racism and
        Intolerance (ECRI) 8, 161, 164,
        184–5, 223–4, 316
European Convention on Human Rights
        (ECHR) 27, 213, 215, 286
    Article 2 (right to life) 233, 236, 241–2, 244
    Article 3 (prohibition of torture) 31, 234,
        235, 236, 238, 241–2, 244
    Article 8 (right to private life) 239
    Article 9 (freedom of thought, conscience
        and religion) 236–7
    Article 10 (freedom of expression) 259–60,
        264, 270
    Article 13 (right to an effective remedy) 236
    Article 14 (prohibition against
        discrimination) 18, 31, 235–7, 241–2,
        244, 316
European Court of Human Rights
        (ECtHR) 18, 31, 32, 38, 215, 218,
        233–44, 316
    *Abdulaziz, Cabales and Balkandali v United
        Kingdom* (1985) 242
    Anguelova v Bulgaria (2002) 233–4
    Antayev and Others v Russia (2014) 239–40
    Assanidze v Georgia (2004) 237
    deliberation 42
    dignitarian conception 40–1
    Dudgeon v United Kingdom (1981) 234
    Hoffmann v Austria (1993) 242
    Identoba and Others v Georgia (2015) 32,
        40–1, 42, 234, 235
    Karaahmed v Bulgaria (2015) 236–7
    McCann and Others v United Kingdom
        (1995) 241
    Moldovan and Others v Romania (No 2)
        (2005) 238
    Nachova and Others v Bulgaria (2005) 18,
        216, 234, 235, 239
    Orsus and Others v Croatia (2010) 242
    reluctance in addressing complaints 235–7
    Sidiropoulos and Others v Greece (1998) 239
    Soering v United Kingdom (1989) 241
    Stoica v Romania (2008) 31, 235
    universally recognized as impermissible
        under international law 286

Europeanization 175, 177
European Network Against Racism 165, 215
European Social Survey 90
European Union 27, 51, 53n, 82, 184, 191, 204,
        226, 239, 268
    integration process 143, 146–8, 153
European Union Agency for Fundamental
        Rights (FRA) 15, 20, 32, 152, 185,
        216–18, 220–4, 226–7, 258n, 316
    Annual Report (2011) 220
    cyberhate 268, 274
    *Fundamental Rights: Challenges and
        Achievements in 2013* 225
    international law 298
    psychosocial impact 103
    spatial impact 99–100
European Union Framework Decision
        on Combating Racism
        Xenophobia 19, 54, 162, 164, 216–18,
        224–8, 273–4, 297
*European Union Minorities and
        Discrimination Survey*
        (EU-MIDIS) 221
European Union Monitoring Centre on
        Racism and Xenophobia (EUMC)
        RAXEN network 220

family responsibility 23, 25
far-right extremism 15, 22
fascism 22
fear 59, 102, 112, 121, 256
Feldman, M. 84, 89, 111
Female Genital Mutilation 254–5
Fernández-Guede, E. 85
Finland 20, 82, 84–5, 221
Foley, J. 100
former Yugoslavia 250
Framework Decision on Combating Racism
        Xenophobia (European Union) 19,
        54, 162, 164, 216–18, 224–8, 273–4, 297
France 24n, 204
    antisemitism 15, 98
    banning of niqab 116
    Charlie Hebdo massacre (2015) 2, 84,
        96, 114
    Front National 15
    homophobia 3
    Islamophobia 114, 120
    Ministry of Interior 98
    Paris attacks 2015 2, 99
    spatial impact of hate violence 99, 100
    terrorism events and retaliatory hate
        crime 82

freedom of expression *see* free speech and freedom of expression
freedom of opinion 254, 257
freedom of peaceful assembly and association 254
freedom of the press 267
Freeman, S.M. 176
free speech and freedom of expression 2, 35, 56, 61, 130, 176, 183, 245–61, 264, 266, 267, 269–70, 271, 272, 273, 274, 306, 317
see also Article 10 (freedom of expression) *under* European Convention on Human Rights (ECHR)
Friedrichsen, G. 43
Funnell, C. 6, 315

Gardner, J. 44
Garland, J. 6, 18, 25, 51n, 315
Gavrielides, T. 309
gay marriage 128
gays 2, 177, 221, 281
see also Lesbian, Gay, Bisexual, Transgender (LGBT)
gender 23, 24, 25, 97n, 123, 127, 145, 149, 151, 157, 180–1, 219, 242, 269, 279, 282–5, 288
gender-based violence 132, 239, 268–9
see also sexual assaults; sexual violence
gender identity/expression 23, 24–5, 143, 153, 175, 180–1, 182, 185, 218, 219, 281
genocide 19, 25, 35–6, 147, 184, 226, 249, 259
geographic clustering 81, 82
Gerards, J. 240
Germany 21, 99, 184, 185, 204, 217
antisemitism 15
collective identity 73
differing understandings and protected characteristics 22
discrimination 255
freedom of expression v public order 251
international variations in legislation 25
Islamophobia 114, 120
nationalism 68
National Socialist Underground (NSU) 43
terrorism events and retaliatory hate crime 90
white supremacy 77
Giannasi, P. 9
Githens-Mazer, J. 119
global events *see* terrorism events globally and retaliatory hate crime

globalization 1–3, 5, 7, 281, 306, 317
cyberhate: online hate speech 269–70, 274, 572
Global Terrorism Database 91
Godzisz, P. 8–9, 315, 316
Goebbels, J. 43
Golden Dawn (Greece) 15, 68–9, 70, 72, 75
Goodall, K. 297
Good, A.N.M. 132
Goodwill Zwelithini, King 130, 132
Grattet, R. 52, 55n
Greece 21, 82, 84, 120
Golden Dawn 15, 68–9, 70, 72, 75
Greer, S. 241
Griffin, J. 41
group identity 35, 98, 103, 122
Grumke, T. 73

Habermas, J. 44
Hall, N. 5, 9, 33, 203
Hammerberg, T. 227
Hamm, M. 4
Hanes, E. 84
harassment 115, 116, 198, 224
Hardy, S. 18
harm, causing 58–9, 264–5, 268
hate crime
conceptions of 34–5, 49–50, 52–7, 62–3, 142
discrimination 55–6
effect 56–7
expression - 'symbolic' crimes 56
intention 54–5, 57
motive 54, 57
international definitions 15–27
differing understandings and associated protected characteristics 22–3
human rights framework 18–20
legislation: international variations 23–6
monitoring levels of hate crime 20–2
'politics of justice' framework 26–7
theoretical conceptualizations 16–18
see also bias-motivated crimes
hate incidents 2, 99, 200, 222, 247, 298, 300, 305, 308
see also terrorism events globally and ensuing hate incidents
hate propaganda 25
hate speech 2, 3, 35, 126, 129–30, 131, 132, 157, 176, 178–9, 181, 182, 247–61, 277
civil-political generation of hate speech (direct incitement to genocide and war crimes) 248, 249–50, 256–7, 259–60

hate speech (*cont.*)
  collective-developmental generation
      of hate speech (incitement to
      discrimination and attacks on
      human dignity) 248, 253–60
  criminalization 279
  Europe 224
  freedom of expression 247–50,
      251–3, 255–60
  free speech 247–51, 256, 258–61
  'generations' of hate speech 248–9
  socio-economic generation of hate speech
      (direct incitement to violence and
      endangering public order) 248,
      251–3, 254, 256–7, 259–60
  South Africa 126, 129–30, 131, 132
  'symbolic' crimes 56
  see also cyberhate: online hate speech
Haynes, A. 8, 114
health sector 23, 105
Hess, R. 255
heterosexism 145
heterosexuality 17
Heyns, C. 259–60
hijab/banning of hijab 82, 88, 111
Hindus 82
HIV-infected persons 182, 240
Hodkinson, P. 18
Holocaust 191, 226
homelessness 23, 25, 182
homophobia 17, 32, 316
  Europe 224
  France 3
  Ireland 160, 162, 165, 167
  Poland 175–8
  Russia 3, 15, 20, 240, 244
  Turkey 152
  Uganda 3
homosexuality 128, 176, 240
  criminalization 278, 280
  see also homophobia
hostility of hatred 213
human dignity 105, 256, 258, 260, 266, 287
humanitarian crises 3, 101, 131
human rights 18–20, 31–46, 126, 128, 146, 147,
      149, 159, 179, 180–1, 204, 205–6, 214,
      215, 217, 226, 288, 315, 316
  advocacy 287
  deliberation 41–4
  dignitarian conception 39–41
  framework 18–20
  organizations 186
  politics of justice 27

  power-regulative conception 38–9
  treaties 285–6, 289
  tribunals 278
  universalism, cultural relativism and
      postcolonialism 280, 281–2
  universally recognized as impermissible
      under international law 286
  violations 37–8, 303, 306
  see also European Convention on Human
      Rights (ECHR); European Court
      of Human Rights (ECtHR);
      international human rights;
      Office for Democratic Institutions
      and Human Rights (ODIHR);
      Universal Declaration of
      Human Rights
Human Rights Committee (HRC) 32, 181,
      184, 250–2, 284, 286
  General Comment No.34 256
Human Rights First 32, 136
Human Rights Watch 32, 101, 136
human trafficking 2, 239

identity 17, 24, 70, 127
  building 72–4
  collective 35, 66–7, 68, 70, 72–4
  cultural 17
  ethnic 17, 100, 143, 149, 151–2
  multicultural 193
  politics 19, 26–7, 175, 177, 184
  religious 17, 100, 143, 306
  sexual 17, 97n, 146, 149
  social 102–3
  transgender 263
  see also gender identity/expression; national
      identity
ideology, politics of 238–9
Iganski, P. 5, 7, 58, 314
immigration/anti-immigration 3, 71, 84–5,
      90–1, 193, 215, 259
incitement of hatred 199
incitement to racial discrimination 255
India, Hundu Jat and Muslim communal
      violence (2013) 101–2
individual justice model (European Court of
      Human Rights) 241
inhuman or degrading treatment 41, 42
  see also torture
institutional racism 184n
  see also Stephen Lawrence Inquiry/
      Macpherson Report
integration programmes 257
intentions 54–5, 57, 59–60

Inter-American Commission on Human
Rights 286
Inter-American Convention on Human
Rights 259
Inter-American Court of Human
Rights 38, 286
interconnectedness of societies 1, 114
intergovernmental agencies 223, 226
International Criminal Court
(ICC) 280–1, 283–7
International Criminal Tribunal for Former
Yugoslavia (ICTY) 250
International Criminal Tribunal for Rwanda
(ICTR) 249–50, 282
Appeals Chamber 279
internationalization of crime control 295–6
International Law Commission (ILC) 285
international law and hate crime 297–8
International Lesbian, Gay, Bisexual,
Trans and Intersex Association
(ILGA) 23, 215
International Military Tribunal (IMT) 279
International Network against Cyberhate
(INACH) 274
International Network for Hate Studies
(INHS) 4
Internet see World Wide Web
inter-regional agencies 214
intimidation 115
intolerance 162, 223, 242
Iraq 2, 80
Yazidi ethnic and religious minority 100–1
Ireland 21, 32, 157–71, 306–7
An Garda Síochána (police service) 158,
165, 167
conflict between official and Central
Statistics Office (CSO) data 165–6
Garda (Police) Inspectorate 160, 165–6
Report Crime Investigation 167
impact on victims and their
communities 169–70
investigation and prosecution 168
legal position 158–60
recording and monitoring 167
response of the state 163–5
sentencing 168–9
Sentencing Information System 160
Islamic State (IS/Isis/Isil) 2, 80, 100–1
Islamization 2, 306
Islamophobia 2, 254–5, 259, 314
Europe 227
hijab (headscarf)/banning of hijab 82,
88, 111

niqab (face covering)/banning of niqab 82,
112–14, 116, 119–20, 122–3
restorative justice 307, 308
South Africa 131
terrorism events and retaliatory hate
crime 81, 82
see also Islamophobia against veiled Muslim
women (United Kingdom)
Islamophobia against veiled Muslim women
(United Kingdom) 1, 5, 20, 111–23,
133, 217, 221, 242–3, 314
collective impacts 121–3
confidence and self-esteem issues 117, 123
emotional, psychological, behavioural,
physical and financial effects 117, 123
fear and anxiety 118–19
individual impacts 117–21
long-term impacts 117
methodology 112–13
personal experiences 113–17
physical markers of 'Muslimness'
(hijab, niqab) 82, 88, 111–14, 116,
119–20, 122–3
spatial impact of hate violence 98–9
vulnerability 112, 119, 121, 123
Israel 5, 27, 68, 99
Tel Aviv University Kantor Centre
antisemitism Worldwide report
(2014) 99
see also Israeli–Palestine conflict
Israeli–Palestine conflict 2, 15, 80, 99,
306, 307n
Italy 21, 82, 99, 120

Jacobson, J. 122
Jeffery, J. 135
Jenness, V. 52, 55n
Jews 68, 81, 82, 96, 98, 100, 252
Europe 222
South Africa 127–8
see also antisemitism; Holocaust
Johannes, I. 133
judicial cooperation on criminal matters 218
jus cogens obligations 248
Justice and Home Affairs Council 224, 226
Council Conclusion on Combating Hate
Crime 226

Kaplan, J. 4–5
Kato, D. 278
Kelly, R. 5
Kenya 281
King, R.D. 83

Kurds 147, 149, 234
Kuwait 120

Lambert, R. 119
Langman, L. 65–6
language 23, 25, 123, 221
    Turkey 146, 147, 149, 151
La Rue, F. 257
Latvia 103
    Centre for Human Rights 97–8
Lausanne Treaty (1923) 144, 146, 151
law enforcement agencies *see* police services
Lawrence, D. (Baroness Lawrence of
        Clarendon) 197
Lawrence, F. 54–5, 58, 242
Legewie, J. 84–5
legislation, international variations 23–6
Lesbian, Gay, Bisexual, Transgender
        (LGBT) 5, 23
    Europe 221, 222, 234
    Poland 180
    rights groups 3
    South Africa 126–7, 129, 131–5, 136–8
lesbians 2, 133, 221, 281
Levin, J. 5, 88, 97n
Lieberman, M. 176
Lilith88 76
Lin, O. 305
Lisbon Treaty 19
Littler, M. 84, 89, 111
Luxembourg 82
Lynch, I. 8, 315

Macedonia 297
Machin, S. 84
Mackic, J. 9–10, 316
Macpherson definition 167
Macpherson Report (1999) 21, 24, 184n, 194
macro-level responses to state-sponsored
        hate 302–5
Maghan, J. 5
Makau, D. 134
Makhutle, T. 133
Malawi 128
Malema, J. 130
Mandaville, P. 122
marginalization 52, 127, 142–3
margin of appreciation 241–2
Mason, G. 17, 24, 26–7, 152–3, 176
mass murder 178
    see also crimes against humanity; genocide
mass rapes 104
Matthews, I. 8, 315

Mauritania 277n, 278
media coverage 84, 89–90, 306
media incitement 101
Mendel, R. 253
mens rea 55, 59
mental health impacts *see* emotional and
        psychological consequences
'message crimes' 61–2, 105, 122
Middle East 80
Mill, J.S. 264
minorities
    national 219
    sexual 127, 153, 180
    see also ethnic minorities
mobilizing hate 274–6
mob justice 278
monitoring levels of hate crime 20–2, 41,
        53, 57, 62, 129, 135–6, 137, 160, 185,
        239, 286
    see also recording hate crime
moral foundations 58–63
    bad characters 62
    bad intentions 59–60
    bad motives 60
    discrimination 60–1
    harm 58–9
    'message crimes' 61–2
    vulnerable/disadvantaged victims 61
motives 54, 55, 57, 60
multiculturalism 69, 70, 184, 193
Munthe, C. 31
Muslimness: physical markers (hijab,
        niqab) 82, 88, 111–14, 116,
        119–20, 122–3
Muslims 81, 82, 222
    see also Islamophobia
Myanmar 101

Nagel, T. 43
national identity 122, 143, 177
nationalism 68
nationality 97n, 127, 149, 151, 159, 178–9, 279
national origin/ancestry 19, 23, 24, 25, 55,
        152, 159
National Point of Contact (NPC) on hate
        crime 223
Nazi mass atrocities 36
neighbourhood theory 81
Nel, J. 8, 315
neo-Nazism 4, 22, 224
Netherlands 15, 20, 215, 221, 252
    terrorism events and retaliatory hate
        crime 82, 84, 90

New Zealand 1, 5, 16, 23, 86
Nhamuave, E. 135
Nielsen, J.S. 84
Nigeria 277n, 278
niqab 82, 111–14, 122–3
  banning 116, 119–20
Nkonyana, Z. 133, 134
Noble, G. 82, 121
'no go' areas 98, 121, 123
Nogwaza, N. 137
non-discrimination 19, 280, 287
  see also Committee on the Elimination of
    Racial Discrimination (CERD);
    Article 14 (prohibition against
    discrimination) under European
    Convention on Human Rights
    (ECHR); International Convention
    on the Elimination of All Forms of
    Racial Discrimination (ECERD)
non-governmental organizations (NGOs) 4,
    50, 215, 223, 257
  Europe 215, 223
  Poland 180, 183, 185, 186
  South Africa 129, 131, 133, 134
  Turkey 148
  United Kingdom 205
non-nationals: South Africa 126–7, 128, 129,
    131–5, 136, 138
Nordic states 217
normative considerations 50–2, 57
Northern Ireland 129, 194
  Criminal Justice Inspectorate 128
Norway 255
Nuremberg Charter 279
Nuremberg Trials 303n

objective aspects of crime 58
O'Dwyer, C. 177
Office for Democratic Institutions and
    Human Rights (ODIHR) 16, 27, 32,
    162–3, 185, 222–3, 315, 317–18
  Annual Report (2012) 222
  cyberhate 273
  differing understandings and protected
    characteristics 22
  discrimination 258n
  Hate Crime Data-Collection and Monitoring
    Mechanisms 224–5
  monitoring levels of hate crime 20
  punishment enhancers 296–7
Oikawa, M. 76
Olsson, P. 31, 41, 267–8
Oman 120

O'Neil, M. 67
O'Nions, H. 240
online hate crime see cyberhate: online
    hate speech
Oosterveld, V. 283
oppression 26, 52, 192
'ordinary' hate crimes 38, 39, 45
Organization for Security and Co-operation
    in Europe (OSCE) 16, 32n, 51, 162,
    164, 190, 194, 213, 222–3, 315
  differing understandings and protected
    characteristics 22
  international variations in legislation 24
  Ministerial Decision 9/09 20, 163
  Ministerial Decision (2003) 227
  politics of justice 27
  punishment enhancers 297
  recorded and prosecuted hate crimes 21
  report (2014) 214
  Turkish integration 150, 151
  see also Office for Democratic Institutions
    and Human Rights (ODIHR)
organized crime 2, 239
Other 81, 90, 128, 177, 281, 307, 310
  denigration of 72
  white supremacy 66–7, 70
Othering 17, 278
Otherness 116, 127, 177

Packer, H. 271
paedophiles 26
Palestine see Israeli–Palestine conflict
Palmar, S. 258
Partsch, K. 250
passive condoning of hostility 192
patriarchy and heterosexual
    dominance 284, 288
Pawlocicz, K. 177
Pejchal, V. 10
Pentassuglia, G. 239
perception-based recording 195
Perry, B. 5, 6–7, 17–18, 31, 41, 66, 88, 121, 122,
    142, 157, 206, 267–8, 314
personal appearance 23, 25
petitio principii 37
philosophical beliefs 151
physical assaults/violence/injury 82, 102, 104,
    114, 132
  see also sexual assault; sexual violence
Pickles, E. 99
Pierce, W. 68
Pieta, S. 183
plea bargaining 195–6

Poland 75, 180–2, 183, 185, 316–17
  differing understandings and protected
      characteristics 23
  Lesbian, Gay, Bisexual (LGB) 174–86
    Alliance of Democratic Left party
        (SLD): draft amendment 383/
        2357 180–1, 183
    Campaign against Homophobia (KPH)
        2005 180
    Catholic Church 177
    Civic Platform party (PO): draft
        amendment 1078 183
    Criminal Code (CC) 178, 179, 180–3
    Equality Parade (Warsaw)
        2013 177–8, 180n
    Law and Justice Party (Pis) 177, 181
    legislation for hate crimes 178–83
    model of understanding hate
        crime 183–5
    political homophobia 176–8
    protection, categories of 175–6
    Your Movement party (TR): draft
        amendment 340 180–1, 183
  terrorism events and retaliatory hate
      crime 84
police services 52, 215, 226, 271
  hate crimes committed by 36
    see also secondary victimization
  response to terrorism events and retaliatory
      hate crime 80
    see also policing hate crime under United
        Kingdom
political beliefs/views 23, 133, 151, 279
politics of identity 238–9
politics of ideology 238–9
'politics of justice' framework 26–7
populism 215
Portugal 82, 84
postcolonialism 277, 280–2, 288
post-traumatic stress disorder/
      symptoms 103–4
post-victimization 102–3, 105
Pound, R. 206
power-regulative conception 38–9, 41–4, 45
Poynting, S. 82, 121
prejudice 22, 34, 54
  see also discrimination
prioritarianism 59
privacy rights 272
Problem-Oriented Policing (POP) 271
prosecution services 21, 195–6, 200, 226
Prosecutors and Hate Crimes Training
      Programme (PAHCT) 225

protected characteristics 34–5
psychosocial impact 102–4, 105
public health approach 104–5
Public Interest Law Alliance (PILA) 166
public order offences 198, 265
public security, threat to 266
Pudzianowska, D. 8–9, 315, 316
punishment enhancement 52, 58, 59, 296–7, 298

Qatar 120
queer rights see Lesbian, Gay, Bisexual,
      Transgender (LGBT)

Rabat Plan of Action (RPA) 257–8
race 19, 22–6, 34, 60, 97n, 279
  Australia 86, 88
  cyberhate 263, 265
  Europe 216, 219, 220
  Ireland 159
  Poland 178–9, 185
  South Africa 127
  Turkey 145, 146, 147, 149, 151, 152
  United Kingdom 111, 115, 123, 191, 194, 200, 201
  see also colour; ethnicity/ethnic origin
racial animus model 54
racial difference 70
racial discrimination 55n, 61, 248, 252
  Europe 213, 223
  see also racism
racial hatred 233
racialization 114
racially aggravated offences 198
racial profiling 162
racial segregation 76
racial superiority 254
racism 4, 16, 18, 67, 82, 115, 116, 127, 145, 147,
      152, 159, 174, 213–17, 220, 223–4, 228,
      240, 242, 273, 316
  cultural 113–14, 120
  institutional 184n
  see also European Commission against
        Racism and Intolerance (ECRI);
        Framework Decision on Racist and
        Xenophobic Crime; xenophobia
racist chanting 199
rape 104
  corrective 278
recording hate crime 20–1, 53, 57, 89, 165–7,
      194–5, 298, 317
  Europe 221, 227
  global terrorism events and retaliatory hate
      crime 89
  under-recording 220

rehabilitative approaches in criminal justice system 62

religion/religious beliefs 18, 19, 55, 55n, 60, 61, 86, 88, 111, 115, 131, 145–7, 149, 151, 152, 159, 178–9, 184, 185, 191, 196, 198, 199, 213, 215, 216, 219, 242, 279, 316
  cyberhate 263, 265
  differing understandings and protected characteristics 22, 23
  and gender and physical appearance, link between 116–17
  international variations in legislation 24, 25, 26
  politics of justice 27
  restorative justice 307
  spatial impact of hate violence 97n

religious freedom 146–7

religious hatred 5, 316

religious hostility/violence 174, 198

religious identity 17, 100, 143, 306

religious intolerance 162, 242

religious minorities 148, 175, 184

Renzo, M. 40

reparation 301

repeat victimization 104, 216, 219

resource-threat theories 85

responsibilization 295

restorative justice (RJ) approach 51n, 294–310, 315–16
  communitarian approaches 302
  community, concept of 299–302
  community police officers 300
  emotional and social support 299
  limitation or expectation 309–10
  macro-level responses to state-sponsored hate 301, 302–5, 310
  macro-meso to micro-, from 308–9
  macro- to meso-, from 305–8
  meso-communities 299–300, 301, 310
  micro-level (inter-personal) crimes/conflict 299, 301, 310
  state, role of 300–1
  welfarist approaches 302

retaliatory hate crime see terrorism events globally and retaliatory hate crime

retributivism 19, 295

rights, law 288, 295, 316

right-wing extremism 22–3, 54, 204, 217
  see also far-right extremism

Roma minority 15, 31, 192, 221, 222, 234, 235, 236–8, 243

Rome Statute 277–9, 281, 283–4, 288–9

Rowbottom, J. 268

Rubenstein, W.B. 81

rule of law 146, 226

Russia 273
  homophobia 3, 15, 20, 240, 244

Rwanda 100, 259
  Hutus and Tutsis 249, 282
  see also International Criminal Tribunal for Rwanda (ICTR)

Sable, S.M. 288

Sadurski, W. 257

safety in numbers 119

Sallah, M. 115, 119, 120

Santoro, Father A. 147

Saudi Arabia 120

Saunders, R.A. 122

Schwartz, K.Z.S. 177

Schweppe, J. 8, 151

Scott-Baumann, A. 120

Scrivens, R. 6–7

secondary victimization (by police and other criminal justice agencies) 133–4, 214, 219, 300

sectarianism 165, 167, 307

segregation 127, 254

self-censorship 170

self-segregation 170

September 11 (2001) 79, 81–2, 89, 91

Serbia 21, 22

sexual assaults 100, 132, 165, 221, 239, 278
  psychosocial impact 103–4

sexual harassment 116

sexual identity 17, 97n, 146, 149

sexuality see sexual orientation

sexual minorities 127, 153, 180

sexual orientation 17, 34, 88, 111, 123, 127, 149, 151–3, 157, 159, 174, 175, 176, 179, 180, 181, 191, 196, 198, 199, 218, 287
  in Africa: state-sponsored hatred and persecution 277–89
  actus reus of persecution 278–80
  colonialism 281
  cultural relativism 279–82
  gender, importance of 282–5
  International Criminal Court (ICC) 280–1, 283–7
  postcolonialism 277, 280–2, 288
  Rome Statute 277–9, 281, 283–4, 288–9
  universalism 277, 280–2
  universally recognized as impermissible under international law 285–8
  cyberhate 263, 265

sexual orientation (*cont.*)
 differing understandings and protected
  characteristics 23
 discrimination 55n
 international variations in
  legislation 24, 25, 26
 politics of justice 27
 spatial impact of hate violence 97n
sexual violence *see* sexual assaults
Sharma, D.P. 89
Shepard, M. 184n
Sigsworth, R. 128
Sikhs 82
Sinti 15, 222
Snow, D. 70
social identity 102–3
social interaction 121
social justice movement 65–6
social media 306
 incitement 101
 see also cyberhate: online hate speech
social networking sites 115, 263
social origin 127, 219
social services sector 61, 105
socio-economic status 23, 123
solidarity 72
Somalia 254–5, 278
South Africa 126–83, 315
 AfriForum 130
 Apartheid 127, 252, 254, 259, 303–4
 colonialism 127
 Constitution 126, 127
 Constitutional Court 131, 304
 criminality 133
 Equality Court 130
 hate crime legislation 129–30
 Hate Crimes Monitoring Project 136
 Hate Crimes Working Group (HCWG) 135–6
  Hate and Bias Crime Monitoring Form
   and User Guide 136, 137
 hate speech and hate crime 126, 129–30,
  131, 132
 Human Rights Commission
  (SAHRC) 129–30, 135
 Iranti-org 136
 Joint Working Group 136
 Lesbian, Gay, Bisexual, Transgender
  (LGBT) 126–7, 129, 131–5, 136–8
 lessons learned 136–7
 monitoring hate crime 135–6
 nation-building and social cohesion
  post-Apartheid 127–9
 non-nationals 126–7, 128, 129, 131–5, 136, 138

 *Policy Framework on Combating
  Hate Crime, Hate Speech and
  Discrimination* 130
 racism 129
 South African Police Services (SAPS) 134
  National Visible Policing Unit 135
 Truth and Reconciliation Commission
  (TRC) 303–5
South America 5
South Asian American Leaders of Tomorrow
 (SAALT) 81–2
South-East Asia 86, 101
Spain 82, 221
 Madrid bombings (2004) 84–5, 86, 91
spatial impact 97–102, 105
spatial impact of hate violence 98, 99
Special Representatives of the Chairman in
 Office 222
state power, abuse of 45
state responsibility 39, 45
state-sponsored hatred and persecution 143,
 301, 302–5, 310
 see also sexual orientation in Africa: state-
  sponsored hatred and persecution
Steenkamp, C.K. 128
Stockholm Programme (2010-14) 226
Stormfront 73, 75
 Activism 74
 Events 74
Straw, J. 195
subjective aspects of crime 58
subsidiarity principle 242
Sudan 277n, 278
suicide bombing 79
Sullivan, A. 242
surveillance, unlimited and
 indiscriminate 272
Sutton, G.M. 83
Swahn, M.H. 82
Sweden 20, 21, 37, 51, 55, 99, 221
 collective identity 73
 cyberhate 273
 Islamophobia 114
 National Council for Crime Prevention 22
 terrorism events and retaliatory hate
  crime 82
Sweiry, A. 7, 314
'symbolic' crimes 56
Syria 2, 100
 Islamic State campaign 80

Tajpan, B. 180
Taylor, C. 43

Taylor, S. 159, 160n
Tell MAMA (Measuring anti-Muslim
        Attacks) 84, 90
terrorism 2, 54, 239
    emotional 121
terrorism events globally and ensuing
        hate incidents 79–92, 96–7, 200
    media, role of in retaliatory hate
        crime 89–90
    psychosocial impact 102–4
    public health problem 104–5
    relationship between terrorism and hate
        crime 80–5
        one incident, global reactions 82–3
        retaliatory hate crime post-2001 83–5
        September 11 (2001) 81–2
    spatial impact of hate violence 97–102
    terrorist impact of hate violence
        globally 96–7
theoretical conceptualizations 16–18
Tokyo Charter 279
tolerance 120
Tolerance and Non Discrimination
        Information System
        (TANDIS) 222–3
torture 38, 41, 184, 278, 284
    see also Article 3 (prohibition of torture)
        under European Convention on
        Human Rights (ECHR)
Torture Special Rapporteur 284
Training against Hate Crimes for Law
        Enforcement (TAHCLE)
        programmes 225
transgender 24, 111, 133, 152, 180, 196–9, 221,
        263, 287
    identity 263
    international variations in legislation 24
    see also Lesbian, Gay, Bisexual,
        Transgender (LGBT);
        transphobia
transnational crime control policies 3
transnationalism 114
    see also 'ummah' (transnational Muslim
        community)
transphobia 165, 167, 224, 316
Travellers (Ireland) 159
Treaty of the European Union 226
Treaty on the Functioning of the European
        Union (TFEU) 213, 218
'trigger events' 2
    see also terrorism events globally and
        ensuing hate incidents
Tulkens, F. 259

Turkey 316–17
    Armenian, Kurdish and Alevi
        communities 149
    cyberhate 273
    Islamophobia 120
    problematization of hate crime
        legislation 142–54
    'Citizen, Speak Turkish!' campaign 144
    Constitution 144
    democratization package 149–50
    European integration process/
        Europeanization 146–8, 153
    ideal citizen, creation of 143–6
    Incident of Reserves 145
    Kurds 147, 149
    legislative response to hate crime
        phenomenon 148–51
    Lesbian, Gay, Bisexual, Transgender
        (LGBT) 144, 148, 150, 151–2
    relationship with Greece over
        Cyprus 145
    selective victimhood 151–3
    Turkification process 144
    Working Group 149
    suppression and mass violence 149
Tutsis and Hutus 249, 282
Tutu, Bishop D. 305

ubuntu 281
Uganda 3, 279, 280, 281, 283
'ummah' (transnational Muslim
        community) 121–3, 314
under-reporting 225
unemployment 85
United Kingdom 98–9, 227, 308, 309
    asylum seekers 240, 244
    Coalition Action Plan (2012) 196
    Coalition Government Action Plan (2012) 23
    College of Policing 22, 23, 111
    Community Security Trust 215
    Crime Survey 97, 202
    Cross-Government Hate Crime
        Programme (previously Race for
        Justice Programme) 197, 199–200
    Crown Prosecution Service (CPS)
        guidance 195, 200
    culture 202–3
    cyberhate 265–6, 273
    defamation law 271–2
    Department for Communities and Local
        Government Citizenship Survey 85
    Director of Public Prosecutions
        guidance 195

United Kingdom (*cont.*)
English Defence League (EDL) 71
governance 197
Hate Crime Action Plan 205
Hate Crime Manual (Association of Chief
        Police Officers) 195, 205
hate incidents 200
Home Secretary's Action Plan
        (1999) 195–6
Home Secretary's Annual Report
        (2000) 195
Independent Advisory Group (IAG) 197,
        200, 205
internationalization of crime
        control 295–6
international variations in legislation 23,
        24, 24n
Labour administration action plan
        (2009) 196
Law Commission 198
legislation 198–9
    enhanced sentencing legislation for any
        offence 199
    positive duty on agencies 199
    racially or religiously aggravated
        offences 198
    specific offences that will always be
        classified as hate crime 199
London bombings (July 2005) 84–5, 86, 91
'Monitored Hate Crime' 197
National Crime Statistics 200
perception-based recording 195
policing hate crime 190–207, 459
    changes 198
    recording hate crimes 21, 195
    Stephen Lawrence Inquiry/
        Macpherson report (1999) 184n,
        193–7, 200–2
    Stephen Lawrence Steering
        Group 197, 199
    Strategy Board 197
    True Vision 204–5
    under-reporting issues 195
policy 199–202
    agreed criminal justice
        definitions 200–2
    hate crimes 200–2
    hate incident 200
    hate motivation 200
    prosecution 202
    transferability to other countries 203–7
        accessible routes for reporting 204
        accuracy of hate crime data 204

inclusive and coordinated
        governance 203
    political leadership 203
    transparency of policy 203
    victim involvement in policy 203
political leadership 196–7
racist element and plea bargaining during
        prosecutions 195–6
Scotland 194, 240
Sophie Lancaster Foundation 25
terrorism events and retaliatory hate
        crime 82, 90, 91
Victim's Fund 205
victim surveys 194
white supremacy 77
see also Islamophobia against veiled Muslim
        women (United Kingdom)
United Nations 43n, 223, 275, 286
    *Basic Principles on the Use of Restorative
        Justice Programs in Criminal Matters*
        (2002) 302
**United Nations Commission for Human
        Rights** 101
**United Nations Committee against Torture
        (CPT)** 181, 286
**United Nations Committee on Economic,
        Social and Cultural Rights
        (CESCR)** 286
**United Nations Committee on the
        Elimination of Racial
        Discrimination (CERD)** 51, 129,
        162, 163–4, 252, 254, 255, 316
**United Nations Convention Against Torture
        (CAT)** 38, 184
**United Nations Convention on the
        Elimination of all Forms of
        Discrimination against Women
        (ICEDAW)** 283–4
**United Nations Convention on the
        Elimination of All Forms of
        Racial Discrimination (ECERD)
        (United Nations)** 162, 191, 214, 252,
        253–4, 273
**United Nations Convention on the
        Prevention and Punishment of the
        Crime of Genocide** 249
**United Nations Convention on the Rights
        of Persons with Disabilities
        (UNCRPD)** 316
**United Nations Covenant on Civil and
        Political Rights (ICCPR)** 162, 179,
        184, 214, 250, 251, 255–6
cyberhate 273

gender, importance of 284
universally recognized as impermissible
under international law 286
**United Nations Educational, Scientific
and Cultural Organization
(UNESCO)** 272
**United Nations General Assembly
(UNGA)** 214
*Basic Principles and Guidelines on the
Right to a Remedy and Reparation
for Victims of Gross Violations
of International Human Rights
Law and Serious Violations of
International Humanitarian
Law* 304
**United Nations High Commissioner for
Refugees (UNHCR)** 214, 284, 287
**United Nations Human Rights Council
(UNHRC)** 137, 138
Universal Periodic Review (UPR)
process 32, 162, 164
United Nations Refugee Agency 136
**United Nations Special Rapporteur on the
Human Rights of Migrants** 129
United States 1, 2, 4, 5, 15, 19, 52, 73, 161,
242, 315
American Association of University
Women survey 268–9
American Border Patrol 71
Charleston African American white
supremacist attack (2015) 15
concepts of hate crime 53
Constitution 258
cyberhate 265–6, 270, 272, 273
FBI 81
Uniform Crime Report 83
First Amendment: right to free
speech 264, 270
internationalization of crime
control 295–6
international variations in
legislation 24–5
Islamophobia 114
John Doe subpoenas 271
Lesbian, Gay, Bisexual, Transgender
(LGBT) and non-nationals 132
Minuteman Project 71
nationalism 68
recorded and prosecuted hate crimes 21
restorative justice 308
Supreme Court 55n, 56, 265
terrorism events and retaliatory hate
crime 79, 82, 83, 90, 91

Uniform Crime Reports 81
white supremacy 77
**Universal Declaration of Human Rights
(UDHR)** 40, 191, 192, 254, 280, 287
universalism 277, 280–2
universality 288
universally recognized as impermissible
under international law 285–8
universal model of hate crime 317–18
unreported crimes 219

Valji, N. 128
Van den Wyngaert, C. 42
Van Gogh, Theodoor (Dutch film-maker)
murder (2004) 90
Vasak, K. 248
verbal abuse 82, 114–15, 259
see also hate speech
victimization 1, 4, 17, 18, 19, 52, 112, 116, 117,
118–29, 130, 136, 145, 152, 170, 181–2,
214, 217, 220, 221
differing understandings and protected
characteristics 23
effect 57
future victimization and psychosocial
impact 102
international variations in legislation 25
psychosocial impact 103
repeat victimization 104, 216, 219
restorative justice 300, 307
secondary 133–4, 214, 219, 300
surveys 226
terrorism events and retaliatory hate
crime 81, 82, 83
vicarious or *in terrorem* 80
vulnerable/disadvantaged victims 61
victimization surveys 226
**Victims' Directive (Directive establishing
minimum standards on the rights,
support and protection of victims
of crime) (2012)** 19, 216–17, 218–19,
226, 228, 239, 302–3
victims' rights movements 19, 175
victim support 52
violence
religious 174, 198
see also physical assaults/violence/injury;
sexual assault; sexual violence
vulnerability and risk of being targeted 57, 61
discrimination 253, 255
hate speech 247
international variations in legislation 25–6
Poland 182

**vulnerability and risk of being
        targeted** (*cont.*)
  South Africa 133
  Turkey 152–3
  United Kingdom 112, 119, 121, 123

Waldorf, L. 305
Waldron, J. 266–7
Walters, M.A. 10–11, 51n, 309, 315–16
war crimes 19
  Europe 216
  Israel and Palestine 2
  Poland 181
war on terrorism 306
Weller, M. 238
Whine, M. 9, 316
White, I. 307
**white supremacists worldwide: use of
        cybermedia** 65–77
  alternative media, alternative
        messages 67–9
  collective identity 66–7, 68, 70, 72–4
  mobilizing hate 74–6
  separating 'us' from 'them' 70–2
Wilkins, R.G. 288

women, crimes against *see* gender; sexual
        assaults; sexual violence
Woods, J.B. 23
World Values Survey (2011) 153
World Wide Web 215, 314, 316–17
  online hate crime monitoring systems 160
  online incitement to hate crime 226
  see also cyberhate: online hate speech
wrongfulness 264

xenophobia 22, 54, 71–2, 116, 129, 130, 131–2,
        133, 134–5, 136, 137, 161–2, 163–4,
        165, 166, 167, 174, 213, 216, 217, 223,
        224, 254–5
  cyberhate 273
  see also Framework Decision on Racist and
        Xenophobic Crime

Yemen 120
Yilmaz, H. 153

Zempi, I. 7–8, 314
Zionist Occupied Government (ZOG) 68
Zozo, D. 133, 134
Zuma, J. 128